ACT®
English, Reading & Writing Prep

Fourth Edition

Related Titles for College-Bound Students

AP Biology
AP Calculus AB & BC
AP Chemistry
AP English Language & Composition
AP English Literature & Composition
AP Environmental Science
AP European History
AP Human Geography
AP Macroeconomics/Microeconomics
AP Physics B & C
AP Psychology
AP Statistics
AP U.S. Government & Politics
AP U.S. History
AP World History
ACT Premier
ACT Strategies, Practice & Review
8 Practice Tests for the ACT
ACT Math & Science Prep
SAT Premier
SAT Strategies, Practice & Review
SAT Total Prep
8 Practice Tests for the SAT
Evidence-Based Reading, Writing, and Essay Workbook for the SAT
Math Workbook for the SAT
SAT Subject Test: Biology E/M
SAT Subject Test: Chemistry
SAT Subject Test: Literature
SAT Subject Test: Mathematics Level 1
SAT Subject Test: Mathematics Level 2
SAT Subject Test: Physics
SAT Subject Test: U.S. History
SAT Subject Test: World History

ACT®

English, Reading & Writing Prep

Fourth Edition

New York

Published by Kaplan Publishing, a division of Kaplan, Inc.
750 Third Avenue
New York, NY 10017

Printed in the United States of America

10 9 8 7 6 5 4 3 2 1

ISBN-13: 978-1-5062-1442-9

Kaplan Publishing books are available at special quantity discounts to use for sales promotions, employee premiums, or educational purposes. For more information or to order books, please call the Simon & Schuster special sales department at 866-506-1949.

Contents

CHAPTER 1

Understanding the ACT

Congratulations! By picking up this workbook, you're making a commitment to yourself to learn about the ACT and how you can do your very best on the English, Reading, and optional Writing tests. The information in this chapter will tell you what you need to know about the ACT. You'll know what to expect on Test Day, so you can walk into your test center feeling confident and prepared. Going into the ACT with that positive attitude is crucial. Familiarizing yourself with the test structure and working through practice problems are a huge part of creating the mind-set that will help you ace the ACT. Let's get started.

ACT STRUCTURE

The ACT is divided into five tests: English, Mathematics, Reading, Science, and Writing. You can elect to take the ACT with only the first four tests, which make up the multiple-choice portion of the ACT. The fifth test, in which you produce an essay, is an optional test.

PREDICTABILITY

No matter where or when you take the ACT, the order of the tests and the time allotted for each is always the same. This consistency works in your favor: the more you know about what to expect on Test Day, the more confident you'll feel. You may know that one section of the exam, let's say, Reading, usually seems more challenging for you, but at least you know that Reading will always be third. The ACT won't surprise you by making the Reading section the first thing you see when you open your exam booklet. Knowing the structure of the ACT will help you feel in control of your test-taking experience.

The following table summarizes the predictable structure of the ACT:

Test	Time Allotted	Number and Type of Questions
Section 1: English	45 minutes	75 multiple choice
Section 2: Mathematics	60 minutes	60 multiple choice
Section 3: Reading	35 minutes	40 multiple choice
Section 4: Science	35 minutes	40 multiple choice
Section 5: Writing	40 minutes	1 essay prompt

WHAT IS A STANDARDIZED TEST?

Here's your first ACT practice question:

> One of the most important ways to succeed on a standardized test is to:
>
> **A.** do nothing but practice problems in your spare time the week before the test.
>
> **B.** talk to anyone who will listen about how nervous you are.
>
> **C.** choose choice (C) for any multiple-choice question you're unsure about.
>
> **D.** understand what a standardized test is and why taking it doesn't have to be a demoralizing experience.

Which answer did you choose? Although some of the choices may have made you groan or grimace if you recognized they weren't true, we hope you spotted that choice (D) is the best answer.

As you use this book and apply the Kaplan strategies to work through practice problems, you'll come to see that the test experience need not be demoralizing at all. Right now, however, you may be apprehensive for a variety of reasons. Your own teachers didn't write the test. You've heard the test maker includes trick answers. You feel weak in one of the content areas and don't know how you can possibly improve enough to do well on that test section. Thousands of students will be taking the test. All of these things can seem very intimidating.

Let's look carefully at that last reason. The simple fact that thousands of students from different places take the ACT is actually a good thing. It means that the test is necessarily constructed in a deliberate and predictable way. Because it's a standardized test, the ACT must include very specific content and skills that are consistent from one test date to another. The need for standardization makes it predictable, not intimidating. It's predictable not only in the layout of the test sections in the booklet, but also in the topics that are tested and even *in the way those topics are tested.* Working the practice problems in this book will help you understand not only how each topic is tested but also how to approach the various question types.

If you feel anxious about the predominance of multiple-choice questions on the ACT, think about this fact: For multiple-choice questions, there has to be *only one right answer*, and it's *right there in front of you* in the test booklet. A question that could be interpreted differently by students from different schools, even different parts of the country, who've had different teachers and different high school courses, would never make it onto the ACT. Each question on the ACT is designed to test a specific skill. Either the question or the passage it's associated with (for English, Reading, and Science) *must* include information that allows all students to determine the correct answer.

There can be no ambiguity about which answer is best for a multiple-choice question on a standardized test. This workbook will teach you proven Kaplan strategies for finding that answer. The Kaplan strategies, along with your understanding about the structure and writing of the test, will put *you* in control of your ACT Test Day experience.

ACT SCORING

SCORING FOR THE MULTIPLE-CHOICE SECTIONS: RAW SCORE, SCALED SCORE, AND PERCENTILE RANKING

Let's look at how your ACT composite score is calculated. For each multiple-choice section of the test (English, Mathematics, Reading, and Science), the number of questions you answer correctly is totaled. No points are deducted for wrong answers. The total of correct answers for each section is called the *raw* score for that section. Thus, the highest possible raw score for a section is the total number of questions in that section.

Because each version of the ACT is different (more in the wording of the questions than in the types of questions or skills needed to answer them), a conversion from the raw score to a *scaled* score is necessary. For each version of the ACT that is written, the test maker generates a conversion chart that indicates what scaled score each raw score is equivalent to. The conversion from raw score to scaled score is what allows for accurate comparison of test scores even though there are slight variations in each version of the test. The scaled score ranges from a low of 1 to a high of 36 for each of the first four sections. Scaled scores have the same meaning for all the different versions of the ACT offered on different test dates.

The score for each of the first three sections of the ACT is broken down further into subscores. The subscores for a particular section do *not* necessarily add up to the overall score for the section. The following table lists the subscores that are reported for each section.

Test Section	Subscore Categories
English (75 questions)	Production of Writing; Knowledge of Language; Conventions of Standard English
Mathematics (60 questions)	Preparing for Higher Mathematics; Integrating Essential Skills; Modeling
Reading (40 questions)	Key Ideas and Details; Craft and Structure; Integration of Knowledge and Ideas
Science (40 questions)	Interpretation of Data; Scientific Investigation; Evaluation of Models, Inferences, and Experimental Results
Writing (1 essay prompt)	Ideas and Analysis; Development and Support; Organization; Language Use and Conventions

What most people think of as the ACT score is the composite score. Your composite score, between 1 and 36, is the average of the four scaled scores on the English, Mathematics, Reading, and Science sections of the test.

In addition to the raw score, scaled score, and section subscores, your ACT score report also includes a *percentile ranking*. This is not a score that indicates what percentage of questions you answered correctly on the test. Rather, your percentile ranking provides a comparison between your performance and that of other recent ACT test takers. Your percentile ranking indicates the percentage of ACT test takers who scored the same as or lower than you. In other words, if your percentile ranking is 80, that means that you scored the same as or higher than 80 percent of the students who took the test.

A raw-to-scaled score conversion chart is necessary to take into account slight variations in the difficulty levels of different versions of the test. In other words, it's not possible to say that for every ACT test date if you answer, for example, 55 of the 75 English questions correctly, your scaled score will be always be 24. However, you should know that the variations in each test version—and therefore in the raw-to-scaled score conversion chart—are very slight and should not concern you. The following table gives some *approximate* raw score ranges for each section, the associated scaled score, and the likely percentile ranking.

Raw Score and Scaled Score Approximate Equivalences					
Scaled Score	**English Questions Correct (Total = 75)**	**Mathematics Questions Correct (Total = 60)**	**Reading Questions Correct (Total = 40)**	**Science Questions Correct (Total = 40)**	**Percentile Ranking**
32	70	55–56	34–35	35–36	99
27	61–63	45–47	27–28	30–32	90
24	53–56	36–39	22–25	26–28	75
20	42–46	31–32	18–20	20–21	50

Don't get bogged down by the numbers in this table. We've put it here to help you relax. The big-picture message of the chart is that you can get a good ACT score even if you don't answer every question correctly. In terms of how many questions you need to get right, reaching your ACT score goal is probably not as difficult as you might think.

SCORING FOR THE WRITING SECTION

The ACT essay subscores range from 2 to 12 points, with 12 being the highest. To determine the essay subscores, two trained graders read your essay and assign it a score between 1 and 6 for each of the four domains: Ideas and Analysis, Development and Support, Organization, and Language Use and Conventions.

Not all colleges and universities require the ACT Writing test for admission, so the fifth section of the ACT is optional. Not every student takes it, and therefore the Writing score has no effect on the composite score. However, if you opt to take the Writing section of the ACT, you will receive three scores in addition to your composite score. First, you will see your essay subscores, between 2 and 12. Second, you will see a Writing section score, which is the average of the four subscores. Third, you will see an ELA score, which is a weighted composite of your Reading, English, and Writing scaled scores. This score also ranges from 1 to 36. If you choose not to do the Writing section, you will not receive essay subscores, an essay scaled score, or an ELA score.

ADDITIONAL SCORES

In addition to an ELA score, you will also receive a STEM score. This is the average of your Math and Science scaled scores and ranges from 1–36.

ACT REGISTRATION

All the information you need about ACT registration is available on the test maker's website at www.actstudent.org. There are two ways to register for the ACT: You can do so online, or you can use a registration packet and send your forms in by mail. If you need a registration packet, you should be able to get one from your school counselor, or you can request one directly via the test maker's website.

Choosing a test day that is right for you depends on admission deadlines. Most students take the test during their junior spring and senior fall semesters, although some opt to take the ACT as early as freshman or sophomore year if they have completed most of the academic skills that are tested by the ACT. The earlier you take the test, the more opportunities you have to take the test again and increase your composite score. Check the websites of colleges to which you are applying, as well as scholarship agencies, to solidify a test date. The ACT website, www.actstudent.org, provides a list of colleges with information about standardized testing policies. It takes about three to eight weeks to receive your scores, so be sure to check college admission deadlines before you choose a test date.

If you think that registering for the ACT on time is simply a matter of logistics and fees, think again. Individual testing centers have limited space. When you know that you're interested in a particular test date at a particular location, it is worthwhile to register as soon as possible. The earlier you register, the more likely it is that you'll be able to test at your preferred location. Many students prefer to test at their own high schools, in a familiar setting. The morning of Test Day will go much more smoothly if you don't have to worry about directions to get to an unfamiliar location. Planning ahead for ACT registration can help you avoid such unnecessary distractions.

When you register, you should read all the information the test maker provides. Learn specifically about what to bring with you, including forms of ID, pencils, acceptable calculators, and snacks for the breaks. You should also pay attention to what behaviors are and are not acceptable during the test. The more you know ahead of time about what to expect on test day, the more relaxed and confident you'll be going into the test. When you put that confidence together with the Kaplan strategies and practice you'll get from this book, you can look forward to higher scores on your ACT!

CHAPTER 2

ACT Strategies

Taking a strategic approach to the ACT will help you earn the highest score possible. This chapter presents several kinds of strategies. Some are general test-taking strategies, and some are specific to a particular section of the test. Pay special attention to the Kaplan Methods for the English, Reading, and Writing tests. You should practice these methods as you work through the test questions in this workbook. The Kaplan Methods, building on the general strategies, give you a firm foundation on which to base your plan of attack for each ACT question you'll see on test day. Taking a strategic approach means you'll know *how to think about* each question.

GENERAL TEST-TAKING STRATEGIES

1. **Make sure you answer the easy questions first!** It's important to understand how the ACT is scored. Each question in a section is worth the same number of points, whether it is tough or easy. Attack easy questions, the ones you know you can get correct, first. Work carefully to avoid making careless mistakes on these questions.

2. **Don't spend too much time on any one question.** You must be constantly aware of the clock to pace yourself well. No single question will make or break your ACT score, so no question deserves a disproportionate amount of your time and attention. Don't let yourself get bogged down. If you're stuck on a question, circle the number in your test booklet and come back to it at the end of the section if you have time.

3. **For the multiple-choice sections, circle the letter of your answer choice in the test booklet, and enter your answers onto the answer grid in a logical way, not one question at a time.** You don't get any credit for any marks you make in the test booklet, only for answers you place on your answer sheet. Still, the habit of circling answers in the booklet and transferring them onto your answer sheet in a logical unit, either by

page or by passage, will save you time, allow you to focus more easily on answering questions, and reduce the likelihood that you'll make errors filling in the wrong answer bubbles. For the English and Reading tests, it makes sense to work on one passage at a time. When you come to the end of a passage, with answers circled in your test booklet, carefully fill in each answer on the grid. You'll get a mini-break from thinking about test content, and you can concentrate on filling in the grid accurately. As you fill in each bubble on the answer grid, silently voice the question number and answer choice letter to yourself: "Number 1 is B. Number 2 is H . . ." If you're leaving some questions blank so that you can return to them later, this strategy of marking a passage worth of questions all at the same time helps you to avoid making mistakes on the answer grid.

4. **Be aware of the ending time for the section you're working on, and make sure you grid in an answer—even if it's only a blind guess—for each question.** You don't lose any points for incorrect answers on the ACT, so it's to your advantage to answer every question. If you're nearing the end of the section—your test administrator will let you know—and you have questions that you skipped or haven't tried yet, be sure to select an answer for those questions.

5. **If you have time, guess strategically on questions you're not sure about.** Strategic guessing, in which you can rule out one or more answers, is preferable to blind guessing. Still, on the ACT English and Reading tests, for which only four answer choices are offered, even with a blind guess, you have a one-in-four chance of choosing the correct answer. Pay attention to the clock and make sure you grid in an answer for every question, even if it's a strategic or a blind guess.

6. **Get in the habit of using your pencil to help you work through test questions.** This strategy, which we call "thinking with your pencil," is invaluable. While you don't get points for anything you write in your test booklet, there's no rule saying that you have to turn in a clean, blank booklet at the end of the test. Many people who wouldn't dream of working on the Math section without using their pencils to do some scratch work to arrive at the answer never make a single mark in the Verbal sections of the test booklet. This is a mistake. In any multiple-choice section, you can use your pencil to cross out the letters for answer choices you've ruled out. In the English section, it's helpful to circle nonunderlined words in the passage that help you determine what the best answer is. For English questions that have a question stem, you can underline key words in the question. In the Reading section, you should jot down brief notes as you read each passage. (You'll learn more about this in the Reading Overview section.) You can also underline key words if that helps you. For the Writing section, try taking notes before you start the actual essay. You should keep your pencil in your hand throughout the test, not just when you're filling in your answers on the grid.

7. **For multiple-choice questions that are presented with a question stem (all Reading questions and some English questions), read the question stem carefully.** It may seem too obvious to say, but if you don't know what a question is asking, you're not likely to find the correct answer. Specific advice in the English and Reading introduction chapters will help you make sure you understand the stem before you try to answer the question.

As you work through the practice questions in this workbook and refine your strategic approach, remember that your goal in practicing is not simply to arrive at correct answers. You should also develop an awareness of the best way to approach each question. On Test Day, you won't see the same questions that are in this workbook. However, because the ACT is a standardized test that covers a specific and limited set of skills, you know that you'll see very similar questions. The more comfort you develop with strategic thinking as you practice, the more confident you'll be that you can work through the questions you'll see in your ACT booklet on Test Day.

Let's take a moment to think about what it means to take a strategic approach. When you use a strategy, you don't approach a problem blindly. Instead, you have a plan for the best way to attack it. Taking a strategic approach and knowing what skills and content each test section covers go hand in hand. The Kaplan Methods for English and Reading are designed to help you focus on determining what each question is asking you to do. For each question, it helps to ask: What knowledge or skill is this question testing? When you combine the strategic approach with an understanding of the content covered by each test section, you'll be confident going into Test Day.

STRATEGIES FOR THE ENGLISH SECTION

THE KAPLAN METHOD FOR ACT ENGLISH

You'll use this three-step method for every question that includes an underlined part of the passage and for most questions that appear with a question stem:

1. READ until you have enough information to identify the issue.
2. ELIMINATE answer choices that do NOT address the issue.
3. PLUG IN the remaining choices and choose the one that is the most correct, concise, and relevant.

Recall the timing for the English test: You have to get through five passages, including a total of 75 questions, in 45 minutes. You need to work efficiently to get through all the questions, and the first step of the Kaplan Method addresses the efficiency challenge. Step 1 of the method provides an alternative to the approach that's recommended in the directions for the ACT English test. Those directions include the words, "Read each passage through once before you begin to answer the questions that accompany it."

Our advice, on the other hand, is to answer each question as soon as you've read far enough in the passage to do so. Let's look in detail at Step 1 of the Kaplan Method. It says, "Read until you have enough information to identify the issue." What do you think "the issue" means here? You might be tempted to say "the error," but remember that for some English questions "NO CHANGE" will be the best answer. Not every ACT English question includes an underlined part of the passage, and even for a question that does, the underlined portion is not necessarily wrong. Therefore, instead of reading the passage and looking for an error, think about what issue the question is testing. In other words, "the issue" is the reason that the test maker included the question.

Right now, you may feel as though you have no idea what issues are likely to be tested in the English section. The ACT is a standardized test, so it covers predictable issues. With practice, you *can* know what to expect. The information in the English Overview chapter includes rules and guidelines that are tested on the ACT. To succeed on the ACT English section, you don't need to know every rule in the grammar book. You only need to know what issues are tested and how to recognize them as they appear on the ACT.

Now that you know what "the issue" refers to in Step 1 of the Kaplan Method for ACT English, let's look at how you know when you've read far enough in the passage to identify the issue. Consider the following excerpt from an ACT English passage, in the standard form. Question 1 asks you to identify which of the four choices would fit best in the sentence. Question 2 asks you to identify the sentence that would fit best in the rest of the paragraph. Read until you have enough information to identify the issue (Step 1), and then skip down to the explanation.

Mice are <u>small, they are</u>[1] easy to maintain. They breed readily, producing litters of up to 8 or 10 young at a time. Because of their small size and short lifespan, mice do not require a large financial investment. Perhaps most important, however, particularly in certain areas of medical research, is that the mouse has a genetic makeup that is similar to the human's genetic characteristics. [2]

1. **A.** NO CHANGE
   B. small, being that they are
   C. small, most are
   D. small and

2. Which of the following is the most effective first sentence for this paragraph?
   F. Mice are among the smallest of the mammals.
   G. Mice are considered by most people to be vermin.
   H. Mice are used frequently in scientific experiments for several reasons.
   J. Scientists have found that many antibiotics that are effective in mice are also effective in humans.

If you stopped reading at the end of the first sentence, terrific! The underlined part comes in the middle of the sentence. It should be pretty easy to determine that reading through to the end of the sentence is enough here. Can you tell what the issue is? On the ACT, an underlined comma in the middle of a sentence is often a clue that sentence structure is the issue. Indeed, that is the case here; the sentence as written is a run-on.

Now that you've identified the issue, move on to Step 2 of the Kaplan Method for ACT English. Step 2 is to eliminate answer choices that don't address the issue. Can you spot any other answer choices that, like A, create a run-on sentence by using a comma? Choice C also forms a run-on. You can eliminate this choice because it doesn't address the issue you identified in Step 1. Having eliminated two choices, you can now plug each remaining choice into the sentence.

Step 3 of the Kaplan Method for ACT English gives you three criteria on which to judge the results of plugging each answer choice in: The best answer uses wording that is correct, concise, and relevant. "Plugging in" means simply reading the answer choice in the sentence in place of the underlined portion. You are left with B and (D), so examine the difference between these choices. Plug in (D) first; because it is shorter than B, it is more likely to be the best answer. With (D), the sentence reads as a compound sentence: *Mice are small and easy to maintain.* Even if you didn't notice that the conjunction *and* makes this choice the correct answer, you should have noticed that B is considerably longer and more wordy. Because conciseness is one of the issues that's tested on the ACT, a good guideline is *if in doubt,start with the shortest answer.* The shortest answer choice won't always be correct, but it often is.

Now, refer back to Question 2 in the passage. The numeral 2 appears in a box at the end of a paragraph. Questions such as this ask about the meaning of a paragraph or about the purpose of the passage. This question is presented not as an underlined portion of the passage, but instead with a question stem. For these questions, it's important to know what the question is asking. Reading carefully will help you identify the issue. For Question 2, because the question stem asks you to choose the best first sentence for the paragraph, relevance—more so than correctness or conciseness—is likely to be the issue. To address the issue, think about what the first sentence of a paragraph should do: It must introduce the topic of the paragraph. How much of the passage do you think you need to read to determine the best answer? You should consider the whole paragraph, but nothing beyond it.

Ask yourself what the purpose of the paragraph is. Certain words in the paragraph, especially *because* and *most important,* indicate that the paragraph is listing reasons. Choice (H) uses the word *reasons,* and it is the best answer for this question. In this case, the best answer choice hinges on relevance rather than correctness or conciseness.

TIME MANAGEMENT STRATEGIES FOR THE ENGLISH TEST

Knowing how the ACT is written will help you manage your time in each section. Recall that the English section contains five passages. The passages are all very similar in length, and each passage has 15 associated questions. Given that you have 45 minutes, you have roughly 9 minutes per passage. That's a little less than half a minute per question.

On Test Day, as you pace yourself on the English section, be aware of the time you spend on each passage. Some English questions can be answered more quickly than others can. Often, questions that are presented with a question stem take a little longer to answer than those made up of an underlined segment with various revisions. As you practice in this book, stay focused on Step 1 of the Kaplan Method for English: Always be thinking about how much of the passage you need to read to identify the issue for a particular question. Identifying the tested issue is the key factor in learning to manage your time efficiently in the ACT English section.

ACT English Test Time Guidelines
45 minutes for 5 passages, 15 questions per passage
Overall: 9 minutes per passage
Reading: 2 minutes per passage
Answering Questions: 7 minutes per passage, about 30 seconds per question

STRATEGIES FOR THE READING TEST

THE KAPLAN METHOD FOR ACT READING

Follow this method for each passage in the Reading section. Step 1 addresses what to do on your first read-through of the passage. Steps 2 and 3 provide a plan of attack you take for each individual question. Here's the Kaplan Method:

1. READ the passage, taking notes as you go.
2. EXAMINE the question stem, looking for clues.
3. PREDICT the answer, and select the answer choice that best matches your prediction.

Let's consider each step in detail. Why should you take notes as you read the passage? You may think that taking notes will take too much time. However, the notes you take on an ACT Reading passage will be different from note-taking you do in school. Your ACT passage notes should be brief. They should summarize main ideas only, *not* supporting details. The purpose of your notes is to provide a passage map. Think of your notes as signposts guiding you to where in the passage you'll find the answer to a particular question.

One important thing to know about the Reading section is that the questions don't appear in any particular order. For example, the first question for a passage won't necessarily ask about something from the first part of the passage; it may ask about something from the end. Therefore, because the ordering of ACT Reading questions doesn't give you any clues about where in the passage you'll find the answer, you need to create your own passage map to help you find the information you need quickly. Your notes will provide this guidance.

The best way to work through each ACT Reading passage is to read actively. Reading actively simply means asking yourself questions as you read and jotting down a brief note after you read each paragraph. Read a paragraph quickly; then pause to identify briefly the purpose of the paragraph. Ask yourself: Why did the author write this paragraph? How does it contribute to her purpose in the passage as a whole? Working with these questions will help you generate brief, appropriate notes to help you remember what information is located where in the passage. The specific details aren't important for your notes. A short description, often only a word or two that labels the information in the paragraph, rather than a long note that restates the information, is what you want here.

We suggest that you actually jot your notes for each paragraph in its margin. You may be wondering, wouldn't it be quicker simply to underline a few words in the passage? Underlining is possibly a little quicker, but there's a danger involved. If you read through a paragraph thinking you'll underline what's important, you may find yourself underlining too many details. On the other hand, when you read each paragraph with the goal of determining the author's purpose for that paragraph, there's a certain discipline involved. The mental processing required to decide on a note to jot down in the margin is more likely to help you develop a good overall understanding of the passage. Writing a quick note in your own words in the margin is a more active approach than simply underlining words in the passage.

Though you must guard against the dangers of too much underlining, there is a limited use for underlining in Step 1. While you shouldn't use underlining to take the place of your own hand-written notes in the margin, it can be helpful to underline an occasional word or phrase on your first read-through. Good words to underline are those that indicate an opinion, such as *fortunately* and *regrettably.* Other words to underline are phrases that direct the logical flow of the passage. These include words that show contrast, such as *however* and *on the other hand,* and words that show cause and effect, such as *as a result of* and *because.* You can also underline names and dates if you feel that's helpful. It may not be necessary, however, because it's usually easy to skim for names and dates if you need to find them to answer a question.

Perhaps the biggest trap that unprepared students fall into with underlining is trying to anticipate on a first reading what specific questions may be for this passage. This is a waste of your time. Your goal in reading through the passage is to get a big-picture understanding. Remember the key questions to guide your active reading: What is the author's purpose here, and how is this information organized? Rely primarily on your passage map notes, and use underlining sparingly. If you practice in this way on all the Reading passages in this workbook, then by Test Day, active reading will have become a habit.

Step 1 of the Kaplan Method for ACT Reading guides you as you read the passage. Once you finish reading, apply Steps 2 and 3 of the method for each question. Step 2 is to examine the question stem, looking for clues. The question stem is the part of an ACT problem that appears before the answer choices. The stem of an ACT Reading question can contain two kinds of clues. First, the test maker uses certain phrases repeatedly in question stems.

You'll frequently see phrases such as *As stated in the passage* and *The author suggests*. These phrases, along with others that you'll learn about in the Reading introduction, help you recognize exactly what a question is asking you to do. This is important because to answer a question correctly, you need to know what it's asking.

Another kind of clue that the question may provide is an indication of where to look back to in the passage to locate the answer. Occasionally, an ACT Reading question stem provides a line reference. If present, a line reference can be a great clue about where to research the passage for the answer. What if the question stem doesn't give you a line reference? In that case, the passage map you created in Step 1 is invaluable. If a question stem includes the phrase *Marc Brown's early education,* and you've made a note in the margin saying, *Brown's childhood,* your note guides you to the right spot in the passage to find information about Brown's early education. Thus, important words in the question stem give clues that work with your passage map notes to help you find *where* in the passage you need to read to find the correct answer.

While Step 2 helps you understand what a question is asking and where you need to read to answer it, Step 3 helps you avoid the temptation of wrong answers that the test maker includes among the choices. In Step 3, you predict (that is, state in your own words) what you think the best answer to the question will be. It's important to make your prediction *before you read any of the multiple-choice answers.* This helps because when you go through the process of predicting in your own words, you do so by focusing your attention on the words in the passage. The correct answer is always based on the passage itself. Predicting will help you avoid thinking too much and falling for a wrong answer that introduces material that isn't in the passage. Predicting also helps you avoid an answer choice that includes a detail from the passage that doesn't answer this particular question.

For nine out of ten questions, an effective prediction will help you easily spot the right answer quickly when you read through the four answer choices. Think of it this way: The process of predicting does take some time, but if you predict, you're certain to spend less time reading and thinking about each answer choice. In the long run, predicting is the best way to work efficiently through the ACT Reading questions. Remember, predict before you peek.

As you do the practice problems in this workbook, you might want to note your prediction before you even read through the answer choices. You shouldn't write out your prediction on test day, because doing so uses valuable time. However, jotting down your prediction in practice will help you develop the skill of predicting. Another strategy, which you can use on Test Day, is to get into the habit of covering the answer choices with your hand until you've verbalized your prediction.

TIME MANAGEMENT STRATEGIES FOR THE READING TEST

Again, the most important things are to know the test and to be aware of the clock as you work through a section. The ACT Reading section always includes four passages. All four are roughly the same length, and each has exactly ten questions. With four passages to get through in 35 minutes, you should spend less than nine minutes per passage.

Aim to spend no more than three minutes on your first read-through of the passage, including the time you spend jotting down your notes. This breakdown allows you about six minutes to spend attacking the questions. You'll have half a minute per question. If you practice all three steps of the Kaplan Method, you'll gain a lot in efficiency. Some questions won't take you even half a minute to answer. The time you save is time that you can spend on a more difficult question that may take you a little longer to answer. When you consider timing issues for any multiple-choice section of the ACT, it's crucial to make sure that you answer the easier questions first so you can spend more time on the harder questions. Skip around within the passage but not within the whole Reading test—chances are you won't remember one passage once you move on to the next.

Here's another point to consider in managing your time for the Reading test: You don't necessarily have to work through the Reading passages in the order they appear in your test booklet. Another order could work better for you. For example, you can choose to focus on each subsection and tackle the Sciences passages or the Arts/Literature passages first. As you practice in this workbook, you may find that you are more experienced and confident with some passage types than others. If that is true, work on those passages and questions first.

Some people don't find any particular passage type in general to be more challenging than any other, but many people find one particular passage on a given ACT to be harder. It can be useful to take a very *quick* glance at each of the four passages in the Reading section and determine if one seems as if it will be more difficult. If so, it makes sense to leave that passage for last. This can help prevent you from getting bogged down and spending too much time on a particularly tough passage early on. Manage your time wisely, and make sure you answer the questions that are likely to be easiest for you first.

ACT Reading Test Time Guidelines

35 minutes for 4 passages, 10 questions per passage

Overall: About 9 minutes per passage

Reading: about 3 minutes per passage

Answering Questions: 6 minutes per passage, about 30 seconds per question

STRATEGIES FOR THE WRITING TEST

THE KAPLAN METHOD FOR ACT WRITING

You can think of the steps of the Kaplan Method for ACT writing as the four *P*'s: Prompt, Plan, Produce, and Proofread. Here's what each step involves:

1. Read the **prompt,** underlining key words that you can use in your essay to maintain your focus on the topic.

2. Jot down a short **plan** in the test booklet that lists your major pieces of evidence and the order in which you'll present them.

3. **Produce,** or write, your essay on the pages provided in the answer booklet, developing your ideas logically and specifically.

4. **Proofread** your essay, making any necessary changes to clarify your meaning and correcting any obvious errors.

TIME-MANAGEMENT STRATEGIES FOR THE WRITING TEST

Because you have only 40 minutes to work on your ACT essay, you need to manage your time carefully. A little time spent planning *before* you actually start to write your essay will pay off. You have to understand the question in the prompt, and then think about how you can answer it effectively. This takes a few minutes of planning. Plan what to say before writing and the result will be a focused and organized ACT essay. We recommend taking a couple of minutes to read the prompt carefully and then spending between four to six minutes planning (Steps 1 and 2, prompt and plan). This is long enough to read the question, consider possible ways to answer it, and jot down very brief notes about what your two or three main pieces of evidence will be. When you know what you're going to discuss *before* you start writing, you can think about the best order to present your main points in.

The time you spend on Step 3, when you actually write your essay in the answer booklet, will go more smoothly if you're working from a well-thought-out written plan. You should spend about 30 minutes on the writing stage.

When you've finished writing, use the remaining time, which should be about two to three minutes, to proofread your essay. At this point, you're not looking to make major revisions. You should simply read your essay with a careful eye, looking for small errors or omissions that affect the readability. If you can correct a few grammatical errors, make sure that each sentence clearly conveys what you mean it to, and insert any transitional words or phrases (such as *however, in contrast, in addition,* etc.) that help your argument flow more logically, your proofreading time will be well spent. Leaving time to proofread ensures that your essay is easy for the graders to read and understand, which means you'll get the best score possible.

ACT Writing Test Time Guidelines

Step 1: Prompt—3 minutes
Step 2: Plan—5 minutes
Step 3: Produce—30 minutes
Step 4: Proofread—2 minutes

CHAPTER 3

Introduction to ACT English

All ACT English questions are passage-based. This means that every decision you make about an answer should be considered in light of the passage's context. The ACT writers divide questions into two broad categories: Mechanics and Rhetorical Skills. Mechanics questions address grammatical issues, matters such as using the correct pronoun or verb form. Generally, you can determine the correct answer for a Mechanics questions simply by reading a single sentence. Rhetorical Skills questions, on the other hand, often require you to take a larger part of the passage into account. These questions ask you to consider the author's style, tone, purpose, and organizational structure. The ACT mixes both Rhetorical Skills and Mechanics questions together throughout the English section. That fact is what gives rise to Step 1 of the Kaplan Method for ACT English. As you work through an English passage, you need to constantly ask yourself how much of the passage you need to read (or consider) to determine the best answer to this question.

Remember from chapter 2 that each ACT subject test has a Kaplan Method, designed specifically to help you maximize your score for that test. As you practice for the English test, don't hesitate to refer to chapter 2 for the Kaplan Method for ACT English. Applying Kaplan Methods and strategies as you work through the practice passages is crucial to your success, so you'll find references to it throughout this chapter.

THE KAPLAN METHOD FOR ACT ENGLISH

Pause for a moment to write down what you can remember about the Kaplan Method for ACT English:

1. ______________________________

2. ______________________________

3. ______________________________

Here's a quick review:

1. READ until you have enough information to identify the issue.
2. ELIMINATE answer choices that do NOT address the issue.
3. PLUG IN the remaining choices, and choose the one that is most correct, concise, and relevant.

Working through these steps in succession will be the key to answering each problem correctly. As you work through an English passage, you need to constantly ask yourself how much of the passage you need to read (or consider) to determine the best answer to each question.

MECHANICS QUESTIONS

First, let's consider Mechanics questions in light of the Kaplan Method for ACT English. Step 1 tells you to read until you have enough information to identify the issue. For a Mechanics question, the issue should be apparent as soon as you come to the end of the sentence containing the underlined portion. Sometimes you'll recognize the issue even before you reach the end of the sentence. Step 2 tells you to eliminate answer choices that don't address the issue. In other words, if the underlined part contains an error, eliminate any other answer choice that repeats the error. Step 3 of the Kaplan Method tells you to plug in the remaining answer choices and select the most correct, concise, and relevant one.

Recall that the Kaplan Method works for all types of ACT English questions. For Mechanics questions, however, the most important word to keep in mind during Step 3 is *correct.* Mechanics issues are those that are either correct or incorrect. You can determine the correct answer by knowing which grammar rule to apply. Don't worry, though, you won't need to memorize a lot of rules. The ACT tests a limited set of rules, and this section goes over all of them.

SENTENCE STRUCTURE QUESTIONS

Before we discuss how the ACT tests sentence structure, you need to be comfortable with just a few grammatical terms. A **sentence** is a group of words that contains a subject and a predicate verb and expresses a complete thought. You will see about 18 questions about sentence structure on the ACT English test. On test day, you should be an expert at observing how a sentence is constructed. A sentence is made up of one or more clauses. A **clause** is a group of words that contains a subject and a verb. A clause may constitute a complete sentence, but it doesn't necessarily have to. If a clause can stand alone as a sentence, it's called an *independent clause.* If a clause cannot stand alone as a sentence, that is, if it doesn't express a complete thought, it's called a *dependent clause.* See if you can label the clauses below as either dependent or independent:

1. ________________ because she was my friend

2. ________________ she is my friend

3. ________________ that I will go to the library

4. ________________ I will go to the library

5. ________________ although Dana is working tonight

6. ________________ Dana is working tonight

7. ________________ that all will be well

8. ________________ all will be well

9. ________________ when I return from vacation next week

10. ________________ I return from vacation next week

11. ________________ if Dawn and Terri are going skating

12. ________________ Dawn and Terri are going skating

13. ________________ whereas most people will be driving

14. ________________ most people will be driving

15. ________________ while my grandmother is visiting over the summer

16. ________________ my grandmother visited over the summer

In this exercise, all of the even-numbered questions are independent clauses. All of the odd-numbered questions are dependent clauses. In each odd-even pair of problems in the exercise, the independent clause actually contains fewer words than the dependent clause. Take a minute to go back to the odd-numbered questions, and circle the first word in each.

When you see words such as *because, that, if, whereas,* and *while* in an underlined part of an ACT English passage, keep in mind that sentence structure may be one of the issues that problem is testing. Remember, just because a group of words in the passage starts with a capital letter and ends with a period, that doesn't necessarily mean it's a complete sentence. Be on the lookout for a dependent clause that isn't joined to an independent clause. A dependent clause by itself is a **sentence fragment,** which must be revised by adding a noun or predicate verb.

Another kind of sentence structure error is a **run-on sentence.** A run-on sentence contains two or more clauses that are incorrectly strung together. A well-formed sentence can have more than one clause, but the clauses must be joined in a way that follows the principles of correct sentence structure. Before we review the rules for sentence structure, test your present understanding by considering the following incorrect sentence:

> My history teacher requires us to use at least two books in our research, I have to go to the library this weekend.

Can you tell why the sentence structure is wrong here? Take a minute to see if you can find one or more ways to correct it:

____

____

____

____

The sentence is a run-on. If a sentence contains two parts that could each stand alone as a sentence (two *independent clauses),* then it's incorrect to join those two parts with just a comma. Doing so creates a run-on sentence. There are several ways to correct a run-on like this one. However, on the ACT, you won't have to choose which one is best; for each question, only one correct choice will be presented.

RUN-ON SENTENCE RULES

Use one of these three ways to correctly combine two independent clauses in a single sentence:

1. Use a comma and a FANBOYS conjunction *(for, and, nor, but, or, yet, so).*

   My history teacher requires us to use at least two books in our research, ***so*** *I have to go to the library this weekend.*

2. Use a semicolon between the two clauses. After a semicolon, it is not correct to use a FANBOYS word, but it is acceptable to use a transitional word such as *however, moreover,* or *nevertheless.*

   My history teacher requires us to use at least two books in our research; ***therefore****, I have to go to the library this weekend.*

3. Break the run-on into two separate sentences by changing the comma to a period and starting a new sentence.

   My history teacher requires us to use at least two books in our research. I have to go to the library this weekend.

4. Change one of the independent clauses to a dependent clause by adding a word such as *although, because, despite,* or since.

   Because *my history teacher requires us to use at least two books in our research, I have to go to the library this weekend.*

In addition to the rules listed here for combining clauses in a sentence, there's one more sentence structure issue that you should be aware of. Fortunately, there's a clue to help you spot it.

> **Be ready for sentence structure issues by checking an underlined portion for a verb that ends in *-ing.* Verbs like these often create sentence fragments.**

SENTENCE STRUCTURE RULE

The verb form ending in *-ing* cannot be used without a helping verb, such as *is, was, has, had,* or *have been,* as the main verb in a clause.

Here's an example. *The monkey swinging from tree to tree* is incorrect as a complete sentence because *swinging* is used alone as the main verb in the clause. A helping verb is needed. Depending on the context, you might say something like, *The monkey* is swinging *from tree to tree* or *The monkey* had been swinging *from tree to tree.*

Try these ACT-like questions that test sentence structure:

1. Two of our team's best players were injured at the beginning of the season, our team has not been doing well. (1: "season, our")

A. NO CHANGE
B. season, therefore, our
C. season; so our
D. season; therefore, our

The tested issue here is sentence structure: A makes the sentence a run-on. After identifying this issue, check the answer choices and eliminate those that don't follow the rules for correcting a run-on. Choice B is incorrect because a comma cannot join two independent clauses and a word such as *therefore.* Choice C is wrong because the semicolon is not the correct punctuation mark to use when you join two independent clauses by a FANBOYS word. Because C uses *so,* a comma is needed instead of the semicolon here. Choice (D) correctly joins two independent clauses with a semicolon and no FANBOYS word. Recall that it is acceptable to use *therefore* after a semicolon.

2. The library, which functioning at times as a social center, is more than just an academic resource.
2

F. NO CHANGE

G. library, which functions

H. library it functions

J. library having the function

The issue here is sentence structure; notice the *-ing* verb in the underlined section. The sentence as written isn't a run-on, but there is a problem in the way that it's structured. The phrase *which functioning* probably sounds wrong to your ear. One way to fix the issue is to remove *which,* thus making the sentence structurally correct. However, this choice is not presented in the answer choices. Plug in the remaining answer choices to see if any of them fix the structural problem in a different way. Choice (G) doesn't create a problem and is the correct answer. Choice H contains the word *it,* which is unnecessary here. Choice J doesn't work in the context because it creates the idiomatically incorrect phrase *having the function...as.*

3. My school's French club planning to go to Paris this spring.
3

A. NO CHANGE

B. planning on going

C. is planning going

D. is planning to go

Did you notice that an *-ing* verb was used in this question, too? The underlined portion includes *planning,* but a helping verb does not precede this *-ing* verb. A **helping verb**, like *has* or *was*, is a verb that does not show action by itself, but can "help" the main verb show action. Because this is the case, you should have identified sentence structure as the issue. Choice B does not address this issue. Both C and (D) address the issue by adding the helping verb *is.* Read each choice into the sentence to determine that the best answer is (D).

Sentence structure is one aspect of how sentences are tested on the ACT. Another aspect is clarity. For these ACT questions, you had to ask yourself if the sentence was constructed properly, and whether its clauses were joined correctly. Now we'll talk about another important consideration: is the meaning of this sentence clear and unambiguous? If an ACT sentence doesn't make sense or you're not sure what it's supposed to mean, then there's a problem with the sentence. Whenever you notice that an entire sentence is underlined in an ACT English passage, take that as a clue that it may be testing overall clarity of the sentence. The other possibility is that the sentence may be testing relevance, which you will read about in the Rhetorical Skills section.

Here's an example. Suppose you see this entire sentence underlined in an ACT English passage:

> Tangled in the leash, the door closed on her dog as Samantha was going into the house.

This sentence isn't written in the clearest way possible. Think about what the sentence is trying to say, and see if you can come up with an effective revision here:

____

____

As it's originally written, the sentence suggests that *the door* is *tangled in the leash.* If you think about it, you realize that, logically, it's the *dog* that is *tangled in the leash.* Moving that phrase and adjusting the wording slightly creates a more logical sentence. Here's an example of how to correct the sentence: *As they went into the house, the door closed on Samantha's dog, which was tangled in the leash.*

Whenever the sentence that contains an underlined part starts with a verb that ends in *-ed* or *-ing,* that's a clue that the question may be testing sentence structure.

A third consideration about sentences on ACT English has to do with how the sentence works in the context of the passage: is this sentence consistent with the nonunderlined parts of the sentences around it? Verbs and pronouns are the primary issue here. Consider the following excerpt, and see if you can determine how the underlined parts should be corrected:

> When you get ready to travel, there are many things <u>one has to</u> [1. __________] take care of in advance. If you're going outside the country, <u>one</u> [2. __________] must plan ahead to ensure that you'll get your passport on time. Of course, there <u>was</u> [3. __________] the packing to be done, though this can wait until closer to your departure day. If you have pets, however, you should <u>have thought</u> [4. __________] ahead about finding a pet-sitter. There is, though, one thing you *must* do at the last minute: Don't forget to lock your door!

You must pay attention to the nonunderlined context to help you make the necessary corrections here. Here is the passage reprinted with correct answers filled in. Notice that certain nonunderlined words are printed in bold, because they are the context clues that help you make the corrections:

> When **you** get ready to travel, there **are** many things <u>one has to</u> [1. you have to] take care of in advance. If **you**'re going outside the country, <u>one</u> [2. you] must plan ahead to ensure that **you**'ll get your passport on time. Of course, there <u>was</u> [3. is] the packing to be done, though this **can wait** until closer to your departure day. If **you have** pets, however, you should <u>have thought</u> [4. think] ahead about finding a pet-sitter. There **is**, however, one thing you must do at the last minute: Don't forget to lock **your** door!

The following two rules needed to be applied to this exercise.

SENTENCE STRUCTURE CONSISTENCY RULES

1. Avoid *pronoun* shift. That is, do not switch needlessly between *one* and *you* within a passage.
2. Make sure the primary verb tense is consistent throughout the passage. If the passage is written primarily in one tense, do not shift to a different tense unless there is a logical reason to do so.

You'll see a reminder about this issue of sentence structure consistency later in the sections on pronouns and verbs.

PUNCTUATION QUESTIONS

Some of the easiest questions to recognize are Punctuation questions. When you look at the answer choices, you'll see that they all use the same or nearly the same words. This is your clue to think about punctuation rules. The great thing about the ACT is that it tests a limited number of punctuation rules. Expect about 10 questions that test commas, dashes, colons, semicolons, periods, question marks, exclamation points, and apostrophes. Comma usage is tested most frequently, followed by semicolon usage.

COMMA RULE

Use commas:

1. To separate introductory words from the main part of the sentence.

   Before you leave the house, you should make sure you've eaten a healthy breakfast.

2. To set off words or phrases that aren't essential to the sentence structure.

   Sonia, who will be playing the role of the lawyer, is a skilled actress.

3. To separate two independent clauses when they're joined by a FANBOYS word (*for, and, nor, but, or, yet, so).*

   Many of my friends drink coffee, but I do not.

4. To separate items in a series.

   Steps involved in a research paper include choosing a topic, conducting the research, writing a first draft, and doing at least one round of revisions.

These four examples are the only uses of the comma that the ACT tests. Learn to recognize when each rule should be applied, and keep in mind the following additional hint.

COMMA HINT

Avoid unnecessary commas. Sometimes your task on an ACT punctuation question is to remove commas that disturb the flow of a sentence.

SEMICOLON RULE

Use a semicolon to link two independent clauses that are *not* joined by a FANBOYS word.

> I will be missing school to visit colleges; however, my teacher said I will not have to make up the Spanish quiz I will miss.

Be aware of certain words that are frequently used to connect two independent clauses. These words are acceptable to use after a semicolon:

furthermore	**moreover**
however	**nevertheless**
in fact	**therefore**
indeed	**thus**

Do not use these words after a semicolon:

although	**which**
despite	**where**
whereas	**that**
who	

DASH RULE

Use em dashes:

1. To indicate a break in thought.
   You did see the movie—am I right about that?
2. To set off parenthetical information from the main part of a sentence.
   Many people find that small necessary items—a wallet, a cell phone, a transit card—are unfortunately very easy to misplace.

APOSTROPHE RULE

Use an apostrophe:

1. To take the place of one or more missing letters in a contraction.

   You can't be late.

2. To show the possessive form of a noun.

   My sisters' teams both won games this weekend. (This is correct if you're using the plural form, two sisters who play on two separate teams.)

   My sister's friends are coming to the party. (This is correct if you're using the singular form, one sister.)

As you work through an ACT English passage, notice when a question is testing punctuation. When it is, think about how the various parts of each sentence relate to one another. Ask yourself what the main part of the sentence is, and consider whether some phrases might be nonessential information. If a sentence has more than one clause, think about whether each could stand alone as a sentence. If that's the case, recall the rules about commas and semicolons and which words are acceptable with each to join two clauses. Keep these ideas in mind as you try the questions below. To increase your understanding, read each answer explanation before you move on to the next question.

I'm unusual among my friends because I don't like, to drink coffee. (4) I do enjoy going with them to

4. **F.** NO CHANGE
   G. like, to drink, coffee
   H. like to drink coffee
   J. like to drink, coffee

coffee shops because, oddly enough, (5) I appreciate the smell of coffee.

5. **A.** NO CHANGE
   B. shops, because, oddly enough,
   C. shops because oddly, enough,
   D. shops because oddly enough

The convivial atmosphere of our local coffee brewer is also quite appealing to me so, (6) I enjoy spending time there with friends.

6. **F.** NO CHANGE
   G. me, so
   H. me; so
   J. me, so,

Fortunately,

I can get a pretty good cup of tea there, in fact
7
I even order hot chocolate.

7. A. NO CHANGE
B. there in fact
C. there: in, fact,
D. there; in fact,

In addition to the socializing and refreshment,
8
the coffee shop offers daily amusement.
8

8. F. NO CHANGE
G. refreshment, the coffee shop, offers,
H. refreshment the coffee shop, offers
J. refreshment; the coffee shop offers

I have to laugh at the wide array of available coffee drinks—regular, decaf, espresso, cappuccino, latte, to name just a few, and the
9
amount of time it takes my friends to decide what to order.

9. A. NO CHANGE
B. to name just a few—
C. to name, just a few,
D. to name just a few:

I'm baffled by how my very busy friends can give so much time and attention to a beverage that, no matter how its' made, still tastes like
10
coffee.

10. F. NO CHANGE
G. it's made,
H. it's made
J. it's made,

4. In this sentence, the comma after *like* disturbs the flow of the clause, *I don't like to drink coffee.* Eliminate answer F and G. Are you stuck choosing between the last two answer choices? In this question, remember the hint about avoiding unnecessary commas. The correct answer is (H).

5. Here, the phrase *oddly enough* is not essential to the sentence. If you remove it, the remaining words still make up a correctly formed sentence. Commas set off nonessential phrases, so the best answer is (A).

6. To answer this question correctly, consider the structure of the sentence as a whole. It contains two independent clauses, joined by the FANBOYS word *so.* The first clause (*the convivial atmosphere of our local coffee brewer is also quite appealing to me*) can stand alone as a sentence. The second clause (*I enjoy spending time there with friends*) can also stand alone as a sentence. Use a comma after the first independent clause when you're joining two independent clauses with a FANBOYS word. The correct answer, (G), uses the conjunction *so,* which connects the clauses and places the comma in the right place.

7. Again, think about sentence structure. You have two independent clauses here. The first is *I can get a pretty good cup of tea there.* The second is *I even order hot chocolate.* The words between the two clauses, *in fact,* are not FANBOYS words, so you need a semicolon rather than a comma to join these two independent clauses. The correct answer is (D).

8. This sentence contains only one independent clause. This independent clause, *the coffee shop offers daily amusement*, forms the main part of the sentence. The earlier part of the sentence (*In addition to the socializing and refreshment*) is not a clause. It is an introductory phrase. Use a comma to set off an introductory phrase from the main part of the sentence. The correct answer is (F).

9. Be careful here. The incorrect punctuation used in A can make this sentence confusing to read and understand. Take the sentence apart to determine which words make up the main part of the sentence. The independent clause is *I have to laugh at the wide array of available coffee drinks…and the amount of time it takes my friends to decide what to order.* The words that follow the nonunderlined dash (*regular, decaf, espresso, cappuccino, latte, to name just a few*) constitute parenthetical information that is not part of the sentence's main clause. A dash must be used at the end of the parenthetical expression to properly set it off. The correct answer is (B).

10. This question tests both comma and apostrophe usage. Whenever you see that an underlined portion of an English passage contains an apostrophe, always check that it is used correctly. The spelling *its'* is never correct. If an apostrophe is called for, as it is here, the correct spelling is *it's.* Remember that this spelling is correct whenever it could be replaced by the words *it is.* You have to think about comma rules for this question also. The words *no matter how it's made* are nonessential information. Because you must use commas to set off nonessential information from the rest of the sentence, a comma is required here after *made.* The correct answer is (J).

PRONOUN QUESTIONS

You probably remember this definition: A **pronoun** is a word that either takes the place of or refers to a noun or another pronoun. Train yourself to spot pronouns immediately in the underlined portion of an ACT English passage. See if you can identify the pronouns in each underlined part of the following paragraph and write them on the lines provided.

My mother and her work friends, nurses in a large emergency room, have many interesting stories <u>about their</u> (1) experiences. Some of these stories are about the challenges patients face, but some of the funniest stories are about interactions <u>her and the other nurses have</u> (2) with various staff members. Whenever Mom and <u>I have</u> (3) friends over at the same time, my friends and <u>me always wind up</u> (4) laughing at the things we hear. The story about the doctor who thought <u>their cell phone had been</u> (5) "borrowed" by a nurse was hilarious. Mom and her friends have <u>given we</u> (6) teenagers some good advice: One should not go into the medical field <u>if you don't have</u> (7) a good sense of humor.

1. ______________
2. ______________
3. ______________
4. ______________
5. ______________
6. ______________
7. ______________

How did you do at picking out the pronouns? These are common pronouns you should feel ready to tackle on the ACT.

1. their
2. her
3. I
4. me
5. their
6. we
7. you

Let's do a quick review of what you need to know about pronouns for the ACT. Any pronoun can be described in terms of two things: case and number. Pronoun **case** refers to how the pronoun is used in a sentence—as a subject or an object. In the sentence *I will call you later,* the pronoun *I* acts as the subject, while the pronoun *you* acts as the object. A pronoun's **number** is either singular or plural. Most personal pronouns take a different form (that is, a different word is used) depending on whether they are used as the subject or object in a sentence and depending on whether they are singular or plural. The following table shows the personal pronouns for which you must consider both case and number.

	Singular	**Plural**
Subject	I, he, she, it,	we, they
Object	me, him, her, it	us, them

Generally, your ear tells you which form of a personal pronoun is correct. The ACT often makes a pronoun question trickier by using a personal pronoun in a combination with *and.* You would never say, Me *went to the store.* On the ACT, you might see something such as Me *and Jesse will do the project together.* By reading this sentence without the words *and Jesse* your ear helps you determine that *Me* should be changed to *I* in this sentence.

Examples of correct pronoun usage as subjects and objects:

1. **We** must be respectful in this class, or the teacher will give *us* detention.
2. Kevin and **I** are going skating tonight.
3. The guests said **they** were thankful for the help that *we* volunteers provided.
4. Ginny told **me** there was no need to return the book to *her.*
5. Can you believe my parents said **they** will give *us* the car for the weekend?

Did you notice that the table of personal pronouns doesn't include the pronoun *you*? The reason for this is that the pronoun *you* takes the same form whether it's used as the subject or object in a sentence. Here's an example:

> *You* must be respectful in the class, or the teacher will give *you* a detention.

However, the ACT does test the pronoun *you* in a different way, by using the word *one* in a sentence that also uses *you.*

PRONOUN-SHIFT RULE

Avoid the *one-you* shift: Do not needlessly shift between the words *one* and *you* in the same sentence or paragraph.

Here's how the *one-you* shift might look on the ACT:

> When <u>one is</u> planning for college, you need to keep many factors in mind.

Here, because the nonunderlined part of the sentence uses the word *you,* the underlined part of the sentence should be corrected to *you are.*

In addition to the personal pronouns and the *one-you* shift, another aspect of pronoun usage that's tested on the ACT is the correct use of *who, whom,* and *which. Who* and *whom* intimidate many people, but it's not hard to use them correctly if you keep in mind the issue of pronoun case. As with the personal pronouns shown in the previous table, the key to using *who* and *whom* correctly is to think about how each word functions in its sentence or clause. Think about whether it is a subject or an object. Here's a hint: If you can correctly substitute the pronoun *he* into a phrase or sentence, then *who* is correct. If you can correctly substitute the pronoun *him* into a phrase or sentence, then *whom* is correct. ACT questions that test *who, whom,* and *which* aren't questions that most people can easily answer just by thinking about what sounds correct. Learn to apply the rule:

WHICH/WHO/WHOM RULE

- Use *which* only to refer to things, never to refer to people.
- Use *who* in a sentence context where either *he* or *she* would be correct.
- Use *whom* in a sentence context where either *him* or *her* would be correct.

See if you can circle the correct word in the following sentences:

1. My brother, *who/whom* attends the state university, is majoring in history.
2. The baby, *who/which* is only nine months old, has already started walking.
3. A public speaker should keep in mind the audience *who/whom* she is addressing.
4. The company president is the person *which/whom* you need to contact.
5. The principal said that all students *who/whom* skip the pep rally will receive a detention.
6. The head librarian is the one to *which/whom* you must send your résumé.
7. The painting of *which/whom* I write is the work of an unknown genius.

Here are the correct answers, along with explanations in case you need help applying the rules:

1. *Who* is correct because you'd say He *attends the state university.*
2. *Who* is correct, because *the baby* is a person, not a thing.
3. *Whom* is correct because you'd say She *is addressing the audience.*
4. *Whom* is correct because you're referring to a person and you'd say *You need to contact* him.
5. *Who* is correct because you'd say He *skip[s] the pep rally.*

6. *Whom* is correct because you're referring to a person and you'd say *You must send your résumé to* him.

7. *Which* is correct because you're referring to the painting, a thing, not a person.

Now let's return to the paragraph you saw at the beginning of this section. This time, it's presented as a testlike passage with multiple-choice answers such as those that appear on the ACT. Use it to test your understanding of the various pronoun issues.

My mother and her work friends, nurses in a large emergency room, have many interesting stories <u>about their</u> [11] experiences. Some of these stories are about the challenges patients face,

11. **A.** NO CHANGE
B. about there
C. on they're
D. on their

but some of the funniest stories are about interactions <u>her and the other nurses have</u> [12] with various staff members.

12. **F.** NO CHANGE
G. her and the other nurses were having
H. she and the other nurses having
J. she and the other nurses have

Whenever Mom and <u>I have</u> [13] friends over at the same time,

13. **A.** NO CHANGE
B. I would be having
C. me have
D. me had

my friends and <u>me always wind up</u> [14] laughing at the things we hear.

14. **F.** NO CHANGE
G. I always wind up
H. I always winding up
J. me always winding up

The story about the doctor who thought <u>their cell phone had been</u> [15] "borrowed" by a nurse was hilarious.

15. **A.** NO CHANGE
B. there cell phone had been
C. they're cell phone had been
D. her cell phone had been

Mom and her friends <u>have given we</u> teenagers
16
some good advice:

16. F. NO CHANGE
G. having gave we
H. have gave us
J. have given us

One should not go into the medical field <u>if you</u>
17
<u>don't have</u> a good sense of humor.
17

17. A. NO CHANGE
B. if they don't have
C. without having
D. if you aren't having

11. The possessive pronoun *their* is underlined. It is plural, so it correctly refers to *my mother and her friends.* Following Step 2 of the Kaplan Method, you can eliminate choices B and C, which use the incorrect spelling: *there* and *they're.* The correct spelling of the pronoun is *their.* Follow Step 3 and plug in remaining choices, (A) and D. Choice D uses the incorrect preposition, *on,* so the correct answer is (A).

12. You should notice immediately that the underlined portion uses the pronoun *her.* Ask yourself if it's used correctly. Remember that you should be especially careful whenever you see an underlined pronoun near the word *and.* Think about how the pronoun sounds in context when you momentarily ignore the word that follows *and.* Does it sound correct to say *interactions* her *[has] with other staff members*? No, you would say *interactions* she *has with other staff members.* The issue here is pronoun case. You can eliminate F and G. Following Step 3, and reading H and (J) into the sentence, you should notice a verb error in H. The correct answer is (J).

13. Notice the underlined pronoun *I* and determine how it's used in the sentence. Here, *I* is used correctly as the subject of the clause *I have friends over.* Based on pronoun usage, you can eliminate C and D. Then, if you read B into the sentence, you can hear that it introduces a verb problem. The correct answer is (A).

14. The underlined portion contains the pronoun *me,* so first you should check to see if it's used correctly. It functions as a subject in the clause *me always wind up laughing.* Pronoun usage is definitely the issue here: the subject pronoun *I* is needed instead. Identifying the issue lets you eliminate F and J. Read the other choices into the sentence, and you'll hear that H introduces a verb error. The correct answer is (G).

15. There's an error in this sentence as it's written, but it's not an easy one for your ear to detect. Still, you should notice that the pronoun *their* is underlined, so find the matching antecedent in the passage. Who does *their* refer to? *Their* refers to the word *doctor.* The problem is *doctor* is singular, but *their* is plural. Because *doctor* is not underlined, you can't change it, so you have to change the pronoun *their.* Notice that B and C don't eliminate the pronoun; they simply substitute a different word that sounds the same.

Only (D) correctly uses a singular pronoun (*her*) to refer to the singular noun *doctor.* The correct answer is (D).

16. Your ear might help you easily identify the issue here. If not, notice that the underlined portion contains the pronoun *we,* and determine how it's used in the sentence. The fact that the pronoun immediately follows the verb *given* indicates that it's used here as an object; however, *we* is the form to use for a subject, so *we* is incorrect here. Thus, you can eliminate F and G. Read the other two choices. Both correctly use the objective pronoun *us,* but H introduces a verb error. The correct answer is (J).

17. The issue in this question is the *one-you* shift. That can be a difficult issue to recognize unless you think to look for it. The fact that the underlined portion includes the pronoun *you* should serve as a red flag. Whenever you notice this word underlined, check the surrounding context for consistency. Because the nonunderlined part of the sentence uses the word *one,* it's incorrect to use *you* in the same sentence. Remembering this rule allows you to eliminate A and D. Read the remaining choices into the sentence. Choice B uses the plural pronoun *they* to refer to the singular *one,* so it can't be correct. The correct answer is (C).

VERB QUESTIONS

You probably remember that a **verb** is a word, such as *draw*, *eat*, or *walk*, that expresses an action or a word, such as *is*, *were*, or *was*, that expresses a state of being. Though it can get pretty complicated to discuss every grammatical point relating to verbs, there are really only three verb usage rules that are tested on the ACT:

1. A verb must agree with its subject.
2. A verb's tense must be logically consistent with time-related phrases in the sentence and other verbs that are used in the passage.
3. Some verbs can form the past tense in a way other than using *-ed.*

An easy way to know if you have to apply one of these rules is to get used to noticing underlined verbs in the ACT English section, and when you do notice one, ask yourself the following questions:

- What is the subject of this verb? Does the underlined verb agree with its grammatical subject?
- Does the tense of the underlined verb make sense in relation to other words in the sentence? Is the underlined verb consistent with other verb tenses used in nearby sentences and the passage as a whole?
- Does this verb form the past tense correctly? Does it sound right?

What is the subject of this verb? Does the underlined verb agree with its grammatical subject?

A key thing to remember is that the noun immediately before the verb may not actually be the verb's subject.

In this example of incorrect subject-verb agreement, see if you can circle the subject and jot down the correction for the underlined verb in the space provided:

> Many of my friends, including everyone in the brass section of the band, is [__________] planning to come to my party.

Recall that the subject is who or what is doing the action that the verb expresses. In the sentence, you should have circled the word *Many,* which is the subject of this sentence. Detecting the incorrect subject-verb agreement here can be tricky because the subject, *many,* is separated from the verb by several phrases. As you work through English questions, both in your practice and on test day, circle the subject that goes with the underlined verb. Then read the subject and the verb without the words that appear between them. When you do this, you'll hear a mistake more easily. You wouldn't say, Many is *planning to come.* The correct subject-verb agreement here is Many are *planning to come.*

Does the tense of the underlined verb make sense in relation to other words in the sentence? Is the underlined verb consistent with other verb tenses used in nearby sentences and the passage as a whole?

To determine if an underlined verb makes sense within its own sentence, watch for time-related phrases and nonunderlined verbs. In the following example of illogical verb tense usage, circle the time-related word, and write down the correct verb tense in the space provided:

> Before my parents will let me take the car by myself, I had to [__________] improve my grade-point average considerably.

Here, you should have circled the time-related word *before* and the nonunderlined verb *will let.* If you focus on these words, you should see that the underlined *had,* in the past tense, is not logical in this sentence. Possible corrections are *have to, must,* and *will have to.* On the ACT, only one correct answer will be presented among the answer choices.

Does this verb form the past tense correctly? Does it sound right?

See if you can make the necessary correction in this sentence:

> Hemingway, along with several other Americans, had went [__________] to Paris to write.

The verb error in this sentence could be corrected in two ways, depending on the context. The key thing to spot here, though, is that *had went* is never correct. It's a good idea to train your ear to recognize several past tense forms that are common errors. The following forms are never correct: *had did, had flied, had wrote, had took.* You don't need to memorize every verb that forms the past tense irregularly (that is, with a spelling other than simply adding *-ed*), but you should be aware that this type of error is sometimes tested on the ACT.

WORD-CHOICE QUESTIONS

Many of the Mechanics questions on the ACT hinge on verb and pronoun usage, but there are a couple of other word-choice issues that you need to be aware of: modifiers, comparatives and superlatives, and idiomatic usages.

A **modifier** is something that describes or provides more information about a word. Two different parts of speech, adjectives and adverbs, function as modifiers. In addition to these single-word modifiers, phrases can also serve as modifiers. Let's look at the two modifier rules that are tested on the ACT.

SINGLE-WORD MODIFIER RULE

An **adjective** must be used only to modify a noun or a pronoun. An adverb must be used only to modify either a verb, an adjective, or another adverb.

Try the following exercise. Underline the adjective or adverb, and circle the word it logically modifies. Then determine whether the modifier is used correctly. If it isn't, put an *X* in the space provided.

1. ________________ Caitlin drove careful on the highway.

2. ________________ Carlos worked diligently on the project.

3. ________________ I am certainly that the show starts at 8:00.

4. ________________ Sarah found it was extreme cold in the tent.

5. ________________ Sonnesh is extremely happy.

6. ________________ Diligent work leads to success.

You should have identified questions 1, 3, and 4 as being incorrect. Question 1 incorrectly uses the adjective *careful* to modify the verb *drove.* (It should be *carefully*). Question 3 incorrectly uses the adverb *certainly* to modify the pronoun *I.* (*Certain* is correct here). Question 4 incorrectly uses the adjective *extreme* to modify the adjective *cold.* (*Extremely* is needed here). The other questions are correct. Question 2 uses the adverb *diligently* to modify the verb *worked.* Question 5 uses the adverb *extremely* to modify the adjective *happy.* Question 6 uses the adjective *diligent* to modify the noun *work.*

MODIFYING PHRASE RULE

A **modifying phrase** should be placed as close as possible to the word it modifies. Specifically, when a sentence begins with a modifying phrase, the next noun or pronoun in the sentence must be the word that that phrase logically modifies.

You can easily spot most introductory modifying phrases because they usually begin with a verb that ends in *-ed* or *-ing*.

You can easily spot most introductory modifying phrases because they usually begin with a verb that ends in *-ed* or *-ing*. If you remember this, you'll have no trouble at all with introductory modifiers on the ACT. Let's look at an example:

18. Having just returned from three weeks of primitive camping, sleeping in his own bed was what Matt looked forward to most.[18]

F. NO CHANGE
G. being home in his own bed was what Matt looked forward to most.
H. Matt most looked forward to sleeping in his own bed.
J. the thing Matt looked forward to most was sleeping in his own bed.

If you notice that the sentence starts with a modifying phrase (*Having just returned from three weeks of primitive camping*), and you ask yourself who or what this phrase logically describes, you'll find this question easy to get right! Logically, the introductory phrase can only be modifying *Matt*. Therefore, *Matt* must immediately follow the phrase, so you can eliminate all choices except (H). The key here is paying attention to the nonunderlined context of the sentence and using it to determine what the best answer is.

Like some modifier questions, another issue tested on the ACT also relates to adjectives. This is the issue of comparative and superlative adjectives. Generally, comparative adjectives end with *-er,* and superlative adjectives end in *-est.* You determine whether the **comparative** or **superlative** form of an adjective is correct by asking how many items are being compared.

COMPARATIVE AND SUPERLATIVE RULE

Use the comparative form of an adjective (for example, *older* or *shorter*) when only two people or things are being compared. Use the superlative form of an adjective (for example, *oldest* or *shortest*) when comparing three or more people or things.

Because the ACT cannot include a question without an unambiguously correct answer, the context surrounding a comparative or superlative must always make it clear how many things are being compared. In the following question, look for a phrase that clues you in on, or indicates, how many people are involved. Here's an example:

19. Of all my friends, I think Johanna is the most likely to become a doctor.[19]

A. NO CHANGE
B. more likely to become a doctor.
C. most likely becoming a doctor.
D. most likeliest to become a doctor.

If you focused on the word *all,* good for you! The phrase *of all my friends* tells you that three or more people are being discussed here. This means that the superlative form *most* is correct. Eliminate choice B and plug the remaining choices in. Choice C correctly uses the superlative *most likely,* but it creates a sentence structure problem by changing the verb to *becoming,* so eliminate C. You should eliminate D because the idea of the superlative is already included in the word *most,* so it's incorrect to change *likely* to *likeliest.* Thus, (A) is the correct answer.

The other word-choice issue that's tested on the ACT is idiomatic usage. An **idiom** is an expression that is conventionally phrased in a particular way. Most often, correct idiomatic usage hinges on prepositions like *over, between, among, through,* and *by.* For example, you would never say, "I'm traveling *at* school." You'd say, "I'm traveling *to* school." In different contexts, though, a different preposition can be correct. For example:

I'm in the math club _____ school.

Your ear should tell you that *at* is correct here. In fact, for idioms, it is indeed your ear that you must rely on to get the correct answer. Idioms, by definition, are not constructed by following any general rules. Idiomatic usage isn't heavily tested on the ACT, and in any case, the English language includes so many idioms that it would be impossible to give you a complete list to memorize. Instead, keep the following guideline in mind: whenever you notice that the underlined portion includes a preposition, think about how it sounds in context to make sure it's idiomatically correct.

Whenever you notice that the underlined portion includes a preposition, think about how it sounds in context to make sure it's idiomatically correct.

Sometimes, when you've eliminated two answer choices and are trying to choose the better one of the remaining two, thinking about correct idiomatic usage will help you select the correct answer.

RHETORICAL SKILLS QUESTIONS

Rhetorical Skills questions on the ACT demand a different approach from the Mechanics issues previously discussed. You can think of Mechanics questions as those that have black-and-white answers, governed by specific conventions that you can learn and apply. Rhetorical Skills questions, on the other hand, are not as simple.

To determine the best answer for a Rhetorical Skills question, you have to call upon some of the same skills you use for the Reading Comprehension questions in the ACT Reading section. Often, for Rhetorical Skills questions, you need to take a big-picture view of the passage. Whereas Mechanics questions can be answered by looking at a small part of the passage, often one sentence, and determining what is right and wrong, Rhetorical Skills questions demand that you consider broader aspects of the passage. As you determine the best answer for a Rhetorical Skills question, you may need to consider one or more of these points:

- What is the author's purpose in writing this passage?
- What effect does choosing one word or phrase instead of another create for the reader?
- What is the overall organizational structure of the passage?
- Would changing the order of sentences in a paragraph or the order of paragraphs in the passage make the writing easier to follow and understand?

As you'll see when you work on the Reading practice in this workbook, you'll need to address some of these same questions in order to choose the best answer for a Reading Comprehension question. Thus, it may be helpful to think of Rhetorical Skills questions as Reading questions that just happen to appear in the ACT English test.

RECOGNIZING A RHETORICAL SKILLS QUESTION

If the fact that the test maker puts Reading-like questions in the English section seems intimidating at first, don't worry. It is true that one of the biggest challenges of the ACT English section is that Mechanics and Rhetorical Skills questions are interspersed. As you begin your English practice, one thing you'll have to get used to is determining how much of the passage you need to consider when answering a given question. The first step of the Kaplan Method for ACT English—read until you have information to identify the issue—illustrates how important it is to know *how much of the passage you must consider* in order to get to the best answer.

There is, however, a general guideline that will help you greatly. While Mechanics questions are usually presented with just the question number and the four multiple-choice answers, Rhetorical Skills questions very often appear with a question stem, that is, something you must read between the question number and the multiple-choice answers. Therefore, you should take the presence of a question stem in the English section as a strong clue that the question is likely a Rhetorical Skills question, requiring you to consider the author's purpose and methods instead of right-or-wrong grammar and usage issues. One notable exception to the rule that Rhetorical Skills questions generally come with question stems is the category of questions that we call *Connections.* We will discuss Connections questions more in the next section.

WRITING STRATEGY QUESTIONS

Writing Strategy questions always appear with a question stem. A Strategy question asks you to choose which phrasing most effectively accomplishes a particular purpose. The most important thing you need to do is to **consider the question stem carefully!** You must read actively, and often it helps to "think with your pencil." When you read the question stem, think about which words most clearly express what the particular question is asking for. Quickly underline those words to help you focus. When you focus clearly on what the question is asking, the best answer will usually stand out among the offered choices.

In the following Strategy question, underline the key words in the stem *before* looking at the answer choices:

The biologist worked painstakingly for more than a year [20] before her research project yielded any publishable results.

20. To most effectively convey that the biologist relied on cooperation with other scientists the underlined portion should read:

F. NO CHANGE

G. needed to discuss methodology with her colleagues

H. planned many experiments

J. needed to order several pieces of costly equipment

If you focused on the words *cooperation and other scientists,* it's likely that (G) jumped out as the best answer. Choices F, H, and J are not incorrect for any grammatical reasons, but they do not fulfill the purpose identified by this question stem. When you're answering Writing Strategy questions, it's helpful to know that, for these questions, the test maker doesn't put ungrammatical or otherwise incorrect language in the answer choices. If you read through the answer choices looking for what sounds best, you won't get very far. The question stem of a Strategy question is crucial, so read it carefully before you look at the answer choices.

For most Writing Strategy questions, you can find a key phrase in the question stem. Get in the habit of looking for a key phrase and underlining it to help you focus on what the question is asking for.

Two kinds of Writing Strategy questions for which you will *not* find a key phrase to underline in the question stem are questions that ask about the effect of adding or deleting a certain phrase or sentence. For questions that ask about deletion, focus on the given phrase, asking yourself what effect it creates for you as a reader. Consider this example:

> The construction site was littered with debris. Scraps of wood, drywall, and various types of nails were scattered on the ground. Even large sheets of roofing materials, some still packaged as they came from the supplier, were lying against the unfinished exterior walls. [21]

21. The author is considering deleting the following sentence:

Scraps of wood, drywall, and various types of nails were scattered on the ground.

What would be lost if the author made this deletion?

A. Information about how long the building site had been unattended
B. A description of what materials are needed in construction
C. A suggestion about how to clean the site
D. Specific details that provide information about what the site looks like

To answer this question, consider the given sentence in the context of the passage. The previous sentence describes the site as *littered with debris,* and the sentence in question lists items that make up that debris. Because it offers specific details describing the debris, (D) is the best answer. If you focus on the given sentence's relation to the sentences around it and how it adds to your understanding of the author's purpose, you shouldn't fall for the wrong answer traps.

For Writing Strategy questions that ask about the effect of deleting information, consider the context and determine how the information contributes to the writer's purpose.

ORGANIZATION QUESTIONS

Organization questions test your understanding of logical sequence. It's easy to recognize an Organization question, because it usually involves sentences or paragraphs that are labeled with bracketed numbers in the text of the passage. Some Organization questions ask you to rearrange the order of the sentences within the paragraph (think of these as scrambled sentences questions) or the order of the paragraphs within the whole passage (think of these as scrambled paragraphs questions). Other Organization questions present a sentence to be added to the passage, and then ask you to determine the best location for it.

The important thing to keep in mind about Organization questions is that **they are based on logic**. The test maker can't present an Organization question unless there is a clearly discernable order to the particular paragraph or passage. Remember that each question on the ACT can have only one possible correct answer. Therefore, the way to succeed with an Organization question is first to recognize that it's testing logical sequence, and then to search carefully in the passage for particular words and phrases that provide the key to the correct sequence.

Sometimes a passage is organized according to a rough outline structure. For example, in a passage on nutrition, you might find separate paragraphs that discuss proteins, carbohydrates, fats, and antioxidants. If you were asked where to add a sentence about the antioxidant potential of a particular fruit, you'd put it in the fourth paragraph, the one focusing on antioxidants. Remember to use your reading skills to help you find the best answer to a question like that.

Another organizational format is the **chronological sequence**. As you read through an English passage that includes an organization question, be alert for specific dates and time references, such as *in 1750* or *before the American Revolution.* Dates and time references can serve as key clues when you need to determine the best location to add new information.

Another organizational format, similar to the chronological one, is the description of *sequence* in a process. As you read, notice words such as *first, second, then, next, last,* and *finally.* These words serve as clues to help you keep track of sequencing and can be useful if you need to find the best spot in the passage to add information.

As you work on this ACT-like Organization question, underline key words that help you determine the logical sequence, as in this example:

[1] If you're like most people, you may find that applying to college is a complicated process. [2] This in itself can be time-consuming; you need to search through guidebooks, learn about colleges from their websites, and talk to admissions officers at college fairs. [3] You also need to take standardized tests and continue to maintain your high school grade point average. [4] Then, by the fall of your senior year, you must actually start filling out applications and arranging to have supporting documentation sent to the colleges. [22]

22. Upon reviewing the paragraph and realizing that some information has been left out, the writer composes the following sentence:

> The first challenge is to narrow down a list of places you'd like to study.

The most logical placement for this sentence would be:

F. before sentence 1.

G. after sentence 1.

H. after sentence 2.

J. after sentence 3.

Did you find any words to underline in the paragraph? The word *then* in sentence 4 is one indicator of sequence. The sentence to be added, which is stated in the question stem, also contains a sequence clue: *first.* This word indicates that the sentence should most likely be added somewhere near the beginning of the paragraph. Plug the new sentence into the passage at the locations described by the answer choices, and think about how it sounds in each context. Notice that sentence 1 introduces the topic of the paragraph. Therefore, it wouldn't make sense to place the additional sentence before that. Read the new sentence after sentence 1, and continue reading sentence 2. The additional sentence fits perfectly here because sentence 2 lists several things that must be done in order to *narrow down a list of places.* You can quickly plug the sentence in at the other locations if you have time, but you should feel pretty confident that you've found the best answer in (G).

When you notice that a passage is presented with numbered paragraphs (the numbers will be in brackets, centered above each paragraph), be aware as you're working through the passage that the paragraphs may not be printed in the most logical order. The other possibility when a passage is printed with numbered paragraphs is that a later question will ask where in the passage is most appropriate to add extra information. If such a question is present for the passage, the paragraphs will be printed in the most logical order, and you will not see a scrambled paragraphs question for this passage.

For an Organization question that asks you to determine the best ordering of paragraphs, there are several points you should consider. First, glance at each paragraph to determine its topic. You might want to make a brief note in the margin or circle a word or phrase in each paragraph to help you identify the main idea. Second, ask yourself which of the paragraphs sounds like it would make the best introduction to the passage. Third, ask yourself which paragraph sounds most like a concluding paragraph. Usually, simply identifying the most logical introductory and concluding paragraphs is enough to let you determine the best sequence for all the paragraphs. Sometimes, you may have to consider the topics and relationships among the body paragraphs as well.

Consider the following scrambled paragraphs question. Even though we give you only the skeleton of a passage to work with, you should be able to find clues that allow you to determine the best sequence for the paragraphs.

[1]

Carbohydrates in food…

[2]

Protein comes from several sources…

[3]

With each passing decade, scientists learn more about how the components of food affect our health. Nutrition researchers have been aware of the basic building blocks, fats, carbohydrates, and proteins, for years. Fats are….

[4]

While nutritionists have been studying the three building blocks of food for years, they frequently turn their attention to new areas. Cholesterol, for example, came to the attention of nutritionists in the 1970s. It was discovered that heart disease…

[5]

In another development in nutrition, antioxidants began creating a stir in 2000 when…

Question 23 asks about the preceding passage as a whole.

23. For the sake of logic and coherence, paragraph 3 should be placed:

A. where it is now.
B. before paragraph 1.
C. after paragraph 1.
D. after paragraph 5.

Remember, an Organization question is testing your reading skills. Start by thinking about how paragraph 3 relates to the topics of the other paragraphs. Paragraph 1 discusses carbohydrates; paragraph 2 discusses proteins; paragraph 4 treats cholesterol; and the topic of paragraph 5 is antioxidants. Now read paragraph 3 carefully. Notice the second sentence: it mentions *carbohydrates* and *proteins,* topics of two of the other paragraphs. Therefore, paragraph 3 would make a good first paragraph because it introduces, at least partially, the rough outline structure of the passage. The best answer is (B).

CONNECTIONS QUESTIONS

Connections questions differ from the other types of Rhetorical Skills questions in that they generally don't appear with a question stem. Therefore, one of the most helpful things you can do to answer Connections questions correctly is to learn to recognize certain transitional words and phrases that appear frequently on the ACT. To find the best connections word or phrase to use in a specific context, you must read carefully in the nonunderlined part of the passage. Sometimes you need to read only the sentence that contains the underlined portion, but sometimes you must go back and carefully read the sentence before it as well.

Connections words and phrases are those that express a relationship between ideas. The two most common types of connections tested on the ACT are cause and effect connections and contrast connections. Other connections that are tested are sequence and emphasis. You should thoroughly familiarize yourself with the words and phrases in the following table. Whenever you see a connections word underlined, you can expect that the other answer choices will also be various connections words and phrases. Spotting a connections word on the ACT is a red flag that you need to think about logical relationships.

Connections Words and Phrases	
Connections that show addition, continuation, emphasis, or examples	additionally and for example for instance furthermore indeed in addition in fact likewise moreover
Connections that show cause and effect	as a result because consequently leading to since so therefore thus
Connections that show contrast	although but despite even though however nevertheless rather though whereas while
Connections that show sequence	finally first if...then last later next second then

Let's look at some examples of how connections words and phrases are tested on the ACT.

24. Many of my friends enjoy team sports; <u>*however*,</u> I prefer individual activities such as running and yoga.
24

F. NO CHANGE

G. but

H. therefore

J. in addition

If you train yourself to recognize the connections words and phrases shown in the table, you'll have no trouble identifying that this question tests connections. Whenever you notice that a connections word or phrase is underlined, read carefully in the surrounding context to determine how the ideas are related. This sentence has two parts. The first is *many of my friends enjoy team sports.* The second is *I prefer individual activities.* Ask yourself how the two ideas are related. Because *team sports* are different from *individual activities*, the relationship is one of contrast. When you first read the sentence, it should sound logical because *however* is a contrast connection. Indeed, (A) is the best answer here. You can eliminate C and D because they do not express contrast. Choice B does express contrast, but it is not appropriate here because a semicolon is used between the two independent clauses.

25. Although (25) she has a strong interest in Renaissance art, Elizabeth is eagerly anticipating her trip to Rome.

A. NO CHANGE
B. While
C. Since
D. Indeed

The presence of an underlined connections word here should alert you that you need to consider the relationship between ideas in the sentence. There are two ideas here: Elizabeth's interest in Renaissance art and her eager anticipation of her trip to Rome. Ask yourself how these ideas are connected. There is a lot of Renaissance art in Rome, so Elizabeth's interest in it leads her to be excited about visiting there. The relationship is one of cause and effect. You can eliminate F because it's a contrast connection. Eliminate B for the same reason. Eliminate D because it's an emphasis connection. Choice (C) is the best answer.

26. Restricting sodium in the diet is important to protecting one's health. A main source of dietary sodium can be found in canned, microwavable, and other prepared foods. Despite this (26), another source is the salt people add to their own food at the table.

F. NO CHANGE
G. However
H. In addition
J. For example

The underlined portion here is a connections phrase, one that shows contrast. Read the surrounding context carefully to determine if that is the appropriate kind of connection here. In this case, you must read not only the sentence that contains the underlined portion, but the sentence before it as well. The previous sentence lists one source of dietary sodium. The sentence containing the underlined segment lists *another source.* The appropriate connection here is one that expresses addition or continuation. Choice (H) is the only one of the answer choices that expresses continuation, so it's the best answer. Eliminate F and G because they're contrast connections. Eliminate J because it indicates an example rather than addition or continuation.

27. I would have called you, rather I couldn't—I lost my cell phone.
27

A. NO CHANGE

B. but

C. moreover

D. while

What do you do when you notice a connections word underlined? You're right, you read the sentence looking for the relationship between ideas! Here, ask yourself how losing the cell phone is related to not calling. The writer is saying that *if* she'd had her cell phone, she would have called. Not having the phone prevented the calling. The appropriate kind of connection here is contrast. This question illustrates the importance of reading the answer choices into the sentence. Notice that A, *rather,* is indeed a contrast connection, but it doesn't sound right here. Choice D, *while*, is also a contrast connection that doesn't work in the context. Choice (B), a contrast connection that fits perfectly in the context, is the best answer. Eliminate C because it's not a contrast connection.

Once you learn to recognize the various connections words, you should have no trouble with Connections questions on the ACT. Just let the presence of any underlined connections word remind you to consider the kind of logical relationship expressed in the sentence. Don't worry if a question includes more than one choice that's in the right category of connections. If that's the case, your ear will tell you which one is appropriate.

WORDINESS QUESTIONS

Wordiness questions on the ACT can be tricky if you're not prepared for them. As you work through the English section, it's important to remember that **concise writing is valued on the ACT**. In other words, sometimes one answer choice will be better than another *simply because it's shorter.* It can be easy to lose sight of this fact when you're working through the English section encountering so many questions—such as the Mechanics questions—that seem to have clear right-or-wrong answers.

There are two types of wordiness errors you can expect to see on the ACT. The first type is **redundancy.** Redundancy means saying the same thing twice, not literally, but saying something one way and then repeating the meaning in different words. For example:

My little brother worked hard on and put a lot of effort into building his sand castle.

You probably noticed here that *worked hard on* and *put a lot of effort into* mean pretty much the same thing. Only one phrase or the other should be used, not both. Remember, when you say the same thing twice *and you repeat yourself,* you're being redundant!

Fortunately for you, many redundancy questions come with a built-in clue that wordiness is the tested issue: the "OMIT the underlined portion" answer choice. Whenever you see that "OMIT" is provided as a choice, always start by asking yourself: Is the underlined portion truly necessary and would anything valuable be lost if the underlined portion were taken out? If the answers to these questions are "no," then you can confidently select OMIT as the best answer choice. You should note that OMIT, if it's offered as an answer choice, always appears as the fourth choice. (Remember, the ACT is highly predictable.)

Questions with OMIT as the last choice come with an added bonus. They can save you time. It means you often have to consider only two, not four, answer choices. If you read through a question and notice that OMIT is a choice, and if you determine that the underlined portion can indeed be omitted, then that's your answer. If you're going to leave something out, you don't have to choose the best way to word it, so you don't need to consider the middle two answer choices. Let's look at an example here:

28. My older sister, who is a sibling of mine, is studying to be a surgeon.
28

F. NO CHANGE

G. , who is of course one of my relatives,

H. , one of my siblings,

J. OMIT the underlined portion.

First, notice that OMIT is an answer choice. Remember, that's your clue to ask yourself whether the underlined portion is necessary! Read around the context to see if the underlined information is already expressed by other, nonunderlined words. That is the case here, because a sister, by definition, is a sibling. You can eliminate F and know that (J) is the best choice *without even taking the time to read* G and H.

Now let's consider another kind of Wordiness question, one that is not always as easy to recognize. This second kind of question is the Wordiness question for which OMIT is not offered as an answer choice. For this kind, you don't have the handy red flag to alert you that wordiness is the issue. Generally, instead of redundancy, this type of question tests **verbosity.** Verbosity means using more words than are necessary. Verbosity results when a long, drawn-out expression is used in place of a shorter one. Read this verbose sentence, and come up with a shorter way of expressing its meaning:

The student council held a meeting for the purpose of determining what would be the most profitable kind of fund-raising event.

___

___

___

Here's a more concise way to express the idea: *The student council met to determine the most profitable kind of fund-raising event.* You may have come up with a different version. The key thing is to notice the wordy phrases that could be replaced with shorter alternatives. Here's how a verbosity question might look on the ACT:

29. Jonathon wanted to write his history paper in the amount of time that would be the shortest possible. (29)

A. NO CHANGE

B. way that would take up the smallest amount of his time possible

C. in the least possible time

D. time that would be the least he could possibly spend on it

You may or may not notice wordiness as the issue here when you read the underlined portion. The problem with a wordy construction isn't grammatical (and grammatical issues are often easier to spot). Wordiness is a style issue, and that's more subtle. Therefore, you should always work through an English passage remembering that the best ACT style is *concise.* While there's no OMIT choice to serve as a warning here, there is another clue you might notice: (C) is considerably shorter than the other answer choices. When this is the case, it's often an indication that the issue is wordiness. If you can't determine anything really wrong with one or more answer choices, choose the shortest one. There's a good chance you'll be right. In this question, (C) is the correct answer because it's most concise. Eliminate the three other choices because they're verbose.

Let's look at one more example of an ACT Wordiness question. In this one, the sentence is wordy because it's redundant, but you won't find OMIT as an answer choice:

30. The intricate figures along the edge of the garden were created and sculpted by (30) the owner of the house.

F. NO CHANGE

G. sculpted by

H. were the creative work of a sculptor who is

J. the original creation of

Let's look at some ways you can identify that this question tests wordiness, even though OMIT is not the last answer choice. First, if you're reading carefully, your ear will tell you that *created and sculpted* is redundant, so you can eliminate F. Here, although *created* doesn't mean exactly the same thing as *sculpted,* the idea of *created* is part of the definition of *sculpted.* Second, you should notice that (G) is shorter than all the others are. Remember, when the meaning of the choices is basically the same, you should always go with the most concise one. Choice (G) is the best answer here. Eliminate H because it's both redundant (using *creative* and *sculptor,* similarly to F and verbose. Eliminate J because it's not as concise as (G).

PASSIVE-VOICE QUESTIONS

Like wordiness, the issue of passive voice relates to writing style. For matters of style, you have to use judgment to determine which choice sounds best; you can't simply apply a rule. Most sentences in English are worded in what we call the **active voice**. When a sentence is in the active voice, the subject of the sentence is the person or thing doing whatever action the verb expresses. On the other hand, when a sentence is in the passive voice, the subject of the verb is *receiving* the action instead of *doing* it. In other words, when an active sentence is written in the passive, the subject becomes an object. Some examples will make the difference clear. In the following sentences, the subjects are printed in upper case and the objects are underlined.

Active Voice: My FAMILY packed the <u>car</u> carefully before we left for vacation.
Passive Voice: The CAR was packed carefully by my <u>family</u> before we left for vacation.
Active Voice: My AUNT gave me a new <u>phone</u>.
Passive Voice: A new PHONE was given to me by my <u>aunt</u>.

Most of the time, we speak and write in the active voice. The active voice puts the emphasis on the subject, which is desirable most of the time. Occasionally, a speaker or writer who wants to emphasize the object, rather than the subject, chooses to use the passive voice. Generally speaking, however, it's preferable to use the active voice. Once in a while, you may come across an ACT question that tests whether you can recognize this. Here's an example:

31. <u>Her knowledge of knitting having been taught to me by my grandmother, I have expanded my skills even further.</u> 31

A. NO CHANGE
B. My grandmother taught me everything she knows about knitting, and I have expanded my skills even further.
C. Having been taught everything she knows by my grandmother, my knowledge of knitting has been expanded even further.
D. My grandmother taught me everything she knows about knitting, and my knowledge has been expanded by my own reading.

In A, the preposition *by* alerts you to check for the passive voice. The verb in the first part of the sentence is *taught*. The grammatical subject is *knowledge*. The person doing the teaching, however, is *my grandmother*. Because the subject is not doing the action, this is a passive construction. Examine the answer choices to see if an active voice wording is offered. It is. In (B), both the first and second parts of the sentence are written in the active voice, so (B) is the best answer. In C, in the second part of the sentence, the verb is *has been expanded* and the subject is *knowledge*, but it's not knowledge that is doing the expanding. The same thing is true in the second part of D, which also has *knowledge* as the subject and *has been expanded* as the verb.

You should note that while the active voice is preferable if all other things are equal, there are some situations in which other grammatical issues make the passive voice the only correct choice. The most common instance is in a sentence that begins with a modifying phrase. Consider this example:

32. Tattered and worn after years of use, the old book of poems was still treasured by my grandfather.
32

F. NO CHANGE

G. the poems in the old book were still treasured by my grandfather

H. my grandfather still treasured the old book of poems

J. the poems were treasured by my grandfather in the old book

The word *by* in the underlined portion is a clue that the expression is in the passive voice. Remember, though, it's not an absolute rule that the passive voice is always wrong. Sometimes, as in this question, the nonunderlined part of the sentence leaves you with no choice but to go with a passive construction. Choice (F) is actually the best answer here. Let's look at the other choices to see what's wrong with them. Choice G starts with *the poems.* Think about this in light of the context. The opening part of the sentence, *tattered and worn after years of use,* is an introductory modifier. Remember the rule from the Mechanics section that when a sentence opens with a modifier, the thing it logically describes must be the next noun in the sentence. Eliminate G because it is not *the poems* that are *tattered and worn,* but the *book.* Similarly, H, although written in the active voice, creates an illogical situation. (The meaning here is not that it's *my grandfather* who is *tattered and worn after years of use.*) Consider J. Like (F), it is written in the passive voice, but the phrase *in the old book* is not placed where it should be, after *poems.* For all these reasons, (F) is the best answer.

ENGLISH WRAP-UP

Now try your hand at the sample practice passages in the following chapters. Practice using the Kaplan Method just as you will on test day. Some of the practice passages here may be slightly longer than the ones you'll see on the actual ACT. On test day, each passage will be followed by 15 questions; to give you extra opportunities for practice, our passages in this book contain 17 problems, including two additional testlike questions to further hone your skills.

To get the most benefit from the practice passages, don't just answer the questions and check your answers against the answer key. Give some attention to *why* you got the questions wrong. Some questions to consider as your read the detailed answer explanations include:

- Is a preposition used? Is it idiomatically correct?
- Is there a verb that ends with *-ed* or *-ing* in the introductory modifier? If so, does the subject follow?

- What is the subject of this verb? Do the two agree?
- Are verb tenses used correctly? Is punctuation used properly?
- Is this the most concise answer choice?

The most effective way to get ready for the ACT is to spend time working on practice passages. We hope you've gotten a sense that the ACT English test is like a game, with easily identifiable rules that you can both learn and apply. As with any game, you are sure to improve with practice.

CHAPTER 4

English Practice Set I

Directions: In the following passage, certain words and phrases have been underlined and numbered. You will find alternatives for each underlined portion in the column to the right. Select the one that best expresses the idea, that makes the statement acceptable in standard written English, or that is phrased most consistently with the style and tone of the entire passage. If you feel that the original version is best, select "NO CHANGE." You will also find questions asking about a section of the passage or about the entire passage. For these questions, decide which choice gives the most appropriate response to the given question. For each question in the test, select the best choice, and fill in the corresponding space on the answer folder. You may wish to read each passage through before you begin to answer the questions associated with it. Most answers cannot be determined without reading several sentences around the phrases in question. Make sure to read far enough ahead each time you choose an alternative.

THE WEDDING CAKE HOUSE

Locals in Kennebunk, Maine, have built up a legend around an unusually 19th-century house [1] in that seaside town.

1. A. NO CHANGE
   B. a house unusually of the 19th century
   C. a house unusual of the 19th century
   D. an unusual 19th-century house

In contrast to [2] the frothy white ornamentation that covers much of the house's exterior, it is known as the Wedding Cake House. Furthermore,

2. F. NO CHANGE
   G. Due to
   H. Despite
   J. A consequence of

the wooden carvings were made, the legend suggests, by a newlywed sea captain, [3] who plied his woodworking talent

3. A. NO CHANGE
   B. a newlywed sea captain, the legend suggests, made the wooden carvings
   C. the legend suggests that the elaborate wooden carvings were made by a newlywed sea captain
   D. it has been suggested according to the legend that the wooden carvings were made by a newlywed sea captain

during lonely hours at sea [4] to surprise his bride upon his return home.

4. The author is considering deleting the underlined phrase. If this deletion were made, the essay would primarily lose:
   F. a fact that describes the house.
   G. a detail that enhances the romantic nature of the legend.
   H. relevant information about the sea-captain's job.
   J. a historical detail.

The reality is that the truth about the house departs from the appealing legend about the lovelorn sailor. The owner of the house, shipbuilder George Washington Bourne, brought his bride, Jane, to the house in 1825. The original house was an example of the balance and typifying symmetry on the Federalist architecture of the time. The two-story house, with a low hipped roof, multiple large casement windows spanning the front facade, and the area above the front door taken up by a large Palladian window, exemplified geometrical balance. The elaborate frosting-like designs being a later addition to this neoclassical house, though they didn't come about in the way the romantic legend describes.

5. A. NO CHANGE
B. reality of the situation is that
C. actual honest
D. OMIT the underlined portion.

6. F. NO CHANGE
G. Bourne, brought, his bride Jane,
H. Bourne brought his bride Jane,
J. Bourne brought his bride, Jane

7. A. NO CHANGE
B. symmetry that was typical on
C. symmetrical type of
D. symmetry that typified

8. F. NO CHANGE
G. a large Palladian window occupying the area above the front door
H. the area above the front door being occupied by a large Palladian window
J. taking up the area by above the front door, a large Palladian window

9. A. NO CHANGE
B. were being
C. were
D. making up a

[1] The transformation of the house from an example of neoclassic restraint to a building with so many Gothic overlays that it looked like a wedding cake resulting from (10) an accident. [2] In 1852, a fire destroyed the barn and shed (11) that were connected to the house. [3] The shipbuilder, now retired, decided on spending (12) his leisure hours carving wooden trim that he could apply to the main house so that its style, on the surface at least, would harmonize with (13) the style of his new Gothic barn. [4] Thus, the Wedding Cake House is technically not an example of the Gothic architecture it appears to emulate; moreover, (14) it remains a neoclassical

10. **F.** NO CHANGE
G. was being caused by
H. had been causing by
J. was the result of

11. **A.** NO CHANGE
B. the barn and shed were destroyed by a fire
C. the barn and shed burning down
D. a fire destroying the barn and shed

12. **F.** NO CHANGE
G. decided to spend
H. decided that to spend
J. deciding he would spend

13. **A.** NO CHANGE
B. be in harmony to
C. create the appearance of harmony with
D. harmonizes with

14. **F.** NO CHANGE
G. however
H. rather
J. therefore

Federal style house that displays multiple touches of Gothic styling: buttresses arches cornices, and pinnacles. 15 [16]

15. A. NO CHANGE
 B. styling; buttresses, arches, cornices, and pinnacles.
 C. styling, buttresses: arches, cornices, and pinnacles.
 D. styling: buttresses, arches, cornices, and pinnacles.

16. Upon reviewing this paragraph and finding that some information has been left out, the writer composes the following sentence incorporating that information:

 Bourne, well-traveled and an admirer of the Gothic architecture he had seen in Europe, rebuilt the barn with five tall pinnacles reminiscent of those on the Milan cathedral.

 This sentence would most logically be placed after sentence
 F. 1.
 G. 2.
 H. 3.
 J. 4.

Question 17 asks about the preceding passage as a whole.

17. Suppose the writer's goal had been to write a brief essay describing a house with features of two different architectural styles. Would this essay fulfill that goal?
 A. Yes, because the Wedding Cake House includes elements from both the Federalist and the Gothic styles.
 B. Yes, because the original Federalist style house was associated with a legend.
 C. No, because the Wedding Cake House was originally built in the Federalist style.
 D. No, because the carvings that gave the Wedding Cake House its name are in only the Gothic style.

ANSWERS AND EXPLANATIONS

1. D	**10. J**
2. G	**11. A**
3. C	**12. G**
4. G	**13. A**
5. D	**14. H**
6. F	**15. D**
7. D	**16. G**
8. G	**17. A**
9. C	

1. **D**

The issue is word choice. Choice A incorrectly uses the adverb *unusually* to modify the adjective *19th-century.* If you recognize this error, your eye will probably be drawn to (D), which corrects the modifier error. Just to make sure, plug in the other two choices. Eliminate B because it incorrectly uses the adverb *unusually* to modify the noun *house.* Eliminate C because *unusual **of*** is the wrong preposition (*unusual **for*** is correct) and because it's wordy.

2. **G**

The issue is connections. You should recognize that the underlined segment, *in contrast to,* is a connections phrase. That's a signal to read the sentence carefully for meaning and look for what the logical connection between ideas is. Here, *the frothy white ornamentation* on *the house's exterior* provides the reason that the house is called the Wedding Cake House. The relationship is one of cause and effect. Having identified this, you can eliminate F and J, both of which are contrast connections. To decide between (G) and J, plug them into the sentence. Choice J is not as concise as (G), so (G) is the best of the four choices.

3. **C**

The issue is sentence sense. Pay attention here to the nonunderlined context. Ask yourself what the introductory modifier, *furthermore,* means. Then ask yourself what word must come next in the sentence. It is *the legend* that builds *on this name.* Because (C) makes *legend* follow the phrase that describes it, it is correct.

4. **G**

The issue is writing strategy. Think about the meaning expressed by the phrase under consideration, *during lonely hours at sea.* Read through the answer choices to see which one works. Choice F is wrong because the phrase does not describe the house. Choice (G) is the best because it implies that the sea captain is missing his bride. Choice H may be tempting, because the sea captain's job does include *lonely hours at sea,* but the paragraph's focus is more on the sea captain and his bride than it is on his job. Choice J is wrong because the phrase does not include a historical detail.

5. **D**

The issue is wordiness. Remember, whenever OMIT is an choice, consider it first. The sentence makes sense without the underlined phrase. Indeed, the word *reality* in A and B repeats the idea of *truth* in the nonunderlined portion. Choice C is also redundant. There is no need to say *actual honest* before *truth.* Choice (D) is the best answer.

6. **F**

The issue is punctuation. This sentence contains two nonessential phrases that must be set off by commas. The basic part of the sentence is *The owner of the house...brought his bride...to the house in 1825.* The descriptive phrase *shipbuilder George Washington Bourne* and the name *Jane* are nonessential information. Choice (F) correctly uses commas to set off this nonessential information. A comma in G incorrectly separates the verb *brought* from its object *his bride.* Choice H is incorrect because it leaves out the two necessary commas after *Bourne* and *bride.* Choice J is incorrect because it omits the necessary comma after *Bourne.* The best answer is (F).

7. **D**

The issue is word choice. The phase *symmetry* ***on*** is not idiomatically correct here. Identifying that lets you eliminate A and B. Read the other two choices into the sentence. Though the phrase *symmetry* ***of*** would be the correct idiom, C, *symmetrical type of* doesn't make sense. Choice (D) is the best answer.

8. **G**

The issue is sentence sense, specifically parallelism. Check the nonunderlined context. This sentence includes a list that starts *a low hipped* ***roof****, multiple large casement* ***windows****....* Because the list is made up of nouns that describe features of the house, parallelism is best established by putting *large Palladian* ***window*** next in the list. If you recognize this, you can eliminate every choice except (G). Choice H repeats the parallelism error in F. Choice (J) is better than F and H, but it still doesn't establish parallelism as clearly as (G), which is the best answer.

9. **C**

The issue is sentence sense. Whenever you notice an *-ing* verb underlined, check to make sure that, if it is used as the main verb in a clause, it has a helping verb with it. Choice A is incorrect because *being* is used here without a helping verb as the main verb of the sentence. Eliminate D for the same reason. Plug the remaining choices into the sentence. Eliminate B because *being* is not necessary with *were*. Choice (C) is the best answer.

10. **J**

The issue is sentence sense. Choice F uses the *-ing* verb *resulting* as the main verb of the clause without a helping verb, so eliminate it. Read the other choices. Choice G is wordy because the word *being* is not necessary here. Choice H is wrong because *had been causing* is not the right verb form in context. Choice (J) is the best answer.

11. **A**

The issues are sentence sense and passives. The best answer is (A). Choice B is not the best answer because the statement is in the passive voice. Eliminate C because it uses *burning*, an *-ing* verb, without a helping verb, as the main verb in a clause. Eliminate D because it also uses an *-ing* verb, *destroying*, as the main verb without a helping verb.

12. **G**

The issues are sentence sense and idioms. You should be able to recognize that F, *decided* ***on spending***, is not the correct idiomatic usage. Choice (G), *decided* ***to*** *spend,* corrects the idiom error and is the best choice. Read H into the sentence. You should hear that it creates sentence structure problems. Eliminate J because it uses the *-ing* verb *deciding* as the main verb of a clause. The best choice is (G).

13. **A**

The issues are idioms, wordiness, and sentence sense. There is no error in (A), so it is the best answer. Read the other choices into the sentence to confirm this. Choice B contains incorrect idiomatic usage, *be in harmony* ***to***, and is wordy. Choice C is wordy. Choice D uses the present tense *harmonizes* and so is not consistent with the context of the passage, which requires a past tense verb here.

14. **H**

The issue is connections. Whenever you notice a connections word underlined, such as *moreover* here, remember that you need to read the sentence carefully for meaning to determine the best logical connection. Choice F, *moreover,* is a transition that expresses emphasis, which is not appropriate here. The first part of the sentence states that the Wedding Cake House is not an example of Gothic architecture. The second part states that the house's style is neoclassical federal. This calls for a contrast connection. Eliminate J, *therefore,* because it is a cause-and-effect connection. Choices G and (H) are both contrast transitions, but you must read them in the sentence to tell which is best. Choice (H), *rather,* sounds best in the context here.

15. **D**

The issue is punctuation. Notice that A uses a colon to introduce a list. This is correct, but there is another problem here. The word *buttresses*, one of the items in the list, needs to be followed by a comma. Eliminate A. Having identified that the colon is correct, you should be drawn to (D) as the best answer. It corrects the comma problem in A. Choice B is incorrect because it uses a semicolon when what follows is not an independent clause. Choice C is incorrect because it puts the colon in the wrong place.

16. **G**

The issue is organization. The best way to handle a question like this is to read the sentence to be added into the passage at the locations indicated by the answer choices. Choice F seems a possibility, but it is not the best answer. The additional sentence introduces Bourne's Gothic-style barn, so it makes sense to add this sentence *before* the existing mention of the *new Gothic barn.* Eliminate H because the *new Gothic barn* has already been mentioned in sentence 3. Eliminate J because sentence 4 discusses the house, not the barn. Choice (G) is the best answer.

17. **A**

The issue is writing strategy. The key words to focus on in the question stem are *describing a house with features of two different architectural styles.* The essay certainly does this, so eliminate C and D. Now look at the reasons given in (A) and B. The reason provided in (A) relates directly to the question asked in the question stem, so (A) is the correct answer. The reason given in B is true according to the passage, but it doesn't address the question in the question stem.

CHAPTER 5

English Practice Set II

Directions: In the following passage, certain words and phrases have been underlined and numbered. You will find alternatives for each underlined portion in the column to the right. Select the one that best expresses the idea, that makes the statement acceptable in standard written English, or that is phrased most consistently with the style and tone of the entire passage. If you feel that the original version is best, select "NO CHANGE." You will also find questions asking about a section of the passage or about the entire passage. For these questions, decide which choice gives the most appropriate response to the given question. For each question in the test, select the best choice, and fill in the corresponding space on the answer folder. You may wish to read each passage through before you begin to answer the questions associated with it. Most answers cannot be determined without reading several sentences around the phrases in question. Make sure to read far enough ahead each time you choose an alternative.

FANTASY LITERATURE: IT'S MORE THAN HARRY POTTER

J. K. Rowling, author of the immensely popular Harry Potter series, has wrought her own special magic in the fantasy genre. Though she may be the best-known fantasy writer to the current generation, she [1] is hardly the first. A number of authors, many of which, [2] like Rowling, are British, wrote fantasy novels before J. K. Rowling was born.

One such writer is George MacDonald, a Scottish minister, best known for his novels *Phantastes* and *Lilith.* MacDonald's work, similar to Rowlings', [3] showed that fantasy literature could hold appeal for older children and even adults. In *Phantastes*, a young man named Anodos journeys through a fantasy land where he experiences magical adventures. While [4] *Phantastes* is a relatively light story, *Lilith*, a much later work by MacDonald, is a more darker and more provocative [5] tale. In this

1. **A.** NO CHANGE
   B. generation: she
   C. generation; she
   D. generation. She

2. **F.** NO CHANGE
   G. of which many,
   H. many of whom,
   J. many being those whom,

3. **A.** NO CHANGE
   B. like Rowling's
   C. as with Rowlings'
   D. like with Rowling's

4. **F.** NO CHANGE
   G. Because
   H. Despite that
   J. Given that

5. **A.** NO CHANGE
   B. most provocatively dark
   C. darker and most provocative
   D. darker and more provocative

novel a character, called Mr. Vane travels through a fantasy land. There he encounters Lilith, an attractive but troubling fairy princess. In describing Mr. Vane's experiences, MacDonald explores the questions of
6

6. F. NO CHANGE
G. novel, a character called
H. novel a character called
J. novel, a character called,

how meaning is found in the condition of being human and how redemption might be possible.
7

7. A. NO CHANGE
B. human nature and what that means
C. what it means to be human
D. how being human has meaning

Another British fantasy writer, C. S. Lewis, acknowledged
8

8. The writer is considering deleting the underlined portion. If this deletion were made, the paragraph would primarily lose:
F. a description of C. S. Lewis's work.
G. a fact about C. S. Lewis's ethnic origin.
H. a phrase that relates C. S. Lewis to the novelists discussed above.
J. a description showing contrast between C. S. Lewis and George MacDonald.

the fact that he felt indebted to George MacDonald. It was MacDonald's mythmaking, rather than his writing style, that Lewis admired. Lewis's *Chronicles of Narnia*, a tale with mythic power, is a group of seven books tied together
9

9. A. NO CHANGE
B. his feelings of owing a debt to
C. his feeling of being really indebted to
D. that he felt indebted to

more than the fictional world they describe than by the narration of a particular character's experiences. Narnia is a magical place where animals can talk and
10

10. F. NO CHANGE
G. rather more than
H. more by
J. more with

time seemed to progress at its own rate. Like Harry
11
Potter and his mates at Hogwarts, the characters

11. A. NO CHANGE
    B. time progresses
    C. time would be progressing
    D. the progress of time is

whom inhabit Narnia struggle with the conflicting
12
forces of good and evil.

12. F. NO CHANGE
    G. which inhabits
    H. who inhabits
    J. who inhabit

Yet another fantasy series, occupying fewer printed pages

but treating its material in the same broad scope that
13
Rowling does, is J. R. R. Tolkien's *Lord of the Rings*.

Here, the tension

13. A. NO CHANGE
    B. and
    C. however
    D. thus

between good and evil are played out in epic scale; the
14
series describes a fellowship of nine characters who journey together in a quest to dispose properly of the ring in the title. As Lewis does with Narnia, Tolkien

14. F. NO CHANGE
    G. among good and evil is
    H. between good and evil is
    J. between good or evil are

was inventing a universe, which he calls Middle Earth,
15
and fills it with a range of characters from mortal humans to

15. A. NO CHANGE
    B. inventing
    C. invents
    D. invented

immortal elves and horrifying creatures called "orcs"
16
and "uruk-hai."

16. F. NO CHANGE
G. elves who are immortal
H. more immortal elves
J. elves being immortal

Question 17 asks about the preceding passage as a whole.

17. Suppose that the writer had been assigned to write a brief essay describing the influence of earlier fantasy novelists on J. K. Rowling. Would this essay successfully fulfill that goal?
A. Yes, because three fantasy authors are discussed along with J. K. Rowling.
B. Yes, because the issue of an author's indebtedness is discussed.
C. No, because J. K. Rowling is the most recent of the writers discussed, and she is the only woman.
D. No, because the essay mentions other fantasy novelists, but does not discuss particular ways that J. K. Rowling was influenced by them.

ANSWERS AND EXPLANATIONS

1. **A**
2. **H**
3. **B**
4. **F**
5. **D**
6. **G**
7. **C**
8. **H**
9. **D**
10. **H**
11. **B**
12. **J**
13. **A**
14. **H**
15. **C**
16. **F**
17. **D**

1. **A**

The issue is punctuation. Choice (A) correctly uses a comma to set off introductory information from the main part of the sentence. If you don't spot this right away, plug the other choices into the sentence. Choice B incorrectly uses a colon to introduce something that is not a list, example, or explanation. Eliminate C because it incorrectly uses a semicolon after a dependent clause. Eliminate D; while it puts a period after a dependent clause, this is incorrect because a dependent clause cannot stand alone as a sentence. Choice (A) is the correct choice.

2. **H**

The issue is pronouns. Whenever you see a pronoun underlined, check to see that it's used correctly. In F, the pronoun *which* is used incorrectly to refer to people. Recognizing this, you can eliminate F and G. Plug in the other choices to determine the best one. Choice J is awkward and certainly wordy compared to (H). Choice (H) is the best answer.

3. **B**

The issue is punctuation, specifically the apostrophe. Eliminate A because *Rowling,* a singular noun, does not form the possessive by adding *s'*. Knowing this, you can also eliminate C. Plugging the remaining choices into the sentence, you should be able to tell that D is wordy, adding an unnecessary *with* after *like*. This leaves (B) as the best answer choice.

4. **F**

The issue is connections. When the underlined portion includes a connections word like *which*, determine the logical relationships that the sentence expresses. The sentence here conveys the contrast between a *light story* and a *darker and more provocative tale*. Choice (F) is appropriate because *while* expresses this contrast. Eliminate G and J because they are both cause-and-effect connections. Choice H is a contrast connection, but it is not suitable in this particular context. Choice (F) is the best answer.

5. **D**

The issue is word choice. When you see a comparative adjective (one that ends in *-er)* underlined, check to make sure it's used correctly. Here, using the comparative *darker* instead of the superlative *darkest* is correct, because two things are being compared. This line of thinking should help you eliminate B and C, which incorrectly use the superlative *most*. To eliminate A, remember that a comparative adjective, like *darker,* should never be preceded by another comparative word, like *more*. Choice (D) is the best answer.

6. **G**

The issue is punctuation. In F, you should notice that the sentence contains the introductory phrase *in this novel*, which should be set off by a comma. Knowing this, you can eliminate F and H. Plug (G) and J into the sentence. Choice J is incorrect because it uses a comma after *called*, incorrectly separating a verb from its object. The correct answer is (G).

7. **C**

The issue is wordiness. Choice A is wordy. If you don't recognize this immediately, plug in the other choices. Choice B is awkward and also a bit wordy. Choice (C) is concise and is the best answer. Choice D is wordy and awkward.

8. **H**

The issue is writing strategy. When a question stem asks about what would be lost by deleting a portion, read that portion carefully and consider how it functions in its context. Also, note that the question stem includes the word *primarily.* This means you should determine the most important aspect of the underlined portion. Here, F is considered a trap answer since the underlined portion does recognize that Lewis was a fantasy author. Choice G is also tempting because the phrase does indicate Lewis's ethnic origin. Choice (H), however, is even better than either F or G. The phrase in question opens the paragraph, and the word *another* shows continuity between Lewis and the writers discussed in earlier paragraphs. Eliminate J because the phrase compares, but does not contrast. Choice (H) is the best answer.

9. **D**

The issue is wordiness. As with many wordiness problems, you may not immediately identify the issue simply by reading A. Still, read the other choices in the sentence. Choice (D) is the most concise and direct among the others, so it is the best choice.

10. **H**

The issue is idioms. Choice F uses an incorrect idiomatic expression, *tied together...**than***. Recognizing this, you can eliminate F and G. The correct idiom here is *tied together **by***. If you know this, you can recognize (H) is the best answer. If not, read (H) and J in the sentence. Train your ear to "hear" the idiom error in J; the preposition *with* is incorrect. The best answer is (H).

11. **B**

The issue here is sentence sense, particularly as it relates to verb tenses. Whenever you notice an underlined verb, one of the things to check for is whether its tense is consistent with the other tenses in the surrounding context. In A here, the past tense verb *seemed* is inconsistent with the present tense verbs *is* and *describe* used elsewhere in the sentence. Knowing this, you can spot the inconsistency in C as well, which uses *would be.* Having eliminated A and C, you should plug the other two into the sentence. Choices (B) and D both correctly use the present tense, but (B) is the better choice because D is wordy.

12. **J**

The issue is pronouns. When you notice an underlined pronoun, one of the things to check is how it functions in the sentence. Here, *whom* is used incorrectly as the subject of the verb *inhabit.* The pronoun form *who* is required here. You can eliminate G because the pronoun *which* is used only to refer to things, never to people. Read the remaining choices in the sentence to decide which is better. The pronoun *who* can refer to nouns that are either singular or plural. In this case, *who* refers to *characters,* which is plural. The correct verb form, therefore, is *characters who **inhabit***. Choice (J) is the best answer.

13. **A**

The issue is connections. Whenever you notice a connections word underlined (in this case, *but*), consider carefully the relationship between the ideas around it. This sentence sets up a contrast: Tolkien's series has a shorter page count, yet treats its material in a broad scope. The word *but* nicely expresses this contrast. Consider the other choices. Choice B, *and,* is a simple joining word; it doesn't express contrast, so eliminate it. Choice C correctly expresses contrast, but it doesn't work in the structure of this particular sentence. Eliminate D because *thus* is a cause-and-effect, rather than a contrast, connections word. The best answer is (A).

14. **H**

The issues are word choice and verb usage. When you notice that the word *between* is underlined, pause to ask yourself how many things are being talked about. Here, two things, *good and evil,* are being discussed, so *between* is correct. *Among* refers to more than two compared objects, which eliminates G as a possible answer choice. Notice, though, that the underlined portion includes the verb *are.*

One thing to check for when you see an underlined verb is subject-verb agreement. Ask yourself what the subject of *are* is. It is *tension*, so the correct verb form here is *is*. Knowing that *between* is correct here and that the correct verb is *is*, you can eliminate F and J.

15. **C**

The issue is sentence sense, especially as relates to verb tense. When you see an underlined verb, remember to check that its tense is consistent with the tense used in the surrounding context. In the nonunderlined part of this sentence, you find the present tense verbs *does* and *calls*. This is an indication that a present tense verb is needed. Eliminate A and D because they use the past tense. Eliminate B because it uses an *-ing* verb alone as the main verb of a clause without a helping verb. Eliminate D because it uses the past tense. The best answer is (C).

16. **F**

The issue is wordiness. You may not be able to identify this issue until you read all of the answer choices. Choice (F) is clearly the most concise, so it is the best answer.

17. **D**

The issue is writing strategy. The key words to focus on in the question stem are *describing the influence of earlier fantasy novelists on J. K. Rowling*. Ask yourself what the purpose of the essay is. It mentions three fantasy writers who worked before Rowling, but it doesn't specifically describe how they influenced her. Knowing this, you can eliminate A and B. Now consider the reasons provided in C and (D). In C, the fact that Rowling is the most recent of the writers does not mean that the influence of the previous writers must be discussed, and the fact that Rowling is a woman is irrelevant. The reason given in (D) specifically addresses the question posed by the question stem. Choice (D) is the best answer.

CHAPTER 6

English Practice Set III

Directions: In the following passage, certain words and phrases have been underlined and numbered. You will find alternatives for each underlined portion in the column to the right. Select the one that best expresses the idea, that makes the statement acceptable in standard written English, or that is phrased most consistently with the style and tone of the entire passage. If you feel that the original version is best, select "NO CHANGE." You will also find questions asking about a section of the passage or about the entire passage. For these questions, decide which choice gives the most appropriate response to the given question. For each question in the test, select the best choice, and fill in the corresponding space on the answer folder. You may wish to read each passage through before you begin to answer the questions associated with it. Most answers cannot be determined without reading several sentences around the phrases in question. Make sure to read far enough ahead each time you choose an alternative.

GAMELAN MUSIC

The gamelan is an Indonesian musical ensemble traditionally heard in variously ritualistic settings [1]. Unlike a symphony orchestra,

1. A. NO CHANGE
   B. in various ritual settings
   C. in settings that are varied and ritualistic
   D. ritually in variously settings

which being composed of [2] the same kinds of instruments as those used in any other symphony orchestra, each gamelan is made up of a unique set of instruments.

2. F. NO CHANGE
   G. composing
   H. is composed of
   J. had been composing of

These instruments are made [3] and tuned to be played together in a particular grouping.

3. A. NO CHANGE
   B. constructed, made
   C. built, made
   D. constructed and built

An instrument made for one gamelan, however, [4] cannot be used in a different gamelan.

4. F. NO CHANGE
   G. therefore
   H. on the contrary
   J. as a consequence of this

Percussion instruments play a significant role in any gamelan; for [5] some of these have a melodic component as well. However, the main melody of a piece is carried by stringed instruments, such as the rebab,

5. A. NO CHANGE
   B. gamelan,
   C. gamelan for
   D. gamelan, for

or by wind instruments. Such [6] as the bamboo flute. Whereas in a symphony orchestra all melodic instruments are tuned to the same key,

6. F. NO CHANGE
   G. instruments: such
   H. instruments; such
   J. instruments, such

melodic instruments in a gamelan are [7] tuned to be complementary with, but not necessarily to match, the tuning system used by other instruments in the gamelan. In addition to the wind instruments,

7. A. NO CHANGE
   B. instruments in a gamelan were
   C. instruments' in a gamelan were
   D. instrument's in a gamelan are

parts for the human voice may be present additionally [8] in a gamelan composition.

8. F. NO CHANGE
   G. may be present
   H. being also present
   J. likewise being included

Gongs are an important component of a gamelan. [9] These include metallophones, gong chimes, hanging gongs, xylophone-like instruments called gambang, and drums.

9. Which choice would make the most effective and appropriate introductory sentence for this paragraph?
   A. NO CHANGE
   B. Several types of percussion instruments are used in a gamelan.
   C. The hand and the mallet are two methods of playing.
   D. There is not a set number of instruments in a gamelan.

The metallophones, used for both percussion and melody, consists in a series of tuned metal
10
bars that are struck with a mallet.

10. F. NO CHANGE
G. consist in
H. consists of
J. consist of

Gong chimes are gong sets of gongs that are
11
largely placed horizontally on stands, while
11
hanging gongs drop vertically from a stand. Gambang are similar to metallophones, but with keys made of wood rather than metal.

11. A. NO CHANGE
B. standing large gongs set horizontally in places
C. large gong sets that are placed on horizontal stands
D. horizontal placed large gong standing sets

A gamelan's drums are constructed in asymmetrical pairs, with the larger one on the right.
12

12. F. NO CHANGE
G. with the larger one being
H. with the largest one
J. the largest one being

The drums are typically played with the hands.

While gamelan music today is frequently
13

13. Which of the following choices would NOT be acceptable as an alternative to the underlined portion?
A. Whereas
B. Although
C. Because
D. Even though

performed <u>of its</u> own sake at concerts, it was
14
traditionally intertwined with social life.

14. F. NO CHANGE
G. for its
H. of its'
J. for it's

The gamelan was a part of various ritual activities, <u>between</u> theatrical performances, shadow
15
puppet plays, and coming-of-age ceremonies.

15. A. NO CHANGE
B. including
C. among
D. despite

Gamelan music also <u>accompanied, dances at</u>
16
<u>religious temples, the royal court,</u> and village
16
festivals.

16. F. NO CHANGE
G. accompanied dances, at religious, temples, the royal court,
H. accompanied dances: at religious temples, the royal court
J. accompanied dances at religious temples, the royal court,

Question 17 asks about the preceding passage as a whole.

17. Suppose the writer's goal had been to write an essay persuading the reader that gamelan music is more complex than symphonic music. Would this essay fulfill that goal?

A. Yes, because various aspects of both the symphony orchestra and the gamelan are discussed in the essay.
B. Yes, because the writer describes several differences between the gamelan and the symphony orchestra.
C. No, because the essay is descriptive only and does not attempt to persuade the reader.
D. No, because only complexities of the symphony orchestra are described.

ANSWERS AND EXPLANATIONS

1. B	**10. J**
2. H	**11. C**
3. A	**12. F**
4. G	**13. C**
5. D	**14. G**
6. J	**15. B**
7. A	**16. J**
8. G	**17. C**
9. B	

1. **B**

The issue is modifiers. Logically, the adverb *variously* is not meant to modify the adjective *ritualistic*. Identifying the issue allows you to eliminate A and D. Then plug the remaining choices into the sentence. Choice (B) is the best. The two adjectives *various* and *ritual* both modify the noun *settings*. Choice C is not the best because it's wordy.

2. **H**

The issue is sentence sense. The verb form *being composed of* is not an acceptable form as it is used in the dependent clauses, beginning with *which*. If you notice that the problem is with the *-ing* form of the verb, you can also eliminate G and J. The best answer is (H) because it uses the correct verb form in the dependent clause.

3. **A**

The issue here is redundancy, but you may not be able to identify it right away because the underlined part doesn't contain an error. If you don't notice the redundancy as you look through the answer choices, try plugging each into the sentence. Choices B, C, and D all introduce redundancy, because *built, made,* and *constructed* all mean roughly the same thing.

4. **G**

Notice that the underlined word *however* is a connections word. Whenever you see such a word underlined, that's a clue that you should read the nonunderlined context carefully to determine the logical relationship between two ideas. Think about the meaning of the sentence before this one: If the instruments are designed to be used together in a *particular grouping*, then the instruments for *one* gamelan cannot be used in a *different gamelan*. You need a connections word that expresses cause and effect. Eliminate F and H because they both express contrast. Because (G) and J both express cause and effect, you must read each into the sentence to determine which is best. You should eliminate J because it's wordy, leaving (G) as the best answer.

5. **D**

The issues here are punctuation and sentence structure. You should be able to recognize that A is wrong because the semicolon cannot be used with the word *for* to join two independent clauses. Read the other choices into the sentence to test them for correctness. Choice B is wrong because it creates a run-on by joining two independent clauses with only a comma. Choice C creates a punctuation problem, because a comma is required before *for,* a FANBOYS word, when it's used to join two independent clauses. Choice (D) is best because it correctly uses *for* with the comma.

6. **J**

The issues here are punctuation and sentence structure. Choice F is incorrect because it punctuates *Such as the bamboo flute* as a complete sentence when it's just a phrase. If you recognize this, you may be able to spot immediately that (J), using the comma, is correct. If not, plug each choice in. Choice G is wrong because what follows the colon is not an explanation. Choice H is wrong because what follows the semicolon is not an independent clause.

7. **A**

The issues are punctuation (the apostrophe) and sentence sense. Choice (A) avoids the incorrect apostrophe used in C and D. Choice (A) also correctly uses the present tense verb *are,* which matches the overall tense of the passage. Choices B and D incorrectly use the past tense verb *were*.

8. **G**

The issue is redundancy, though this may be hard to spot at first. The underlined word *additionally* unnecessarily repeats the meaning of the nonunderlined phrase *in addition* at the beginning of this sentence. Eliminate H and J, because they both create redundancy with the words *likewise* and *also*. Choice (G) is the best answer because it eliminates the redundancy.

9. **B**

The issue is organization. Because the question asks about the best introductory sentence, you should read through the whole paragraph before deciding on your answer. As you read through the paragraph, you can answer questions 10, 11, and 12 and then come back to answer question 9. What is the topic of this paragraph? This paragraph describes some of the percussion instruments used in a gamelan. Choice (B) is the most general of the choices; it is broad enough to relate to everything in the paragraph. Choice A is too specific: gongs are mentioned in the paragraph, but so are other instruments. Choice C does relate to the paragraph's topic of percussion instruments, but if you read it into the context, it doesn't flow smoothly with the sentence that follows. Choice D is too general and doesn't lead into the paragraph's focus on percussion instruments. Choice (B) is the best answer.

10. **J**

The issues are verb usage and idioms. When you notice an underlined verb, one of the things you should check for is agreement with its subject. The subject here is *metallophones,* which is plural. Thus, the verb form needed is *metallophones* ***consist***. Identifying this issue lets you eliminate F and H. Plug G and (J) into the sentence. The idiomatically correct phrase here is *consist* ***of***. Plugging G into the sentence should help you hear this. Choice (J) is the best answer.

11. **C**

When you read through the sentence as written, it should sound confusing. The issue here is sentence sense. The adverb *largely* doesn't really modify *placed,* so the word order is mixed up. Read the other choices back into the sentence to determine which makes the most sense. The order of words in B also make the sentence confusing. Choice (C), even though in this case it's longer than the other choices, is the most sensible, logical wording. *Large* correctly modifies *gong sets*, and *horizontal* modifies *stands.* You should be able to eliminate D because it's not correct for the adjective *horizontal* to modify the verb *placed.* Choice (C) is best.

12. **F**

The issue is superlative and comparative adjectives. Whenever you notice that a word ending in *-er* or *-est* is underlined, that's a red flag that you should ask yourself how many things are being compared. Here, the phrase *of the pair,* which is used earlier in the sentence, clearly indicates that two items are being compared. For two items, the comparative form, *larger,* is correct. Recognizing this lets you eliminate H and J. Plugging G into the sentence, you should notice that it is slightly longer than (F). Because it's more concise than G, (F) is the better answer. (Note that of all *four* choices, we would say that (F) is the *best* answer.)

13. **C**

Be careful when an English question stem includes the word *NOT.* For most English questions, you're looking for the choice that sounds best. For this question, you need to determine which choice does *not* sound correct. Notice that the underlined word here, *while,* is a connections word. This is a signal that you must pay attention to the meaning and logic of the sentence. This sentence expresses contrast, the difference between gamelan music as it's played *today* and how it was played *traditionally.* Choices A, B, and D would all fit acceptably here because they're all contrast connections. Choice (C) would not be acceptable because it indicates a cause-and-effect transition. Thus, (C) is the best answer.

14. **G**

The issues here are idioms and punctuation (the apostrophe). Start with the punctuation. You know contractions are tested on the ACT, so whenever you see the words *its, it's*, or even *its'* (which is never correct) underlined, check the context to determine the correct spelling. In the context here, *its own sake*, the word *its* is correctly spelled for use as a possessive pronoun. Recognizing this lets you eliminate F and J. You should also recognize that the spelling used in H, *its'*, is never correct. Even if you're unsure about the correct spelling of *its* here, your ear may tell you that the phrase *performed* ***of*** is idiomatically incorrect, allowing you to eliminate F and H. However you get to it, (G) is the best answer.

15. **B**

The issue is word choice. When you notice that either *between* or *among* is underlined, that's a signal to check the context to determine how many things are being talked about. In this context, a list of three things follows:...*performances,...plays, and... ceremonies.* The word *between* is not correct here, so you can eliminate A. Plug the other choices into the sentence. You might think that C, with *among*, would be correct, because more than two things are discussed, but it's not the best wording here. Choice C is a little awkward and not as concise as (B). You can eliminate D because it indicates a contrast. The best answer is (B).

16. **J**

The issue is punctuation. Notice that the underlined portion and its surrounding context include a list: *religious temples, the royal court, and village festivals.* Commas are needed to separate the items in this list, but nowhere else in the sentence. Eliminate F because the comma after *accompanied* incorrectly separates the verb from its object, *dances.* Eliminate G because the commas around the phrase *at religious* incorrectly break up the flow of the sentence. Eliminate H because the colon is unnecessary and breaks up the flow of the sentence. Choice (J) is the best choice.

17. **C**

The issue is writing strategy. The key words in the question stem are *persuading the reader that gamelan music is more complex than symphonic music.* Think about the tone of the essay, and consider whether it is persuasive. No, it is not. The essay does make some comparisons between gamelan music and symphonic music, but the writer makes no attempt to say that one is more complicated than the other is. Thus, you can eliminate A and B. Now look at the reasons in (C) and D. Choice (C) is the better answer because it acknowledges that the tone of the essay is not persuasive.

CHAPTER 7

English Practice Set IV

Directions: In the following passage, certain words and phrases have been underlined and numbered. You will find alternatives for each underlined portion in the column to the right. Select the one that best expresses the idea, that makes the statement acceptable in standard written English, or that is phrased most consistently with the style and tone of the entire passage. If you feel that the original version is best, select "NO CHANGE." You will also find questions asking about a section of the passage or about the entire passage. For these questions, decide which choice gives the most appropriate response to the given question. For each question in the test, select the best choice, and fill in the corresponding space on the answer folder. You may wish to read each passage through before you begin to answer the questions associated with it. Most answers cannot be determined without reading several sentences around the phrases in question. Make sure to read far enough ahead each time you choose an alternative.

IT'S THE LITTLE THINGS THAT MATTER

[1]

I've lived, in New York City for my entire life. 1 I'm not happy to leave

1. A. NO CHANGE
   B. lived, in New York City, for my entire life.
   C. lived in, New York City, for my entire life.
   D. lived in New York City for my entire life.

even though 2 my mom got a great new job three states away.

2. F. NO CHANGE
   G. the reason being
   H. being for the reason
   J. because of the reason

Theirs a lot 3 about my life here that I'll miss. It will be awful having to complete senior year in a

3. A. NO CHANGE
   B. Their's a great deal
   C. There's a lot
   D. Theres a lot

strange place without my friends. 4 That's only part of it, though.

4. All of the following choices would appropriately convey the writer's concerns about a new school EXCEPT:
   F. it will be awful without my friends.
   G. it's a place where I won't know anyone.
   H. it's in a different state.
   J. it's a new place with unfamiliar classmates.

Being that cell phones and computers are so common, 5 it's easier than ever to communicate over a distance. I know my buddies and I will stay in touch.

5. A. NO CHANGE
   B. Cell phones and the computer being so common,
   C. Among cell phones and the computer,
   D. Between cell phones and the computer,

[2]

Moving means leaving more than my friends. I'll be leaving and abandoning my childhood home behind. It
6
may be hard for someone

6. **F.** NO CHANGE
   G. saying goodbye to
   H. leaving
   J. parting with and leaving

who's never lived in a city to perceive a city community as
7
intimate, but my neighborhood is far from impersonal. It really does have the feel of a village. There are lots of people

7. **A.** NO CHANGE
   B. never having lived
   C. who hadn't ever lived
   D. which hasn't ever lived

who, though they are not exactly friends are a regular
8
part of my life. Unlike my friends, these aren't people I know well enough

8. **F.** NO CHANGE
   G. who, though they are not exactly friends, are
   H. who, though they are not exactly, friends, are
   J. who though they are not exactly friends, are

staying in contact with after I move. This may sound
9
odd, but I'll miss them.

9. **A.** NO CHANGE
   B. to stay in contact
   C. so that staying in contact
   D. for the keeping in touch

[3]

There's Joe, the old guy who's been the superintendent of my apartment building ever since I can remember. He's always out sweeping the hallway or cleaning the laundry room, and also he's just a call away to fix a
10
clogged sink or change a lightbulb in a tall fixture. Joe has a warm smile and is incredibly nice. I have to admit, I love that he always keeps a few fun-size chocolate bars in his tool box, and he's happy to share his stash with

10. **F.** NO CHANGE
    G. room. And
    H. room;
    J. room,

my sister and I as well. Sure, I can come back
11
and check on Joe when I visit New York,

11. **A.** NO CHANGE
    B. me and my sister
    C. my sister and I
    D. I and also my sister

and it just won't be the same.
12

12. **F.** NO CHANGE
    G. so
    H. but
    J. despite that

[4]

I'll also miss Gen, the quiet woman which
13
runs the green grocer on the corner.
13

13. **A.** NO CHANGE
    B. who runs
    C. who had run
    D. which had been running

I think most New Yorkers would agree that
14
the corner grocery is indispensable. Whenever
14
I run in for a drink or a snack, it seems she's there at the cash register with her lively kindergarten son, Tang, and now her new baby. I feel like I've watched Tang grow up.

14. **F.** NO CHANGE
    G. For most New Yorkers, the corner grocery store is a great convenience.
    H. The average New Yorker probably could not live with the convenient corner grocery.
    J. OMIT the underlined portion.

How old when I come back to visit, who
15
knows, will his baby sister be?
15

15. **A.** NO CHANGE
    B. Who knows how old his baby sister will be when I come back to visit?
    C. When his baby sister comes back to visit, who knows how old I will be?
    D. Who knows, when his baby sister comes back to visit, how old I will be?

Will the family even still be here? It's so strange to think that <u>people who are seen by me</u> every day may just vanish from my life. I'll miss these small connections with people almost as much as I'll miss my friends.
16

16. F. NO CHANGE
G. people I have been seeing
H. people I see
J. I'm seeing people

Question 17 asks about the preceding passage as a whole.

17. For the sake of logic and coherence, paragraph 3 should be placed:
A. where it is now.
B. before paragraph 1.
C. after paragraph 1.
D. after paragraph 4.

ANSWERS AND EXPLANATIONS

1. D	**10. H**
2. F	**11. B**
3. C	**12. H**
4. H	**13. B**
5. D	**14. J**
6. H	**15. B**
7. A	**16. H**
8. G	**17. A**
9. B	

1. **D**

The issue is punctuation. Choice A uses a comma after *lived* that incorrectly breaks up the flow of the sentence. In fact, the sentence functions well without any commas at all, which means you can also eliminate B and C. Choice (D) is the best answer.

2. **F**

The issue is word choice. The words *even though* used in (F) are appropriate because what follows describes a condition. In addition, G and H incorrectly use the verb form *being*. Choice J is redundant: There is no need to say *the reason* with *because*. Choice (F) is the best answer.

3. **C**

The issue is word choice. Whenever you see *theirs* underlined, check that it's used correctly. The word *theirs* is a possessive pronoun, which is incorrect in this sentence. The word needed here is *there's* because its meaning is *there is*. Recognizing this, you should eliminate all choices except (C), which is the correct answer.

4. **H**

The issue is writing strategy. The key words to focus on in the question stem are *the writer's concerns about a new school*. Choices F, G, and J all include phrasing that expresses the writer's nervousness about going to school with a different group of students. Choice (H) does not, and because this question asks for the one choice that does not express the writer's concerns, (H) is the best answer.

5. **D**

The issue is word choice. Beware whenever you see the phrase *being that* on the ACT. *Being that* is not an acceptable way to say *because*. You can eliminate A and plug in the other choices to look for something better. Eliminate B because it uses the *-ing* verb *being* without a helping verb as the main verb in a clause. Eliminate C because it incorrectly uses *among* when only two things are being discussed. Choice (D), which correctly uses the word *between* when two things are discussed, is the best answer.

6. **H**

The issue is wordiness. Eliminate F because *leaving* and *abandoning* mean the same thing, so the phrase is redundant. Eliminate J for the same reason. Plug in the remaining choices. Choice G probably sounds okay to your ear, but (H) is the better choice because it's more concise.

7. **A**

The issues are pronouns and verb tense. Address the pronoun issue first: whenever you see *who's* underlined, make sure that it's in a context in which either *who is* or *who has* makes sense. In this sentence, *who's* correctly stands for *who has*. Now look at verb tense. In this sentence, the past tense verb *has...lived* is correct. Check the other choices just in case. Eliminate B because it uses the *-ing* verb *having* without a helping verb as the main verb in the clause. Eliminate C because the past tense verb *had...lived* is not the appropriate one here. Eliminate D because it incorrectly uses the pronoun *which* to refer to a person. The best answer is indeed (A).

8. **G**

The issue is punctuation. Think about how the sentence is structured and where the commas are needed. The main part of the sentence is *there are lots of people...who are a regular part of my life*. The phrase *though they are not exactly friends* is nonessential information and should be set off with commas. Eliminate F because it doesn't place a comma after *friends*. Eliminate H because, though it correctly sets off the nonessential phrase, it unnecessarily inserts a comma after *exactly*, which breaks up the flow of the sentence. Eliminate J because it doesn't use a comma after *who*. The best answer is (G).

9. **B**

The issue is idioms. There is an error in A because the correct idiomatic usage here is *enough* ***to stay*** *in contact*. Eliminate A. If you identified the idiom issue, (B) should stand out as the best choice. If not, plug in the remaining choices. Choice C introduces a sentence structure problem with *so that*, which doesn't lead to a complete thought. Choice D uses the awkward phrasing *for the keeping*. Choice (B) is the best answer.

10. **H**

The issues are sentence structure and punctuation. Choice F correctly uses a comma and the FANBOYS word *and* to join two independent clauses, but the additional modifier creates a run-on sentence. Choice G incorrectly begins a sentence with *and*. Choice (H) correctly uses a semicolon to join two independent clauses. Choice J creates a run-on sentence by using only a comma, without a FANBOYS word, to join two independent clauses. The best answer is (H).

11. **B**

The issue is pronouns. Whenever you spot an underlined pronoun, check to make sure it's used correctly. In most answer choices, the pronoun *I* is used incorrectly as the object of the preposition *with*. Recognizing this, you should eliminate A, C, and D. Choice (B) correctly uses the object pronoun *me* and so is the best answer.

12. **H**

The issue is connections. Choice F uses *and*, which is a generic connections word that doesn't express any particular logical relationship. Read the sentence carefully to see if a more specific connections word would be appropriate. There are two ideas in this sentence. First is that the writer can come back to visit, and second is that it won't be the same. The second idea expresses some disappointment, so a contrast connections word is appropriate. Eliminate G because *so* expresses cause and effect. Choices (H) and J both convey contrast. Read each in the sentence. Choice (H) works best here.

13. **B**

The issues are pronouns and verb tenses. When you notice the word *which* underlined, remember that it should refer only to things, never to people. Here, *which* is used incorrectly to refer to *Gen*. Recognizing this, you can eliminate A and D. Notice that C and (B) use different verb tenses, so plug these choices into the sentence. Pay attention to the broader context of the passage. The predominant tense is the present, so eliminate C, which uses a past tense. Choice (B) is the best choice.

14. **J**

The issue is wordiness, specifically relevance. Whenever you notice that an entire sentence is underlined, check to see if OMIT is offered as an answer choice. If it is, that's a clue that you should ask yourself whether the sentence is relevant to the topic of the paragraph. The focus of this paragraph is how much the writer will miss the family at the green grocer. Therefore, a sentence about how most New Yorkers find the green grocer indispensable is not relevant. Choice (J) is the best answer choice. Having determined this, you don't even need to worry about G and H. If a sentence is irrelevant, don't consider the best way to word it; simply take it out.

15. **B**

The issue is sentence sense. If an entire sentence is underlined and OMIT is not offered as an answer choice, that's a clue that you need to find the choice that is most logical and easy to understand. Pay attention to the order of the words and phrases.

Choice A probably sounds confusing when you read it, another good clue that sentence sense is the issue. Choice (B) is clear and makes sense, but you should consider the other choices just in case. Choices C and D are both misleading because it is the writer, not the *baby sister,* who will come *back to visit.* Choice (B) is the best choice.

16. **H**

The issue is sentence sense. Choice F is probably not going to be the best choice because it uses the passive voice. Read through the answer choices looking for the active voice. Choice (H) is written in the active voice. Choice G is wrong because it inappropriately uses a past tense that isn't consistent with the context. Choice J is wrong because it uses a present tense (*am seeing*) that isn't consistent with the simple present and future tenses that are used in the context. Choice (H) is the best answer.

17. **A**

The issue is organization. To answer a question that asks you to determine the best ordering of paragraphs, think about which would make the best introduction and which would make the best conclusion. Here, paragraph 1 introduces the topic and serves as the best introduction. Paragraph 4—especially the last two sentences—make it the best conclusion for the essay. Recognizing this lets you eliminate B and D. To decide between (A) and C, consider the relationship between paragraphs 2 and 3. Paragraph 2 discusses in general the people the writer will miss. Paragraph 3 discusses Joe, a specific example of one of those people. Therefore, it makes sense to keep paragraph 3 after paragraph 2, making (A) the best answer.

CHAPTER 8

English Practice Set V

Directions: In the following passage, certain words and phrases have been underlined and numbered. You will find alternatives for each underlined portion in the column to the right. Select the one that best expresses the idea, that makes the statement acceptable in standard written English, or that is phrased most consistently with the style and tone of the entire passage. If you feel that the original version is best, select "NO CHANGE." You will also find questions asking about a section of the passage or about the entire passage. For these questions, decide which choice gives the most appropriate response to the given question. For each question in the test, select the best choice, and fill in the corresponding space on the answer folder. You may wish to read each passage through before you begin to answer the questions associated with it. Most answers cannot be determined without reading several sentences around the phrases in question. Make sure to read far enough ahead each time you choose an alternative.

[1]

In recent years, however, a number of psychologists have turned there attention away from illness and depression, choosing to focus instead on health and happiness. Their work has gained

1. A. NO CHANGE
   B. turning their
   C. have turned their
   D. who have turned there

the attention of that group of people we call the public. Kay Redfield Jamison, in *Exuberance: The Passion for Life,* describes exuberance as a temperamental trait.

2. F. NO CHANGE
   G. people known as
   H. those we call
   J. OMIT the underlined portion.

Through a series of biographical sketches of both famous and less well-known figures, Jamison explores the nature of exuberance.

3. A. NO CHANGE
   B. sketches of both famous, and, less well-known figures, Jamison
   C. sketches of both famous and less well-known figures, Jamison,
   D. sketches, of both famous, and less well-known, figures Jamison

Her subjects, what they have in common being energy, passion, and a sense of play and joy that guide their work and even recreation throughout their lives.

4. F. NO CHANGE
   G. What her subjects have in common are
   H. The common thing for her subjects is
   J. Having this in common, her subjects are

[2]

At one time, the word psychologist may have evoked an image of a bespectacled and bearded doctor encouraging a reclining patient to explore her deepest fears,

5. A. NO CHANGE
   B. had been evoking
   C. may have been evoking
   D. is evoking

desires that felt most repressed, 6 and darkest dreams. The groundbreaking work of Dr. Sigmund Freud did indeed have a negative orientation,

6. **F.** NO CHANGE
G. most repressed desires
H. those desires that had been most repressed
J. desires that she had been most repressing

focused on treating patients who's 7 behavior showed symptoms of emotional or mental illness. This orientation toward pathology directed the work of psychologists for many decades.

7. **A.** NO CHANGE
B. patients' who's
C. patients whose
D. patient's whose

[3]

Another investigating psychologist, who finds value in healthy mental states, Martin Selig man is one. 8 Seligman's work is guided by the idea that the role of the psychologist is not simply

8. **F.** NO CHANGE
G. Martin Seligman, also finding value in healthy mental state investigation, is another psychologist.
H. Another psychologist, Martin Seligman, is one who finds value in investigating healthy mental states.
J. Another psychologist who finds value in investigating healthy mental states is Martin Seligman.

to help people in the effort of avoiding 9 pain and pathology, but to help them attain feelings of happiness, engagement, and fulfillment.

9. **A.** NO CHANGE
B. avoid
C. who need to avoid
D. in the avoidance of

Seligman has encouraged 10 his colleagues in academic psychology to focus research on

10. **F.** NO CHANGE
G. which has encouraged
H. who has encouraged
J. encouraging

these areas.

He has also written books accessible to (11) a wide audience of readers,

11. Which of the following alternatives to the underlined phrase would NOT be acceptable?

A. accessible on

B. that are accessible to

C. available to

D. that can be understood by

including *Authentic Happiness, Learned Optimism*, and *The Optimistic Child.* [12]

12. At this point the writer is considering adding the following sentence:

> In fact, it was a casual remark by a child that inspired Seligman to write *The Optimistic Child.*

Assuming this statement is true, would it be a relevant and appropriate addition to the essay?

F. Yes, because it explains where Seligman got the title for *The Optimistic Child.*

G. Yes, because child development is an important branch of psychology.

H. No, because casual remarks are not mentioned anywhere else in the essay.

J. No, because it distracts from the focus of the paragraph.

[4]

Academic interest in happiness continues to grow, not only for those, in the field of psychology, but, (13) also for students in other fields.

13. A. NO CHANGE

B. grow not only, for those in the field of psychology, but

C. grow, not only for those in the field of psychology but

D. grow not only, for those in the field of psychology but,

Recently, a course that students have (14) called "Positive Psychology," taught by Harvard Professor Tal-Ben Shahar, has drawn more students

14. F. NO CHANGE

G. that is

H. that some have

J. OMIT the underlined portion.

than a <u>popularly perennial economics introduction</u> (15) class. Shahar's class,

while grounded in rigorous <u>research; encourages</u> (16) students to reflect on their own assumptions about happiness.

15. **A.** NO CHANGE
B. perennially popular introductory economics
C. economically popular perennially introductory
D. popular perennial and introductory economics

16. **F.** NO CHANGE
G. research: is encouraging
H. research, encourages
J. research—encourages

Question 17 asks about the preceding passage as a whole.

17. For the sake of logic and coherence, the best order for the paragraphs in this essay is:
A. as they are now.
B. 2, 1, 3, 4.
C. 1, 4, 2, 3.
D. 3, 2, 1, 4.

ANSWERS AND EXPLANATIONS

1. **C**
2. **J**
3. **A**
4. **G**
5. **A**
6. **G**
7. **C**
8. **J**
9. **B**
10. **F**
11. **A**
12. **J**
13. **C**
14. **J**
15. **B**
16. **H**
17. **B**

1. **C**

The issues are pronouns and sentence sense. When you see *there* underlined, make sure it is not being used incorrectly in place of the possessive pronoun *their.* That is indeed the case here. Eliminate A and D. Plug the remaining choices into the sentence. You should hear the error in B: it incorrectly uses an *-ing* verb without a helping verb as the main verb in a clause. Choice (C) is the best answer.

2. **J**

The issue is wordiness. Remember to check for wordiness whenever you notice that OMIT is offered as an answer choice. The underlined words are unnecessary, so the best answer is (J).

3. **A**

The issue is punctuation. When you can tell that commas are being tested, as is the case here, consider the sentence structure. The first part of the sentence, *Through a series of biographical sketches of both famous and less well-known figures*, is an introductory phrase and so should be separated from the rest of the sentence by a comma. Choice (A) correctly does this. Eliminate D because it does not. Choice B is wrong because the commas around *and* disturb the flow of the sentence. Choice C is wrong because the comma after *Jamison* incorrectly separates the subject from the verb *explores.* The best choice is (A).

4. **G**

The issue is sentence sense. This sentence lacks a proper verb, so eliminate F. Eliminate H because it's awkward. Eliminate J because it doesn't flow smoothly with the remainder of the sentence. The best choice is (G).

5. **A**

The issue is verb tense. You can probably tell that (A) doesn't seem to contain an error. Nevertheless, consider the other choices, just to be sure. Choice B incorrectly uses *had been evoking*, a verb tense that should be used only to describe an action that took place prior to another past action. Choice C incorrectly uses *may have been evoking*, a form that should be used only for an action that continues into the present. Choice D is incorrect because it uses the present tense *is evoking*, which is not consistent with the phrase *at one time* used in this sentence.

6. **G**

The issue is wordiness. You may not spot this issue immediately, but considering all the answer choices should make it apparent. Notice that (G) is much shorter than the others are. Choice (G) makes sense in the context and it's the most concise, therefore, it is the best answer. Choices F, H, and J are all wordy.

7. **C**

The issues are punctuation (the apostrophe) and pronouns. Whenever you notice an underlined word that contains an apostrophe, check that it's being used correctly. Here, it doesn't make sense to substitute *who is* or *who has* for *who's*, so eliminate A. Eliminate B for the same reason. Now consider (C) and D, reading them into the sentence. It doesn't make sense for the word *patient's* to be possessive here, so eliminate D. The best answer is (C).

8. **J**

The issue is sentence sense. When an entire sentence is underlined and OMIT is not offered as an answer choice, you must think carefully about the meaning of the sentence and choose the wording that is clearest and most logical. Eliminate F because of the way the sentence is constructed. Starting with *another* and ending with *is one* is awkward. Eliminate G because the focus of the sentence is at the end, *is another psychologist*, and this doesn't fit with the focus of the passage, which is psychologists who investigate *healthy mental states*. Choice H is better than F and G, but it is not as good as (J). Choice (J), because it uses *who* instead of *is one*, is a more direct and concise statement.

9. **B**

The issue is wordiness. When one answer choice is considerably shorter than the other three, it is the best answer if no significant meaning is lost. This is the case here. Choices A, C, and D are all wordy. Choice (B) is the best answer.

10. **F**

The issue is sentence sense. Choice (F) is correct. Eliminate G and H because it is incorrect in this context to put a pronoun such as *who* or *which* between the subject and the verb. Another red flag for H is that *which* should never be used to refer to a person. Eliminate J because it incorrectly uses *encouraging* without a helping verb as the main verb in the sentence.

11. **A**

The issue is idioms. When an English question stem includes the word *NOT*, remember that you are looking not for an answer that sounds good but for one that sounds bad. Read all choices into the sentence to find the one that is not acceptable for some reason. Choice (A), even though it is shorter than B and D, is the answer you're looking for. Choice (A) is incorrect because *accessible **on*** is incorrect idiomatic usage. Either *accessible **to*** or *available **to*** would be acceptable here. The correct answer is (A).

12. **J**

The issue is writing strategy. When you're asked if an additional sentence would be relevant, consider the main topic of the paragraph. This paragraph focuses on Seligman's interest in positive psychology and his role in promoting it among colleagues and the public. The mention of the book *The Optimistic Child* is a supporting detail, so it would not be relevant to add a sentence that explains the source of inspiration for it. Eliminate F and G.

13. **C**

The issue is punctuation. When commas are underlined, think about how the sentence is structured. The main part of this sentence is *academic interest in happiness continues to grow.* What follows, *not only for those in the field of psychology but also for students in other fields*, is considered nonessential information and so should be set off by commas. Knowing this, you can eliminate B and D. Eliminate A because the flow is disturbed by the commas after *those* and *psychology.* Choice (C) is the best answer.

14. **J**

The issue is wordiness. Always consider wordiness when you notice that OMIT is one of the answer choices. Because the sentence reads smoothly and makes sense without the underlined portion, (J) is the best answer.

15. **B**

The issue is sentence sense. Often, when adverbs and adjectives are underlined in the same question, it's a clue that sentence sense is the issue. Eliminate A because it doesn't make sense for the word *popularly* to modify *perennial.* Eliminate C because it creates even more confusion with modifiers. It doesn't make sense for *economically* to modify *popular* or for *perennially* to modify *introductory.* Eliminate D because it uses *perennial* to modify *economics*, which doesn't make sense. Choice (B) is the best answer because it correctly uses *perennially* to modify *popular* and *introductory* to modify *economics.*

16. **H**

The issues are sentence structure and punctuation. Choice F uses a semicolon. To determine if that is correct, consider whether the word that come before and the words that come after the semicolon each stand alone as sentences. The answer here is no; in fact, neither grouping of words forms a complete sentence. Eliminate F because the semicolon is used incorrectly. Think about the structure of the sentence to determine what punctuation is needed. The main part of the sentence is *Shahar's class... encourages students to reflect on their own assumptions about happiness.* The phrase *while grounded in rigorous research* is nonessential information and so should be set off by commas. Knowing this, you can spot that (H) is the best answer.

17. **B**

The issue is writing strategy. When you're asked about the order of paragraphs, start by determining which would make the best introduction and which would make the best conclusion. Notice the chronological element in this passage. The passage discusses psychology from *Freud* to *recent years.* It makes sense, then, to organize this passage chronologically, putting the paragraph that discusses Freud first. Only (B) does this. Choice (B) also puts paragraph 4, which treats the present (as evidenced by the words *continues to grow* and *recently*) last, which makes sense in the chronological sequence. Choice (B) is the best answer.

CHAPTER 9

English Practice Set VI

Directions: In the following passage, certain words and phrases have been underlined and numbered. You will find alternatives for each underlined portion in the column to the right. Select the one that best expresses the idea, that makes the statement acceptable in standard written English, or that is phrased most consistently with the style and tone of the entire passage. If you feel that the original version is best, select "NO CHANGE." You will also find questions asking about a section of the passage or about the entire passage. For these questions, decide which choice gives the most appropriate response to the given question. For each question in the test, select the best choice, and fill in the corresponding space on the answer folder. You may wish to read each passage through before you begin to answer the questions associated with it. Most answers cannot be determined without reading several sentences around the phrases in question. Make sure to read far enough ahead each time you choose an alternative.

My camping trip in the wilderness land of Canada[1] was everything I'd expected and more.

1. A. NO CHANGE
   B. at the Canadian wilderness
   C. in the Canadian wilderness
   D. to the wilderness at Canada

I had known their would be[2] challenges: I'd have to carry heavy supplies, face some difficult hiking trails,

2. F. NO CHANGE
   G. there would be
   H. their might have been
   J. there are challenges

and of course, deal with[3] wildlife and the unpredictability of the weather.

3. A. NO CHANGE
   B. I'd also have to deal with
   C. dealing with
   D. to deal with

With[4] my previous camping experience and the training I'd done for cross-country, I felt well-prepared.

4. Which of the following alternatives to the underlined portion would be LEAST acceptable?
   F. As a result of
   G. Despite
   H. Because of
   J. Owing to

I now realize that the challenges I'd anticipated were created by myself. Annoying bugs, heavy rains. The[5] exertion of miles of hiking every day for a week—I'd thought about all these things and knew that I would push myself to get through them.

5. A. NO CHANGE
   B. rains: the
   C. rains; the
   D. rains, the

As it turned out, nonetheless, the most significant challenges weren't the physical ones I'd expected, but the emotional ones that happened to catch even me by surprise.

6. F. NO CHANGE
   G. moreover
   H. however
   J. consequently

7. A. NO CHANGE
   B. caught me by surprise
   C. were very surprising to me
   D. surprised me

A city kid, I who had lived in urban areas my whole life, found that the beauty of nature was utterly overwhelming. I'd been in the woods before, but I'd never been in a vast area of pristine wilderness.

8. F. NO CHANGE
   G. who had lived my entire life in a single urban area,
   H. accustomed to urban experiences,
   J. OMIT the underlined portion.

[9] It's hard for me to describe what I saw without resorting to clichés and exaggeration. The snow-covered mountains,

9. The writer is considering deleting this sentence:

   It's hard for me to describe what I saw without resorting to clichés and exaggeration.

   If the writer removed this sentence, the essay would primarily lose:

   A. a reason that that the writer valued the time in the wilderness.
   B. an indication that the writer has given some thought to how the reader will react to the description.
   C. a contradiction of the statement made in the previous sentence.
   D. an explanation of what a cliché is.

trees with foliage in at least a thousand different[10] shades of green, a sky that looked bluer and cleaner than any I'd ever seen, and the graceful flight of eagles high overhead—words feel

10. F. NO CHANGE
G. at least, a thousand, different
H. at least a thousand, different
J. at least a thousand, different,

inadequate for the purpose of conveying[11] my experience, but I'm not sure photographs or videos would do much better. To really understand, you have to experience it.

11. A. NO CHANGE
B. to convey
C. to convey and express
D. in the attempt at conveying

When you're exposed to beauty like this, one starts to realize[12] how magnificent nature is and how human beings aren't really in control the way we like to think we are. At times on my trip,

12. F. NO CHANGE
G. one start to realize
H. you started to realize
J. you start to realize

I felt spine-tingling chills[13] and a light-headed panic. The ultimate stillness,

13. A. NO CHANGE
B. was aware of chills causing tingling along my spine
C. felt a chilled feeling that tingled my spine
D. experienced a feeling of spine-tingling chills

punctuated only by the wind's slow movement of the leaves,[14] and the occasional clear, piercing bird call, even the freshness of the air, moved me beyond belief.

14. Which of the following phrases provides the MOST specific detail about sounds the writer experienced?
F. NO CHANGE
G. along with the color of the leaves
H. in addition to the moss I saw on the trees
J. reminding me of a peaceful dream

The feeling of being <u>overpowered at</u> 15 nature changed how I see myself. My simple camping trip indeed <u>turned out, to be humbling, but in ways</u> 16 I had never expected.

15. A. NO CHANGE
B. overpowered by
C. taken over by the power of
D. overpowered with

16. F. NO CHANGE
G. turned out to be humbling, but in ways
H. turned, out to be humbling, but in ways
J. turned out to be, humbling but in ways

Question 17 asks about the preceding passage as a whole.

17. Suppose the writer's goal had been to write a brief essay describing an experience of a human battling nature's physical hazards. Would this essay successfully fulfill that goal?

A. Yes, because the essay mentions bugs and rainfall.
B. Yes, because the essay discusses the writer's anticipation of facing wildlife.
C. No, because the essay focuses more on the writer's internal, not external, experience of nature.
D. No, because the essay mentions only aspects of nature that exist in the Canadian wilderness.

ANSWERS AND EXPLANATIONS

1. C
2. G
3. A
4. G
5. D
6. H
7. D
8. J
9. B
10. F
11. B
12. J
13. A
14. F
15. B
16. G
17. C

1. **C**

The issues are wordiness and idioms. Choice A unnecessarily uses the word *land*, and the preposition *in* is not idiomatically correct in this context. Choices B and D, using *to* and *at*, also form incorrect idioms. Choice (C) uses the idiomatically correct preposition *in* and is appropriately concise.

2. **G**

The issues are word choice and verb tense. *Their* is a possessive pronoun and is not interchangeable with *there.* Choice (G) addresses this issue. Choice H incorrectly uses *their* and also introduces a verb tense problem. Choice J correctly uses *there* but incorrectly changes *would be* to the present tense *are.*

3. **A**

The issues are wordiness and parallelism. Choice B is wordy. Choice C doesn't use parallel structure because *dealing* doesn't match the form of *carry* and *face* that are in the nonunderlined part of the passage. Choice D is likewise not parallel because it adds the word *to* before *deal.*

4. **G**

The issue is transitions. Choices F, H, and J all include a word or phrase that correctly expresses the relationship of cause and effect. Choice (G) is wrong because it inappropriately uses a contrast word, *despite.*

5. **D**

The issue is punctuation. Choice A uses a period when no complete sentence is present. Choice B uses the colon incorrectly because what follows the colon here is not an explanation. Choice C is wrong because the semicolon should be used only to join two independent clauses. Choice (D) correctly uses a comma after *rains*, the second item in the series *bugs, heavy rain, and the exertion.*

6. **H**

The issue is connections. Choice F uses the appropriate kind of connection, a contrast word, but this particular word doesn't fit in this context. Choice (H), *however,* works better. Choice G is incorrect because *moreover* is not a contrast word. Choice J is wrong because *consequently* is not a contrast word.

7. **D**

The issue is wordiness. Choices A and C are unnecessarily wordy. Choice B is better, but it is not as concise as (D).

8. **J**

The issue is redundancy. Choice F is not the best answer because the phrase *who had lived my whole life in urban areas* repeats the meaning expressed by the nonunderlined phrase *a city kid.* Choices G and H simply reword the redundant phrase. Only (J) eliminates the redundancy.

9. **B**

The issue is writing strategy. Focus on the sentence in question: *It's hard for me to describe what I saw without resorting to clichés and exaggeration.* Here, the writer is self-consciously reflecting on what the reader will think of his words. Only (B) comes close to getting at this idea. Choice A doesn't answer the specific question posed in the question stem. Choice C is wrong because there is no contradiction here. Choice D is wrong because the sentence in question doesn't define *cliché.*

10. **F**

The issue is punctuation. Choice (F) is correct because it does not use any unnecessary commas. All other choices insert unnecessary commas that inappropriately break up the flow of the sentence.

11. **B**

The issue is wordiness. Choice A uses the filler phrase *for the purpose of*, which causes this version to be wordy. Choice C is redundant because *convey* and *express* mean the same thing. Choice D unnecessarily uses the phrase *in the attempt*, which leads this version to be wordy.

12. **J**

The issue is word choice. Choice F is wrong because the nonunderlined part of the sentence uses the word *you*. Therefore, *one* is incorrect in this sentence. Choice G is wrong because it also uses *one*. Choice H corrects the *one-you* shift but introduces a new error with the past tense *started*.

13. **A**

The issue is wordiness. Choice B uses the extraneous phrases *was aware of* and *along my spine* that lead to this version being longer than necessary. Choice C uses unnecessary repetition with *felt…a feeling*. Choice D is wordy because of the phrase *experience a feeling*.

14. **F**

The issue is writing strategy. Pay attention to the question stem. It helps to underline the words *most specific details about the sounds the writer experienced* to help you focus on what the question is asking for. Only (F), with the words *punctuated* and *wind*, addresses the issue of sound. Choice G, with *color*, addresses only something that can be seen. Choice H explicitly uses the phrase *I saw*. Choice J provides no details related to sound.

15. **B**

The issue is idioms. Choices A and D use *at* and *with*, both incorrect prepositions with the word *overpowered*. Choice C is not idiomatically incorrect, but it's not as concise as (B).

16. **G**

The issue is punctuation. Choice (G) correctly uses a comma to separate the nonessential phrase *but in ways I had never expected* from the main part of the sentence. Choices F and H use a comma to set off the nonessential phrase, but they also introduce other unnecessary commas that disturb the flow of the sentence. Choice J fails to use the necessary comma and inserts an unnecessary one elsewhere.

17. **C**

The issue is writing strategy, so pay attention to the question stem. You should have underlined the phrase *describing an experience of a human battling nature's physical hazards*. This question asks you to think about the purpose of the passage. The main point is the writer's surprise at his emotional response to the wilderness. Thus, you can eliminate A and B. Choice D is wrong because the question stem doesn't ask about nature in any specific geographic area. Choice (C) is best because the word *internal* accurately describes the author's emotional response that forms the centerpiece of this passage.

CHAPTER 10

Introduction to ACT Reading

Like the ACT English test, the ACT Reading test is passage-based. All the information you need to answer the questions correctly can be found in the passage, so think of it as an open-book test. Nevertheless, it does not mean that it's easy. Getting through the Reading section in the time allowed is a challenge for most people. You, however, will find it much less intimidating because you're using this Kaplan workbook. After doing the practice exercises and the sample passages, you'll know what to expect on test day in terms of passage topics and structure, question types, and typical wrong answer traps. This chapter fills you in on all those aspects of the Reading section.

Remember from chapter two that for each section of the ACT, we have a Kaplan Method designed specifically to help you maximize your score. As you practice for the Reading section, don't hesitate to refer to chapter two for the Kaplan strategies for ACT Reading. Applying the Kaplan Method as you do the practice passages is crucial to your success, so you'll find references to it throughout this chapter.

THE KAPLAN METHOD FOR ACT READING

Pause for a moment to write down what you can remember about the Kaplan Method for ACT English:

1. ______________________________

2. ______________________________

3. ______________________________

Here's a quick review:

1. READ the passage, taking notes as you go.
2. EXAMINE the question stem, looking for clues.
3. PREDICT the answer and select the answer choice that best matches your prediction.

Handling Step 1 well is the foundation of answering each reading question correctly, so let's look at what you should be thinking about as you read the passage and take notes. The key is to read actively.

ACTIVE READING

Take a minute to consider what you think "active reading" might mean. Write down your ideas:

____

____

____

____

GUIDE TO ACTIVE READING

1. Focus on the big picture; note the purpose of each paragraph, and do not get bogged down in details.
2. Pay close attention to the first and last paragraphs. They often give great clues for determining the purpose of the passage as a whole.
3. Notice phrasing that indicates an example such as *an illustration of, for example, for instance, this...can be seen when,* and *to illustrate.* Remember that the example is a detail, but the general statement or principle it's illustrating is more general and could be a main idea.

4. Ask yourself questions as you read:
    a. What is the writer's purpose? Is he merely describing and explaining, or does he try to persuade the reader? Notice whether the writer is taking a side on an issue.
    b. What is the tone of the passage? Do you notice any phrasing that is approving, critical, or sarcastic?
    c. What is the internal logic of the passage? Do you notice features of a chronological structure or an outline structure or some of each?
    d. Who else is mentioned in the passage? What perspectives, other than the author's, are included?
5. Read for contrast, noting when the writer points out differences and contradictions. Pay attention to connections words and phrases that show contrast, such as *although, appears, but, by claims, despite, even though, however, in spite of, on the other hand, some...others, though*, and *yet*.
6. Read for comparison; note when the writer points out similarities in two things.
7. Notice where and when the writer states an opinion.
8. Notice where and when the writer makes an argument. What is her evidence? What point is the evidence supporting? Notice words that direct the flow of an argument, such as *as a consequence, as a result, because, consequently, resulting in, therefore*, or *thus*.

The idea behind active reading is that it puts *you* in charge. When you learn to read actively for the ACT, you're not at the mercy of the test maker's choice of complicated passages about unfamiliar topics. With practice, you'll know a lot about what to expect in an ACT Reading passage. On test day, you don't have time to read each passage as slowly and carefully as you might like to. You need to read the passage only to get a sense of the writer's purpose and determine its structure. You don't have to understand every detail the author discusses.

No matter what the author's purpose for writing the passage is, *your* only purpose for reading it is to understand the passage well enough to be able to answer the ten questions about it. The ACT is not a memory test; the passage is right there in the test booklet for you to refer to as you answer the questions. On your first reading, you need only to get a sense of what is where. Step 1 of the Kaplan Method directs you to make notes so that you can more easily locate the information you need when you go to answer the questions. The principles of Active Reading guide your note-taking and tell you what to focus on during your first read-through.

There's a reason this chapter refers to your first "read-through" instead of your first "reading" of the passage. What we mean by read-through is a delicate balance of the words *reading* and *skimming*. We don't advise you to skip the passage all together, or merely skim it, and go right to the questions. On the other hand, we don't advise you to read the whole passage slowly and thoroughly. If you read too slowly, you won't have time to make it through the entire Reading test.

Instead, we recommend that you do a quick read-through of the passage before you start answering the questions. Use a combination of skimming and reading to read some parts of the passage more slowly than you do others. At the beginning of the passage, you should read carefully, just until you're confident you've got a sense of what the writer is trying to do. Look for repetition of key words and ideas. After that, you probably won't have to read the rest of the passage slowly, word for word. If you can tell how a paragraph relates to the one that came before it, jot down your passage map note and move on. You don't have to eyeball every word of that paragraph. As a general—though not absolute—rule, it's often a good idea to read the first and last sentences of the middle paragraphs fairly carefully. Those sentences tend to give you the purpose of the paragraph and make connections with the previous and succeeding paragraphs.

Surprised to hear that you shouldn't read each paragraph carefully before you look at the questions? Remember, the passage isn't going anywhere. The answer is right there in the test booklet for you to refer to as you answer the questions, and you *should* refer to it. You'll score the most points on test day if you let the questions themselves direct you to the parts of the passage you need to read and understand thoroughly in order to answer the questions.

UNDERSTANDING THE STRUCTURE OF THE PASSAGE

As you'll recall from chapter one, one feature of a standardized test is its predictability. The ACT writers can't pick any random piece of writing and create ACT Reading questions for it. Only a passage that has a clearly discernible organization and internal logic will appear as one of the three nonfiction passages on the ACT. (See the section on prose for information about the structure of a fiction passage.) Determining this structure is your task in Step 1 of the Kaplan Method.

ORGANIZATIONAL STRUCTURES IN ACT READING PASSAGES: OUTLINE AND CHRONOLOGICAL DEVELOPMENT

On your first read-through, you should read actively, asking yourself questions about the writer's purpose and viewpoint. Understanding the structure helps you to determine the writer's purpose. Therefore, you should get in the habit of noticing key words and phrases that are clues to the passage's structure. Two key organizational structures to keep in mind are the outline structure and the chronological structure. By *outline*, we don't mean the highly structured notes you may have had to prepare before writing a paper for school. For our purposes here, *outline structure* simply means that one broad topic is divided into several narrower aspects. A *chronological structure* is in place when a writer treats the topic in terms of development over time, most often starting with an earlier time period and moving toward more recent time periods.

Here's an exercise to help you think about the organizational structure of a passage. Consider each sentence and decide whether it points to a chronological or an outline structure. Underline key words or phrases that help you decide.

1. ________________ In the middle ages, few ordinary people knew how to read and write.

2. ________________ Three American writers exhibited this fascination with nature in their poetry.

3. ________________ By the early twentieth century, various groups had become interested in promoting women's right to vote.

4. ________________ A turning point came in 1859 when Charles Darwin published *Origin of Species*.

5. ________________ By the beginning of the next decade, the vaccine had become almost universal.

6. ________________ Another aspect of residential architecture to be considered is the use of stained glass windows.

7. ________________ The second factor in the education debate is funding.

8. ________________ The time period of the musician's works can be classified as one of three major eras.

This exercise should have you thinking about which words to pay attention to on a first reading in order to help you identify a passage's structure.

Of course, not every ACT Reading passage you encounter will have a simple outline or chronological structure. A writer might combine the two or use a different kind of organizational format that allows for an effective development of the topic. Still, you should always be alert on your first read-through for any time-related words, phrases, and key words that indicate a writer is dividing a larger topic into smaller subtopics. In addition, words that express contrast and logic can also provide quick clues about a passage's organizational structure.

OTHER STRUCTURAL FACTORS TO CONSIDER: LOGIC AND CONTRAST

While some ACT passages feature a strictly chronological flow or follow a basic outline format, not every passage can be described so simply. However, you can expect each nonfiction passage to have its own internal logic. To determine this internal logic, you need to pay attention to words and phrases that express relationships between ideas. The very same words and phrases described under the connections heading in the English introduction also appear in passages in the Reading test. When you spot these words in your first read-through of an ACT Reading passage, take note. It's even a good idea to underline them. They provide important clues about the author's purpose and the structure of the passage. Refer to the following table for a list of some of these words:

KEY WORDS THAT INDICATE CAUSE AND EFFECT OR CONTRAST

Cause and Effect	Contrast
as a result	but
as shown by	claims (may suggest that a "claim" isn't true)
because	difference
consequently	however
evidence shows	in contrast
for this reason	nevertheless
it follows that	on the other hand
so	some...others
therefore	whereas
thus	while

Of course, the words in the table don't form an exhaustive list, but they do give you an idea of the kinds of words to pay attention to when you need to determine the logical flow and notice what contrasts the writer presents. One thing to notice is that these words are not subject-specific. This is precisely why connections words and phrases are so important. They show up repeatedly in all three nonfiction ACT passages, no matter what topic the passage discusses. You can't predict the exact content of the Reading passages you'll see on test day, but you can be certain that cause-and-effect and contrast words and phrases will be present and crucial to your understanding of the passage.

ANSWERS AND EXPLANATIONS

1. chronological; *in the middle ages*
2. outline; *three American writers*
3. chronological; *by the early twentieth century*
4. chronological; *a turning point, 1859*
5. chronological; *by the beginning of the next decade*
6. outline; *another aspect of*
7. outline; *the second factor*
8. chronological; *can be classified; three major eras*

ACT READING QUESTION TYPES

A crucial part of scoring points on the ACT is **understanding what the particular question is asking**. You'll read more about typical wrong answer traps later on, but for right now, you should know that the test maker includes details from the passage among the wrong answer choices. You won't necessarily find the correct answer to a question simply by selecting an answer that is familiar from the passage. To find the right answer, you have to make sure it answers the question posed by the question stem. It's for this reason that we've broken down ACT Reading questions into six different types: Detail questions, Inference questions, Big Picture questions, and Vocabulary-in-Context questions. As you read about these common question types, remember, you don't score points for correctly identifying a question type. The purpose of recognizing different question types is to help you understand *what each question is asking* because that's the first step in determining the best answer.

DETAIL QUESTIONS

A Detail question asks about a specific detail in the passage. These questions are very straightforward. You don't have to draw a conclusion or make an interpretation; you simply have to locate the particular detail in the passage and restate it. Sometimes the correct answer choice for a Detail question uses virtually the same wording that's used in the passage. At other times, the correct answer is a paraphrase of the wording from the passage.

Certain phrases in the question stem serve as clues that a particular question is asking about a detail directly from the passage. These phrasings include:

- *As stated in the passage,*
- *According to the author,*
- *According to the passage,*
- *The passage states that*
- *The writer states that*
- *All of the following are cited in the passage EXCEPT*

What all these phrasings have in common is that they refer you back to the passage, and they ask about something that is stated directly rather than something that is implied.

Although Detail questions are easy to answer when you know where in the passage to look, it can be challenging to locate the part of the passage that contains the answer. Therefore, it's very important to take good notes for your passage map on your first read-through of the passage. Remember that passage map notes should not include specific details but instead should note the location of details. For example, if a paragraph discusses the career of an artist, don't take notes about specific paintings and critical reactions. Instead, write a short note that describes the general purpose of the paragraph, such as *early career—critics admired.*

For such a paragraph, some people like to underline the names of specific paintings or critics on the first reading. You might find as you practice that this kind of underlining helps you. However, we recommend that you **underline sparingly**. Each ACT reading passage includes many details, but the test presents only ten questions for each passage. Many of the details in a given passage will not be relevant to any of the ten questions. The purpose of your first read-through is to *focus on the big picture.* Do *not* try to psyche out the test maker by trying to guess which details will show up in the question and underlining them. Though this advice may seem counterintuitive at first, the best way to score points on Detail questions is by not getting too wrapped up in particular details on your first read-through of the passage.

Keep Detail questions in perspective. Of all the question types, they appear most frequently on the ACT Reading test: roughly one-third of the questions are Detail questions. If you're attacking the questions and you have difficulty locating a particular detail, don't sweat it. Just circle the question number in your test booklet and make an initial guess. If you have time before the section ends, you can come back to the circled question. Remember that you don't have to answer every single question correctly to get a good score. This is especially important to keep in mind for Detail questions. Do your best, but don't obsess. No single question is worth more of your time than any other is.

INFERENCE QUESTIONS

Inference questions ask about something that is implied, or suggested, in a small part of the passage. You may be tempted to think that such questions are a matter of opinion, that *anything* could be implied, but this is not the case. Although it's true that Inference questions, unlike Detail questions, ask you to draw a conclusion that's not directly stated in the passage, the correct answer to an Inference question will not be a huge logical step away from what is stated in the passage. In other words, to answer an Inference question correctly, do not go too far beyond what's in the passage. You do have to make an inference, but you can't get carried away. The best answer to an Inference question, like the best answer to all ACT Reading questions, is strongly grounded in the words of the passage.

You can learn to recognize Inference questions by spotting key phrases in the question stem. Common wordings used in Inference questions include:

- *It may be inferred from lines…that*
- *The author implies about…that*
- *The phrase…suggests that*
- *In lines…the author most likely means that*
- *It is most reasonable to infer from lines…that*

Notice from these phrasings that an Inference question refers you to a specific line, phrase, or location in the passage. To answer an Inference question, you must read that part of the passage and come up with a prediction based on what is stated there. Thus, Inference questions refer to a small, localized part of the passage.

BIG PICTURE QUESTIONS

Big Picture questions look a lot like Inference questions. The two are similar in that they both require you to draw a logical conclusion based on what you read in the passage. The difference between them lies in how much of the passage you need to consider for each. We've defined Inference questions as those that refer to a small, particular part of the passage, such as a phrase or sentence. An Inference question stem directs you exactly to the part of the passage it's asking about. A Big Picture question, on the other hand, asks you about a larger part of the passage, which may or may not be clearly identified by the question stem. It may address a whole paragraph or the passage as a whole. To answer a broadly worded Big Picture question, you sometimes need to draw on material from multiple parts of the passage, say the beginning, middle, and end. In this case, keep the overall purpose of the passage in mind. Whenever a question stem refers to the passage as a whole, you must choose an answer that fits with the passage as a whole, not with just one part of the passage, such as a single sentence or paragraph.

The same key words that appear in the question stem for an Inference question are also used for Big Picture questions. For both question types, you'll see words such as *probably, most likely, implies, inferred,* and *suggests.* When you spot these words in a question stem, don't worry about explicitly determining whether you're dealing with an Inference or a Big Picture question. Remember, identifying question types doesn't score points on the ACT; answering questions correctly does! We distinguish between Inference and Big Picture questions only to remind you that the first refers to a smaller, narrower part of the passage, while the second refers to a larger part of the passage or to the passage as a whole. The main point for you is that you always need to read the question stem carefully. (Remember Step 2 of the Kaplan Method: Read the question stem looking for clues.) With a careful reading of the question stem, you'll know what the question is asking you to do (for both Big Picture and Inference questions, that's drawing a conclusion) and how much of the passage you should consider when you make your prediction.

VOCABULARY-IN-CONTEXT QUESTIONS

A Vocabulary-in-Context question asks about the meaning of a word or phrase as it's used in the passage. The word or phrase is always printed in italics, and a line number reference is always provided. The line reference is a terrific help; the question stem tells you exactly where in the passage you need to look to answer the question. The following steps will help you answer Vocabulary-in-Context questions:

1. Look in the line referenced by the question stem, and pretend that the word you're looking to define is actually a blank line in the sentence.

2. Read that sentence and look for clues to help you determine what word or phrase would make sense in the blank. Use that word or phrase as your prediction for this question.
3. Look at the answer choices and choose the one closest to your prediction.

Here are some other points to help you with Vocabulary-in-Context questions:

- **Do *not* skip the prediction.** Words used for Vocabulary-in-Context questions are often chosen because they have more than one meaning. The first meaning that comes into your mind or the most common meaning is not necessarily the appropriate meaning in the context of the passage. As its name suggests, the Vocabulary-in-Context question relies on the context of the word as it's used in *this* passage.
- Occasionally predicting seems tough: You may not find any clues within the sentence where the word is used. If that's the case, look at the sentences before and after it. In nearly every case, one of these three sentences contains specific clue words to let you predict the meaning of the blank.
- Connection words and phrases are often the key to making your prediction. Pay particular attention to words such as *yet, but*, and *however.* These contrast clues may tell you that your prediction should be the opposite of another word that's used in the sentence.

You should learn to love Vocabulary-in-Context questions. They don't appear frequently on the ACT (you'll probably see between one and three on any given test day), but they're easy to spot and fairly easy to answer quickly once you know how. Because of this, always look for Vocabulary-in-Context questions and try to answer them. If you have to guess on any question, guess on a harder question that would take you more time to answer. Make use of any Vocabulary-in-Context questions you find in order to rack up a few easy points quickly.

TYPICAL WRONG ANSWER TRAPS ON THE ACT READING TEST

Think for a minute about one of the most important things you're learning about the ACT: It is predictable. You can prepare and know what to expect on test day precisely because the ACT is a standardized test. You've learned that the format is always the same and the question types are predictable. Now we'll look at how you can even know what to expect when it comes to incorrect answer choices! The test maker uses several types of wrong answer choices. We call these wrong answer traps. If you know what kinds of traps to expect, you'll be better prepared to avoid falling for them. We call these wrong answer traps misused details, distortions, extremes, contradictions, and out-of-scope answers.

MISUSED DETAILS

A misused detail refers to a detail that actually is used in the passage. When you spot a misused detail among the answer choices, it may jump out at you and look very tempting because it concerns something you remember reading about in the passage. If it's used in the passage, then why is it wrong? Remember that you have to choose the best answer to the question posed in this particular question stem. If a detail doesn't directly answer the question you're dealing with, it can't be the best answer to this question, even though it may be a true statement according to the passage. Remember Step 2 of the Kaplan Method for ACT Reading: Predict the answer in your own words *before* you look at the answer choices. Predicting, along with reading the question stem carefully, is your best defense against falling for misused details.

DISTORTIONS

The distortion is a wrong answer choice that uses a detail from the passage but phrases the detail in such a way that it's distorted, or twisted, into something that doesn't match what's in the passage. A distortion may combine two details from the passage in an inaccurate way, or it may combine a detail from the passage with something else that doesn't appear in the passage at all. As with misused details, it's much easier to avoid falling for a distortion if you make a prediction about the best answer to the question before you even read the answer choices.

The distortion trap is similar in some ways to the misused detail trap. You may be wondering how to tell the difference between these two. That's a good question, but you shouldn't worry if you can't identify a particular wrong answer as either a distortion or a misused detail. Remember, on the ACT, you don't score points for correctly labeling the kinds of wrong answer traps. You score points for identifying the correct answer!

EXTREMES

As its name suggests, an extreme answer choice uses language that's too extreme. This means that the answer choice may be something that is along the right lines to answer the question but is worded in a way that goes too far. Certain kinds of words appear frequently in extreme answer traps. Here are some words and phrasings that can indicate extreme answer traps:

- *absolutely*
- *always*
- *all*
- *best*
- *certainly*
- *ever*

- *in every case*
- *largest*
- *never*
- *no*
- *none*
- *smallest*
- *worst*
- *without a doubt*

An answer choice that contains words or phrases such as those listed is not *necessarily* the wrong answer. However, if an answer choice does contain extreme language, you should consider it a trap unless the extreme language is also used in the passage. For example, suppose a writer says, "Isaac Newton was one of the one most brilliant scientists of his time," and you encounter a question that asks about the writer's opinion of Newton. Consider the following answer choices. Circle any extreme words you notice, and see if you can pick out which one is correct and which are extreme:

A. Isaac Newton was the most brilliant scientist ever to have lived.
B. Isaac Newton displayed much brilliance in his scientific work.
C. Isaac Newton was more brilliant than any of his contemporaries were.
D. Isaac Newton was the most brilliant scientist of his day.

What did you identify for extreme language? You should have spotted the following words:

A. *most...ever*
B. no extreme words
C. *more...than any*
D. *most*

If you noticed the extreme language, it should be easy to see that (B) is the correct choice.

CONTRADICTIONS

A contradiction is a wrong answer trap that goes against what's stated in the passage. We sometimes call this an *opposite* answer trap. Think about why an opposite trap would be a tempting answer choice. It addresses something that is indeed found in the passage, so it will contain words that may tempt you much as a misused detail or distortion does. A contradiction trap doesn't come out of left field; it's clearly related to the topic of the passage. The problem with a contradiction is that it completely turns around what is stated in the passage. To avoid contradiction traps, read carefully both in the passage as you make your prediction and in the answer choices when you look for a match for your prediction. Little words such as *no* and *not* are sometimes the keys to spotting a contradiction. They reverse the meaning of a sentence, giving it a 180-degree turn.

OUT-OF-SCOPE ANSWERS

The *scope* of a passage refers to the information that is covered in the passage. A passage that touches on a few key aspects of a large topic has a scope that is broad. A passage that treats a smaller topic in greater depth and detail has a scope that is narrow. Because the correct answer to an ACT Reading question is always based on what is in the passage, you should pay close attention to the scope of the passage when you're considering answer choices and looking for the one that best matches your prediction.

An out-of-scope trap goes beyond what is stated in the passage. If you see an answer choice that brings up something you don't even remember seeing in the passage, you can usually eliminate that as an out-of-scope trap. Occasionally, the best answer to a Big Picture question may appear to bring up something that isn't directly in the passage. Remember to read the question carefully to determine what it's asking. Let's consider some choices that are wrong because they go beyond the scope of the passage. Big Picture questions that ask about the passage as a whole frequently include this trap among the answer choices. Suppose you see a passage that discusses two medieval philosophers followed by this question:

The primary purpose of this passage is to:

A. give an overview of medieval philosophy.

B. discuss the merits of a medieval philosopher.

C. argue that medieval philosophy has been more influential than ancient Greek philosophy.

D. describe the work of two medieval philosophers.

Did you spot three out-of-scope answer traps here? Choice A is out-of-scope because it's too broad. A passage that discusses only two philosophers can't be an overview of all medieval philosophy. On the other hand, B is too narrow. While one or more paragraphs does concern a single medieval philosopher, B addresses only part of the passage and so is out-of-scope. Choice C cannot be correct because the passage discusses only medieval philosophy, not ancient Greek philosophy. Because Greek philosophy isn't addressed at all in the passage, it can't be part of the best answer for this question. Choice (D) is the best answer here.

THE FOUR DIFFERENT PASSAGE TYPES

In addition to knowing the kinds of questions to expect and the kinds of wrong answer traps you'll see repeatedly on the test, it helps to have some familiarity with the different passage types. Generally, the three nonfiction passage types will be organized according to a clearly identifiable structure that is based on an outline, chronology, or logical argument. Occasionally, you'll encounter a nonfiction passage written in a more narrative structure that has something in common with the prose fiction. Here, we'll look at the passage types in the order in which they appear on the ACT.

PROSE FICTION

The prose selection is taken from a novel or short story. Because the Prose Fiction passage is centered on characters' thoughts, moods, behaviors, and relationships, it's quite different from the three nonfiction passages. As you do the practice passages in this book, get a feel for your own comfort level with prose passages. Do you find them as easy as or even easier than the other three passages? If so, then jump right into the ACT Reading test at the beginning and work on the prose passage first. On the other hand, if you're generally less comfortable with the prose passage, it would be wise for you to work through the other three passages first and come back to do the prose passage last. Remember that you need to manage your time carefully during the Reading section if you want to answer each question. If you attempt to do the prose passage first even though you're not comfortable with prose, chances are that you'll get bogged down and spend too long on it. This leaves less time to work on passage types that may be easier for you. You don't want to run out of time and wind up guessing on questions for a passage type that would have been easy for you to answer if only you'd had more time to spend on it.

One aspect of the Prose Fiction passage that can be challenging is that you must infer much of the meaning. Typically, fiction writers don't come right out and make explicit statements. They tend to *show* rather than *tell.* Thus, your ability to understand a prose passage hinges largely on your ability to make appropriate inferences. If you find this challenging, think about watching a movie. The writer and director don't often tell you what to think. Instead, they show you a situation. The music, lighting, and camera angles all affect how you interpret what the characters say and do. Obviously, a piece of literature doesn't use music and cinematography to impart meaning. Nonetheless, a prose passage may be easier for you to understand if you try to visualize it as a movie. Trying to visualize the characters as if they were on film, and not just words on a page, can help you develop a fuller understanding of the prose passage.

Recall that scoring points on this ACT section requires you to read actively, which means asking yourself questions as you read. For the prose section, the questions you need to keep in mind are different from the questions that help you understand a nonfiction passage. Ask yourself:

- Who are the characters?
- What do specific details about a character help you understand about that person? The ways the character looks, moves, and speaks can give you important clues.
- How are the characters related? You can think of this first in a literal way: Are they friends, relatives, acquaintances, or strangers who are meeting here for the first time? You can also think of this in a more psychological way, asking what connects them: Are they accepting and approving of each other, or are they tied together by a more negative emotion?
- What is the overall tone of the passage? Is the mood upbeat and joyful or serious and reflective? Do any words create a sense of tension, drama, or excitement?

- What contrasts does the passage present? Is one character portrayed as being sharply different from another in personality, background, or values?

Often, the ACT prose passage focuses on only a few main characters, but it may include several minor characters as well. As you read through the prose passage, one of the most important things you must do is develop your understanding of the main characters. If you come across a character that seems more minor, you can underline the name, but don't get distracted by giving equal attention to all the characters. Focus on the most important ones.

SOCIAL STUDIES

The Social Studies, or Social Sciences, passage always appears second in the ACT Reading test. It may cover a topic relating to history, anthropology, archaeology, education, psychology, political science, biography, business, geography, sociology, or economics. Because social science is a nonfiction passage, remember to apply the active reading questions listed at the beginning of this chapter. Look for the connections words that illustrate the logical progression of the passage. Topics you might see in a Social Science passage include:

- A reinterpretation of the traditional understanding of a historical event
- A discussion of several scholars who've done work in the field and similarities and differences in their viewpoints
- A presentation of one scholar's view on a topic and argument explaining why the writer disagrees with that view
- An explanation of a concept or idea and why it's important in the field of study
- A discussion of the causes of a historical event
- An overview of the work of an important person in the field

This list is merely representative; it certainly doesn't include everything you might find in a Social Science passage. No matter what the topic, your task on your first read-through is to grasp the author's purpose for writing. As you read each paragraph, ask yourself how it broadly contributes to the overall purpose. Don't focus on particular details until later, when a question directs you to do so.

HUMANITIES

The Humanities passage is always the third passage in the ACT Reading test. Broadly speaking, you can think of the humanities as areas that relate to human creativity. Obviously, the visual arts, such as drawing, painting, and sculpture, fall into this category, but so do other areas, such as literature, theater, music, dance, philosophy, language, communications, film, literary criticism, radio, television, and architecture. As you read the Humanities selection, you should apply all of the active reading questions that you'd use for any nonfiction selection. Some examples of topics that you might be likely to find in a Humanities passage include:

- A discussion of the style of one or more artists and characteristics of the artist's work that make it noteworthy or unique
- A discussion relating to the development of a particular art form, what the origin of the form was, and how it changed over time as different artists used it
- A critical assessment of the work of a particular artist, how the artist's work was received in his own lifetime, and whether scholars in the field have maintained that view or come to a different view
- A chronological tracing of a particular artist's work over time, what the characteristics of the artist's early work were, what periods or stages scholars use to categorize the artist's work, and whether the work of a particular period is valued more highly than work from the other periods

Again, this list is not exhaustive. Notice, however, that the outline form and the chronological structure appear in some way in each example. Even though you can't predict the topic you'll see in the Humanities passage, and you may find yourself on test day facing a topic you have little familiarity with, you don't need to be intimidated. The practice you get in this workbook looking for the main purpose and the relationships among ideas will prevent you from getting lost in the details.

NATURAL SCIENCE

The Natural Science passage is always the fourth (and last) passage type in the ACT Reading test. Areas that might appear in a Natural Science passage include botany, zoology, natural history, biology, chemistry, earth sciences, physics, anatomy, astronomy, ecology, geology, medicine, meteorology, microbiology, physiology, and technology. Don't worry if a science passage includes technical terms that you aren't familiar with. If you need to understand a technical term to answer a question correctly, then that term will be explained somewhere in the passage. Some examples of the way a topic might be treated in an ACT science Reading passage include:

- A concept is introduced and several different understandings of it are presented. (Remember to keep straight who says what.)
- A historical view of a scientific concept is contrasted with a contemporary view.
- Several different ways of investigating a particular phenomenon are discussed.
- A first-person narrative discusses personal experience investigating a scientific concern.
- A detached presentation of facts discusses what is known in a particular field.
- A description of the current understanding of a concept is discussed, and suggestions of what researchers might investigate next are presented.

While science passages may seem challenging if you don't know much about the particular topic, you should be especially careful with passages that address topics you *are* familiar with. If you've just studied a particular group of elements in your chemistry class and you find a passage that discusses those elements, your first read-through of the passage will go pretty quickly and comfortably because you've had some previous exposure to the material. When you attack the questions, however, don't rely on your previous knowledge. The correct answer is always based on something that's stated in the passage. Even when you're familiar with a topic (in fact, *especially* when you're familiar with it), it's very important to carefully read the question stem and make sure that your prediction is grounded in this passage.

If you've attacked the passages in the order in which they appear on the test, you may be feeling tired and rushed by the time you get to the science passage. Don't lose sight of the big picture. Read the passage through once quickly, looking only to discern the writer's main purpose. Make brief passage map notes, and get to the questions as soon as possible. Avoid spending time trying to understand every detail in the passage. You score points only for answering questions correctly, not for coming to a complete and thorough understanding of the passage.

PAIRED PASSAGES

It is important that you also prepare for Paired Passages on the Reading Test. Paired Passages provide two passages that deal with the same topic or related topics. Some questions ask about only one of the passages, while others ask you to consider both. The passage or passages each question addresses is clearly labeled. When you see Paired Passages, they will replace one of the single passages, and will make up about 25% of your Reading score.

If you are tackling a set of paired passages, you want to follow the Kaplan Method for Paired Passages in which you divide and conquer.

THE KAPLAN METHOD FOR PAIRED PASSAGES

STEP 1: Read Passage A and answer the questions about it.

STEP 2: Read Passage B and answer the questions about it.

STEP 3: Answer questions asking about both passages.

The ACT will make clear which questions relate to Passage A, Passage B, and both Passages A and B, which is very helpful. By concentrating on one passage a time before you tackle questions that discuss both, you can avoid trap answer choices that refer to the wrong passage.

ACT READING REVIEW AND WRAP-UP

What are some of the most important things to take away as you move on to practice with the sample questions in this workbook? How can you work with these guidelines in a way that will maximize your chances of answering questions correctly? Take a moment to skim through this chapter and note some of the suggestions that you think will be most helpful to you:

____

____

____

____

Now, try our quiz to make sure you can recall the Kaplan Method and other strategies.

REVIEW QUIZ

1. The Kaplan Method for ACT Reading is:

Step 1: Read the ________________, taking ________________ as you go.

Step 2: Examine the ________________, looking for ________________.

Step 3: ________________ the answer in your own words, and ________________ the answer choice that ________________.

2. What should you do on your first read-through of the passage?

____

____

3. What should you do when you can't easily locate the right lines to answer a question?

____

____

4. What kinds of words and phrases tell you that a chronological structure is important in the passage?

____

____

5. What kinds of words tell you that the passage is organized like an outline?

____

____

____

6. What kind of logical relationship is indicated by words such as *because, thus, consequently,* and *therefore*?

____

7. What kind of logical relationship is indicated by words such as *on the other hand, however, but, while,* and *although*?

____

8. True or False? The details are the most important part of any ACT Reading passage.

9. What question type is each of the following phrasings associated with?
   a. *According to the passage,* ______________________________
   b. *The primary purpose of this passage is to* ______________________________
   c. *The author uses the phrase...in order to* ______________________________
   d. *As used in the passage,...most nearly means* ______________________________
   e. *It may be inferred from lines...that* ______________________________
   f. *Which of the following statements would the author most likely agree with?* ______________________________

10. List the five common wrong answer traps that the test maker includes among the answer choices:
    a. ______________________________
    ____
    b. ______________________________
    ____
    c. ______________________________
    ____
    d. ______________________________
    ____
    e. ______________________________
    ____

READING WRAP-UP

We trust you did well on the quiz. Now try your hand at the sample practice passages in the next chapters. Practice using the Kaplan Method just as you will on test day. Because the passage map notes are so crucial to your success, we've included suggested passage map notes as part of the Answers and Explanations for each passage. Your own notes need not match these exactly to be effective, but your notes for each paragraph should address the purpose of the paragraph as a whole and not recite details.

On test day, each passage will be followed by 10 questions; for the sake of practice, each practice passage in this book contains 12 problems, including two extra testlike questions to further hone your skills.

To get the most benefit from the practice passages, don't just answer the questions and correct them. Give some attention to the questions you get wrong. Read the answer explanation and try to determine *why* you got the question wrong. Some questions to consider include:

- Did you read the question stem carefully?
- Did you find the most appropriate part of the passage to refer back to before making your prediction?
- Were you focusing on the wrong words when you referred to the passage?
- Did you try to answer the question from memory or skip the prediction step?

Occasionally, a particular question may give you trouble because you don't know the meaning of a word used in the passage. If this happens to you, don't panic. You don't always need to know the meaning of every word in the passage to answer all the questions correctly. If you think you do need to know a word's meaning, see if you can deduce the meaning from the other words around it (just as you do to answer a Vocabulary-in-Context question). If you find yourself stumbling over a lot of unfamiliar words, plan to add some vocabulary study to your ACT prep time. A great way to start is to look up any unfamiliar words in the practice passage. You can keep a running vocabulary list, write the words on flashcards, or add them to an electronic device that you can use for study and review. However, don't let vocabulary study distract you from working through practice passages and applying the Kaplan Method and strategies. While some vocabulary study can be helpful for everyone, the most effective way to get ready for the ACT is to spend time working on practice passages.

We hope you've gotten a sense that the ACT Reading test is like a game with easily identifiable rules that you can learn and apply. As with any game, you are sure to improve with practice. Have fun!

ANSWERS AND EXPLANATIONS

1. Step 1: passage; notes
   Step 2: question stem; clues
   Step 3: Predict; select; best matches your prediction
2. Focus on the big picture, determine the author's purpose for writing; avoid getting bogged down by details.
3. Drop it and move on! Circle the question number in your test booklet, fill in a guess when you grid answers for that page, and come back to take a second look at the question if you have time left when you've finished the section.
4. Dates and time-related phrases such as *during the 1800s, after the Revolutionary War,* and *before the 20th century.*
5. A sentence near the beginning of the passage that breaks a large topic into smaller parts, such as *Beethoven's work can be divided into three periods;* words such as *groups, categories,* and *classification* also suggest an outline structure.
6. Cause and Effect
7. Contrast
8. False: The details are important only if they help you determine the author's purpose or if a particular question asks about a detail.
9. a. Detail
   b. Big Picture
   c. Vocabulary-in-Context
   d. Inference
10. a. Misused Detail
    b. Extreme
    c. Opposite (or contradiction)
    d. Distortion
    e. Out-of-Scope Perhaps one thing that occurred to you is that active reading is not passive. Reading actively means doing something. What you need to do on your first reading is ask yourself questions and look for certain elements that you'll be expecting in an ACT passage. We do recommend that you actually read the passage, not merely skim it, but in your first reading, you should focus more on some aspects of the passage than on others.

CHAPTER 11

Reading Practice Set I—Prose Fiction

Directions: This test contains a passage, followed by several questions. After reading the passage, select the best answer to each question. You are allowed to refer to the passage while answering the questions.

PROSE FICTION: *This passage is adapted from the novel The House of Mirth, written by Edith Wharton and published in 1905. This excerpt concerns Mr. Gryce and Miss Lily Bart and other guests who are visiting at Bellomont, the home of the Trenors.*

The observance of Sunday at Bellomont was chiefly marked by the punctual appearance of the smart omnibus destined to convey the household to the little church at the gates. Whether any one got into the omnibus or not was a matter of secondary importance, since by standing there it not only bore witness to the orthodox intentions of the family, but made Mrs. Trenor feel, when she finally heard it drive away, that she had somehow vicariously made use of it.

It was Mrs. Trenor's theory that her daughters actually did go to church every Sunday, but their French governess's convictions calling her to the rival fane, and the fatigues of the week keeping their mother in her room till luncheon, there was seldom anyone present to verify the fact. Now and then, in a spasmodic burst of virtue—when the house had been too uproarious overnight—Gus Trenor forced his genial bulk into a tight frock-coat and routed his daughters from their slumber, but habitually, as Lily explained to Mr. Gryce, this parental duty was forgotten till the church bells were ringing across the park, and the omnibus had driven away empty.

Lily had hinted to Mr. Gryce that this neglect of religious observances was repugnant to her early traditions, and that during her visits to Bellomont she regularly accompanied Muriel and Hilda to church. This tallied with the assurance, also confidentially imparted, that, never having played bridge before, she had been "dragged into it" on the night of her arrival and had lost an appalling amount of money in consequence of her ignorance of the game and of the rules of betting. Mr. Gryce was undoubtedly enjoying Bellomont. He liked the ease and glitter of the life and the luster conferred on him by being a member of this group of rich and conspicuous people. However, he thought it a very materialistic society; there were times when he was frightened by the talk of the men and the looks of the ladies, and he was glad to find that Miss Bart, for all her ease and self-possession, was not at home in so ambiguous an atmosphere. For this reason, he had been especially pleased to learn that she would, as usual, attend the young Trenors to church on Sunday morning. As he paced the gravel sweep before the door, his light overcoat on his arm and his prayer-book in one carefully gloved hand, he reflected agreeably on the strength of character which kept her true to her early training in surrounds so subversive to religious principles.

For a long time Mr. Gryce and the omnibus had the gravel sweep to themselves, but, far from regretting this deplorable indifference on the part of the other guests, he found himself nourishing the hope that Miss Bart might be unaccompanied. The precious minutes were flying, however. The big chestnuts pawed the ground and flecked their impatient sides with foam. The coachman seemed to be slowly petrifying on the box and the groom on the doorstep, and still the lady did not come. Suddenly, however, there was a sound of voices and a rustle of skirts in the doorway, and Mr. Gryce, restoring his watch to his pocket, turned with a nervous start, but it was only to find himself handing Mrs. Wetherall into the carriage.

The Wetheralls always went to church. They belonged to the vast group of human automata who go through life without neglecting to perform a single one of the gestures executed by the surrounding puppets. It is true that the Bellomont puppets did not go to church, but others equally important did—and Mr. and Mrs. Wetherall's circle was so large that God was included in their visiting list. After them Hilda and Muriel struggled, yawning and pinning each other's veils and ribbons as they came. They had promised Lily to go to church with her, they declared, and Lily was such a dear old duck that they didn't mind doing it to please her, though for their own part they would much rather have played lawn tennis with Jack and Gwen, if she hadn't told them she was coming. The Misses Trenor were followed by Lady Cressida Raith, a weather-beaten person in Liberty silk and ethnological trinkets, who, on seeing the omnibus, expressed her surprise that they were not to walk across the park. At Mrs. Wetherall's horrified protest that the church was a mile away, her ladyship, after a glance at the height of the other's heels, acquiesced in the necessity of driving, and poor Mr. Gryce found himself rolling off between four ladies for whose spiritual welfare he felt not the least concern.

It might have afforded him some consolation could he have known that Miss Bart had really meant to go to church. She had even risen earlier than usual in the execution of her purpose. She had an idea that the sight of her in a grey gown of devotional cut, with her famous lashes drooped above a prayer-book, would put the finishing touch to Mr. Gryce's subjugation and render inevitable a certain incident which she had resolved should form a part of the walk they were to take together after luncheon. Her intentions in short had never been more definite, but poor Lily, for all the hard glaze of her exterior, was inwardly as malleable as wax. She was like a water-plant in the flux of the tides, and today the whole current of her mood was carrying her toward Lawrence Selden. Why had he come to Bellomont? Was it to see herself?

1. As it is used in line 49, the word *ambiguous* most nearly means:

   A. misty.

   B. contradictory.

   C. wealthy.

   D. unclear.

2. From the third paragraph, it can be inferred that Mr. Gryce is attracted to Lily because:

   F. she embodies the ease and luster that he enjoys at Bellomont.

   G. he is intrigued by her ambiguous behavior and the apparent complexity of her intellect.

   H. she does not appear to fit in completely in her surroundings.

   J. she learns to play games quickly.

3. In this passage, Mr. and Mrs. Trenor are primarily characterized as being:

   A. widely known for their generous hospitality.

   B. somewhat hypocritical in their concern for appearances.

   C. overly concerned about the religious practices of their guests.

   D. unreasonably controlling of their two daughters.

4. The phrase "It was Mrs. Trenor's theory" (line 12) is used primarily to indicate that:

   F. Mrs. Trenor doesn't care whether or not her daughters attend church.

   G. Mrs. Trenor's understanding and that of the French governess contradict each other.

   H. Mr. and Mrs. Trenor have different beliefs about how best to manage their daughters.

   J. Mrs. Trenor would like to believe that Muriel and Hilda attend church regularly.

5. The author uses the phrase *spasmodic burst* (line 19) in order to emphasize that:

   A. Mr. Trenor's overweight condition is affecting his health.

   B. the Trenors are consistent in providing their guests with transportation to church.

   C. parties given by the Trenors are known to be uproarious.

   D. Mr. Trenor does not regularly attend church.

6. Lily's admission to Mr. Gryce that she "had lost an appalling amount of money...betting" (lines 36–39) is used in the passage mainly as:

   F. an indication that Lily's financial status is significantly lower than that of her hosts.

   G. a detail that Mr. Gryce uses to justify his admiration of Lily.

   H. evidence of the contrast between Lily, who is not at home at Bellomont, and Mr. Gryce, who enjoys his visit there.

   J. an example of the Trenors' tendency to manipulate Lily.

7. According to the passage, the Wetheralls' attitudes and habits regarding church attendance are accurately described in all of the following EXCEPT:

   A. They attend church regularly.

   B. They view Sunday church attendance as a pressing moral obligation to God.

   C. They feel that they are expected to go to church.

   D. They view church attendance as something similar to a social visit.

8. It can be inferred from the last paragraph that:

   F. Lily never had any intention of meeting Mr. Gryce for church.

   G. Lily is conscious of trying to appear attractive to Mr. Gryce.

   H. Lily's inflexibility can create social problems for her.

   J. Lily's outward appearance of malleability belies her actual resoluteness.

9. The main focus of this passage is:

   A. the hypocrisy of the Trenors and their guests.

   B. the uncomfortable interaction between Mrs. Wetherall and Lady Cressida Raith.

   C. Mr. Gryce's interest in Lily Bart.

   D. the manners and morals of the upper classes.

10. The author includes the information in lines 66–71 mainly for the purpose of:

   F. adding to the visual appeal of the story.

   G. emphasizing Mr. Gryce's impatience.

   H. providing details about the omnibus.

   J. illustrating Lily and Mr. Gryce's common love of nature.

11. From the last paragraph, it is reasonable to infer that Lily does not attend church on this morning because:

   A. her interest in Mr. Gryce is quickly pushed aside by her interest in Lawrence Selden.

   B. she comes to feel that Mr. Gryce is too materialistic and not a person whose spiritual values she shares.

   C. she finds it repugnant to attend church with hypocrites such as Mrs. Wetherall and Lady Cressida Raith.

   D. Mr. Trenor has not woken Lily on time.

12. From the description of the Wetheralls in lines 77–82, the author would most likely agree with which of the following statements?

   F. People who attend church frequently do so to foster their sense of belonging to a community.

   G. Acting on religious principles encourages people to behave like automatons.

   H. Religious belief encourages the view that the subjugation of others is acceptable.

   J. Many people model their behaviors after those of the people around them.

ANSWERS AND EXPLANATIONS

SUGGESTED PASSAGE MAP NOTES

Paragraph 1: Omnibus to take people at Bellomont to church

Paragraph 2: Trenors don't often go to church; conversation between Lily and Mr. Gryce

Paragraph 3: Mr. Gryce mostly likes Bellomont; Lily a bit out of place there; Mr. Gryce approving of Lily

Paragraph 4: Mr. Gryce waits for Lily to come out for church

Paragraph 5: Wetheralls and others (the Trenor sisters and Lady Cressida) come for church

Paragraph 6: Lily has sudden change of heart and doesn't follow through on her plan for church; she's curious about Selden

ANSWER KEY

1.	**B**	**7.**	**B**
2.	**H**	**8.**	**G**
3.	**B**	**9.**	**C**
4.	**J**	**10.**	**G**
5.	**D**	**11.**	**A**
6.	**G**	**12.**	**J**

1. **B**

For Vocabulary-in-Context questions, start by going back to the sentence where the word is used and make a prediction. If you need to, read a little before and after this sentence. Despite Lily's *self-possession*, she isn't quite comfortable in the ____________ *atmosphere*. Here, *ambiguous* means something that would cause discomfort. For more detail, check the two previous sentences. Mr. Gryce likes the *ease and glitter* of life at Bellomont. The word *however* signals a contrast. Here, the contrast is that Mr. Gryce finds the people at Bellomont to be *materialistic*. Thus, your prediction should relate to contrast. A good prediction would be something like *contrasting* or *contradictory*. Choice A is wrong because nothing in the context relates to it. Choice C is a misused detail. Choice D is a common meaning of *ambiguous* but not the meaning used here.

2. **H**

For this Big Picture question, you have to take into account the whole paragraph and make a prediction that's consistent with it. Still, certain phrases are the key. Here, the phrase *he was glad to find…that Miss Bart…was not at home* indicates Mr. Gryce's approval of Lily. In addition, he appreciates that she plans to go to church even though most people at Bellomont do not. Predict something along the lines of *he appreciates that she is different from the hosts and other guests at Bellomont* or *he admires her for planning to attend church.* Choice (H) is the best match. Choice F is a distortion. Though Mr. Gryce enjoys the *ease and luster,* the passage never suggests that Lily embodies it. Choice G combines the distortion and out-of-scope traps. The word *ambiguous* is used, but not to describe Lily, and her intellect is not described at all. Choice J is a contradiction.

3. **B**

For this Inference question, use your passage notes to help you find the appropriate spots in the passage to refer to. Mrs. Trenor is discussed in paragraphs 1 and 2; Mr. Trenor is discussed in paragraph 2. At the end of paragraph 1, we read that Mrs. Trenor appears to like feeling that she *had somehow vicariously made use of* the omnibus that takes people to church. We can infer from this that Mrs. Trenor likes the idea, though not the actuality, of going to church. It pleases her that her family and guests go to church and makes her feel that she has had some part in the process. In paragraph 2, we read that Mr. Trenor goes to church only occasionally (*in a spasmodic burst of virtue,* lines 19–20), usually after a particularly wild party (*when the house had been too uproarious overnight,* lines 20–21). Taken together, it seems that the Trenors view church attendance not as a regular habit but as something they like their guests and family to do to for the sake of appearances. This matches (B). Choice A is out-of-scope. The Trenors do appear to be hospitable, but the passage doesn't say they are *widely known* for hospitality. Choice C is a distortion. Mrs. Trenor does appreciate the fact that some of her guests might go to church, but she isn't *overly concerned.* Choice D is a contradiction. If anything, the Trenors are seen to have relatively little control over their daughters; Mr. Trenor doesn't even always manage to get them to go to church when he wants them to.

4. **J**

For a Vocabulary-in-Context question, look back to the context to make your prediction. Here, *Mrs. Trenor's theory* is something she can't prove. The governess attends a different church (*a rival fane*), and Mrs. Trenor herself stays in her room until lunch, so neither of them can confirm that the Trenor daughters go to church. Consider also the previous paragraph, which mentions that Mrs. Trenor likes to feel that she's attended church *vicariously* through other members of her household. Put the information from these two paragraphs together, and it seems that Mrs. Trenor would like to believe that her daughters go to church, even though she can't prove it. Choices F and G are contradictions. Choice H is out-of-scope. Nothing in the passage supports this.

5. **D**

For a Vocabulary-in-Context question asking about the use of a phrase, read the immediately surrounding context carefully. Notice the phrases *Now and then* (line 19) and *when the house had been…*(line 20). From this context, predict that *spasmodic burst* refers to something that happens only occasionally, under certain circumstances. Choice (D) nicely matches this prediction. Choice A is a distortion. Though Mr. Trenor is described as heavy (*his genial bulk*, line 22), the passage doesn't refer specifically to his health. Choice B is a misused detail. While it's true that the Trenors regularly provide transportation to church, the fact has nothing to do with the phrase *spasmodic burst.* Choice C is a distortion. The word *uproarious* is used (line 21), but the passage doesn't indicate that the Trenors are known for uproarious parties.

6. **G**

As with all Vocabulary-in-Context questions, context is crucial here. Use your passage map notes. Paragraph 3 describes Mr. Gryce's attraction to Lily. The phrase *this tallied with the assurance…that she had been 'dragged into it'* (lines 33–35) gives part of the reason for Mr. Gryce's approval of Lily. Mr. Gryce appreciates *the assurance* that Lily had not willingly involved herself in the bridge game and that she is not an experienced gambler. Therefore, predict that the fact that Lily loses money inspires Mr. Gryce's admiration. This prediction fits with (G). Choice F is out-of-scope. Lily's financial status as compared with that of her hosts isn't mentioned in the passage. Choice H is a misused detail. The contrast between Lily and Mr. Gryce is present in the passage, but it doesn't address this particular question. Choice J is a distortion. Although the passage states that the Trenor sisters *dragged [Lily] into* the bridge game, the passage never says that the Trenors have a tendency to manipulate Lily.

7. **B**

For this Big Picture question, address each point one by one, but consider all statements. Choice A is true: Line 77 states that the Wetheralls *always went to church.* In considering (B), pay attention to lines 84–86, which discuss the Wetherall's *circle* of social acquaintances. Because *God is included in their visiting list*, it can be inferred that while the family felt expected to attend church, they viewed church as more of a social experience than a moral obligation. Therefore, C and D can be eliminated. Choice (B) is false and the correct answer.

8. **G**

For a Big Picture question, consider the specified portion of the passage, and look for particular details that justify your answer. Here, pay careful attention to lines 112–116: *She [Lily] had an idea that the sight of her in a grey gown of devotional cut...would put the finishing touch to Mr. Gryce's subjugation.* The word *subjugation* suggests that Lily wants to use her charms to ensure Mr. Gryce's attraction to her. This prediction best matches (G). Choice F is a contradiction. Choice H combines the contradiction and out-of-scope traps. Lily is described in this paragraph as being prone to sudden change, the opposite of inflexibility. The passage doesn't directly refer to any social problems Lily may have. Choice J is a distortion of lines 121–123, *Lily, for all the hard glaze of her exterior, was inwardly as malleable as wax.* Choice J reverses the details stated here: Lily is actually resolute on the outside but malleable on the inside. Note that *belies* in J means *contradicts*.

9. **C**

For this Big Picture question, consider the relative emphasis the writer gives to the different characters. In the passage, Lily and Mr. Gryce are discussed more than the Trenors and the Wetheralls, so predict that the answer centers on Lily and Mr. Gryce. Only (C) comes anywhere close. Choice A is a misused detail. We can infer that the writer portrays the Trenors and their guests as behaving hypocritically, but this is just part of the passage, not the main focus. Choice B is a misused detail. The interaction between Mrs. Wetherall and Lady Cressida is described, but it is minor. Choice D is out-of-scope. It is too general to apply to this passage.

10. **G**

This is a Detail question, so pay attention to the immediate context. The paragraph describes Mr. Gryce waiting for Lily to appear. He hopes that he will get some time alone with her (*He found himself nourishing the hope that Miss Bart might be unaccompanied,* lines 64–65). He is portrayed as being eager and impatient (*The precious minutes were flying,* lines 65–66). Thus, when the writer describes even the chestnut trees as appearing to behave impatiently, the detail emphasizes Mr. Gryce's impatience. Similarly, he feels that Lily's taking so long is making time pass unrealistically slowly. The detail in the question stem, the coachman and groom *petrifying* (that is, turning to stone) is meant to convey Mr. Gryce's impatience. Choice (G) is the best match. Choice F isn't specific or relevant to the passage; it doesn't take into account the main purpose of the paragraph in the way that (G) does. Choice H is a misused detail. While the detail in the question stem does include a reference to the omnibus's driver, describing the omnibus itself is not the main purpose of the paragraph. Choice J is out-of-scope. The passage never suggests that Lily and Mr. Gryce share a love of nature.

11. **A**

For a Big Picture question, consider the purpose of the whole paragraph and look for details that support the inference you arrive at. The paragraph states that Lily had intended to go to church: *Her intentions...had never been more definite* (lines 119–121). However, she is also described as being *as malleable as wax* and as easily affected by her mood as a water plant is affected by changing tides. The name *Lawrence Selden* (lines 125–126) seems to come out of nowhere. We can infer from the last lines of the passage that Selden is a guest who has recently arrived at Bellomont and that Lily thinks he may have come to see her. Taken together, the details in this paragraph suggest that Lily has been distracted from her intention to attend church with Mr. Gryce because she is curious about Selden. This works well as a prediction and leads us to (A). Choice B includes a misused detail. The word *materialistic* is used in line 44 to describe what Mr. Gryce thinks of other guests at Bellomont, not to describe Lily's opinion of Mr. Gryce. Choice C is out-of-scope. Nothing in the passage suggests that Lily doesn't want to attend church with Mrs. Wetherall and Lady Cressida Raith, nor does the passage indicate that Lily finds them to be hypocritical. Choice D is a distortion. The passage states that Mr. Trenor sometimes doesn't wake up in time to get his daughters (Muriel and Hilda) to church, but the passage doesn't indicate that Lily had been expecting Mr. Trenor to wake her up for church.

12. **J**

For any Inference question, you must infer from the words and context of the passage what the author thinks. For this question, go back to the lines cited in the question stem and pay attention to the context to make your prediction. *They* refers to the Wetheralls, who *always went to church* (line 77). The cited lines describe the Wetheralls as *automata.* Though this word may be unfamiliar to you, use your inference skills to deduce that it means something like automatons, or people who act more because they are copying the behaviors of others than because they are thinking for themselves. According to the passage, *Automata...perform...the gestures executed by the surrounding puppets.* Predict that the author uses the quotation in the question stem to describe people who copy others instead of acting on their own ideas. This prediction best matches (J). Choice F is out-of-scope; there is nothing in the passage to suggest this. Choice G is a distortion that carries the inference too far. The author never suggests that people behave like *automata* because they have religious beliefs. Choice H is a distortion. The word *subjugation* is used in line 116 to describe the effect Lily hopes to have on Mr. Gryce, not in the context of a statement about religious belief.

CHAPTER 12

Reading Practice Set II—Prose Fiction

Directions: This test contains a passage, followed by several questions. After reading the passage, select the best answer to each question. You are allowed to refer to the passage while answering the questions.

PROSE FICTION: *This passage is adapted from the novel* The Woman in White *by Wilkie Collins. It was first published in serial form in 1859 and 1860. The narrator, Walter, is a teacher of drawing. His friend, Pesca, is a native of Italy who teaches Italian in England.*

Pesca's face and manner, on the evening when we confronted each other at my mother's gate, were more than sufficient to inform me that something extraordinary had happened. It was quite useless, however, to ask him for an immediate explanation. I could only conjecture, while he was dragging me in by both hands, that, knowing my habits, he had come to the cottage to make sure of meeting me that night and that he had some news to tell of an unusually agreeable kind.

We both bounced into the parlor in a highly abrupt and undignified manner. My mother sat by the open window laughing and fanning herself. Pesca was one of her especial favorites, and his wildest eccentricities were always pardonable in her eyes. From the first moment she found out that the little Professor was deeply and gratefully attached to her son, she opened her heart to him unreservedly and took all his puzzling foreign peculiarities for granted, without so much as attempting to understand any one of them.

My sister Sarah, with all the advantages of youth, was, strangely enough, less pliable. She did full justice to Pesca's excellent qualities of heart, but she could not accept him implicitly, as my mother accepted him, for my sake. Her insular notions of propriety rose in perpetual revolt against Pesca's constitutional contempt for appearances, and she was always more or less undisguisedly astonished at her mother's familiarity with the eccentric little foreigner. I have observed, not only in my sister's case, but in the instances of others, that we of the young generation are nowhere near as hearty and impulsive as some of our elders. I constantly see old people flushed and excited by the prospect of some anticipated pleasure which altogether fails to ruffle the tranquility of their serene grandchildren. Are we, I wonder, quite such genuine boys and girls now as our seniors were in their time? Has the great advance in education taken rather too long a stride, and are we in these modern days just the least trifle in the world too well brought up?

Without attempting to answer those questions decisively, I may at least record that I never saw my mother and my sister together in Pesca's society without finding my mother much the younger woman of the two. On this occasion, for example, while the old lady was laughing heartily over the boyish manner in which we tumbled into the parlor, Sarah was perturbedly picking up the broken pieces of a teacup, which the Professor had knocked off the table in his precipitate advance to meet me at the door.

"I don't know what would have happened, Walter," said my mother, "if you had delayed much longer. Pesca has been half mad with impatience, and I have been half mad with curiosity. The Professor has brought some wonderful news with him, in which he says you are concerned, and he has cruelly refused to give us the smallest hint of it till his friend Walter appeared."

"Very provoking: it spoils the set," murmured Sarah to herself, mournfully absorbed over the ruins of the broken cup.

While these words were being spoken, Pesca, happily and fussily unconscious of the irreparable wrong which the crockery had suffered at his hands, was dragging a large arm-chair to the opposite end of the room, so as to command us all three, in the character of a public speaker addressing an audience. Having turned the chair with its back towards us, he jumped into it on his knees and excitedly addressed his small congregation of three from an impromptu pulpit.

"Now, my good dears," began Pesca, "listen to me. The time has come—I recite my good news—I speak at last."

"Hear, hear," said my mother, humoring the joke.

"The next thing he will break, Mamma," whispered Sarah, "will be the back of the best arm-chair."

"Among the fine London Houses where I teach the language of my native country," said Pesca, "is one, mighty fine, in the big place called Portland. The golden Papa there, the mighty merchant, says, "I have got a letter from my friend, the Mister, and he wants a recommend from me, of a drawing-master, to go down to his house in the country. Perhaps you know of a drawing master that I can recommend?"

I address myself to the mighty merchant, and I say, "Dear sir, I have the man! The first and foremost drawing-master of the world!"

1. It can be inferred from the first paragraph that:
   - **A.** Pesca frequently visits the narrator's mother.
   - **B.** the narrator does not believe that Pesca shows good judgment.
   - **C.** the narrator fears a hostile confrontation with Pesca.
   - **D.** Pesca visits the cottage fully expecting to meet up with the narrator there.

2. As it is used in line 62, the word *precipitate* most nearly means:
   - **F.** quick.
   - **G.** rude.
   - **H.** faithful.
   - **J.** eccentric.

3. It can be inferred from the passage that all of the following are true of Professor Pesca EXCEPT:
   - **A.** he is familiar with the narrator's daily routine.
   - **B.** he is well trained in public speaking.
   - **C.** the narrator's mother approves of him.
   - **D.** he has not completely mastered the subtleties of the English language.

4. A difference between older people and younger people that the narrator finds remarkable is:
   - **F.** younger people are impulsive, while older people are more deliberate.
   - **G.** older people tend to be more curious than younger people are.
   - **H.** older people fail to display appropriate gratitude toward the young.
   - **J.** older people are more likely than younger people are to anticipate pleasures enthusiastically.

5. According to the passage, the narrator's mother has a high opinion of Professor Pesca because:
   - **A.** she values intellectual pursuits.
   - **B.** Professor Pesca has been instrumental in advancing her son's career.
   - **C.** Professor Pesca feels a grateful attachment toward her son.
   - **D.** she is the sort of person who can easily overlook the faults of others.

6. It can be inferred from the passage that Professor Pesca waits until the narrator's arrival to tell his good news because:
   - **F.** he is afraid that the narrator's mother would spoil the news if she heard it first.
   - **G.** he is uncomfortable around Sarah and is not willing to talk to her unless her brother is not present.
   - **H.** his news has nothing to do with the narrator's mother.
   - **J.** he wants to deliver the good news in an impressively dramatic way.

7. The passage implies that Sarah:
   - **A.** fails to see any good qualities in Professor Pesca.
   - **B.** feels extremely protective toward her brother.
   - **C.** has a strong concern for taking care of material things.
   - **D.** is guilty of neglecting her elderly mother's basic needs.

8. The writer uses the phrase "while he was dragging me in by both hands" (lines 7–8) in order to convey that the narrator:

   F. believes Pesca's actions are characterized by rudeness.

   G. is reluctant to enter his mother's house in the presence of Pesca.

   H. is aware of Pesca's impatience.

   J. is frequently caught off guard by Pesca's eccentric behaviors.

9. When the narrator uses the phrase "strangely enough" (line 27), he suggests that:

   A. he is surprised that Sarah has any respect at all for Pesca.

   B. he would expect her to be more lenient in her judgments than she is.

   C. Sarah reacts in a way that is inconsistent with the advantages she has been given.

   D. he has never known Sarah to admit that Pesca has any good qualities.

10. The narrator's questions at the end of the third paragraph suggest that:

    F. the narrator admires the unreserved way that members of the older generation express their feelings.

    G. the narrator believes that Pesca is overly concerned with appearances.

    H. Sarah disapproves of her mother's attitude toward Pesca.

    J. the narrator judges his own generation to be more genuine than his parents' generation.

11. According to the passage, which event takes place first?

    A. Pesca breaks the teacup.

    B. Pesca arrives at the cottage.

    C. The narrator's mother laughs at the behavior of Pesca and her son.

    D. The narrator enters the cottage.

12. According to the passage, the narrator wonders:

    F. whether advances in education have gone too far.

    G. if Pesca is entirely trustworthy.

    H. why his mother dislikes Pesca.

    J. why Sarah's attitude is one of perpetual revolt.

ANSWERS AND EXPLANATIONS

SUGGESTED PASSAGE MAP NOTES

Paragraph 1: Pesca has good news for narrator

Paragraph 2: Narrator's mom likes Pesca

Paragraph 3: Sarah not fond of Pesca; young/old differences

Paragraph 4: Sarah seems older than mom; broken teacup

Paragraph 5: Mom eager for Pesca's good news

Paragraph 6: Sarah's annoyance

Paragraph 7: Pesca sets stage like preacher

Paragraphs 8–10: Responses to Pesca

Paragraph 11: Pesca knows rich man who needs drawing teacher

Paragraph 12: Pesca excited to know drawing teacher

ANSWER KEY

1.	**D**	**7.**	**C**
2.	**F**	**8.**	**H**
3.	**B**	**9.**	**B**
4.	**J**	**10.**	**F**
5.	**C**	**11.**	**B**
6.	**J**	**12.**	**F**

1. **D**

For a Big Picture question about a paragraph, make sure your answer is consistent with everything in the paragraph. It may be tough to predict, but you should at least refer to your passage map notes and skim the paragraph before reading the answer choices. Choice A is a misused detail from the second paragraph. Choice B is out-of-scope. The narrator never questions Pesca's judgment. Choice C is out-of-scope. Nothing in the paragraph suggests that a confrontation is likely. Choice (D) is the best answer. The phrase *knowing my habits* (lines 8–9) suggests that Pesca knows he will find the narrator at his mother's house.

2. **F**

For a Vocabulary-in-Context question, go back to the sentence and check for context clues that help you predict. The sentence states the Pesca had knocked the teacup off the table while moving to greet the narrator at the door. Paragraph 1 indicates that Pesca is very eager and excited, so predict that he moved *quickly* toward the door. This prediction matches (F). Choice G is a distortion. The passage states that Sarah is *perturbed* by the broken cup, but the narrator doesn't ascribe rudeness to Pesca. Choice H is out-of-scope. Nothing in the sentence or passage indicates that *precipitate* could mean *faithful.* Choice J is a distortion. Although Pesca is described as *eccentric* in this passage, his *advance toward the door* is not necessarily eccentric.

3. **B**

For a broad Inference question, quickly review your passage map notes before considering the answer choices. In this case, you must eliminate choices that *are* supported by the passage. Eliminate A because lines 8–9 (paragraph 1) states that Pesca knows the narrator's habits. Choice (B) is not supported by the passage and is the best answer. Although Pesca consciously uses a dramatic manner to deliver his good news, appearing to act like a preacher addressing his congregation, he does so a bit awkwardly. Nothing in the passage indicates that he is "well trained" as a public speaker. Eliminate C because line 22 states that the narrator's mother *unreservedly* opens her heart to Pesca. Eliminate D because Pesca's statements in the passage do not always show strong command of English. For example, in lines 99–100, Pesca says, *he wants a* recommend *from me* instead of *a* recommendation.

4. **J**

For a Big Picture question about a contrast, review your passage map notes and skim the passage if necessary to find where in the passage to go for your prediction. In this case, your passage map notes may direct you to paragraphs 3 and 4. Predict that *the young generation [is not as] impulsive as some of our elders* (lines 38–40) and that *old people [are] excited by the prospect of some anticipated pleasure* (lines 41–42). This prediction fits well with (J). Choice F is a distortion; the descriptions of young and old are reversed in this answer choice. Choice G is out-of-scope. Nothing in the passage suggests that older people are more curious. Choice H is out-of-scope. Older people are not described as ungrateful.

5. **C**

For a Detail question, check your passage notes or skim the passage to find the words used in the question stem. Here, your passage map notes should direct you to paragraph 2, where lines 19–21 state that the narrator's mother has favored Pesca since *the first moment she found out that the little Professor was deeply and gratefully attached to her son.* Choice A is out-of-scope. The passage says nothing about the narrator's mother valuing intellectual pursuits. Choice B is a distortion. While the passage does concern Pesca's recommending the narrator for a job, the narrator's mother doesn't yet know about this when the passage opens. Choice D is a distortion. The passage states the narrator's mother overlooks Pesca's faults, but it doesn't suggest that she applies this lenient attitude toward everyone.

6. **J**

For an Inference question, read the appropriate part of the passage and draw a conclusion that doesn't stray too far from what is stated. In this case, use your passage notes to direct you to paragraphs 7–10. Pesca is described as wanting to *command us all three, in the character of a public speaker addressing an audience* (lines 80–82). Pesca's words, *The time has come—I recite my good news—I speak at last* (lines 87–88), show that he wants to build a sense of anticipation and drama around what he has to say. This prediction supports (J). Choice F is out-of-scope because the passage doesn't indicate Pesca is afraid the narrator's mother would spoil his secret. As the prediction describes, it is primarily his desire to be dramatic that makes him delay. Choice G is a distortion. Although Sarah displays some discomfort around Pesca (her annoyance at his breaking the teacup), Pesca is not described as feeling at all uncomfortable around Sarah. Choice H is a contradiction. If anything, Pesca seems confident that the narrator's mother will be delighted by his news.

7. **C**

For a Big Picture question about a character, start with your passage map notes. In this case, they should lead you to paragraphs 3 and 4. Quickly look at these paragraphs to get a feel for how Sarah is portrayed. In addition, skim through the passage for the word *Sarah* to see if any other references will help you with this question. Then read through the answer choices and eliminate. Choice A is an extreme. The passage says that Sarah *did full justice to Pesca's excellent qualities of heart, but she could not accept him implicitly* (lines 28–30). This means that Sarah acknowledges that Pesca at least has a good heart, even if she doesn't like everything about him. Choice B is out-of-scope because Sarah is not described as being protective of her brother. Choice (C), the best answer, is justified by lines 73–74, where Sarah is described as *mournfully absorbed over the ruins of the broken cup.* Additional support for this choice is found in lines 91–93, where Sarah is concerned that Pesca will break *the best arm-chair.* Choice D is out-of-scope. The passage says nothing about the basic needs of the narrator's mother not being met.

8. **H**

For a Vocabulary-in-Context question about a phrase, read around the immediate context to make your prediction. Because the narrator suspects that Pesca has come with good news, the narrator probably realizes that Pesca is eager to get him into the house. This prediction fits well with (H). Choice F is out-of-scope. There is no evidence suggesting that the narrator finds Pesca to be rude. Choice G is out-of-scope. Nothing suggests that the narrator wants to resist Pesca or avoid his company. Choice J is a distortion. While the passage does describe Pesca as *an eccentric little foreigner* (line 36), the narrator never says he is caught off guard by Pesca's eccentricities.

9. **B**

For a Vocabulary-in-Context question about a phrase, check the context of the sentence to predict. This sentence contains a comparison, *less pliable* (lines 27–28). Briefly refer back to the previous paragraph to determine that the comparison is between Sarah and her mother. Sarah is described as having *all the advantages of youth.* Given the contrast between mother and daughter, the narrator seems to think that a younger person would be more flexible. This prediction lines up with (B). Choice A is a distortion that doesn't take the contrast between youth and age into account. Choice C is a distortion. The *advantages* in this context are the *advantages of youth,* not particular advantages that have been given to Sarah. Choice D is an opposite. The narrator states that Sarah can see Pesca's excellent qualities of heart (lines 28–29).

10. **F**

For a Big Picture question about a paragraph, use your passage map notes and quickly review the paragraph to see if you can predict. There's a lot in this paragraph. Sarah isn't very comfortable with Pesca; the mother seems more excited to hear Pesca's good news; the narrator compares old and young, wondering if the young are a little too serious. Don't worry which is more important, but be ready to use the information to judge the answer choices. Choice (F) is the best answer. It embraces the differences between old and young and the narrator's surprise at Sarah's attitude toward Pesca. Choice G is a distortion. The passage states that Sarah disapproves of Pesca's lack of regard for appearances (lines 32–33). Choice H is a distortion. Though lines 29–30 indicate that Sarah doesn't share her mother's opinion of Pesca (*she could not accept him implicitly, as my mother did*), Sarah doesn't express disapproval of her mother's attitude. Choice J is a distortion. The narrator asks himself if members of his own generation are *quite such genuine boys and girls now as our seniors were in their time* (lines 45–46), but he doesn't make an explicit statement that his generation is the *more genuine.*

11. **B**

For this Big Picture question, try to determine which event happened first and use that knowledge to eliminate wrong answer choices. In this case, Pesca arrives at the cottage first. This is justified by lines 8–10:*...knowing my habits, he [Pesca] had come to the cottage to make sure of meeting me....* For further elimination, you can determine that the narrator enters the cottage *after* Pesca had arrived and broken the teacup by reading lines 60–62: *the Professor had knocked [the teacup] off the table in his precipitate advance to meet me at the door.* Thus, (B) is the correct answer choice.

12. **F**

For a broadly worded Detail question, your passage map notes and quick skimming may not be much help in directing you to the best part of the passage to refer to. If this is the case, don't spend too much time looking around. Check the answer choices and see if a quick reference to the passage can help you choose the best one. Here, (F) is the best answer, but that may not be immediately apparent. Eliminate G because the narrator never questions Pesca's trustworthiness, making this choice out-of-scope. Eliminate H because it's a contradiction. The author states that his mother has a high opinion of Pesca. Choice J is a distortion. The phrase *perpetual revolt* describes Sarah's opinion of Pesca's *contempt for appearances* (lines 46–48), but it isn't something the narrator wonders about. Working by elimination is effective for this question. Notice, however, that the lines 46–48, *has the great advance in education taken rather too long a stride?,* directly support (F).

CHAPTER 13

Reading Practice Set III—Social Science

Directions: This test contains a passage, followed by several questions. After reading the passage, select the best answer to each question. You are allowed to refer to the passage while answering the questions.

SOCIAL SCIENCE: *This passage is adapted from "Assessing the Values of Cultural Heritage," a report published in 2002 by the Advisory Council on Historic Preservation. This selection, written by Marta de la Torre and Randall Mason, examines the challenges involved in determining the cultural significance of historic sites to various groups, including conservation experts and ordinary citizens.*

In recent decades, the concept of what is heritage has evolved and expanded, and new groups have joined specialists in its identification. These groups of citizens, of professionals from other fields, and of representatives of special interests arrive in the heritage field with their own criteria, opinions, and values—which often differ from our own as heritage specialists.

This democratization is a positive development in our field and bears witness to the importance of heritage in today's society. Nonetheless, this aperture has brought new considerations to the discussions and has made them much more complex. Today the opinions of experts are often a few among many, in an arena where it is recognized that heritage is multivalent and that values are not immutable. In this changed environment, the articulation and understanding of values have acquired greater importance when heritage decisions are being made about what to conserve, how to conserve it, where to set priorities, and how to handle conflicting interests.

As conservation professionals, we are comfortable with the assessment methods used by traditional heritage experts. However, to identify and measure "social" values, we must venture into new areas. The stakeholders of social values are usually members of the public who have not traditionally participated in our work or had their opinions taken into consideration. Today, as we recognize the importance of including all stakeholders in the process, we must turn to other disciplines to bring these new groups into the discussions.

Anthropologist Setha M. Low has introduced ethnographic research as a way of bringing new groups of stakeholders into the values identification process. The field of environmental conservation has a relatively long tradition of consultation with a broad spectrum of stakeholders. Approaches from the environmental field are often held up as examples to be emulated in the heritage field. Theresa Satterfield's work in this area has been a model for assessment tools and methods that might be productively applied in our own field. Economists seem to have the most developed and widely accepted value assessment tools. However, these tools might not be as accurate in measuring cultural values as has been accepted in the past. A number of economists are now searching for ways of honing their tools to make them more useful in the heritage field. The work of researchers in all three of these areas points us toward collaboration with other disciplines.

A discussion of values, of how social contexts shape heritage and conservation, and of the imperative of public participation provides examples of issues that challenge conventional notions of conservation professionals' responsibilities. How to champion conservation principles (traditional ones, centered on the sanctity and inherent meaningfulness of material heritage) while managing an open democratic process that may conclude by underselling conservation in favor of other social goals? This issue gets to the essential nature of the field and of conservation as a profession: Are we advocates? Are we neutral professionals and experts?

Conservation professionals are faced with two particular challenges arising out of these social and political contexts: power sharing and collaboration. Broader participation poses a challenge to the roles and responsibilities of conservation professionals: some suggest that bringing conservation policies and decisions in line with democratic values would undermine the authority of conservation professionals and would even amount to an abdication of professional responsibility. In other words, democratization of conservation decision making could contradict the professional devotion to conservation—what happens when the democracy of voices decides that a heritage site can be destroyed? Do we as conservation professionals have a right, or even a responsibility, to speak against the democratic will?

The probability is not that actual decision making power will be democratized but, rather, that the process of value elicitation will be included. Democratization of the processes of consultation and assessment of heritage values is not likely to be a threat to the sovereignty of the field, but it still requires a change of attitude and training. The inevitability of trade-offs and compromises and the respectful and meaningful gathering of different modes of valuing have to be recognized.

Using new methods from different fields means collaborating with more and different professionals, anthropologists and economists, for instance. Such collaboration raises questions about who is in charge of which part of the process. What are the relative roles and contributions and responsibilities of this different cast of characters? Does the conservation professional's role become that of an orchestrator of specialists or of one specialist among others? It seems that the conservation professional has moved to play the dual role of specialist and orchestrator. The tasks associated with the latter function call for new ways of thinking as well as for new skills. The challenge ahead is to continue searching for the means to serve the public good by preserving material remains of the past.

1. What is the fundamental question addressed by the passage as a whole?
   - **A.** What is the role of the ordinary citizen in determining what conservation professionals should preserve?
   - **B.** What are the best methods to use to ensure reliable conservation of culturally significant sites?
   - **C.** In what ways can anthropologists contribute to the field of conservation?
   - **D.** How is the role of the conservation professional changing in light of social and political concerns about the democratization of conversation activities?

2. This passage is written from the point of view of:
   - **F.** a politician whose main concern is balancing the needs of various interest groups.
   - **G.** an anthropologist who is eager to see her methodology applied in the field of conservation.
   - **H.** a specialist in the field of conservation who believes that conservation professionals have much to contribute.
   - **J.** an economist who is pushing for the value assessment tools used in economics as the basis for conservation decisions.

3. The phrase "democracy of voices" in line 92 most likely refers to:
   - **A.** the opinion of a large number of ordinary citizens.
   - **B.** a government run by the people.
   - **C.** the viewpoint of a citizen who is politically active.
   - **D.** a traditional influence on decisions about heritage conservation.

4. A possible drawback of power sharing and collaboration in the conservation field that the passage refers to is that:
   - **F.** the authority of the specialist would be undermined.
   - **G.** the ordinary citizen lacks knowledge relating to historic sites.
   - **H.** the general public does not express much interest in historic conservation.
   - **J.** most conservation specialists lack the skills needed to lead group collaboration.

5. In the context of the passage as a whole, the questions at the end of the sixth paragraph serve to:
   - **A.** address a concern that the writer will later resolve.
   - **B.** reflect uncertainty about future goals.
   - **C.** expose a flaw in a current theory.
   - **D.** point the way to a clearly defined solution to a problem.

6. The author uses the sentence in lines 62–67 to suggest that:

F. championing traditional conservation principles must be made a priority.

G. conservation professionals' traditional view of their responsibilities did not demand that they take social contexts into account.

H. the field of conservation has been mired in convention for too long.

J. ethnographic research should be used to inform the values identification process.

7. The writer believes that the effect of democratization on the conservation field will:

A. be a threat to the sovereignty of the field.

B. mean that different ways of assessing value will have to be recognized.

C. ultimately lead to conservation decisions being made by the people.

D. serve the public good by completely reforming the practices of conservation specialists.

8. As used in the passage, the word *orchestrator* (line 117) most nearly means:

F. manager.

G. creator.

H. person with particular expertise.

J. musical director.

9. The writer's view of the outlook for the conservation field is:

A. grounded in cynicism.

B. cautiously optimistic.

C. tinged with reservations.

D. fairly pessimistic.

10. According to the passage, the notion of what heritage is has evolved:

F. to reflect a multitude of social changes in recent years.

G. because heritage specialists have been considered too old-fashioned in their values.

H. by recognizing the values of those who aren't professionals in the field.

J. to reflect a growing trend toward democratization in many academic specialties.

11. The phrase "underselling conservation in favor of other social goals" (lines 72–73) is used to describe:

A. the way in which the values of conservation are being neglected because of economic concerns.

B. the priority that has been given to social goals over economic considerations.

C. the fear that inviting a democratic process may dilute the traditional goals of conservation.

D. the challenges that currently face conservation professionals.

12. Setha M. Low and Theresa Satterfield are mentioned in the passage as:

F. conservation professionals who are fighting the democratization of their field.

G. economists who point to the need for heritage professionals to take economic values into account.

H. citizens who are fighting to have their voices heard in decisions that are made about which historic sites are preserved.

J. experts in other fields who have contributions to make as to the direction that conservation should move in.

ANSWERS AND EXPLANATIONS

SUGGESTED PASSAGE MAP NOTES

Paragraph 1: New groups affecting heritage field

Paragraph 2: Democratization positive but complex

Paragraph 3: Importance of determining social "values"

Paragraph 4: Other fields help bring new groups into values ID process

Paragraph 5: Tension between conservation principles and democratization

Paragraph 6: Resulting challenges

Paragraph 7: Democratization requires changes for professionals

Paragraph 8: Collaboration w/ experts outside conservation field

ANSWER KEY

1.	**D**	**7.**	**B**
2.	**H**	**8.**	**F**
3.	**A**	**9.**	**D**
4.	**F**	**10.**	**H**
5.	**A**	**11.**	**C**
6.	**G**	**12.**	**J**

1. **D**

For a broad Big Picture question, keep the overall purpose of the passage in mind. Incorrect answer choices may refer to too small a part of the passage. Predict that the purpose of the passage is to address challenges faced by conservation professionals. Choice (D) best captures this purpose. Choice A is a distortion. It uses several words from the passage, but it puts the emphasis in the wrong place by focusing on citizens instead of professionals. Choice B is out-of-scope. The passage doesn't address particular methods of conservation. Choice C is a misused detail. Paragraph 4 discusses contributions from anthropologists, but the focus of the whole passage is much broader.

2. **H**

For this Big Picture question, take the whole passage into account and don't put excessive emphasis on a particular detail. Lines 26 and 93–94 both use the word *we* with the phrase *as conservation professionals*, making it clear that the writer identifies with this group. Choice (H) is the only choice supported by this prediction. Choice F is a distortion. The passage mentions *political contexts* but does not refer at all to politicians. Choice G is a distortion. The passage mentions Low, an anthropologist, but doesn't describe her as being eager to see her methodology used by conservation professionals. Choice J is a distortion. Although the passage mentions economists, they are not described as pushing to have an influence in the field of conservation.

3. **A**

For an Inference question that asks about the meaning of a phrase, pay close attention to the context of the paragraph. Here, the paragraph refers to *power sharing* (line 80) that might *undermine the authority of conservation professionals* (lines 85–86). There is a tension here between allowing the opinions of new groups into the discussion and maintaining the traditional role of the conservation professionals because it's possible that the new groups would contradict the professionals. This prediction leads to (A). Choice B is out-of-scope. There is nothing in the passage to indicate that *government* works in this context. Choice C is out-of-scope. *Politically active* citizens aren't mentioned in the passage. Choice D is an opposite. The phrase in question refers to those who might oppose the *traditional influence.*

4. **F**

To predict for a Detail question, refer to your passage map notes to direct you to the right spot in the passage. If the notes don't suggest a particular paragraph to research, skim the passage for the words used in the question stem or words with a similar meaning. Here, *power sharing and collaboration* appear in paragraph 6 in the context of *challenges* that are presented by allowing more groups into the discussion. The writer states that *some suggest [that allowing more groups in] would undermine the authority of the conservation professional* (lines 83–86). This prediction leads directly to (F). Choice G is out-of-scope. The ordinary citizen's knowledge of historic sites is not mentioned in the passage. Choice H is out-of-scope. The passage never states that the general public lacks interest in historic sites. Choice J is out-of-scope. The passage doesn't question the leadership skills of *most conservation professionals.*

5. **A**

For a Vocabluary-in-Context question, pay close attention to the context. Read a little above and a little below the cited lines to make your prediction. Here, context of the lines below puts the answers to the questions in a balanced perspective: *The probability is not that actual decision making power will be democratized, but, rather, that the process of value elicitation will be included* (lines 97–100). Predict from this that the questions at the end of paragraph 6 can be answered in ways that are not alarming. This prediction lines up with (A). Choice B is a distortion that doesn't take information from paragraph 7 into account. Although the questions point to *uncertainty,* the writer immediately addresses the issue with a firm expectation that is not uncertain. Choice C is out-of-scope. The passage examines questions and processes but does not mention a theory. Choice D is a distortion. Paragraph 7 does begin to suggest a solution to the problem of how to allow more voices in the discussion of conversation values, but the last sentence of the paragraph, *The inevitability...to be recognized* (lines 105–108), indicates the solution has a tentative, not a *clearly defined*, quality.

6. **G**

To predict for an Inference question, carefully read the cited lines and, if necessary, their immediate context, to draw a conclusion that doesn't stray too far from what is stated. Here, the word *challenge* indicates a tension: the possible conflict between *the imperative of public participation* (line 64) and *conventional notions of conservation professionals' responsibilities.* Predict that the conventional notions did not previously take into account the necessity of public participation. This prediction matches well with (G). Choice F is a contradiction. The whole point of the passage is about finding ways to accept input from outside the realm of *traditional conservation principles.* Choice H is a distortion of the word *conventional* as it's used in the passage. Choice J is a misused detail. This comes from paragraph 5 and doesn't relate to the line that this question stem refers to.

7. **B**

A Big Picture question demands that you keep the overall purpose of the passage in mind. To predict, look for where *democratization* is mentioned in the passage. Your passage map notes should lead you to paragraphs 5 and 7. Read in paragraph 7 to predict that democratization is part of a process of assessing values and will lead to changes for professionals. This prediction supports (B), which is also consistent with the passage overall. Choice A is a contradiction of lines 100–103, *Democratization...is not likely to be a threat...the field.* Choice C is a distortion. While the people will take a greater role, the writer states that it will be in *consultation and assessment* (line 101) rather than in the ultimate decision making. Choice D is an extreme. While the writer does suggest changes in process and attitude, there is nothing in the passage to suggest that the field will be *completely reformed.*

8. **F**

For a Vocabulary-in-Context question, read the sentence carefully, and if necessary, the preceding and following sentences, to search for clues to predict the meaning. In this case, the sentence itself presents a contrast. There are two different possibilities for the role of the conservation professional: first, *an orchestrator of specialists* and second, *one specialist among others.* This contrast suggests that the *orchestrator* somehow places above the other specialists, so predict that it means something like *leader* or *one who takes priority over.* This prediction fits well with (F). Choice G is a distortion that might be tempting if you're thinking of a musical orchestra instead of paying attention to the context. Choice H is a distortion that gives too much emphasis to the word *specialist* in the sentence and misses the idea of the orchestra having a role above and beyond that of *specialist.* Choice J is out-of-scope. It draws on a completely different meaning of the word that is not relevant to this passage.

9. **D**

For a Big Picture question, keep in mind the tone of the passage as a whole. For this question, also research in the passage for the area that discusses *the outlook for the conservation field.* To predict, carefully read the last paragraph. It brings up questions about the role of the conservation specialist, but it also poses an answer: *It seems that...orchestrator* (lines 118–120). It mentions changes that will be necessary to meet *the challenge ahead*, but does not suggest that these challenges will be insurmountable. Therefore, predict something like *concerned but hopeful.* This prediction leads directly to (D). Choice A expresses a bleaker view than the passage justifies. The word *tinged* has a negative connotation that makes it sound as though the *reservations* are the primary factor in the writer's outlook. Choice B is also too negative. The writer mentions the challenges in a hopeful rather than a pessimistic tone. Choice C is out-of-scope. While the author attempts to take a balanced view, looking at both challenges and ways to address them, there is nothing cynical in the tone or approach.

10. **H**

To predict for a Detail question, use your passage map notes or skim the passage for key words in the question stem. In this case, your passage map notes may lead you to paragraph 1. From the first sentence, predict that the concept of heritage has broadened as new groups have influenced its meaning. The next sentence identifies these others as citizens, experts in other fields, and special-interest groups. This prediction matches well with (H). Choice F is a distortion. The passage indicates that the notion of heritage is changing as a result of new social contexts, but it doesn't refer to anything like *a multitude of social changes.* Choice G is out-of-scope. Heritage specialists are clearly attempting to redefine their role, but the passage doesn't state that they have become *too old-fashioned.* Choice J is a distortion. The passage does mention *democratization* but only as it relates to the conservation field, not to any other *academic specialties.*

11. **C**

For a Vocabulary-in-Context question about a phrase, pay close attention to the surrounding sentences. The phrase is used here in the context of asking how to support traditional conservation goals in the face of needing to accept *an open democratic process* (line 71). This is a contrast that leads to the prediction that traditional goals and the *other social goals* are potentially conflicting. Predict that *underselling* indicates fears that the other goals might take precedence over the traditional goals. This prediction matches with (C). Choice A is a distortion. The passage mentions economists in a discussion of determining values but doesn't discuss conservation values as being in conflict with economic values. Choice B is also a distortion. It reverses the terms used in A, but both choices address a tension that isn't present in the passage. Choice D is a misused detail. Although the purpose of the passage is to discuss current challenges, this detail doesn't answer the question posed in the question stem.

12. **J**

For a Detail question, pay close attention to the context in which the detail is mentioned. Passage map notes for the paragraph are usually helpful. In this case, your note may indicate that the paragraph discusses experts in other fields who have done work that might be helpful to conservation specialists. This makes a great prediction that lines up with (J). Choice F is a distortion of two details that are present in the passage: *conservation professionals* and *democratization.* Choice G is a misused detail. *Economists* are mentioned in the passage, but the passage clearly indicates that Low and Satterfield are associated with other fields. Choice H is out-of-scope. The passage doesn't specifically mention any groups who are *fighting to have their voices heard.*

CHAPTER 14

Reading Practice Set IV—Social Science

Directions: This test contains a passage, followed by several questions. After reading the passage, select the best answer to each question. You are allowed to refer to the passage while answering the questions.

SOCIAL SCIENCE: *This passage is adapted from* New Discoveries at Jamestown: Site of the First Successful English Settlement in America *by John L. Cotter and J. Paul Hudson, published in 1957.*

Archeological explorations at Jamestown, Virginia, have brought to light thousands of colonial period artifacts that were used by the Virginia settlers from 1607 until 1699. A study of these objects, which were buried under the soil at Jamestown for decades, reveals in many ways how the English colonists lived on a small wilderness island over 300 years ago. Artifacts unearthed include building materials and handwrought hardware, kitchen utensils and fireplace accessories, furniture hardware, and many items relating to household and town industries.

These artifacts provide valuable information concerning the everyday life and manners of the first Virginia settlers. Excavated artifacts reveal that the Jamestown colonists built their houses in the same style as those they knew in England, insofar as local materials permitted. There were differences, however, for the settlers were in a land replete with vast forests and untapped natural resources close at hand that they used to their advantage.

The Virginia known to the first settlers was a carpenter's paradise, and consequently the early buildings were the work of artisans in wood. The first rude shelter, the split-wood fencing, the clap-board roof, puncheon floors, cupboards, benches, stools, and wood plows are all examples of skilled working with wood.

Timber at Jamestown was plentiful, so many houses, especially in the early years, were of frame construction. During the first decade or two, house construction reflected a primitive use of materials found ready at hand, such as saplings for a sort of framing, and use of branches, leafage, bark, and animal skins. During these early years, when the settlers were having such a difficult time staying alive, mud walls, wattle-and-daub, and coarse marsh-grass thatch were used. Out of these years of improvising, construction with squatted posts, and later with studs, came into practice. There was probably little thought of plastering walls during the first two decades. When plastering was adopted, clay, either by itself or mixed with oyster-shell lime, was first used. The early floors were of clay, and such floors continued to be used in the humbler dwellings throughout the 1600s. It can be assumed that most of the dwellings, or shelters, of the early Jamestown settlers had a rough and primitive appearance.

After Jamestown had attained some degree of permanency, many houses were built of brick. It is quite clear from documentary records and archeological remains that the colonists not only made their own brick but also that the process, as well as the finished products, followed closely the English method. Four brick kilns were discovered on Jamestown Island during archeological explorations.

While some of the handwrought hardware found at Jamestown was made in the colony, most of it was imported from England. Types of building hardware unearthed include an excellent assortment of nails, spikes, stapes, locks, keys, hinges, pintles, shutter fasteners, bolts, hasps, latches, door knockers, door pulls, bootscrapes, gutter supports, wall anchors, and ornamental hardware. In many instances, each type is represented by several varieties. It is believed that wooden hardware was used on many of the early houses.

A few glass window panes may have been made in the Jamestown glass factory, which was built in 1608. Most of the window glass used in the colony, however, was shipped from England. Many of the early panes used were diamond-shaped pieces known as "quarrels" and were held in place by means of slotted lead strips known as "cames." The window frames used in a few of the Jamestown houses were handwrought iron casements. Most of the humbler dwellings had no glass panes in the windows. The window openings were closed by batten shutters, operated by hinges of wood and fitted with wooden fastening devices.

Busy conquering a stubborn wilderness, the first Jamestown settlers had only a few things to make their houses cozy and cheerful. In most cases, their worldly goods consisted of a few cooking utensils, a change of clothing, a weapon or two, and a few pieces of handmade furniture. After the early years of hardship had passed, the colonists began to acquire possessions for more pleasant living; by 1650 the better houses were equipped with most of the necessities of life of those times, as well as a few luxuries of comfortable living.

1. According to the author, artifacts discovered in Jamestown are worthy of study because they:

   A. are made of valuable materials.
   B. offer information about the daily lives of settlers.
   C. indicate that life in Jamestown was not as difficult as had been previously thought.
   D. display a remarkable degree of artistic ingenuity.

2. All of the following are given as examples of skilled woodworking EXCEPT:

   F. puncheon floors.
   G. benches.
   H. kitchen utensils.
   J. stools.

3. The primary purpose of the passage is to:

   A. discuss artifacts found at the Jamestown settlement.
   B. argue that life in Jamestown was harder for the settlers than life in England had been.
   C. persuade the reader to visit Jamestown.
   D. describe the ways in which colonists rejected English traditions when they came to Jamestown.

4. As used in line 36, the word *frame* most nearly means:

   F. outline.
   G. wood.
   H. picture-like.
   J. brick.

5. It can be inferred that "wattle-and-daub" in line 43 refers to:

   A. a type of food consumed by the Jamestown settlers.
   B. decorative hardware used on colonial furniture.
   C. tools the archeologist used in the process of studying the Jamestown settlement.
   D. natural materials used in the construction of houses in Jamestown.

6. Which of the following are NOT examples of hardware found at the Jamestown settlement?

   F. Nails
   G. Curtain rods
   H. Door knockers
   J. Bootscrapes

7. It can be inferred from lines 58–60, *After Jamestown...brick*, that one reason the earliest houses built by the settlers were made of wood was that:

   A. Jamestown lacked facilities for manufacturing brick.
   B. it was initially unclear how long the settlers would remain in Jamestown.
   C. climate conditions in Virginia made it impossible to produce the kind of brick the settlers had been familiar with in England.
   D. the settlers had not brought any building materials with them from England.

8. It can be inferred from the last paragraph that concern with domestic comforts was a priority for the settlers:

   F. because most of them had lived relatively luxurious lives before leaving England.

   G. only after the necessities of basic survival had been addressed.

   H. by the time the Jamestown settlement had been in existence for two years.

   J. because they needed relief from the harshness of the wilderness.

9. According the passage, clay was used for floors:

   A. because the supply of timber was scarce.

   B. exclusively during the early years of Jamestown's existence.

   C. in all types of buildings at the settlement.

   D. for many years in the settlement's more modest houses.

10. As used in the passage, the phrase "replete with" in line 23 most nearly means:

   F. finished by.

   G. lacking in.

   H. filled by.

   J. constrained by.

11. As stated by the author, a glass factory was built in Jamestown:

   A. in 1699.

   B. over 300 years ago.

   C. sometime before 1650.

   D. in 1608.

12. It can be inferred that "there was probably little thought of plastering walls during the first two decades" (lines 46–49) because:

   F. the materials necessary to make plaster were difficult to obtain.

   G. plastered walls were not a requirement of survival.

   H. the studs used at the time were too primitive to hold plaster.

   J. the rough and primitive appearance of unplastered walls was desirable to most settlers.

ANSWERS AND EXPLANATIONS

SUGGESTED PASSAGE MAP NOTES

Paragraph 1: Artifacts at Jamestown

Paragraph 2: Houses—similarities/differences w/ England's

Paragraph 3: Woodworking

Paragraph 4: House construction details—initially wood

Paragraph 5: Brick used for houses—later

Paragraph 6: Hardware imported

Paragraph 7: Windows

Paragraph 8: More comforts by 1650

ANSWER KEY

1.	**B**	**7.**	**B**
2.	**H**	**8.**	**G**
3.	**A**	**9.**	**D**
4.	**G**	**10.**	**H**
5.	**D**	**11.**	**D**
6.	**G**	**12.**	**G**

1. **B**

For a Detail question, start by using your passage map notes to direct you to the right part of the passage to make your prediction. Here, paragraph 1 states that studying the objects found at Jamestown shows *how the English colonists lived* (lines 7–8), and paragraph 2 specifically refers to *the everyday life* (line 16) of the settlers. These ideas form a good prediction, which matches perfectly with (B). Choice A is out-of-scope because the artifacts aren't described as being made from expensive material. Choice C is a distortion. While the passage does refer to the difficulty of the settlers' lives, it doesn't link this difficulty to the artifacts described. Choice D is out-of-scope. The artistic qualities of the objects found at Jamestown are not addressed in the passage.

2. **H**

For a Detail question that uses *EXCEPT*, find support for three answer choices in the passage and eliminate them. The choice that is *not* supported in the passage is the correct answer here. Use passage map notes to refer you to paragraph 3. Here, you find that puncheon floors, benches, and stools are all listed as *examples of skilled working with wood* (lines 32–33). Kitchen utensils are mentioned, but not as examples of hardware. Choice (H) is the best answer.

3. **A**

For a Generalization question about the purpose of the passage, keep the big picture in mind. If you need help predicting, check your passage map notes. Also keep the tone of the passage in mind. This passage discusses the artifacts turned up by archeological explorations in Jamestown and what those artifacts indicate about the settlers' lives. The tone is detached and explanatory. Choice (A) is a good match for this prediction. Choice B is a distortion. The passage does mention some challenges faced by the settlers, but it doesn't discuss the relative difficulty of their lives in England and Jamestown. Choice C is out-of-scope. The passage is meant only to describe the settlement, not to persuade the reader to visit it. Choice D is a contradiction. England is mentioned in regard to housing styles; the passage states that the settlers built their houses in the same style as those they knew in England, insofar as local materials permitted.

4. **G**

For a Vocabulary-in-Context question, read the sentence the word appears in and look for clues to help you predict. In this sentence, the words *timber* and *so* are important to focus on. The sentence states that *timber...was plentiful.* It makes sense, especially given the use of the word *so,* that if wood is abundant in the area then it would be used to build houses. Predict that *frame* as used here means *made of wood.* This prediction matches (G). Choice F is out-of-scope. *Outline* is a common meaning of *frame* but is not justified in this context. Choice H is out-of-scope. It may be tempting to associate *frame* with the word *picture*, but the meaning doesn't fit here. Choice J is a misused detail. Brick is mentioned elsewhere in the passage but not in this context.

5. **D**

For an Inference question, read a little bit before and after the words referred to in the question stem. Make a prediction by drawing a conclusion that doesn't go too far beyond what is stated. Here, the phrase *wattle-and-daub* appears in a list of materials that were used for building. Because the other items mentioned, *mud* and *marsh-grass thatch,* are natural resources, predict that *wattle-and-daub* describes other natural materials used in building. This prediction matches (D). Choice A is out-of-scope. The passage never mentions food. Choice B is a misused detail. Hardware is mentioned elsewhere in the passage but isn't related to this question stem. Choice C is a distortion. The passage concerns archeological topics, but the tools used by archeologists are never mentioned.

6. **G**

For this Detail question, check each item one by one to see if it's mentioned in the passage. The long list of hardware discovered at Jamestown, *Types of building hardware...ornamental hardware* (lines 71–77), includes the items in F, H, and J. The passage never mentions curtain rods.

7. **B**

For an Inference question, read the sentence containing the lines in the question stem, and be ready to read a little before and after that if necessary. Here, the first part of the sentence, *After Jamestown had attained some degree of permanency,* suggests that Jamestown was at first possibly only a temporary settlement. The phrase *of the* early *Jamestown settlers* (lines 55–56) in the previous sentence supports this idea. The prediction matches well with (B). Choice A is contradicted by the passage in lines 65–67. Choice C is a contradiction because the passage states that brick made in Jamestown was similar to brick made in England. Choice D is out-of-scope. The passage doesn't say the settlers didn't bring materials, and (B) follows more directly from the passage.

8. **G**

For an Inference question, read the appropriate part of the passage and draw a conclusion that doesn't stray too far. The first part of the sentence referred to in the question stem describes the settlers as *busy conquering a stubborn wilderness,* (line 96). A few lines later, you read that *the colonists began to acquire possessions for more pleasant living* (lines 104–105) *after the early years of hardship had passed.* Therefore, predict that during the early years, settlers at Jamestown had to focus on basic survival needs more than comfort. This prediction fits well with (G). Choice F is out-of-scope. The passage says nothing about luxuries in England. Choice H is a distortion. This choice gets it right that comfort wasn't a priority for the earliest settlers, but the passage doesn't say that it took the settlers only two years before they could focus on domestic comforts. Choice J is a distortion. Although the passage does mention the *stubborn wilderness*, it is mentioned as something that *prevented* the settlers from thinking about comforts, not as something that *caused* them to do so.

9. **D**

For a Detail question, start by using your passage map notes to determine where to go back and read to make your prediction. Here, your notes should direct you to paragraph 4. The passage says that clay was used for *early floors* (lines 51–52) and *in humbler dwellings throughout the 1600s.* This prediction leads to (D). Choice A is a contradiction. Line 34 says that timber was *plentiful.* Choice B is an extreme. The word *exclusively* is a red flag. This answer choice can't work unless this extreme language is justified by the passage. Choice C is also an extreme because of the word *all.*

10. **H**

Treat a Vocabulary-in-Context question that asks about a phrase just as you would any other Vocabulary-in-Context question: Go back to the sentence and look for clues to help you predict. Here the words vast *forest and* untapped *resources* suggest abundance. This prediction lines up nicely with (H). Choice F is out-of-scope. Nothing in the context suggests an ending. Choice G is an opposite. Choice J is out-of-scope. There is nothing to indicate constraint or limitation in connection with forests or natural resources.

11. **D**

Use your passage map notes to determine where to look to make your prediction for a Detail question. In this case, your notes should lead you directly to paragraph 7. The first sentence states that the Jamestown glass factory was built in 1608. This prediction leads to (D). Choices A, B, and C are all misused details. They use dates that are indeed mentioned in the passage, but not in connection with the glass factory.

12. **G**

For an Inference question, be prepared to read a little before and after the lines cited in the question stem. In this case, your prediction should come from several sentences earlier. If *the settlers were having a difficult time staying alive* (lines 42–43), it makes sense that survival concerns would prevent them from worrying about whether the walls were plastered. This prediction leads to (G). Choice F is a distortion. The passage describes the materials but doesn't imply that they are hard to get. Choice H is a distortion. Studs are mentioned in the passage but are not described as being weak. Choice J is a distortion. The word *primitive* is used in the passage but not as a desirable stylistic feature.

CHAPTER 15

Reading Practice Set V—Humanities

Directions: This test contains a passage, followed by several questions. After reading the passage, select the best answer to each question. You are allowed to refer to the passage while answering the questions.

HUMANITIES: *This passage is taken from a collection of essays about twentieth-century British novelists.*

British novelist Barbara Pym has been described as a novelist of manners, a twentieth-century Jane Austen. Despite this comparison with such a famous literary figure, Pym, for most of her own life, was relatively unknown. She came to the attention of the public only three years before her death when the *Times Literary Supplement* asked for opinions about the "most underrated novelist" of the twentieth century. Barbara Pym was the only novelist to be named by two of the respondents, the novelist and poet Philip Larkin and the literary scholar Lord David Cecil. This recognition led finally to a surge in her popularity, and Pym lived to see the publication of most of the novels she had written previously.

Pym, born in 1913, began writing novels at the age of 16. Her first effort was titled "Young Men in Fancy Dress." In 1931, she entered St. Hilda's College at Oxford, where she read English literature. Following her graduation, she began working on the novel *Some Tame Gazelle,* centered on the daily lives of two women in their fifties. Pym based this story on the way she imagined her life and the lives of her sister and their friends from Oxford as it might be thirty years into the future. Pym completed this novel in 1935 but had no luck in finding a publisher for it. She kept writing, however, producing several novels and short stories by crafting some of her own life experiences into literary form.

During World War II, Pym worked first at the Censorship Office in Bristol, England and later with the Women's Royal Naval Service in Naples, Italy. On her return to England, she worked at the International Africa Institute in London. Her job as assistant editor for the journal *Africa* put her in contact with the world of anthropological scholarship. Her stories include characters who work in academics and are presented in a mostly appreciative and humorous way.

Pym's artistic perseverance paid off when her revision of *Some Tame Gazelle* was finally accepted by Jonathan Cape, who published the novel in 1950. Contemporary critics reviewed this work favorably, so Pym was finally established as a writer. For the next decade, Pym enjoyed some success, seeing the publication of several more novels. *Excellent Women* was published in 1952, and *Jane and Prudence* came out the following year. Every three years until 1961, Pym published a new novel. Scholars see these first six novels as an important body of work marking Pym as a significant author with a unique voice. She wrote about ordinary people living quiet lives, often in provincial locations and small towns in England. The novels include detailed descriptions of characters, clothing, meals, local gossip, and activities of Anglican clergy and church members.

Pym's consistent publishing success throughout the 1950s eventually came to an end. In 1963, when she presented her next novel, *An Unsuitable Attachment,* to her publisher, it was considered out of date and was rejected. Pym, though disappointed, did not give up. She submitted the novel to several other publishers. After receiving several rejections, she revised and resubmitted it. All told, twenty publishers rejected this novel during the 1960s. Over the next fifteen years, Pym fought against losing hope that her writing would ever again be appreciated. She worked on yet another book, *The Sweet Dove Died.* This novel, darker than her earlier ones, about an older woman attracted to a much younger man, was again rooted in Pym's personal experience. Like her previous novel, *The Sweet Dove Died* was not accepted by any publisher.

Even though Pym's rejections were compounded by health crises, including a cancer diagnosis in 1971 and a stroke in 1974, she continued to write. After retiring from her job at the Africa Institute, she wrote *Quartet in Autumn,* her darkest novel yet, about four office workers facing their own upcoming retirement. When Pym submitted this work to publishers in 1976, it was again rejected by all.

Pym's citation by Philip Larkin in the *Times Literary Supplement* pulled her out of obscurity. Macmillan published *Quartet in Autumn* in 1977 and *The Sweet Dove Died* the following year. *Quartet* was nominated for the Booker Prize, Britain's prestigious literary award. When these last two novels attracted critical attention in England, Macmillan reprinted all of Pym's earlier novels. When American audiences discovered Pym's work, Dutton published all of her novels in the United States. Her work was published in translation, bringing her even wider readership. Despite declining health, Pym worked to finish her last novel, *A Few Green Leaves,* before she died in 1980. Following Pym's death, *An Unsuitable Attachment*, the novel earlier rejected, was published, along with two other novels, *Crampton Hodnet* and *Civil to Strangers.* Pym has continued to generate interest among scholars for her philosophical outlook and distinctive voice.

1. The writer of this passage adopts a tone that can best be described as:

   A. detached but mildly appreciative.

   B. zealously enthusiastic.

   C. overtly biased.

   D. impatient and critical.

2. According to the passage, *The Sweet Dove Died* was published in:

   F. 1952.

   G. 1961.

   H. 1977.

   J. 1978.

3. The writer uses the phrase "throughout the 1950s" (line 68) to emphasize that:

   A. the 1950s was a stable time for British society.

   B. Pym's reputation was not consistent throughout her lifetime.

   C. Pym's publishing house saw remarkable success during the 1950s.

   D. *Excellent Women* was one of the novels published during the 1950s.

4. Regarding her life experience, the passage implies that:

   F. Pym's ultimate rejection by Jonathan Cape hurled her into a depression.

   G. Pym's interest in the culinary arts led her to see descriptions of food as being as important as character development in a novel.

   H. Pym was relieved to be named the most underrated novelist of the twentieth century.

   J. Pym did not view her life as something that should be kept entirely separate from her novels.

5. The passage states that all of the following novels were eventually published during Pym's lifetime EXCEPT:

   A. *Some Tame Gazelle.*

   B. *Quartet in Autumn.*

   C. *The Sweet Dove Died.*

   D. *Crampton Hodnet.*

6. The second paragraph functions in the passage primarily as:

   F. a detailed description of the sources of *Some Tame Gazelle.*

   G. an argument that *Some Tame Gazelle* should not have been rejected by Jonathan Cape.

   H. a chronology of significant dates in the first part of Pym's life.

   J. a summary of Pym's literary career.

7. It may be inferred from the last paragraph that:

   A. Pym did not let her declining health interfere with her artistic goals.

   B. Philip Larkin was single-handedly responsible for salvaging Pym's literary reputation.

   C. *Quartet in Autumn* was written after Pym retired from her job at the Africa Institute.

   D. Pym has the most distinctive voice of any twentieth-century novelist.

8. The writer suggests in the first paragraph that:

   F. the article in the *Times Literary Supplement* generated renewed interest in Pym's earlier novels.

   G. the *Times Literary Supplement* rejected several of Pym's short stories.

   H. Pym suffered a stroke in 1974.

   J. Pym enjoyed a long friendship with Philip Larkin and Lord David Cecil.

9. According to the passage, Pym was employed by which of the following companies?

   A. The *Times Literary Supplement*
   B. St. Hilda's College of Oxford
   C. The Women's Royal Army Corps
   D. The journal *Africa*

10. Which of the following novels is NOT mentioned in the passage as being associated in some way with Pym's own life?

   F. *Some Tame Gazelle*
   G. *Civil to Strangers*
   H. *The Sweet Dove Died*
   J. *Quartet in Autumn*

11. The writer uses the phrase *artistic perseverance* (line 46) to show that:

   A. Pym did not give up when her publishers first rejected her work.
   B. Pym worked harder on *Some Tame Gazelle* than she had on *Young Men in Fancy Dress.*
   C. rejection at some point is inevitable for all writers.
   D. Pym's subtle artistry was appreciated by contemporary critics.

12. According to the author, Barbara Pym's literary work may compared to that of:

   F. Philip Larkin.
   G. Lord David Cecil.
   H. Jane Austen.
   J. Jonathan Cape.

ANSWERS AND EXPLANATIONS

SUGGESTED PASSAGE MAP NOTES

Paragraph 1: Pym's work popular late in her life

Paragraph 2: Early efforts at writing

Paragraph 3: Work history

Paragraph 4: Novels finally published

Paragraph 5: Later novels rejected

Paragraph 6: Continued working

Paragraph 7: Eventual acclaim

ANSWER KEY

1. A	**7. A**
2. J	**8. F**
3. B	**9. D**
4. J	**10. G**
5. D	**11. A**
6. H	**12. H**

1. **A**

For this Big Picture question, pay attention to words that indicate the writer's opinion. Here, the overall tone is detached and analytical. The writer appears to admire Pym's persistence, as evidenced by phrases such as *she kept writing, however* (line 31), *Pym's artistic perseverance paid off* (line 46), and *Even though Pym's rejections were compounded...she continued to write* (lines 89–90). Therefore, predict that the tone is primarily detached but colored with admiration. This prediction matches (A). Choice B is out-of-scope. Nothing about the tone of the passage suggests zealousness. Choice C is a distortion. The mild admiration implied by the author is not the same as an overt bias. Choice D is opposite. *Impatient and critical* is the opposite of detached and admiring.

2. **J**

For a Detail question, make sure you refer to the appropriate portion of the passage to make your prediction. You may have to read especially carefully when dates are involved to avoid misused detail traps. Quickly scan the passage for *The Sweet Dove Died.* It appears in line 81 and in line 100. The relevant reference here is line 100. The novel was published in the year *following* 1977, making (J) the correct answer. Choices F, G, and H are all misused details. These dates are all mentioned in the passage but do not correctly answer the question posed by this question stem.

3. **B**

For a Vocabulary-in-Context question asking about a phrase, read the sentence carefully to make your prediction. Here, notice that the sentence describes a contrast: *continued success...came to an end.* Predict that the phrase *throughout the 1950s* is used to develop and emphasize this contrast. This prediction matches well with (B). Choice A is out-of-scope. The passage focuses on Pym and makes no general statements about *British society.* Choice C is a distortion of the word *success* as it's used in the passage. The *success* mentioned in this sentence is Pym's, not that of her publisher. Choice D is a misused detail. It makes a statement that is consistent with the passage, but it doesn't relate to the question posed by the question stem.

4. **J**

For a Big Picture question, remember to keep the big picture in mind. If it's tough to predict, work through the answer choices one by one and eliminate those that don't fit. Eliminate F because it's out-of-scope. Be careful not to read too much into the passage. It doesn't suggest anywhere that the rejection *hurled Pym into a depression.* Eliminate G because it's a distortion. Although the passage does say that descriptions of meals are included in Pym's novels, it doesn't suggest that they are *as important as character development.* Eliminate H because it's an extreme. The passage states that Pym was named as *one* of the most underrated writers, but it would be reading too much in to infer that she is *the* most underrated writer. The process of elimination leaves (J), which is the best answer. It is justified in several places in the passage, including lines 33–34, *by crafting some of her own life experiences into literary form.*

5. **D**

For a Detail question phrased with the word EXCEPT, check in the passage to see which choice is *not* supported by the passage. Choice (D) is the best answer because lines 112–115 indicate that *Crampton Hodnet* was published following Pym's death. Choices A, B, and C are mentioned in the passage as having been published while Pym was still living.

6. **H**

For a Big Picture question that asks about a paragraph, use your passage map notes and think about how the paragraph works in the passage as a whole. The passage describes Pym's literary career, and the second paragraph discusses her early work as a writer. Use this as a prediction and work through the answer choices. Choice (H) is the best choice, even though the prediction is not worded in exactly the same way as this answer choice. The second paragraph does include dates, making *chronology* appropriate here. In addition, the prediction *early work* matches well with the wording *first part of Pym's life* in (H). Choice F is a misused detail. The paragraph does mention *Some Tame Gazelle*, briefly noting its connection to Pym's personal life, but it doesn't give a *detailed* description of the novel's sources. Choice G is out-of-scope. The writer makes no attempt to argue the wisdom of the publisher's decision. Choice J is out-of-scope. The answer choice is much too broad to describe the second paragraph.

7. **A**

For a Big Picture question based on a paragraph, try using your passage map notes or reading the paragraph. There's a lot in this last paragraph, so it may be difficult to predict. Work through the answer choices, being careful not to fall for traps. Choice (A) is the best answer. It's a reasonable inference to make from lines 110–111, *Despite declining health, Pym worked to finish her last novel.* Eliminate B because it's an extreme. Though you can certainly infer that Larkin had a strong influence on Pym's reputation, the passage doesn't justify the notion that he was *single-handedly* influential. Eliminate C because it's a misused detail. It contains a true statement that's mentioned in paragraph 6, but this question stem asks for an inference based on paragraph 7. Eliminate D because it's an extreme. Paragraph 7 does mention Pym's *distinctive voice* but doesn't suggest that it is the *most distinctive voice.*

8. **F**

For a Big Picture question about a paragraph, review your notes and the whole paragraph, if necessary. Predict if possible, and if not, work through the answer choices. For the first paragraph, your passage note may refer to Pym's achieving literary success later in life. This is not an exact match but is consistent with (F), the best answer. Eliminate G because it's a distortion. The passage doesn't suggest that it was the *Times Literary Supplement* that rejected Pym's stories. Eliminate H because it's a misused detail. This answer choice is indeed a true statement from the passage, but it doesn't address the question in this particular question stem. Eliminate J because it's a distortion. The passage mentions both Philip Larkin and Lord David Cecil, but only in the context of the *Times Literary Supplement.* There is nothing in the passage to suggest that either of them was a friend of Pym.

9. **D**

For this Detail question, reference the passage to verify each answer choice. Look for ways to use logic to save you time. For example, in this case, A is not consistent with the passage: Pym was cited by another author, but was not described as an employee of the *Times Literary Supplement.* Additionally, in lines 37–38, the passage states that Pym worked for the Women's Royal Naval Service, not the Army Corps. Line 41 can help you narrow down to the correct answer: Pym worked for the journal

Africa as an assistant editor. (D) is the correct answer choice.

10. **G**

For a Detail question phrased with NOT, refer back to the passage to check each answer choice one by one. Eliminate F because lines 26–27 state that *Some Tame Gazelle* is based *on the way she imagined her life…as it might be.* Eliminate H because lines 83–84 states that *The Sweet Dove Died* was *again rooted in Pym's personal experience*. Eliminate J because *Quartet in Autumn* is described as a novel about retirement that Pym started work on after her own retirement.

11. **A**

For a Vocabulary-in-Context question about a phrase, examine the immediate context to make your prediction. The sentence includes the word *finally* (line 48), which indicates that Pym's success was not immediate. Predict that her *artistic perseverance* is used to show that she kept on writing novels even while working at the Africa Institute. This prediction is a good match for (A). Choice B is a distortion. Both the novel *Some Tame Gazelle* and the unpublished first novel, *Young Men in Fancy Dress*, are mentioned, but the passage doesn't compare how hard Pym worked on one relative to the other. Choice C is an extreme. It uses the word *all* and makes a general statement that is much broader than anything expressed in the passage. Choice D is a distortion. The context here does mention *contemporary critics* (lines 49–50), but the answer choice inappropriately twists the passage's phrasing *reviewed favorably* (line 50) to appreciating *subtle artistry.*

12. **H**

A Detail question like this is hard to predict for. There are no words in the question stem that you can scan the passage for, and passage notes likely guide you to both the first and last paragraphs. The best thing to do in this case is to look at the answer choices and skim the passage for each. Eliminate F because, although Larkin is mentioned in both the first and last paragraphs, Pym's work is not compared to his. Eliminate G for the same reason. Choice (H) is the correct answer and is supported by the first sentence of the passage. Eliminate J because Jonathan Cape is mentioned as a publisher, not as a writer.

CHAPTER 16

Reading Practice Set VI—Humanities

Directions: This test contains a passage, followed by several questions. After reading the passage, select the best answer to each question. You are allowed to refer to the passage while answering the questions.

HUMANITIES: *This passage is adapted from an article on garden design by a landscape architect who is an enthusiast of agriculture. Garden design is defined as the art of planting landscapes.*

A garden is a living work of art that blends elements of space and mass, light and shade, the natural and the manmade, along with color, scent, texture, and climate. As with any other art, the evolution of garden design may be seen as reflecting the interests and values of groups of people living in a particular time and place. It is not surprising, then, that the history of the garden illustrates in various ways the principles of both continuity with and reaction against earlier trends in design. An especially notable example of a reaction against an existing style is the *jardin anglais,* or the English garden, that became popular in France and other parts of Europe during the mid-18th century.

In the early 18th century, French cultural influence dominated Europe, leading to the popularity of the highly formal garden, sometimes known as the French garden. This garden style is characterized by rigidly formulated geometric patterns in which precision, regularity, and proportion are dominant. The garden at Versailles, one of the largest and best known formal gardens, is the epitome of the style that was emulated on a smaller scale at other locations. Typical of the style it represents, the colossal garden at Versailles is based on designs that are strongly geometrical, including areas separated by long straight lines and circular pools dividing symmetrical areas. Canals, fountains, and statuary are used to emphasize the balanced forms.

Versailles, like many formal gardens, made use of the bosquet, a precisely planted grove in which trees are planted so as to be perfectly aligned according to a pattern. Another feature of the formal garden used extensively at Versailles is the *parterre,* a sort of garden-within-a-garden. Several types of *parterres* were used, including the *parterre de broderie,* or embroidered *parterre,* in which neatly trimmed boxwood shrubs were planted in designs suggestive of botanical shapes. In the embroidered *parterre,* the box plantings were set against turf or colored earth. Other types of *parterres* used different kinds of flowers and other plants, but the use of a formal pattern was common to all types of *parterres.*

It was in the context of such highly stylized and classical designs that the English landscape garden came into being. Reaction against formality came in part from the British poet and literary critic Alexander Pope, who in 1713 published an essay on gardening in *The Guardian.* Eschewing the balance, formality, and rigid symmetry popular in gardens of the time, Pope called instead for the creation of gardens that reflect the "amiable simplicity of unadorned nature." Pope argued that the design of a garden should take its cues from local topography rather than starting from a preconceived plan that is artificially imposed on the landscape.

In England, two of the most famous designers of landscape style gardens were William Kent and Lancelot (better known as "Capability") Brown. Kent, a friend of Alexander Pope, drew inspiration from the ideas of the literary critic. Kent, who had studied art in Italy, was highly receptive to Pope's notion that "all gardening is landscape painting." One of the best examples of Kent's work is found in the garden at Rousham House in Oxfordshire. This garden, started in 1738, typifies the landscape principle of making the surrounding countryside an integral part of the experience of the garden. Kent used outlying buildings in a picturesque Gothic style to call attention to the larger surrounding area and the garden's place within it.

Following Kent and achieving even greater fame, Capability Brown was the next great English landscape gardener. Fittingly, Brown earned his nickname from his tendency to talk to his clients about the "capabilities" of their land. Among Brown's most famous works is the landscaping on the grounds of Blenheim Palace in Oxfordshire. Here he created a free-flowing expanse marked by large grassy areas, irregularly shaped bodies of water, and seemingly random plantings of trees, both isolated and in clustered groupings. The naturalistic designs that Brown perfected may be seen as the polar opposite of the highly stylized and artificial designs in the garden at Versailles. Admirers of the more formal gardens such as the one at Versailles have criticized Brown for destroying some of the best examples of formal gardens in England, while those who appreciate the naturalistic style celebrate Brown's achievement.

Capability Brown influenced Humphrey Repton, who continued to create designs that were largely similar to those of his predecessor. In addition, Repton had some literary talent and in the late 18th and early 19th centuries produced several books documenting the landscape styles that were popular at the time. Though the landscape or "English" style garden eventually saw a decline in popularity in its country of origin, it enjoyed further longevity in continental Europe, particularly in France.

1. The writer's tone in this passage is:

   A. critical and judgmental.

   B. scholarly and detached.

   C. overly involved.

   D. decidedly persuasive.

2. According to the passage, all of the following were known for their garden designs EXCEPT:

   F. Alexander Pope.

   G. Humphrey Repton.

   H. Capability Brown.

   J. William Kent.

3. The primary contrast in this passage revolves around:

   A. the relative importance of nature and artificiality in garden design.

   B. the comparative significance of Alexander Pope's and William Kent's garden designs.

   C. two artists working in the same era but producing distinctive though related work.

   D. the dominance of the French culture over the English culture during the 18th century.

4. One inference that may be drawn from the fourth paragraph is that:

   F. British poets in the early 18th century rebelled against formality.

   G. a desire to rebel against formality was a crucial element of Alexander Pope's poetry.

   H. creative pursuits in diverse areas did not always exist in isolation from each other.

   J. knowledge of European painting influenced William Kent's garden designs.

5. Based on the information in the passage, which statement is true about the garden at Versailles?

   A. It was featured in a book of garden designs produced by Humphrey Repton.

   B. The surrounding landscape was considered a crucial part of the garden's design.

   C. It made use of geometric designs that mimicked botanical forms.

   D. Bosquets were not among the pattern designs featured.

6. As used in line 27, the word *epitome* most nearly means:

   F. best example.

   G. balanced plan.

   H. artistic creation.

   J. inevitable result.

7. According to the passage, the work of Capability Brown:

   A. was strongly influenced by the designs of Humphrey Repton.

   B. was a source of inspiration for Alexander Pope's poetry.

   C. is a subject of some disagreement among critics.

   D. exemplifies the use of geometrical forms in garden design.

8. Based on information provided in the passage, which of the following would be LEAST likely to be found in a "French garden"?

   F. Two rows of trees planted in precisely parallel lines

   G. Low trimmed bushes planted in a circular maze design

   H. Four similar statues each placed in the corners of a square *parterre*

   J. A randomly curved stone path surrounding a large grassy area

9. The writer mentions "Rousham House" (line 78) for the purpose of:

   A. describing gardens that contrast with those found at Blenheim Palace.
   B. providing an example of a famous estate in Oxfordshire.
   C. explaining how the principles of French garden design were adapted to the British landscape.
   D. illustrating an important aspect of William Kent's work.

10. In the passage as a whole, paragraph 2 functions as:

   F. a detailed description of the gardens at Versailles.
   G. an explanation of a concept necessary to differentiate between different gardens.
   H. a criticism of the balanced geometrical designs used in the French style garden.
   J. an argument that statuary and lakes are essential features of a formal garden.

11. The writer mentions "Blenheim Palace" (line 94) in order to:

   A. provide an example of one of Capability Brown's most well-known projects.
   B. suggest that it plays a transitional role in the development of European garden styles.
   C. criticize its designer for destroying a valuable example of the formal French garden.
   D. prove that Oxfordshire was home to more landscape-style gardens than any other county in England.

12. The primary purpose of this passage is to:

   F. present a detailed description of some of the most famous gardens of the 19th century.
   G. argue that a palatial residence cannot be considered complete unless it includes an extensive garden.
   H. support the view that the French and English gardens in the mid-1800s had some significant features in common.
   J. discuss two contrasting styles that are important in the history of garden design.

ANSWERS AND EXPLANATIONS

SUGGESTED PASSAGE MAP NOTES

Paragraph 1: Background on garden design; English garden a reaction

Paragraph 2: French garden style; Versailles—geometrical, symmetrical

Paragraph 3: Versailles cont'd—*parterres*

Paragraph 4: Pope started reaction against earlier style, urged focus on nature

Paragraph 5: Kent's work in landscape style

Paragraph 6: Brown; Blenheim Palace—criticized by some

Paragraph 7: Repton; landscape garden style outside of England

ANSWER KEY

1. B	**7. C**
2. F	**8. J**
3. A	**9. D**
4. H	**10. G**
5. C	**11. A**
6. F	**12. J**

1. **B**

For a Big Picture question, consider the passage as a whole. The tone of this passage is descriptive and analytical. It mentions a controversy (the opinions of Capability Brown's work in paragraph 6) in passing but doesn't take a side. Predict that the tone is descriptive and detached. Choice (B) is the best match. Choice A is a contradiction because the writer is not judgmental. Choice C is a contradiction because the writer doesn't take sides. Choice D is a contradiction because the writer is merely explaining, not attempting to persuade.

2. **F**

A Detail question that uses EXCEPT is one of the few question types that you shouldn't spend time predicting for. Instead, go straight to the answer choices and research the passage for each one. Remember that for an EXCEPT question, the correct answer is the one that you do NOT find supported in the passage. Choice (F) is the best answer because, although Pope is mentioned in the passage, he is described as a *poet and literary critic* (line 57), not as a garden designer. Eliminate G because Repton is mentioned in line 110. Eliminate H because Brown is described as a landscape designer in lines 69–72. Eliminate J because Kent is also referred to as a landscape designer.

3. **A**

For a Big Picture question, your answer must be based on the passage as a whole. Use your passage notes to help here. Predict that the primary contrast is between the garden at Versailles and the landscape style garden. The garden at Versailles is described in lines 22–25 as being *characterized by rigidly formulated geometric patterns in which precision, regularity, and proportion are dominant.* Paragraph 4 describes the landscape garden as being a *reaction against formality* (lines 55–56). Predict that the answer has something to do with the difference between a highly formal style and a more natural style. This prediction matches best with (A). Choice B is a distortion. Although Kent is mentioned in the passage as a designer of gardens, Pope is not. Choice C is a distortion. Although three garden designers are mentioned (Kent, Brown, and Repton), their work is described as largely continuous, not *distinctive.* Choice D is a misused detail. The dominance of French culture is cited, but in passing, not as a major element of the passage.

4. **H**

For a Big Picture question about a paragraph, use your passage notes. Paragraph 4 discusses a poet's influence on the field of garden design. The best answer will be consistent with this idea, and

(H) matches well. Choice F combines the out-of-scope and distortion answer traps. It's out-of-scope because the passage focuses on landscape design, not poetry. The phrase *rebel against formality* in F is a distortion of the phrase *reaction against formality* (lines 55–56), which is used in the passage in relation to garden design, not poetry. Choice J is a misused detail. The reference to Kent's study of art in Italy comes in paragraph 5, but this question stem asks about an inference based on paragraph 4.

5. **C**

This Inference question requires that you understand the passage as a whole. This statement is true; lines 45–47, *neatly trimmed boxwood shrubs were planted in designs suggestive of botanical shapes,* justify this statement. Choice B is not true of the garden at Versailles. The surrounding landscape is mentioned in the passage as being important in Kent's landscape style garden (lines 83–86). Choice (C) is not true, either. Though the passage states that Repton *produced several books documenting the landscape styles that were popular at the time* (lines 114–116), Versailles is not described as having a landscape style. Choice D is an opposite: in lines 36–39, the statement is true about the Versailles garden.

6. **F**

For a Vocabulary-in-Context question, pay attention to clues in the sentence that tell you what the word means. In this case, reading the previous sentence is also helpful. The previous sentence describes the style of garden known as the French garden, suggesting that the garden at Versailles is presented as an example of this style. This leads to a prediction of *example*, and (F) matches nicely. Choice G is a misused detail. While the garden at Versailles exhibits a *balanced plan*, that is not the meaning of the word *epitome*. Choice H is a misused detail. Though *artistic style* is relevant to the passage, it doesn't fit in this context. Choice J is out-of-scope. There's no cause-and-effect relationship indicated here, so *result* doesn't work in this context.

7. **C**

For a Detail question, your passage map notes can help you know where to look to make your prediction. For this question, look back to paragraph 6. The question is broadly worded, so it's hard to make a precise prediction. Skim the paragraph so that you're familiar with what it says: The grounds at Blenheim Palace are a famous example of Brown's work, and they reflect the naturalistic style; Brown has been criticized for destroying great examples of formal gardens. Read through the answer choices and eliminate as you go. Choice A is a contradiction. Repton followed Brown, so Brown could not have been influenced by him. Choice B combines the distortion and out-of-scope answer traps. Although Pope is mentioned in the passage, Brown is not discussed as a source of inspiration for Pope's poetry. Choice (C) fits with your general prediction, particularly taking into account lines 103–108, *Admirers of the more formal gardens...Brown's achievement.* Choice D is a contradiction. The passage states that Brown, instead of using geometrical forms, created *a free-flowing expanse, marked by...irregularly shaped bodies of water and seemingly random plantings* (lines 95–98).

8. **J**

For a Big Picture question such as this one, determine what information you need to take from the passage. Your prediction should involve referring to the passage to make sure you're clear about how a *French garden* is described. Your passage map notes direct you to paragraph 2, where the French garden is described as featuring *precision, regularity, and proportion* (line 24). With this in mind, consider each answer choice and eliminate choices that don't match. Choice F is a contradiction because *precisely planted parallel lines* might easily have appeared in a French garden. Choice G is also a contradiction. *A circular maze design* features the geometry that is characteristic of a French garden. Choice H is a contradiction because the statues placed in the four corners of a square exemplify the geometrical form and symmetry found in a French garden. Choice (J) is the best answer. The *random* curve and *large grassy area* do not fit in the highly stylized plan of a French garden as it's described in the passage.

9. **D**

For a Vocabulary-in-Context question, pay attention to context and think about the writer's purpose. Your passage map notes should tell you that the purpose of paragraph 5 is to discuss William Kent's work. The immediate context states that Rousham House is *one of the best examples of Kent's work* (line 50). This makes a great prediction, which nicely fits with (D). Choice A is a misused detail. Blenheim Palace is not discussed in connection with Kent's work. Choice B is a distortion. While Rousham House is indeed described as an example of something, it is not presented as *an example of a famous estate.* Choice C is both a misused detail and a contradiction. French design principles have nothing to do with Rousham House, and the passage never says that French design principles were adapted to the English landscape.

10. **G**

For a Big Picture question that asks how a paragraph functions, use your passage map notes, and consider the passage as a whole. Predict that paragraph 2 discusses the French garden, with the garden at Versailles as an illustration, and that it's used to show the contrasts between the French style and the landscape style used in England. This prediction lines up nicely with (G). Choice H is a distortion. While paragraph 2 does describe the garden at Versailles, the description is brief, and this choice says nothing about how the paragraph fits into the passage as a whole. Choice H is a contradiction. Nothing in paragraph 2 indicates criticism of the French garden style. Choice J is a distortion. It's true that *statuary* is mentioned in paragraph 2, but the author never argues that statues are essential to the style.

11. **A**

For a Big Picture question that asks about a detail, consider the context of the sentences surrounding it. The context states that Blenheim Palace is *among Brown's most famous work* (line 93). Predict that Blenheim Palace is used to illustrate Brown's work. This prediction matches (A). Choice B is a distortion. The passage does treat the development of garden styles, but the focus is on the French style that came *before* the landscape style Brown worked in. If the writer were suggesting that Brown's style is *transitional*, he would have to state what style followed it, and the passage doesn't do this. Choice C is a misused detail. It's true that the paragraph indicates some have criticized Brown for destroying examples of formal gardens, but the writer doesn't say that Brown destroyed a formal garden in carrying out his work at Blenheim. Choice D combines the out-of-scope and extreme traps. The writer never even states, much less attempts to prove, that Oxfordshire has more landscape gardens than anyplace else. The phrasing *more...than any other* in this answer choice should alert you that it may be an extreme trap.

12. **J**

For a Big Picture question about the purpose of the whole passage, use your passage map notes to predict, and avoid tempting wrong answers that address only part of the passage. Here, your prediction should include something about the difference between the two styles of garden design discussed in the passage. Choice (J) is a great match. Choice F is out-of-scope. Its description, *some of the most famous gardens of the 19th century,* is too broad. Choice G is out-of-scope. *Palatial residences* are not mentioned as such and are not the focus of the passage. Choice H is a distortion. Though both garden types are discussed, the author focuses on their differences, not their similarities.

CHAPTER 17

Reading Practice Set VII—Natural Science

Directions: This test contains a passage, followed by several questions. After reading the passage, select the best answer to each question. You are allowed to refer to the passage while answering the questions.

NATURAL SCIENCE: *This passage is adapted from a document describing research done by the United States Geological Survey. The selection below concerns the effects of wind power developments on migrating birds.*

Interest in developing wind power as an alternative renewable energy source has increased in recent years. In the eastern United States, exposed summits or ridge crests in the Appalachian Mountains have high wind power potential, and numerous wind power projects are being proposed. While generally supportive of energy development from renewable sources, the U.S. Fish & Wildlife Service, state wildlife agencies, nongovernmental organizations, and the public are concerned about potential impacts of wind power development on wildlife.

During their seasonal migrations, large numbers of birds and bats cross or follow the mountainous landforms used for wind power. Wind power development could potentially impact populations of several species. Baseline information on nocturnally migrating birds and bats has been collected at some wind power development sites in the Appalachians, generally within a single season. However, a stronger scientific basis is critically needed to assess and mitigate risks at a regional scale.

The United States Geological Survey (USGS) is studying the distribution and flight patterns of birds and bats that migrate at night. Researchers are analyzing weather surveillance radar data (NEXRAD) to allow for a broad view of spring and fall migration through the Appalachians and to assess the response of migrant birds to mountain ridges and other prominent landforms. Although NEXRAD data provide information on the broad-scale spatial and temporal patterns of nocturnal migration through the region, the devices generally do not detect bird or bat targets within the altitudinal zone potentially occupied by wind turbines. Therefore, researchers are using two complementary ground-based techniques, acoustic detection and portable radar sampling, to obtain site-specific information on the abundance and flight characteristics of nocturnal migrants in lower airspace.

USGS is conducting acoustic monitoring at 31 sites scattered throughout the central Appalachians. Researchers are recording the calls made by migrating birds in flight to index the migrants' abundance and species composition at different locations. Data is being collected in the spring and fall. During the most recent season, there has been minimal disturbance from animals to the recording devices, so data from this season are expected to provide more complete coverage.

Researchers are working diligently to process and analyze the sound recordings. Because the recording units operate continuously, 24 hours a day, the first step in the analysis is the identification and separation of the nighttime segments from the recordings. These nighttime recordings are then scanned for flight calls using sound analysis software called XBAT, developed by Harold Figueroa and Matt Robbins. An XBAT extension, developed by Kathy Cortopassi, searches for and flags sounds of a user-specified range of durations with a user-specified range of frequencies. Spectrograms of these sounds are then reviewed to eliminate sounds that are not bird calls. Sound files can also be scrolled through manually, with flight call spectrograms selected and output. Calls are identified by species, when possible, by matching them to a reference set. For each hour of sampling at each site, recorded calls are tallied to index migrant abundance within and among nights.

Researchers are continuing to process these recordings. Preliminary analysis, however, indicates that more flight calls have been recorded at the sites during the fall migrations than during the spring. In addition, during both spring and fall, there is considerable variation among nights, both within and among sites. Researchers have been able to match some of the calls to particular species, but most calls can be placed only in species groups (for example, warblers, sparrows, thrushes) because their spectrograms are not clear. Researchers speculate that this lack of clarity occurs because many of the calls are made by birds flying at the outer limits of the recording. The microphones can record calls up to about 300 meters above ground level.

The acoustic monitoring is supplemented with portable radar sampling at three sites to provide additional data on the passage of migrants, including their flight altitudes and directions. The data from these radar samplings will be used to model the effects of topography, weather, and other variables on migrant abundance and flight to assess where and when migrants might be at risk from wind power development.

The data from all these sampling techniques will collectively allow researchers to understand migrant flight dynamics and behavior and conditions that influence them.

Predicted migrant densities and flight characteristics will be mapped region-wide as a function of topographic characteristics, and densities will be summed across dates within seasons to identify locations over which large numbers of migrants pass, or pass at altitudes within the sweep reach of wind turbine rotors, either consistently or occasionally. This information will be used to develop a summary map of areas where the risk of migrant interactions with potential wind power projects is expected to be low, moderate, or high.

1. Based on the passage as a whole, it can be inferred that the development of wind power in the Appalachians could potentially affect:

   A. warblers, sparrows, and thrushes.
   B. multiple species of birds and bats.
   C. all kinds of wildlife.
   D. several species of deer as well as migrating birds and bats.

2. Which of the following choices is NOT concerned about the effect that wind power developments could have on birds?

   F. State wildlife agencies
   G. The general public
   H. The U.S. Fish & Wildlife Service
   J. Harold Figueroa and Matt Robbins

3. According to the passage, the USGS is currently studying the habits of migrating birds:

   A. all across the country.
   B. on a year-round basis.
   C. during the spring and fall.
   D. by using XBAT to analyze NEXRAD data.

4. It can be inferred from lines 54–59 that:

   F. promising results can be obtained only when more complete coverage becomes available.
   G. there have been some disturbances to the recording devices in previous seasons.
   H. researchers are devising data collection techniques that minimize potential interference from wildlife.
   J. further research will be needed to assess and mitigate the risks wind power developments pose for wildlife.

5. It can be inferred from the passage as a whole that:

   A. the turbines used in generating wind power create well-defined risks for migrating bats.
   B. weather surveillance radar data may be used independently to assess risks to wildlife.
   C. computer technology is an essential part of investigations about the risks of wind power to wildlife.
   D. acoustic monitoring is the best currently available data collection technique for assessing wind power's potential threats to migrating bats.

6. The primary purpose of the passage is to:
   - **F.** discuss ongoing research about the habits of migrating birds and bats to determine how wind power developments will affect them.
   - **G.** persuade the public that the well-being of birds and bats will be threatened by any new wind power developments in the Appalachians.
   - **H.** examine the process of analyzing data collected by acoustic monitoring devices.
   - **J.** argue that XBAT software is essential in investigating the habits of migrating species.

7. The seventh paragraph functions as:
   - **A.** an explanation of how portable radar sampling works.
   - **B.** evidence about the flight altitudes of migrating animals.
   - **C.** a description of how spectrograms are used in acoustic monitoring.
   - **D.** a brief mention of a kind of data collection that is used in conjunction with acoustic monitoring.

8. It can be inferred from the second paragraph that:
   - **F.** the migration path of some animals is along mountain ranges.
   - **G.** more bird migrations occur in the Appalachians than elsewhere in the country.
   - **H.** there have been animal disturbances to the acoustic monitoring equipment used during bird migrations.
   - **J.** birds and bats have numerous similarities in addition to their migrating habits.

9. The writer uses the phrase "lack of clarity occurs…at the outer limits" (lines 96–98) in order to describe:
   - **A.** an error in the researchers' technique.
   - **B.** a condition that is inevitable.
   - **C.** a possible explanation for a situation.
   - **D.** an argument that this more sensitive equipment is essential.

10. The goal of the research described in this passage is to:
    - **F.** provide evidence that wind power developments are detrimental to migrating birds and bats.
    - **G.** make use of some sophisticated data collection and analysis techniques, including NEXRAD and XBAT.
    - **H.** determine which areas in the Appalachians could be used as sites for wind power developments while posing minimal threats to migrants.
    - **J.** assess the concerns of various groups, including the U.S. Fish & Wildlife Service, state wildlife agencies, and nongovernmental organizations, regarding wind power projects.

11. As used in line 35, the word *prominent* most nearly means:
    - **A.** famous.
    - **B.** projecting.
    - **C.** advancing easily.
    - **D.** tree-covered.

12. As stated in the passage, the threats posed by wind power projects to migrating animals:
    - **F.** have been well-documented.
    - **G.** are a source of contention between governmental agencies and the public.
    - **H.** should be assessed after enough data has been collected.
    - **J.** are a problem in all regions of the country.

ANSWERS AND EXPLANATIONS

SUGGESTED PASSAGE MAP NOTES

Paragraph 1: Groups concerned about wind power's effects on animals

Paragraph 2: More info needed to determine risks to bats and birds

Paragraph 3: U.S. studying bird and bat migration using radar and other techniques

Paragraph 4: Acoustic monitoring

Paragraph 5: Software used to analyze acoustic data

Paragraph 6: Preliminary results of acoustic monitoring

Paragraph 7: Portable radar technique

Paragraph 8: Data from all techniques to be combined in map

ANSWER KEY

1. B	**7. D**
2. J	**8. F**
3. C	**9. C**
4. G	**10. H**
5. C	**11. B**
6. F	**12. H**

1. **B**

For a Big Picture question, keep the entire passage in mind. Here, you can predict that the passage describes research about bird and bat migrations. This prediction is a good match for (B). Choice A is a misused detail. Choice C is an extreme. The passage discusses studies about bats and birds only, not *all wildlife*. Choice D is out-of-scope. The passage doesn't refer to *deer* at all.

2. **J**

For this Detail question, your passage map notes should point you toward paragraph 1 to predict your answer. Lines 10–14 mention several groups that are concerned about wind power effects: the U.S. Fish & Wildlife Service, state wildlife agencies, nongovernmental organizations, and the public. Thus, eliminate all choices but (J), which is the correct answer.

3. **C**

For a Detail question, use your passage map notes or skim the passage for key words in the question stem to help you find the right spot in the passage to read for your prediction. Here, either your notes or skimming should direct you to paragraphs 3 and 4. The question is worded broadly, so your prediction might cover a lot: the USGS is studying the habits of migrating birds in the Appalachians, using acoustic monitoring, in the spring and fall. The only choice that matches anything in this prediction is (C). Choice A is out-of-scope. The passage doesn't mention any studies outside the Appalachian area. Choice B is out-of-scope. The passage states that researchers are interested in the habits of migrating bats and birds, and migration doesn't occur all year long. Choice D is a distortion. XBAT is described in the passage as a tool for analyzing the acoustic data.

4. **G**

For an Inference question, read the quoted lines carefully and make a prediction that doesn't stray too far from the text. Here, notice that the sentence in question contains an implied contrast: *during the most recent season* is mentioned, suggesting that there's a difference between this season and previous seasons. Predict that the answer has something to do with this contrast, something like *in previous seasons, there has been significant interference on the recording devices from animals.* Choice (G) is a great match for this prediction. Choice F is an extreme. Nothing in the passage justifies the use of the word *only.* Choice H is out-of-scope. This choice goes too far beyond what's stated in the passage. Choice J opposite. The meaning of the quoted sentence is that this season's data are expected to be much more useful, not that *further research* is needed.

5. **C**

For a Big Picture question, keep the purpose of the whole passage in mind and work through the answer choices, eliminating incorrect ones. The purpose of the passage is to discuss research being done to assess the risks of wind power projects on migrating bats and birds. Choice A is a contradiction. According to the passage, the risks are not yet *well-defined.* The research is being done to get a better handle on what those risks are. Choice B is an extreme because it uses the word *independently.* Weather surveillance radar data are being used, but the passage also mentions two other monitoring techniques that are being used: acoustic monitoring and portable radar sampling. Choice D is an extreme. Acoustic monitoring is certainly important, but the passage doesn't state or imply that it's *the best currently available* technique.

6. **F**

For a Big Picture question that asks about the purpose of the whole passage, use your passage map notes and remember not to focus too heavily on a particular detail. Here, predict that the purpose of the passage is to discuss methods of monitoring the habits of migrating birds and bats in order to determine what threats wind power development may pose to them. Choice (F) is a great match for your prediction. Choice G is a contradiction because the passage does not attempt to persuade the reader, only to inform. Choice H is a misused detail. It's true that the passage contains information about acoustic monitoring, but that is only one of the research techniques discussed in the passage. Choice J is a contradiction based on a misused detail. The passage makes no argument about XBAT being essential and, in any case, XBAT is only a small part of the passage and doesn't address the purpose of the passage as a whole.

7. **D**

For an Inference question about a paragraph, use your passage map notes and consider the context of the previous and following paragraphs. Here, paragraph 7 discusses one technique, portable radar, giving this technique much less attention than acoustic monitoring got in paragraphs 4–6. Paragraph 8 discusses all of the research techniques as a whole. Predict that the purpose of paragraph 7 is to briefly introduce a research technique. This prediction matches well with (D). Choice A is a distortion. While the paragraph does discuss portable radar sampling, it doesn't explain how the technique works. Choice B is a distortion. Paragraph 7 mentions *flight altitudes* as something portable data sampling is used to investigate, but the paragraph doesn't present any evidence about *flight altitudes.* Choice C is a misused detail. Acoustic monitoring and spectrograms are discussed in paragraphs 5 and 6, not paragraph 7.

8. **F**

For a Big Picture question about a paragraph, read the paragraph carefully and draw a conclusion that doesn't go too far beyond what is stated. Use elimination if necessary to work through the answer choices. In this case, elimination is helpful. Choice (F) is the right answer because it sticks closely to what the passage states. It restates the first sentence of the paragraph, using *some animals* where the passage says *birds and bats.* Remember that the correct answer to an Inference question does not necessarily say anything new. Sometimes, as here, just reading the passage and stating the obvious will get you to the correct answer. Choice G is out-of-scope. The passage focuses on migrations in the Appalachians and doesn't say anything specific about migrations in other parts of the country. Choice H is a misused detail from paragraph 4. Choice J is out-of-scope. The only similarities between bats and birds that the passage is concerned with are their migratory behaviors.

9. **C**

For a Vocabulary-in-Context question about a phrase, read carefully in the context, paying attention to the lines before and after the quoted phrase. Here, the phrase appears in a sentence that begins

Researchers speculate. Predict that the phrase is used to describe the researchers' theories about information in the previous line, why some *spectrograms are not clear* (line 95). This prediction matches well with (C). Choice A is out-of-scope. The paragraph doesn't mention any error in carrying out the research. Choice B is out-of-scope. The paragraph simply mentions a problem and a possible explanation; it doesn't state that the problem is unavoidable. Choice D is out-of-scope. While the problem described could probably be remedied by *more sensitive equipment*, the paragraph does not state that better equipment *is essential.*

10. **H**

For a Big Picture question, keep the purpose of the passage as a whole in mind. Predict that the passage examines research about bird and bat migration in the Appalachians to assess the potential risks of wind power development on these animals. Choice (H) closely matches this prediction. Choice F is a distortion. The goal of the research is to determine how detrimental wind power projects could be, not to argue that they *are* detrimental. Choice (H) is a distortion. NEXRAD and XBAT are mentioned in the passage, but the research has a more specific purpose than simply making use of these methods. Choice J is a distortion. All of the groups in J are mentioned in the passage, but the research discussed is research about bats and birds, not about the concerns of the various people.

11. **B**

For a Vocabulary-in-Context question, read carefully in the immediate context looking for clues that help you predict. Here, the context is *other prominent landforms* (line 35). Just before this phrase, the sentence mentions *mountain ridges.* Thus, you know that *prominent* could also be used to describe mountain ridges. Use this knowledge to predict that *prominent* in this context means *elevated.* This prediction matches well with (B). Choice A is out-of-scope. It gives a common meaning of *prominent* that is not justified at all in the context of the passage. Choice C is out-of-scope. There is nothing in the context to suggest that *advancing* is relevant here. Choice D is a distortion. *Tree-covered* might make sense if you think only of mountains, birds, and bats, but it doesn't take into account the clues that relate the word *prominent* to *other...landforms* like *mountain ridges.*

12. **H**

For a Detail question, consider your passage map notes to help you know where to read to predict. Here, your notes should guide you to paragraph 1. Paragraph 1 states that researchers are studying the effects of wind power development on migrating animals. You may need to use this prediction in combination with your understanding of the passage as a whole to eliminate wrong answer traps. Choice F is a distortion. The passage mentions risks, but it discusses methods of assessing risk and does not conclude that risks have been well-documented. Choice G is a distortion. The passage mentions both government agencies and the public but does not state that the two groups are in conflict. Choice J is out-of-scope. The passage doesn't refer to all regions of the country, only to research being done in the Appalachians.

CHAPTER 18

Reading Practice Set VIII—Natural Science

Directions: This test contains a passage, followed by several questions. After reading the passage, select the best answer to each question. You are allowed to refer to the passage while answering the questions.

NATURAL SCIENCE: *This passage is adapted from the paper "Indigenous Uses, Management, and Restoration of Oaks of the Far Western United States." It was issued by the U.S. Department of Agriculture Natural Resources Conservation Service in 2007.*

Today, oaks are plagued with problems. There is lack of regeneration in populations of certain species. Pests such as the acorn weevil and the filbert worm eat away at acorns and prevent germination. By undermining the root systems of seedlings and saplings, ground squirrels, gophers, and other small mammals often prevent these young plants from reaching tree size. Severe diseases, such as sudden oak death, kill many adult oaks. Many mature oaks are having a tough time with fire suppression. In the past, with light surface fires, the oaks had been able to maintain a stronghold where other plants were not able to compete and died out. Now oaks are being toppled by trees that have a higher tolerance for shade and are not fire resistant; earlier such trees would have been killed when Native Americans set fires.

Given all of these challenges, the "old-growth" oaks—the large old valley oaks,

Garry oaks, coast live oaks, and canyon live oaks that have huge girth and large canopies—may become a thing of the past. These oaks in particular are important because there are often more terrestrial vertebrates living in mature oak stands than in seedling and sapling areas. This prevalence of animals occurs because the large crowns of such oaks provide cover and feeding sites for a large variety of wildlife.

The University of California has embarked on an ambitious and necessary research program called the Integrated Hardwood Range Management Program to explore the significant causes of oak decline and offer varied solutions. These include investigating the use of grassing regimes that are compatible with oak seedling establishment, revegetating sites with native grasses to facilitate better germination of oak seedlings, documenting insects and pathogens that attack oaks, and exploring the ways that native people managed oaks in the past. Scientists at the Pacific Northwest Research Station in Olympia, Washington and at Redwood National Park in northern California are reintroducing the burning practices of Native Americans. When used in Garry oak ecosystems, fires keep Douglas firs from encroaching on the oaks and promote the growth of wildflowers that are important food plants. Further investigations about these fire practices may be essential in figuring out how to maintain oaks in the western landscape today, given that the fires address many of the factors that are now causing oak decline—from how to eliminate insect pests of acorns to how to maintain an open structure in oak groves.

Ecological restoration, the traditional approach to woodland maintenance, referred to humans intervening on a very limited time scale to bring back plants and animals known to have existed in an area historically. However, the decline of oaks, one of the most significant plants to Native Americans, shows us that humans may play an integral part in the restoration of oak areas. While animals such as jays have been recognized as crucial partners in oak well-being, human actions through the eons may also have been the key to the oaks' flourishing.

Sudden oak death, for example, although of exotic origin, may be curtailed locally by thinning around coastal oaks and tan oaks and setting light surface fires, simulating ancient fire management practices of Native Americans. Indigenous shrubs and trees that grow in association with oaks are hosts to the sudden oak death pathogen. By limiting the growth of these shrubs, burning that mimics earlier Native American ways may reduce opportunities for disease agents to jump from other plants to oak trees. With a more open environment, it may be harder for sudden oak death to spread.

The oak landscapes that we inherited, which still bear the marks of former Native American interactions, demand a new kind of restoration that complements other forms of ecological restoration. This new kind of restoration could be called *ethnobotanical restoration*, defined as reestablishing the historic plant communities of a given area and restoring indigenous harvesting, vegetation management, and cultivation practices (seedbeating, burning, pruning, sowing, tilling, and weeding) necessary to maintain these communities in the long term.

Thus, this kind of restoration is not only about restoring plants, but also about restoring the human place within nature. Ethnobotancial restoration is viewed not as a process that can be completed, but rather as a continuous interaction between people and plants as both their fates are intertwined in a region. Uniting oaks and people once again through harvesting acorns, making products from all parts of the tree, knocking the trees, and setting light fires may offer us ways to coexist, receive products from, and benefit the long-term health and well-being of the remarkable oak.

1. All of the following challenges to the health of the oak population are mentioned in the passage EXCEPT:
   - **A.** small mammals attacking the root systems of young trees.
   - **B.** sudden oak death caused by a pathogen.
   - **C.** grazing deer removing bark from the tree trunks.
   - **D.** competition from other plants such as shade tolerant trees.

2. As described in the passage, traditional ecological restoration differs from ethnobotanical restoration in that:
   - **F.** ethnobotanical restoration takes place over a longer period of time than ecological restoration.
   - **G.** ecological restoration involves introducing particular plants and management practices, whereas ethnobotanical restoration involves only the introduction of plants.
   - **H.** only ecological restoration follows historically proven ecological principles.
   - **J.** ecological restoration is meant to be used in conjunction with other restorative practices, whereas ethnobotanical restoration is meant to be used in isolation.

3. An important assumption underlying this passage is that:
   - **A.** the decline of the oak population is due primarily to root damage caused by ground squirrels, gophers, and other small mammals.
   - **B.** reinstituting indigenous cultivation practices is likely to be sufficient to restore the health of the oak population.
   - **C.** damage to many species of oak started centuries ago when Native Americans selectively set fires in many areas.
   - **D.** the practices of Native Americans offer lessons to modern researchers about how to promote a healthy oak population.

4. According to the passage, one way to reduce the incidence of sudden oak death is to:
   - **F.** reduce the population of animals that destroy the root systems of the oaks.
   - **G.** control the number of certain shrubs that grow in the vicinity of oak trees.
   - **H.** regulate the importation of the exotic plants that introduced the sudden oak death pathogen to the United States.
   - **J.** plant several varieties of oaks, particularly tan oaks and coastal oaks, to strengthen the oak population in general.

5. The author refers to the "huge girth and large canopies" (lines 24–25) of the old-growth oaks in order to:

   A. provide a description of what the various old-growth oak trees look like.
   B. argue that the old-growth trees are too large to be sustained in a modern ecosystem.
   C. support the explanation of why more vertebrates live in mature oak stands.
   D. indicate that Native Americans valued these trees for their ability to produce shade.

6. The primary purpose of the first paragraph is to:

   F. discuss how oak trees provide a habitat for various animals.
   G. suggest ways in which the declining oak population can be restored.
   H. support the argument that sudden oak death is not as common as rampant forest fires.
   J. describe current challenges to the health of the oak population.

7. Based on the passage as a whole, it is likely that:

   A. human intervention will be crucial in restoring the native oak population.
   B. despite much historical study, it will be impossible to recreate the cultivation practices of early Native Americans.
   C. documentation of the insects and pathogens that attack oak trees is the best way to begin the restoration process.
   D. native shrubs and trees that grow near oaks have served as kindling for many fires that damaged the oak population.

8. The author mentions "trees that have a higher tolerance for shade" (line 17) as an example of:

   F. one type of vegetation that is desirable to plant near oaks.
   G. a currently existing problem that presents a new kind of threat to the oak population.
   H. one of the drawbacks associated with several of the old-growth oak species.
   J. the types of plants Native Americans cultivated.

9. It can be inferred from the third paragraph that:

   A. the oak population in Redwood National Park has faced greater threats than oak populations elsewhere.
   B. native grasses have been shown to deprive oak seedlings of nutrients.
   C. the sudden oak death pathogen has been the primary cause of oak decline.
   D. researchers are interested in finding multiple avenues to restoring the health of the oaks.

10. As stated in the passage, the effect of light surface fires on oaks is to:

    F. promote the health of oaks by limiting vegetation that would compete with them.
    G. reduce the number of oak trees by destroying the acorns before they can seed.
    H. create scars in the bark that allow for the entrance of the sudden oak death pathogen.
    J. harm the oaks by destroying the nests of jays.

11. From the last paragraph, it is reasonable to infer that the author would agree with all of the following statements EXCEPT:

    A. the well-being of people is related to the well-being of plant populations.

    B. it is advisable to complete the restoration of the oaks before turning to other types of ethnobotanical restoration.

    C. human intervention is not always harmful to the health of the natural world.

    D. harvesting parts of the oak tree to make products for human use need not harm the oak population as a whole.

12. The word *curtailed* as used in line 77 most nearly means:

    F. eliminated.

    G. ended.

    H. explored.

    J. limited.

ANSWERS AND EXPLANATIONS

SUGGESTED PASSAGE MAP NOTES

Paragraph 1: Problems facing oak populations

Paragraph 2: Importance of "old-growth" oaks

Paragraph 3: Research being done to learn about problems and solutions

Paragraph 4: Ecological restoration

Paragraph 5: Sudden oak death

Paragraph 6: Def. of ethnobotanical restoration

Paragraph 7: Importance of people in ethnobotanical restoration

ANSWER KEY

1. C	**7. A**
2. F	**8. G**
3. D	**9. D**
4. G	**10. F**
5. C	**11. B**
6. J	**12. J**

1. **C**

For a Detail question that uses EXCEPT, go straight to the answer choices and check the passage for each one. Eliminate A because it's cited in lines 5–9. Eliminate B because *sudden oak death* is mentioned in line 10, and the *pathogen* that causes it is mentioned in line 83. Eliminate D because it's mentioned in line 17. Choice (C) is the correct answer because the passage says nothing about grazing deer.

2. **F**

When a Detail question asks you to describe a contrast, make sure you read enough to determine what the passage says about both things contrasted. Here, research in paragraph 6 to predict that ethnobotanical restoration is a new approach that involves introducing plants and practices that were used in the past and working on long-term maintenance (lines 94–102). Research in paragraph 4 to predict that ecological restoration is used in a limited time frame and refers only to introducing plants and animals that were historically present (lines 62–67). Choice (F) matches perfectly with the time frame the prediction points to. Choice G is a distortion because ecological restoration isn't described as involving *management practices.* Choice H is a contradiction because both types of restoration are described as being historically based. Choice J is a distortion. The descriptions of the two kinds of restoration are reversed in the wording of this answer choice.

3. **D**

A Big Picture question about an underlying assumption may be tough to make a prediction for. Still, try making a quick prediction that at least addresses the purpose of the passage, and then check through the answer choices. In this case, your prediction might be something along the lines of *restoring the health of the oak populations is an important endeavor.* None of the answer choices matches this prediction exactly, but (D) comes very close, and it is true that the writer values the practices of Native Americans. Thus, (D) is the best answer. Choice A is a misused detail. Damage done to oaks by small mammals is mentioned, but it is not described as being the primary cause of the oaks' decline. Choice B is a distortion; you should pay special attention to the word *sufficient* in this choice. While ethnobotanical restoration does include bringing in Native American practices, the passage describes ethnobotanical restoration as something that *complements other forms of ecological restoration* (lines 93–94). Choice C is a contradiction. Lines 19–20 refer to fires set by Native Americans as protecting oaks by limiting the growth of other trees that competed with oaks.

4. **G**

For a Detail question, use passage map notes to guide you to the right part of the passage. Paragraph 5 discusses sudden oak death. It states that a way to reduce the spread of sudden oak death is to limit the growth of shrubs that harbor the sudden oak death pathogen. Choice (G) matches this prediction. Choice F is a misused detail. Animals that destroy the root systems of oaks are described as a problem, but addressing this problem is not mentioned as a way to reduce sudden oak death. Choice H combines a misused detail and out-of-scope traps. Sudden oak death is described as having an *exotic origin* (line 77), but there is nothing in the passage about regulating imports. Choice J combines the misused detail and out-of-scope traps. There is nothing in the passage suggesting that planting tan oaks and coastal oaks will strengthen the oak population in general.

5. **C**

When a Vocabulary-in-Context question asks about a phrase, consider the sentence it appears in and the sentences before or after, if necessary. Here, predict that the phrase *huge girth and large canopies* describes trees in *mature oak stands* (line 28), which the passage states are home to more small animals (the *terrestrial vertebrates* in line 27) than younger trees are. This prediction fits with (C). Choice A is a misused detail. It's true that the phrase describes the appearance of the trees, but that doesn't address the author's purpose for describing this appearance. Choice B is out-of-scope. The passage never says that the trees are too large for a modern ecosystem. Choice D is a misused detail. Both *Native Americans* and *shade* are mentioned in the passage, but not in the context of the oaks' *huge girth and large canopies.*

6. **J**

When a Big Picture question asks about the purpose of a paragraph, keep in mind how its topic relates to the passage as a whole. Here, predict that paragraph 1 introduces the topic by discussing problems facing oak trees. Choice (J) is a great match for this prediction. Choice F is a misused detail. The animals that live in oaks are mentioned in paragraph 2, not paragraph 1. Choice G is a misused detail. This statement is true of the passage as a whole but doesn't relate to the first paragraph. Choice (H) is a distortion. The passage mentions both fires and sudden oak death but doesn't compare their effects.

7. **A**

For a broad Big Picture question, keep the entire passage in mind. Predict that the passage concerns problems facing oaks and proposed solutions. Choice (A) goes just a little beyond this prediction but is consistent with the passage because solutions to the problems involve human intervention. Thus, (A) is the best answer. Choice B is a contradiction. Lines 98–99, discuss *restoring indigenous...cultivation practices* as though it's reasonable to expect that such things can be accomplished. Choice C is an extreme. Though the passage mentions the pathogen and *pests* (line 60), it doesn't say that dealing with them is the *best* way to start the restoration process. Choice D is a distortion. The fires that are mentioned in the passage (e.g., line 13) are described as protecting the oak population, not damaging it.

8. **G**

For this Detail question, focus on the immediate context to make your prediction. Here, pay attention to the first part of the sentence: *Now oaks are being toppled by trees that have a higher tolerance for shade* (lines 16–17). Predict that the shade-tolerant trees are overpowering the oaks. This prediction works well with (G). Choice F is an opposite: because shade-tolerant trees are *toppling* the oaks, it would not be good to plant them near the oaks. Choice H is a distortion. The passage mentions *old-growth oaks* but doesn't describe them as being at all shade-tolerant. Choice J is a distortion. The passage mentions *Native Americans* but doesn't say that they planted the highly shade-tolerant trees.

9. **D**

For a Big Picture question about a paragraph, use your passage map notes and keep the purpose of the paragraph in mind. Here, predict that the best answer will have something to do with finding ways to improve the declining strength of the oak population. Choice (D) fits perfectly with this prediction. Choice A is a misused detail. Redwood National Park is mentioned in the paragraph, but nothing in the paragraph suggests that oaks there are in worse shape than they are elsewhere. Choice B is a contradiction. The paragraph states that native grasses can *facilitate better germination of oak seedlings.* Choice C is a misused detail. Although sudden oak death is mentioned in the passage, nothing is said about it in paragraph 3. (This answer choice also uses the extreme language *primary cause*, which should put you on alert.)

10. **F**

If your passage map notes do not direct you to a particular place in the passage to answer a Detail question, skim the passage quickly for a phrase from the question stem or another phrase that means something similar. Here, the exact phrase *light surface fires* appears in line 13. Read the sentence and predict that *they*, here referring to the oaks, were *able to maintain a stronghold* (line 14) because the fires kept in check plants that competed with the oaks. Choice G is a distortion. The passage does mention acorns, but not in connection with fires. Choice H is out-of-scope. The passage does not say anything about scars forming on the bark of oak trees. Choice J is a distortion. *Jays* are mentioned in the passage, but not in relation to fires.

11. **B**

This Detail question uses EXCEPT in the question stem, so three of the four choices will be supported by the passage. Work through each choice and eliminate as you go. Choice A is justified by line 109 as *both their fates* [i.e., plants' and people's] *are intertwined.* Choice (B) is not justified by the passage and so is the correct answer here. Choice C is supported, particularly in lines 110–114, *uniting oaks and people...offering us ways to coexist.* Choice D is justified by the suggestion that people should [*make*] *products from all parts of the tree* (lines 111–112).

12. **J**

For a Vocabulary-in-Context question, go back to the passage and look for clues in the sentence that allow you to predict what the word means. In this case, information in the rest of the paragraph can also help you eliminate choices. The subject of the sentence where the word appears is *sudden oak death.* Because the passage identifies this disease as a problem facing oaks, and the passage addresses solutions, predict that *curtailed* means something like *minimized* or *reduced.* This prediction matches well with (J), which is the best answer. Choices F and G are both extremes. Nothing in the rest of the paragraph suggests that sudden oak death can be completely eradicated. Choice H is a distortion that might result from putting too much emphasis on the phrase *exotic origin* used in the sentence.

CHAPTER 19

Introduction to ACT Writing

THE BASICS

40 Minutes

1 Prompt

PACING

Take up to 8 minutes to read the prompt and create a plan. Spend about 30 minutes producing the essay. Save 2 minutes at the end for proofreading.

TEST DAY DIRECTIONS AND FORMAT

This is a test of your writing skills. You will have **forty** (40) minutes to read the prompt, plan your response, and write an essay in English. Before you begin working, read all material in this test booklet carefully to understand exactly what you are being asked to do.

You will write your essay on the lined pages in the **answer document** provided. Your writing on those pages will be scored. You may use the unlined pages in this test booklet to plan your essay. Your work on these pages will not be scored.

Your essay will be evaluated based on the evidence it provides of your ability to:

- clearly state your own perspective on a complex issue and analyze the relationship between your perspective and at least one other perspective
- develop and support your ideas with reasoning and examples
- organize your ideas clearly and logically
- communicate your ideas effectively in standard written English

OUTSIDE KNOWLEDGE

No outside knowledge is required. However, you may choose to strengthen your essay with examples from history, science, literature, or even your own experiences.

THE INSIDE SCOOP

This is an optional part of the ACT, as far as your registration for Test Day is concerned. Whether or not it is truly optional depends on whether your high school or the colleges you're applying to require it. *If they do, it isn't optional.* If you're not sure what schools you're applying to, or whether they require it, consider it mandatory—far better to have it and not need it than need it and not have it. Either way, it's an area on which, with some advance practice and planning, you can get a high score, so you should be prepared to take it with confidence.

The ACT Writing test is designed to gauge your ability to compose a clear and logical argument and effectively present that argument in written form.

The essay prompt will present a specific issue and three perspectives. You are asked to analyze multiple perspectives on a complex issue and to arrive at a point of view on that issue. Then you must state your point of view clearly and support it with clear and relevant examples.

The essay is *argument based,* not *fact based.* That is, you're being tested on what you can effectively argue, not what you know about the topic. Does this mean facts aren't relevant? Yes and no—you will not be scored based on whether your facts are *true* or not, but you will be scored based on whether you use facts effectively. In an essay about being active in your community, for example, if you attribute the quote "Ask not what your country can do for you; ask what you can do for your country," to Ronald Reagan, you will be factually wrong, but you will be using an effective piece of evidence anyway. So you will get credit for effective use of information, even though the quote was said by John F. Kennedy.

SMARTPOINTS

As there is only one prompt for the Writing Test, there are no SmartPoints. All strategies apply to the whole section.

THE KAPLAN METHOD FOR ACT WRITING

STEP 1: PROMPT

Read about the issue and be sure you understand clearly what the core arguments are. Getting a high score requires clearly responding to at least one of the three perspectives. Once you've determined what each perspective is arguing, pick a position on the issue. There is no right or wrong answer, and you can partially or fully agree or disagree with the perspectives provided. You should plan a thesis that you can *best defend*, whether that's what you personally believe or not. Be aware that **multiple** sides can be effectively defended; there's no "easy" or "right" side.

STEP 2: PLAN

Take up to eight minutes to complete Steps 1 and 2. You want to be sure to strategically plan your essay before you write. Most students skip this step on Test Day. Take this time to plan so you know what you're trying to accomplish and can put forth your best first draft. Begin by stating your thesis. Because you already decided upon a stance during Step 1, now compose a sentence that states your position clearly. Then, focus on what kinds of reasoning and examples you can use to discuss not only your position but also at least one other perspective provided in the prompt. Choose the best specific, relevant examples you can brainstorm. You'll use one in each body paragraph, and the strongest body paragraphs discuss real-world evidence rather than hypothetical positions.

STEP 3: PRODUCE

Write your draft, sticking closely to your plan. In about 20 minutes, you should aim to produce five well-developed paragraphs with topic sentences and supporting details. You're not scored on how many words or paragraphs you write but on the strength of what you put down. Be very sure to include an introductory paragraph stating your position and a concluding sentence, because without those two framing statements, you're missing fundamental ingredients your essay needs. As you produce your essay, write as neatly as possible—words that cannot be read cannot be scored.

STEP 4: PROOFREAD

Always leave yourself the last couple of minutes to review your work—this time spent proofreading is definitely to your benefit. Very few of us can avoid the occasional confused sentence or omitted word when we write under pressure, and a missed word can affect the meaning of a sentence. Again, graders can only score what they read, not what you might mean. Therefore, always quickly review your essay to be sure your ideas are clearly stated. Also, by leaving yourself this two-minute buffer at the end, you'll avoid having to rush your conclusion. Remember, that's the last thing your essay grader will read, and you want to go out strong.

QUICK TIPS

MINDSET

- **Don't wait until Test Day to practice.** Regardless of what issue is raised in the prompt, the directions and objectives will be the same. Practicing this type of essay beforehand will save you time because you will know what to expect. As other students are looking at the directions for the first time, you will already be reading through the issue and perspectives, ready to start planning the points you will discuss.
- **Refresh your memory about school subjects, current events, personal experiences, and activities—anything.** By doing so, you strengthen mental connections to those ideas and details, making it easier to use them as specific, relevant support for your thesis on Test Day. Again, the important thing to remember is that real-world evidence is far more powerful than hypothetical stances. Saying "This is right because I believe it" will never be as strong as saying "This is right—look at all this evidence."

SPECIAL STRATEGIES

You must be very focused to write a complete, coherent essay in 40 minutes. You can use Kaplan's Essay Template to guide your overall organization.

KAPLAN'S ESSAY TEMPLATE

¶1: Introductory paragraph

- **Introductory statement**
- **Thesis**

¶2: 1st body paragraph

- Describe your **thesis**
- Provide **1st example/reasoning:** include specific, relevant information

¶3: 2nd body paragraph

- Continue supporting your **thesis**
- Provide **2nd example/reasoning:** include specific, relevant information

—***Time valve:*** *If you are running out of time, don't write a 2nd body paragraph. Instead, take the time to write a thorough 3rd body paragraph and a clear conclusion paragraph.*—

¶4: 3rd body paragraph

- Explain how your thesis compares and contrasts with **Perspectives One, Two, and/or Three**
- **Strengths/Weaknesses** of the perspective(s)
    - Insights offered / Insights not considered
    - Persuasive / Not persuasive
- **Example or reasoning:** provide specific, relevant information

✔ EXPERT TIP

The goal of your 4th paragraph (the 3rd body paragraph) is to evaluate and critique at least one perspective provided, and it is often easiest to discuss a perspective that mostly clearly *contrasts* with your thesis.

¶5: Conclusion paragraph

- Recap your **thesis**
- Recap how your thesis compares and contrasts with **Perspectives One, Two, and/or Three**

Stick to the template as you write the essay. Don't change your essay halfway through, even if another idea suddenly comes to you—it might derail the essay! Keep your focus on the issue and don't digress.

TIMING

With only 40 minutes, efficient use of time is critical. Divide your time as follows:

First 8 minutes—Read the prompt and plan your essay.

Next 30 minutes—Write your essay, sticking to the plan.

Last 2 minutes—Proofread and correct any errors.

WHEN YOU'RE RUNNING OUT OF TIME

On the Writing test, you won't be able to guess on the last few questions when you're running out of time, as you can on the other tests. Thus, practice the timing carefully to avoid losing coherence toward the end. If you do start running out of time, don't write a second body paragraph. Instead, take the time to write a thorough final body paragraph and a clear conclusion paragraph. The conclusion is a necessary component of your essay, and its exclusion will cost you more than a strong body paragraph will gain you. Even when you're rushed, try to allow 1 to 2 minutes to proofread for errors that affect clarity.

SCORING

Your essay will be scored according to four domains: Ideas and Analysis, Development and Support, Organization, and Language Use and Conventions. (Notice that these correspond with the four bulleted items in the Essay Task.) What is significant for you, prep-wise, is to make sure you can write an essay that is well developed in each of these four domain areas in order to maximize your Writing test score.

Two trained readers score your essay on a scale of 1–6 for each of the four Writing test domains; those scores are added to arrive at your four Writing domain scores (each from 2 to 12). You will also receive an overall Writing test score ranging from 2 to 12, which is determined by a rounded average of the four domain scores. Essays can receive a zero if they are entirely off-topic, left blank, illegible, or written in a language other than English. If there's a difference of more than 1 point between the two readers' scores (for example, one reader gives the essay a 3 and the other a 5), your essay will be read by a third reader.

Statistically speaking, there will be few essays that score 12 out of 12 for all four Writing test domains. If each grader gives your essay a 4 or 5 for each of the four domains (making your subscores 8–10), that will place you within the upper range of those taking the exam.

METHOD BREAKDOWN

STEP 1: PROMPT

The ACT Writing prompt usually relates to a topic that is broad enough for high school students to be able to relate to it. In most cases, the subject will be something fairly innocuous, like the possible advantages of including mandatory career-readiness programs in high schools. If, by chance, the prompt describes a situation you feel strongly about, be sure to still present your argument in a careful, thoughtful manner. Do *not* write an overly emotional response. You are being gauged on the strength of your argument, not the strength of your feelings.

Here's an example of a typical ACT Writing prompt:

BILINGUAL ACCREDITATION

While the United States has just one official national language, English is certainly not the only language in which Americans communicate. In fact, bilingual fluency is highly desirable in many professions, including business, education, and medicine. In an effort to ready students for success in their future careers, some high schools may consider instituting programs that would offer bilingual accreditation to students who successfully complete a significant portion of their schooling in a language other than English. Because bilingual certification is not a necessary component of traditional education, should schools be expected to explore this option for interested students? As American high schools aim to remain competitive as measured by increasingly rigorous international education standards, innovative programs such as bilingual certification may prove to be essential.

Read and carefully consider these perspectives. Each discusses relevant aspects of offering bilingual accreditation.

Perspective 1	Perspective 2	Perspective 3
Schools should encourage bilingual fluency but should not be expected to offer special classes or programs. School administrators need to work on strengthening the existing curriculum rather than overcomplicating instruction by attempting to incorporate additional programs that do not reinforce traditional education.	Offering bilingual accreditation weakens the core of high school curriculum. A large enough portion of the student population already struggles to maintain passing grades when taught in English, and adding other languages would likely add to that number.	Bilingual accreditation should be offered, but it needs to be thoughtfully implemented. Courses taught in languages other than English need to be carefully selected to ensure that this program does not affect the integrity of the high school diploma.

ESSAY TASK

Write a unified, coherent essay in which you evaluate multiple perspectives regarding bilingual accreditation. In your essay, be sure to:

- clearly state your own perspective on the issue and analyze the relationship between your perspective and at least one other perspective
- develop and support your ideas with reasoning and examples
- organize your ideas clearly and logically
- communicate your ideas effectively in standard written English

Your perspective may be in full agreement with any of the others, in partial agreement, or wholly different. Whatever the case, support your ideas with logical reasoning and detailed, persuasive examples.

PLANNING YOUR ESSAY

You may wish to consider the following as you think critically about the task:

Strengths and weaknesses of the three given perspectives

- What insights do they offer, and what do they fail to consider?
- Why might they be persuasive to others, or why might they fail to persuade?

Your own knowledge, experience, and values

- What is your perspective on this issue, and what are its strengths and weaknesses?
- How will you support your perspective in your essay?

As you read, be sure you understand the argument clearly. In this case, the issue is "Should schools be expected to explore bilingual accreditation for interested students, even though it is not a necessary component of traditional education?" You know you have the right question in this case because it is stated clearly in the prompt, but it may not always be. If the question is not stated this clearly, make sure you think through the issue thoroughly enough that you can take one clear position, being careful not to over-complicate your thesis. Based on the structure of the prompt, you can use the three perspectives to help you determine your position. In this case, you can say, "High schools should promote bilingualism but shouldn't be required to offer bilingual classes," "High schools should avoid bilingual options," or "High schools should offer bilingual accreditation if it is carefully implemented." For this prompt, you do not want to try to argue all three positions because these perspectives feature diverse arguments.

STEP 2: PLAN

Take up to 8 minutes to analyze the prompt (Step 1) and build a plan before you write. This step is critical—a successful plan leads directly to a high-scoring essay. Focus on what kinds of reasoning and examples you can use to support your position.

Note: If you find you have better supporting evidence for a position different from the one you originally thought you would take, *change your position.*

Kaplan's Essay Template is an excellent way to organize your essay before you begin to write. This can easily be done in the 4 to 6 minutes you will invest in planning, and doing so will make the actual production *much* faster and smoother. Take a few minutes to write down notes about the prompt in Step 1. Then organize your notes using Kaplan's Essay Template. Your outline may look similar to the following:

¶1: Introductory paragraph

- Introductory statement
- Thesis—***Schools should offer bilingual accreditation as long as courses offered in languages other than English are carefully selected.***

¶2: 1st body paragraph

- Describe your thesis—***All classes need to be carefully selected so carefully selecting bilingual offerings is not an additional burden for school administrators.***
- Provide 1st example/reasoning: include specific, relevant information—***Even if core classes are given in two languages, all students still study the core curriculum and preserve the integrity of the diploma.***

¶3: 2nd body paragraph

- Continue supporting your thesis—***Offering bilingual accreditation provides an opportunity for schools to offer non-traditional classes for all students.***
- Provide 2nd example/reasoning: include specific, relevant information— ***Every dollar spent to accommodate bilingual education should be matched with equal funding for other types of educational enrichment such as STEM training and career-oriented electives.***

¶4: 3rd body paragraph

- Explain how your thesis compares and contrasts with Perspectives One, Two, and/or Three—***The first perspective argues that schools should encourage bilingual fluency but not add any bilingual classes, which is in direct contrast to Perspective Three.***
- Strengths/Weaknesses of the perspective(s)—***Perspective One doesn't take into account that making the existing curriculum better often means adding additional classes, which bilingual accreditation would accomplish.***
    - Persuasive / Not persuasive—***The argument simply says that these classes would only be for interested students, so it doesn't affect everyone.***
    - Example or Reasoning: provide specific, relevant information—***Most of the world uses English as a second language, and many people speak at least two languages, so to stay competitive, U.S. students should also be fluent in two languages.***

¶5: Conclusion paragraph

- Recap your thesis—***I fully support perspective three because it opens up possibilities for all students without denying anyone a full high school curriculum leading to a meaningful diploma.***
- Recap how your thesis compares and contrasts with Perspectives One, Two, and/or Three—***Recognizing the benefits of being bilingual, and making bilingual courses available but optional, is the best of both worlds.***

Information banks: Don't wait until Test Day to think of examples you can use to support your ideas. Regardless of what question is raised in the prompt, you will draw your support from the things you know best and are most comfortable writing about—things you know a fair amount of concrete detail about.

Refresh your memory about your favorite or most memorable books, school subjects, historical events, personal experiences, activities—anything. By doing so, you strengthen mental connections to those ideas and details, making it easier to connect to the right examples on Test Day.

With that in mind:

- Use an effective *hook* to bring the reader in.
- Use *transitions* regularly—these are the "glue" that holds your ideas together.
- End with a *bang* to make your essay memorable.

Using a "hook" means avoiding an essay that opens (as thousands of other essays will): "In my opinion, . . . because . . ." Your opinion is not compelling to a reader who has graded hundreds of essays on the same subject. Make it something more exciting than that.

In today's global economy, students are looking for ways to ready themselves for an increasingly international future.

A "bang" means a closing that ties the essay together. A good choice can be a clear, succinct statement of your thesis in the essay or a vivid example that's right on point.

Enhancing instruction is always better than restricting learning, especially when the result is effective communication, desirable skills, and valuable experiences.

In summary, a good plan:

- Responds to the prompt
- Has an introduction
- Has strong examples, usually one per paragraph
- Has a strong conclusion

STEP 3: PRODUCE

You are not graded directly on word count, but graders know that filling out a thorough argument takes time and space—it will be hard to present all the elements of a strong argument in a few words or only a couple of paragraphs. Nonetheless, don't think about your *number of words*; instead, think about the *strength of your arguments.*

Organization counts. Graders are far more able to follow—and be compelled by—your argument if they can see its distinct ingredients.

Write neatly. Graders may give you a zero if your essay is impossible to read. If your handwriting is a problem, print.

Stick with the plan. Resist any urge to introduce new ideas—no matter how good you think they are—or to digress from the central focus or organization of each paragraph.

Use topic sentences. Each paragraph should be organized around a topic sentence that you should finish in your mind before you start to write. These may begin as follows:

- *One example . . .*
- *Another example . . .*
- *Therefore, we can conclude . . .*

You don't have to write it this way in the essay, but completing these sentences in your mind ensures that you focus on the idea that organizes each paragraph.

Choose words carefully. Use vocabulary you know well. New or fancy words that you have learned recently often stick out in a negative way. Using unfamiliar words in an essay often produces awkward, confusing thoughts—the opposite of what you want. Instead of impressing the graders, you would obscure your ideas. Two more points to keep in mind:

1. **Avoid using *I* excessively.** You are absolutely allowed to use personal examples ("At my school, we had this issue just last year, and I was very involved in the discussion . . ."), but avoid using your opinions or beliefs *as evidence* ("I really think . . ." "I believe . . ." "In my opinion . . ."). You base your argument on weak ground when it is founded on your thoughts, not what you can prove.
2. **Avoid slang.** Your tone should be personal and natural but academic. This is a school paper. Abbreviations such as those you might use in text messaging, online, or in personal emails are not appropriate here; at best, they're unprofessional, and at worst, the grader won't know what you're talking about.

Use transitions. Think about the relationship between ideas as you write and spell out your concepts clearly. Doing so allows the readers to follow your reasoning easily, and they'll appreciate it. **Use key words from the prompt as well as the kinds of words you've learned about in Reading that indicate contrast, opinion, relative importance, and support.**

Don't sweat the small stuff. Do not obsess over every little thing. If you cannot remember how to spell a word, do your best and just **keep going.** Even top-scoring essays can have minor errors. The essay readers understand that you are writing a first draft and have no time for research or revision.

STEP 4: PROOFREAD

Always leave yourself 2 or 3 minutes to review your work—the time spent will definitely pay off. Very few of us can avoid the occasional confused sentence or omitted word when we write under pressure. Quickly review your essay to be sure your ideas are clearly stated.

Don't hesitate to make corrections to your essay—this is a timed first draft, not a term paper—but keep your writing clearly readable. Use a single line through deletions and an asterisk to mark where text should be inserted.

✔ EXPERT TUTOR TIP

Use a caret (^) or an asterisk (*) to insert a word or words. Write a backward *P* to create a new paragraph. Cross words out with one line. Be neat with your edits: Don't make a mess.

During proofreading, remind yourself that **you don't have time to revise substantially**. This isn't the time for inserting new paragraphs, radically changing your tone, or (worst yet) changing your mind. Use your practice essays to learn the types of mistakes you tend to make and look for them.

COMMON ERRORS

- Omitted words
- Sentence fragments
- Misplaced modifiers
- Misused words—especially homonyms like *their* for *there* or *they're*
- Spelling errors

COMMON STYLE PROBLEMS

- Choppy sentences (combine some)
- Too many long, complex sentences (break some up)
- Too many stuffy-sounding words (replace some with simple words)
- Too many simple words (add a few college-level words)

SUMMARY

In this chapter, we went over the method you can use to write a high-scoring essay on the ACT Writing test.

Remember, the idea is to clearly explain your own perspective and analyze the relationship between your perspective and at least one other perspective. When explaining your thesis, take a distinct stance and support your argument with clear logical evidence.

Make sure to plan. You can get a good score on the ACT Writing test just by presenting clear points and using proper structure. Know what points you are going to make beforehand to avoid writing an essay that sounds like a stream of consciousness.

The ideal structure: Put your thesis and a hook into your first paragraph. Have three body paragraphs, each with a distinct supporting point and evidence. Make sure you don't bring up any new points in your concluding paragraph. Just wrap things up neatly.

Leave yourself a couple of minutes to proofread. Doing so will also give you a time buffer—in case your writing runs long, you won't have to cut your essay short.

In the next chapter, we'll go over each piece of the essay in detail, learning how to craft each piece to maximize your score.

Work on the sections you most need, whether it's crafting a compelling hook for your introduction and a clear thesis or using well-developed evidence to drive a body paragraph home with the reader.

Put the pieces together at the end of these Writing chapters by completing a sample Writing test and reviewing your strengths and weaknesses.

Keep an eye on where you're going. Take a clear side on the issue, create a plan for your essay, and follow through. When you do these things, you're well on your way to mastering the ACT Writing test.

CHAPTER 20

ACT Writing Strategy in Depth

OVERVIEW

Use this chapter to get familiar with how to properly form the pieces of an essay for the ACT Writing test.

We'll go over each in turn, paragraph by paragraph.

For the introductory paragraph, we'll discuss how to create a thesis (the most important sentence of your essay) and how to draw the reader in with a hook.

For the body paragraphs, we'll discuss further how to include coherent analysis and specific evidence. We'll also look at the proper way to discuss your own perspective.

For the concluding paragraph, we'll discuss how to properly bring the essay to a close.

Finally, you'll get a chance to put it all together in response to a prompt, and we'll discuss how your essay will be graded. We'll discuss how the pieces should fit together and flow from one to the next so you can maximize your score potential.

PARAGRAPH BY PARAGRAPH

THE INTRODUCTION

You've likely been writing essays for as long as you've been in school, and you may have had multiple teachers tell you at various points the "one right way" to write an essay. If you've come to suspect there may not really be "one right way," you're in good company. What good essays do have in common, however, is a set of ingredients. Some of these ingredients are optional and vary based on individual taste, but some are necessary to successfully produce an academic essay.

Think about a sandwich. You can have any kind of bread and any kind of fillings you like, but if you don't have a piece of bread on each side and something in the middle, you don't have a sandwich. In a formal essay like this, the introduction and conclusion are your bread, and your body paragraphs are your filling. Exactly what you will put in, what will it look like, and what it will do—all these things are yours to decide. However, without the key ingredients of introduction, conclusion, and body paragraphs, you don't have a sandwich.

Your introductory paragraph needs to fulfill certain roles. It must:

- Introduce the argument. By the end of the first paragraph, a person who has just picked up your essay should know what is being discussed and what the main arguments are.
- Establish your side of the argument. We'll talk more about your **thesis statement** soon, but do know this is where it goes. You may have heard before that your thesis should be the first sentence of the first paragraph, or the last sentence of the first paragraph, or any other sentence, but rest assured that it should just be *somewhere* in the first paragraph. Readers should go into the second paragraph (the first body paragraph) knowing which side you're on.
- Set the tone for the essay. While your essay should be academic in style, that still leaves some wiggle room. Will your essay be fierce and uncompromising? Gentle but persuasive? Personal and humorous? Use whatever tone comes most naturally to you; just make sure to keep it consistent throughout the essay. Sudden changes of voice will distract readers.

If you've included the items listed in this section, then you have an introduction. The thesis is the most important component of this paragraph because it tells readers what to expect from the rest of your essay, so let's dig into it further.

THE THESIS STATEMENT

Before you can create a thesis, you need to understand the issue. Start with Step 1 and read the prompt. To help you focus on the topic, underline key words in the prompt as you read. Key words are the nouns and verbs that form the backbone of the prompt. You'll also use these words in your essay to keep your writing on topic.

After reading the prompt, move to Step 2, making your plan. You should write a brief plan before you start producing your essay, but you don't need to do this immediately after reading the prompt. Take a minute to think about the three perspectives posed in the prompt. Do you have an immediate and strong reaction to them? Sometimes, you'll know right away how you feel about the issue, and ideas and examples will pop into your head even as you're reading the prompt. At other times, you might be a little less certain. Perhaps all three perspectives seem equally valid, and you can think of reasons to support all of them. In this case, don't spend too long deliberating. Remember, the issues posed in ACT prompts are chosen precisely because three reasonable people might have legitimate reasons for supporting those views. Your essay score is not affected by which viewpoint you choose to defend.

Again, don't spend too much time deciding which perspective to support. Choose one viewpoint and jot down a list of evidence you can use to support that viewpoint. Once you've chosen a perspective, you need to formulate a good *thesis statement.* A thesis statement is a clear, simple sentence that describes the position you will support in your essay. A strong thesis statement:

- Answers the question in the prompt
- Leaves no doubt about where you stand on the issue
- Doesn't necessarily contain reasons for your position but does set the stage for your presentation of evidence that will follow

WRITING EXERCISE 1

Using the "Bilingual Accreditation" prompt from the previous chapter, consider each of the following sentences and put an asterisk next to the ones you think would make a good thesis sentence:

1.______ I've always enjoyed learning languages other than English.

2.______ Learning foreign languages serves several educational purposes.

3.______ Bilingual certification is an innovative program that should be offered to high school students.

4.______ Learning languages other than English actually distracts students from learning well.

5.______ Bilingual accreditation would unfairly reward students who already know other languages.

6._______Schools should focus on improving the existing curriculum instead of adding new programs like bilingual certification.

7._______ While students should have the opportunity to learn other languages, bilingual certification should not be offered because teaching classes in languages other than English will make it harder to ensure that every student is receiving the same type and quality of education.

8._______ Teachers tend to give better grades to students they know speak more than one language.

Sentences 3, 6, and 7 are the most appropriate thesis sentences. Sentences 2, 4, and 5 all discuss bilingual programs, but they don't state a position on the question in the prompt. These sentences might be appropriate as part of your argument in the essay, but they can't act as a thesis statement. Sentences 1 and 8 do not relate to the issue in the prompt and should not be featured in your essay.

1. Although this sentence discusses learning languages other than English, it does not state a position relating to the question in the prompt.
2. Although this sentence discusses foreign languages, it does not state a position relating to the question in the prompt. This sentence might be appropriate as part of your argument in the essay, but it can't act as a thesis statement.
3. This is an appropriate thesis sentence.
4. Although this sentence discusses the issue presented in the prompt, it does not state a clear position in regard to the three perspectives. This sentence might be appropriate as part of your argument in the essay, but it can't act as a thesis statement.
5. Although this sentence discusses bilingual accreditation, it does not state a position relating to the question in the prompt. This sentence might be appropriate as part of your argument in the essay, but it can't act as a thesis statement.
6. This is an appropriate thesis sentence.
7. This is an appropriate thesis sentence.
8. Although this sentence discusses bilingual certification, it does not state a position relating to the question in the prompt.

DEMONSTRATING UNDERSTANDING OF COMPLEXITY

One thing an ACT essay grader expects to find in a top-scoring essay is an indication that the writer understands the complexity of the question in the prompt. The strongest ACT essays not only effectively discuss all three perspectives but also illustrate an understanding of the ramifications of each position.

EVIDENCE

Now that you know what an appropriate thesis statement is, let's consider what your evidence should look like. The use of *evidence* (real-world examples) is highly effective, as it takes the argument off the page and grounds it in real issues.

The most important thing to remember when selecting evidence is that it should be specific and relevant to your topic. During Step 2: Plan, identify your examples and reasons in brief notes, but in Step 3: Produce, you'll actually flesh out your evidence. Now it's important to develop your evidence with specifics. A problem many unprepared students have with the ACT essay is not talking in generalities instead of presenting specific evidence that supports their thesis. This happens because they are writing under time pressure without planning sufficiently. With practice, however, you will avoid this common pitfall.

Prepare solid examples by reading newspapers, staying informed about current events (local, national, and world), and reading opinion articles and blogs. Doing so in the weeks leading up to Test Day will both provide you with a wealth of real-world examples and expose you to strong writing examples.

INFORMATION BANKS

Don't wait until Test Day to think about what subjects you can draw on for your examples to create animated and engaging essays. Examples can be drawn from anywhere: your life experience, a story you saw on the news, and so on. So prepare yourself by refreshing your memory about your favorite subjects—collect examples that can be used for a variety of topics.

Don't hesitate to use your examples broadly. If the topic is about school, that doesn't mean you have to use school-based examples. It's better to write about things that you are comfortable with and know a lot about. Just be sure to make clear how they are relevant to the essay's topic.

There you have the pieces of an excellent body paragraph. Before you move on, though, make sure to wrap up.

You'll want to produce an evidence sandwich. In other words, you don't want to just jump into or out of your specific example. You take care of the entry to your evidence with your topic sentence. This gives the reader an idea of the main point that evidence is supporting. Then end your paragraph by reminding the reader what your evidence proved. In other words, put a second piece of bread on that sandwich before moving on.

CONCLUSION

In the last chapter, we discussed the importance of leaving time to write a strong conclusion, even if you need to cut a body paragraph a little short. Remember: Without a conclusion, you don't have a full formal essay, and your score will reflect that. Your conclusion serves several purposes:

- It ties all of your body paragraphs together. ("Considering all of these arguments together . . .")
- It reminds the reader of the centrality of your argument. ("Ultimately, we must remember the most important point . . .")
- It provides a chance to leave a lasting impression on the reader. ("We cannot overlook the importance of this issue . . .")

Make sure your conclusion does all of the following:

- Restates your thesis, not by repeating it word for word but by paraphrasing it to remind the reader of your main idea.
- Summarizes your points. Again, don't repeat them all, but reference them briefly to reinforce their strength and relationship to your thesis.
- Wraps up the argument. By this point in the essay, you should be writing with the assumption that your reader agrees with you. Close with clear language about the rightness and importance of your argument.

PUTTING IT ALL TOGETHER

LANGUAGE

In your practice for the ACT English test, you're learning rules and principles to help you make the best choices about wording in the English passages. It's important that you keep these rules and principles in mind for the ACT Writing test as well. Remember that the last step of the Kaplan Method for ACT Writing is to proofread. If you spend an adequate amount of time on the prompt, plan, and produce steps, you'll have only a few minutes to proofread. Let's give some attention to the best ways to use this time effectively.

BE CAREFUL WITH PRONOUNS

When you're writing under pressure, as you are on the ACT, it's easy to make some grammatical mistakes that affect the logic of your essay. The use of pronouns is an area that many students have trouble with. If you train yourself to pay attention to pronouns and think about what's involved in using them correctly, it will be easier to catch pronoun problems and correct them even when you're proofreading quickly. Everything you know about pronouns that you apply to the English test also holds true for the Writing test. Refresh yourself on the guidelines described here.

PRONOUN REFERENCE RULE

A pronoun refers to a noun or another pronoun. Do not use a pronoun if the sentence it's in or the sentence before it doesn't contain a word for the pronoun to refer logically to.

PRONOUN NUMBER RULE

A pronoun must agree in number with the noun or pronoun it refers to. Do not use a plural pronoun to refer to a singular noun.

PRONOUN SHIFT RULE

Do not switch between the words *one* and *you* in a given context.

For most people, it's easier to spot mistakes in something written by someone else. It can be tough to identify errors in your own writing, but pronouns are an area you can easily work on. Try the following pronoun exercise.

WRITING EXERCISE 2

In the following essay excerpts, watch for errors in the use of pronouns. Circle the mistakes and write down the corrections.

1. When one works hard on academics all semester, you expect to get some kind of recognition.

   ____

2. School authorities shouldn't try to control the lives of students completely. If a student doesn't want to perform community service, they shouldn't have to.

   ____

3. The school administration has given a lot of thought to the value of the honor roll. They feel that by doing away with the honor roll, students will lose motivation to work hard.

   ____

4. Our school administration is debating whether or not to allow the use of films in the classroom. They say that movies are effective at capturing the interest of students.

   ____

5. A girl who has attended a single-sex school is likely to report that they feel teachers take their opinions seriously.

   ____

6. Student council exists to serve the student body. Therefore, they should have the responsibility of electing the representatives.

   ____

7. A bilingual classroom doesn't help a nonnative English speaker learn English quickly. They should get tutoring and extra help, but they should attend classes in English.

____

8. I've read the newspaper every day for the past five months, and they say that education is one of the most pressing issues in the upcoming election.

____

9. Every student deserves the right to wear what they want to, within reasonable boundaries of course.

____

10. Educators, because they have more experience, know what's best for students. They should be the ones who decide about new course offerings.

____

This exercise should have increased your awareness of sloppy pronoun usage. Question 1 is wrong because it shifts between *one* and *you.* Many of the others are wrong because the pronoun *they,* which is plural, appears without a plural noun that it can logically refer to. Here are some corrections you could have made. Note that you might have come up with different revisions that effectively correct the pronoun errors.

1. When one works hard on academics all semester, **one expects** [*not* you expect] to get some kind of recognition.
2. School authorities shouldn't try to control the lives of students completely. If a student doesn't want to perform community service, **he or she** [*not* they] shouldn't have to.
3. The school administration has given a lot of thought to the value of the honor roll. **Administrators** [*not* They] feel that by doing away with the honor roll, students will lose motivation to work hard.
4. Our school **administrators are** [*not* administration is] debating whether or not to allow the use of films in the classroom. They say that movies are effective at capturing the interest of students.
5. A girl who has attended a single-sex school is likely to report that **she feels** [*not* they feel] teachers take **her** [*not* their] opinions seriously.
6. Student council exists to serve the student body. Therefore, **students** [*not* they] should have the responsibility of electing the representatives.
7. A bilingual classroom doesn't help **nonnative English speakers** [*not* a nonnative English speaker] learn English quickly. They should get tutoring and extra help, but they should attend classes in English.

8. I've read the newspaper every day for the past five months, and **many reporters and columnists** [*not* they] say that education is one of the most pressing issues in the upcoming election.

9. **All students deserve** [*not* Every student deserves] the right to wear what they want to, within reasonable boundaries of course.

10. **Educators, because they have more experience, know what's best for students and should be the ones who decide about new course offerings.** [The problem is that *they* in the original sentence could logically refer to either *students* or *educators*. You could also correct the problem by simply changing *they* to *educators* instead of rewriting the whole sentence.

AVOID SLANG AND CLICHÉS

Although some slang words and expressions are acceptable in ordinary conversation, you should avoid slang in your ACT essay. The purpose of the essay is to present a logical argument based on reasoning and evidence, and the language you choose should reflect the seriousness of the task. As you practice, become sensitive to the tone of various expressions. If you think something is slang or too informal, ask yourself if there's a more appropriate phrasing.

Like slang, clichéd language is best avoided in your ACT essay. A cliché is a worn-out, overused expression. Your essay should show that you're taking a fresh and thoughtful approach to the question posed, and the overuse of clichés undercuts the serious and thoughtful attention you bring to your argument.

WRITING EXERCISE 3

In the following sentences, circle slang and clichéd expressions. Write an alternative in the space provided.

1. Most kids don't have time to hold jobs during the school year.

____

2. The idea of making math teachers give writing assignments to students is just crazy.

____

3. Politicians say they have everyone's best interests in mind, but those guys don't really see the big picture.

____

4. It's true that some kids do act like jerks, but the entire student body shouldn't have to pay for the misbehavior of a few bad apples.

____

5. If this change is implemented, all students will have the chance to get the best ever education.

____

6. It's been shown over and over again that everyone needs encouragement.

____

Phrases such as "kids" and "crazy" and "best ever" detract from your argument by sounding far too casual. You're trying to gain points for seriousness and care, so your language should reflect maturity of writing. Here are some corrections you could have made. Note that you might have come up with different revisions that also avoid slang or clichés.

1. *Kids* is slang. Change to *teens, teenagers, high school students*, or *adolescents.*
2. *Just crazy* is slang. Change to *unrealistic, unworkable*, or *impractical.*
3. *Those guys* is slang. Change to *they* or *most of them.*
4. *Kids* and *jerks* are slang, and *a few bad apples* is a cliché. Rewrite the sentence as something like, *It's true that some students do act inappropriately, but the entire student body shouldn't have to pay for the mistakes of a few.*
5. *The best ever* is a cliché. Change to *a sound* or *an excellent.*
6. *Over and over again* is a cliché (and it's wordy). Change to *repeatedly.*

USE CORRECT AND VARIED SENTENCE STRUCTURE

Sentence structure is tested directly in the ACT English test, but it's also very important for the essay you produce in the Writing section. To apply the principles of correct sentence structure in your essay, think about how you combine groups of words into sentences. You can avoid sentence fragments by making sure that each sentence includes a subject and a verb and expresses a complete thought. You can avoid run-ons by making sure that ideas are joined with proper punctuation and connections (transitions) words. The following exercise is designed to help you review what you learned about sentence structure in the English section.

WRITING EXERCISE 4

The following is a run-on sentence. Write out three acceptable ways to correct it.

Teenagers value driving as a privilege, most work hard to be safe drivers.

1. ____

2. ____

3. ____

Here are our answers, each followed by a general guideline.

1. Because teenagers value driving as a privilege, most work hard to be safe drivers. [Use a connections word to introduce the first clause.]

2. Teenagers value driving as a privilege, so most work hard to be safe drivers. [Use a comma followed by a FANBOYS word to combine the two clauses.]

3. Teenagers value driving as a privilege; therefore, most work hard to be safe drivers. [Use a semicolon and a non-FANBOYS connections word to combine the two clauses.]

Varied sentence structure means sentences of different lengths. Your essay shouldn't use all short, choppy sentences, but you should use some shorter sentences to provide variety among longer, complicated sentences. During the proofread step, you're likely to find spots in your essay where you can make a few quick adjustments, say, inserting a word or changing the punctuation, to help you improve your sentence structure. If you follow the guidelines for properly combining clauses into sentences, your essay's sentence structure should be in good shape.

AVOID UNNECESSARY REPETITION

When you're writing an essay under very tight time constraints, as you must on the ACT, it's easy to find yourself using the same words and phrases frequently. Such repetition can detract from the effectiveness of your essay. You need to stay focused on the topic, that's true. However, if you use the same words and phrases repeatedly, it's a sign that you may not be developing your ideas thoroughly. Thus, the first remedy for needless repetition comes in the planning stage: Make sure you've reflected carefully about your viewpoint. To earn a high score, you must go beyond the ideas offered in the prompt; you must expand upon your own position with reasoning and evidence. Thinking through your plan and writing brief notes in the test booklet help to ensure that you'll develop your ideas adequately during the production step. It can also help if you think of some synonyms for key words and phrases that are important to the topic.

WRITING EXERCISE 5

Imagine that the topic of your essay question somehow relates to academic success. Take a few minutes to write down some words and phrases that might be relevant in the space provided:

____

____

____

____

There are no right or wrong answers here, and of course, the ones you choose to use in your essay will depend upon the focus of the particular question and the angle from which you approach it. Some phrases that relate to "academic success" are *academic achievement, excellence, scholarship, academic arena, intellectual development, effective learning strategies, motivation, diligence.*

> Though thinking carefully during the planning step can help you minimize repetition in your essay, repetition is still something you should watch for when you're proofreading. Making a slight change in a word or phrasing is quick to do and can introduce greater variety and effectiveness in your choice of vocabulary.

WRITING EXERCISE 6

The following examples all include unnecessary repetition. Some could be made more concise. In each example, underline the repeated words and phrases, and then rewrite the examples to be less wordy and more varied in word choice.

1. Funding arts programs is important to student achievement. Studies show that musical training leads to increased student achievement.

____

____

2. Bilingual education is an important topic in education today. Bilingual education is necessary for students whose first language is not English.

____

____

3. My school allocates too much money to sports programs. I know many students who don't participate in sports. Money allocated for sports programs doesn't benefit them. The school could achieve a better balance by allocating more money to programs that promote social activities and creative pursuits.

____

____

____

4. School newspapers serve several important functions. One of them is to let students decide what is worthy of publication and what is not. This function of a school newspaper would be completely taken away if a panel of teachers were to take over the decisions about what is worthy of publication.

____

____

____

For many students, proofreading is the most difficult part of writing. Remember, the ACT essay graders don't expect your essay to be flawless. However, you can improve your writing even by making only a few small corrections during the proofreading step. Don't worry if you didn't make the same corrections that we did. However, do work on identifying repetition and wordiness in your own writing. Here are some possible ways of correcting the examples. We've reprinted them and highlighted repetition and wordiness in boldface type.

1. Funding arts programs is important to **student achievement**. Studies show that musical training leads to increased **student achievement**.

   Funding arts programs is important because studies show that musical training leads to increased student achievement [or "academic performance"].

2. **Bilingual education** is an important topic in **education** today. **Bilingual education** is necessary for students whose first language is not English.

   Bilingual education is an important topic today because public schools serve many students whose first language is not English.

3. My school **allocates** too much **money** to **sports programs**. I know many students who don't participate in **sports**. Money allocated for **sports programs** doesn't benefit them. The school could achieve a better balance by **allocating** more **money** to **programs** that promote social activities and creative pursuits.

   My school allocates too much money to sports programs. This funding doesn't benefit the many students I know who are not athletically inclined. The school could achieve a better balance by directing more resources to social activities and creative pursuits.

4. **School newspapers** serve several important **functions**. One of them is to let students decide **what is worthy of publication and what is not**. This **function** of a **school newspaper** would be completely taken away if a panel of teachers were to take over the decisions about **what is worthy of publication**.

   School newspapers serve several important functions, one of which is giving students the opportunity to decide what is appropriate for publication. This function would be removed if the determination about what is worthy of publication were made by a panel of teachers instead of students.

SCORING

Step	A High-Scoring Essay	A Low-Scoring Essay
Step 1: Prompt	Clearly develops a position on the prompt	Does not clearly state a position
Step 2: Plan	Supports with concrete, relevant examples	Is general, repetitious, or overly simplistic
Step 3: Produce	Maintains clear focus and organization	Digresses or has weak organization
Step 4: Proofread	Shows competent use of language	Contains errors that reduce clarity

Kaplan has found this approach useful in our many years of experience with hundreds of sample essay statements on a wide range of tests. Let's look at what the test makers tell you about how the essays are scored.

To score a 4, you must:

- Answer the question
- Support ideas with examples
- Show logical thought and organization
- Avoid major or frequent errors that make your writing unclear

Organization and clarity are key to an above-average essay. If the reader can't follow your train of thought—if ideas aren't clearly organized or if grammatical errors, misspellings, and incorrect word choices make your writing unclear—you can't do well.

To score a 5, all you have to add to a 4 is:

- Address the topic in depth

In other words, offer more examples and details. The test graders love specific examples, and the more concrete your examples are, the more they clarify your thinking and keep you and your essay focused.

To score a 6, all you have to add to a 5 is:

- Make transitions smoother and show variety in syntax and vocabulary

Use words from the prompt to tie paragraphs together rather than rely exclusively on connectors like *however* and *therefore*. Vary your sentence structure, sometimes using simple sentences and other times using compound and complex ones. Adding a few college-level vocabulary words will also boost your score.

Scoring the essay	In your essay, you must ...	Your essay will not be affected by ...
• The essay is scored by two readers, who each assign a score between 1 and 6. • The scores are added to generate a final essay score that is between 2 and 12. • Your ACT essay score is *not* included in your ACT Composite score. When you take this optional Writing test, you receive an additional score called an ELA score, which is a weighted composite of your Reading, English, and Writing scaled scores.	• answer the assignment question. • show an understanding of the issue. • show an understanding of the complexity of the issue. • have a distinct introduction and conclusion. • use effective organization • have effective development of ideas. • maintain sustained focus • demonstrate effective language use. • use effective transitions • not have errors that detract from clarity and readability.	• which point of view you choose to defend. • factual errors. • a few minor spelling or grammatical errors.

VIEW FROM THE OTHER SIDE: GETTING YOUR SCORE AND GRADING ESSAYS

GETTING YOUR SCORE

We've referenced the idea a few times that your essay score is *holistic*—that is, that it reflects the grader's overall impression of your writing skill, rather than a strict equation of "right" and "wrong" answers. There is not, for example, an automatic point deduction for a misspelled word or a misused punctuation mark. However, an essay riddled with poor punctuation and spelling will be harder for a grader to give a high score. Still, there are elements essay graders consistently look for as hallmarks of strong writing. The grading criteria include:

- Is the author's own perspective clearly stated?
- Does the body of the essay assess and analyze an additional perspective?
- Is the relevance of each paragraph clear?
- Does the author start a new paragraph for each new idea?
- Is each sentence in a paragraph relevant to the point made in that paragraph?
- Are transitions clear?
- Is the essay easy to read? Is it engaging?
- Are sentences varied?
- Is vocabulary used effectively? Is college-level vocabulary used?

While a perfect essay will address all of these points, a strong essay that gets a 4 or 5 from each grader will have to do fairly well on most of the points. An essay that misses any of them completely or does many of them at a very low level will have a hard time getting a high score, and the more basic the requirement, the more it affects your score. For example, while an otherwise-strong essay that has only basic transitions can still do well, an essay that doesn't directly answer the question cannot score higher than a 2 from each grader.

GRADING ESSAYS

Let's look at some sample essays based on the "Bilingual Accreditation" prompt we've seen. Evaluate each essay against the points we've discussed, and give it a score.

SAMPLE ESSAY 1

Some people think schools should encourage bilingualism but should not be expected to offer special classes or programs. Other people think offering bilingual accreditation weakens high school classes. Others say bilingual accreditation should be offered but it needs to be thoughtfully implemented. In my opinion, schools should definitely give the option of bilingualism.

Firstly, schools should always encourage bilingualism. Students better in life with more than one language. Second, weakening high school doesn't make sense. More languages mean more learning.

Finally and most importantly, there should be bilingual accreditation. Students won't be able to cognizant and value diverse languages if not given the opportunity. Extra certification on diplomas is good for getting kids into college. So high schools should have bilingual accreditation.

Score:______/6

It should have been fairly easy to see that this isn't a strong essay. This essay would get a score of 2 or 3 out of 6. The author does state a clear opinion, but half of the essay is a direct copy of the prompt—the graders will notice this and those sentences won't help the score. The time and space spent just quoting the prompt was completely wasted—it earned the writer zero points.

The rest of the essay is organized and uses transition words (*firstly* and *finally*). The author states her thesis, acknowledges the three perspectives provided in the prompt, and then offers a conclusion. However, none of this is discussed fully enough—no concrete details or examples are given. In the second paragraph, for instance, the author should have added examples that demonstrate how encouraging bilingual education is both beneficial to students and not a threat to the quality of high school curriculum.

The language is understandable, but there are significant errors affecting clarity. For instance, the second sentence of paragraph 2 is a fragment—there is no verb. Some vocabulary words are used without a clear understanding of their meaning: In paragraph 3, "won't be able to cognizant" is incorrect; perhaps the student meant "won't be able to understand."

It is possible that the writer couldn't think of good ideas to support each point, waited too long to start writing, and had to write in a hurry.

Let's look at another essay. Read it quickly and decide how you would score it.

SAMPLE ESSAY 2

Some people think that schools should provide enough education in a different language for students to be certified as bilingual. Others think this will weaken the curriculum. Still others think the accreditation should be offered but carefully administered so that graduation from that school would indicate the completed high school curriculum, and this is the option I agree with.

The third perspective posits that while students should be given the opportunity to learn in other languages and be accredited as bilingual, the courses given need to be carefully selected. In reality, all classes need to be carefully selected so this is not a problem for bilingual classes. And if the classes selected were all optional, not required, it would not affect students who still want to learn everything in English.

As schools work to accommodate students who wish to pursue a bilingual education, administrators must keep in mind that students who do not want an additional bilingual accreditation should still have every opportunity to excel as they work toward their high school diplomas. Given the rigorous demands of the current job climate, students will greatly benefit from any additional marketable skills that they can acquire during their high school career.

The first perspective argues that schools should encourage bilingual fluency but not add any bilingual classes, which is in direct contrast to my position. Instead, the school administrators should make the existing curriculum better so that traditional education is really good. Certainly a high school curriculum should be as good as it can be and we should always be looking for ways to make it better. That often means adding new courses.

Being bilingual in a world with international interaction can't help but be useful. I fully support perspective three. Expanding courses offered in a curriculum is always better than restricting them, especially when they serve such an important need as the ability to communicate with others in their own language.

Score:______ /6

This essay is pretty good—it would earn a 4. The position is clearly stated, and some supporting reasoning is given.

However, the reasoning is too general and the writing is too ordinary to earn the top score. Let's see how it could be improved.

TURNING A 4 INTO A 6

The essay plunges right into the first point of view offered in the prompt. It could be improved by introducing the issue with a general statement, such as:

> In today's world where international education standards are very high and the U.S. needs to remain competitive, educators are looking for ways to enhance high school curriculum. One way is offering classes in languages other than English.

In the last sentence of the first paragraph, the writer indicates that she agrees with Perspective 3. It is good to include your thesis in the introductory paragraph, but it would be better to make it clear where the position from the prompt ends and the author's position begins, perhaps like this:

> Still others think the accreditation should be offered but carefully administered so that graduation from that school would indicate the completed high school curriculum, and this is the option I agree with. I would further argue that schools should not only carefully implement bilingual programs to suit students who want to become fluent in two languages, but also provide supplemental non-traditional courses for students pursuing their entire education in English.

The second paragraph is relevant and organized—it covers one of the three positions offered in the prompt. However it would be better if the writer discussed this perspective using real-life information, such as:

> Since core classes might be given in two languages, and students select which one they want, all students still study the core curriculum and preserve the integrity of the diploma. Schools have always taught languages in high school so a French or Spanish course taught as a bilingual class makes perfect sense. Bilingual classes are also advantageous for students who do well and want to challenge themselves. So a French literature class can be taught in French while students read in French also.

The third paragraph addresses Perspective 2. Discussing concrete ideas would bolster the essay. Plus, graders look to see if writers are able to provide analysis regarding how the perspectives relate to each other. For example:

> Every dollar spent to accommodate bilingual education should be matched with equal funding for other types of educational enrichment such as STEM training and career-oriented electives. That way, every student can benefit from classes that go beyond traditional education, whether the classes concentrate on language, science, technology, engineering, mathematics, or future careers.

Paragraph four is pretty good, but expanding the discussion helps to increase your score. For instance:

For instance, computer courses didn't exist a few years ago, but they are in schools now because it's important for people to be able to use computers. It's the same thing with bilingual courses. Most of the world uses English as a second language, and many people speak at least two languages. So it's only right that to stay competitive, U.S. students should also be fluent in two languages; this is particularly important in careers that require international work. Also, the argument simply says that these classes would only be for interested students, so it doesn't affect everyone. And finally, how can the schools encourage bilingual fluency if they don't provide a place for students to practice another language?

The fifth paragraph reiterates the writer's thesis, but it could benefit from reorganization and additional development, such as:

Being bilingual in a world with international interaction can't help but be useful. I fully support perspective three <u>because it opens up possibilities for all students without denying anyone a full high school curriculum leading to a meaningful diploma. Recognizing the benefits of being bilingual, and making bilingual courses available but optional, is the best of both worlds.</u> Expanding courses offered in a curriculum is always better than impeding them, especially when they serve such an important need as the ability to communicate with others in their own language.

Here's how this essay would look with the improvements we've suggested.

In today's world where international education standards are very high and the U.S. needs to remain competitive, educators are looking for ways to enhance high school curriculum. One way is offering classes in languages other than English. Some people think that schools should provide enough education in a different language for students to be certified as bilingual. Others think this will weaken the curriculum. Still others think the accreditation should be offered but carefully administered so that graduation from that school would indicate the completed high school curriculum, and this is the option I agree with. I would further argue that schools should not only carefully implement bilingual programs to suit students who want to become fluent in two languages, but also provide supplemental non-traditional courses for students pursuing their entire education in English.

The third perspective posits that while students should be given the opportunity to learn in other languages and be accredited as bilingual, the courses given need to be carefully selected. In reality, all classes need to be carefully selected so this is not a problem for bilingual classes. And if the classes selected were all optional, not required, it would not affect students who still want to learn everything in English. Since core classes might be given in two languages, and students select which one they want, all students still study the core curriculum and preserve the integrity of the diploma. Schools have always taught languages in high school so a French or Spanish course taught as a bilingual class makes perfect sense. Bilingual classes are also advantageous for students who do well and want to challenge themselves. So a French literature class can be taught in French while students read in French also.

As schools work to accommodate students who wish to pursue a bilingual education, administrators must keep in mind that students who do not want an additional bilingual accreditation should still have every opportunity to excel as they work toward their high school diplomas. Every dollar spent to accommodate bilingual education should be matched with equal funding for other types of educational enrichment such as STEM training and career-oriented electives. That way, every student can benefit from classes that go beyond traditional education, whether the classes concentrate on language, science, technology, engineering, mathematics, or future careers. Given the rigorous demands of the current job climate, students will greatly benefit from any additional marketable skills that they can acquire during their high school careers.

The first perspective argues that schools should encourage bilingual fluency but not add any bilingual classes, which is in direct contrast to my position. Instead, the school administrators should make the existing curriculum better so that traditional education is really good. Certainly a high school curriculum should be as good as it can be and we should always be looking for ways to make it better. That often means adding new courses. For instance, computer courses didn't exist a few years ago, but they are in schools now because it's important for people to be able to use computers. It's the same thing with bilingual courses. Most of the world uses English as a second language, and many people speak at least two languages. So it's only right that to stay competitive, U.S. students should also be fluent in two languages; this is particularly important in careers that require international work. Also, the argument simply says that these classes would only be for interested students, so it doesn't affect everyone. And finally, how can the schools encourage bilingual fluency if they don't provide a place for students to practice another language?

Being bilingual in a world with international interaction can't help but be useful. I fully support perspective three because it opens up possibilities for all students without denying anyone a full high school curriculum leading to a meaningful diploma. Recognizing the benefits of being bilingual, and making bilingual courses available but optional, is the best of both worlds. Expanding courses offered in a curriculum is always better than restricting them, especially when they serve such an important need as the ability to communicate with others in their own language.

This is now a 6 essay. It addresses the task both fully and concretely. The first paragraph introduces all the lines of reasoning that will be used, demonstrating to the reader that the writer knew right from the start where this essay was headed. The development of ideas is clear and logical, and the paragraphs reflect this organization.

The author shows a high level of skill with language. The transitions between paragraphs are clear and guide the reader through the reasoning. The sentence structure varies throughout the passage and is at times complex.

So what did we do to our 4 to make it a 6?

- We added examples and detail.
- We varied sentence structure and added stronger vocabulary (*advantageous, accomodate, enrichment*).
- While length alone doesn't make a 6, we've added detail to our original essay.

SUMMARY

In this chapter, we went over all of the necessary pieces of a great essay for the ACT Writing test. Use this chapter to work on the individual pieces.

Then, we saw how those pieces are put together into an overall essay, and you had a chance to work on some general skills.

Finally, you learned the details of how an essay is scored and had a chance to put that into practice and score some essays yourself.

Use this knowledge as you practice your essay with prompts in the next chapter. Time yourself accurately, and score your essays honestly. That will help you find which aspects are your areas of opportunity.

Remember to keep practicing. Use Kaplan's Essay Template each time you work on an essay so that you will be able to easily organize your ideas on Test Day. If you're unable to fairly assess yourself, get a second opinion. Have someone else help you by reading your essay and assessing how clear it is.

Refine the pieces and practice the flow. Soon enough, you'll be able to master the ACT Writing test.

CHAPTER 21

Writing Prompt I

Here we go!

Treat the following essay like the one you'll encounter on Test Day and see how you do.

Starting the moment you read the prompt, keep track of your time. Allot 40 total minutes, divided up according to the Kaplan Method. Remember to take a good 3 minutes to read and fully understand the prompt so you can respond to it effectively, another 5 minutes to plan your essay so you know you have all the pieces, about 30 minutes producing, and the last 2 minutes proofreading and making *minor* edits.

Finally, take the time to read and evaluate your essay, asking yourself the same questions the graders will on Test Day, and give yourself a grade. If you'd like a second opinion on your score, get one! An English teacher or friend or family member with strong writing skills can help you fine-tune your skills. Use this practice essay to focus your energy for the Practice Tests at the end of the book.

Remember the Kaplan Method—Understand the Prompt, Make a Plan, Produce Your Essay, and Proofread.

Directions: This is a test of your writing skills. You will have **forty** (40) minutes to write an essay in English. Before you begin planning and writing your essay, read the writing prompt carefully to understand exactly what you are being asked to do. Your essay will be evaluated on the evidence it provides of your ability to:

- clearly state your own perspective on the issue and analyze the relationship between your perspective and at least one other perspective
- develop and support your ideas with reasoning and examples
- organize your ideas clearly and logically
- communicate your ideas effectively in standard written English

Essay Task

Write a unified, coherent essay in which you evaluate multiple perspectives on experiential education. In your essay, be sure to:

- clearly state your own perspective on the issue and analyze the relationship between your perspective and at least one other perspective
- develop and support your ideas with reasoning and examples
- organize your ideas clearly and logically
- communicate your ideas effectively in standard written English

Your perspective may be in full agreement with any of the others, in partial agreement, or wholly different. Whatever the case, support your ideas with logical reasoning and detailed, persuasive examples.

Planning Your Essay

Use a blank sheet of paper to generate ideas and plan your essay. You may wish to consider the following as you think critically about the task:

Strengths and weaknesses of the three given perspectives

- What insights do they offer, and what do they fail to consider?
- Why might they be persuasive to others, or why might they fail to persuade?

Your own knowledge, experience, and values

- What is your perspective on this issue, and what are its strengths and weaknesses?
- How will you support your perspective in your essay?

Experiential Education

Experiential education is a philosophy that holds that students learn best through direct experience. Hands-on learning is said to promote deeper understanding because students are able to apply concepts and theories to physical situations. Rather than being required to memorize facts, students are given the opportunity to create physical evidence of logical reasoning and are thus better equipped to apply the same reasoning to new situations. Since all teachers aim to impart critical thinking in their classrooms, should they be expected to provide more hands-on learning opportunities? As educators aim to continuously improve the quality of the education they offer to students, consideration should be given to better incorporating hands-on learning.

Read and carefully consider these perspectives. Each suggests a particular approach regarding experiential education.

Perspective One	Perspective Two	Perspective Three
Some argue that to accept a theory without experiencing it is to learn nothing at all. Teachers need to provide opportunities for experiential involvement if they expect students to truly comprehend each lesson plan objective.	Experiential education is an integral part of readying students to pursue careers in the science, technology, engineering, and math fields, but not all disciplines. If students are expected to perform skill-based tasks in these fields after they graduate, they should be provided a strong foundation on which to build their careers. However, teachers should not be expected to supply experiential learning where it is not appropriate.	Schools cannot be expected to offer hands-on learning for students. Not only is it costly, but also it may not be effective for all learners. Students will be better served if schools invest money in other educational models and opportunities.

ANSWERS AND EXPLANATIONS

MODEL ESSAY

SCORE OF 6

Here's one possible way to approach this essay prompt. Remember that the opinion you express is less important than the way you present it. Notice that this response includes a logically arranged argument with specific examples.

Response:

Teachers often tell us that learning is fun, and the best way to convince us that learning is enjoyable is to give us activities that keep us engaged (and awake). The issue here is whether teachers should provide more hands-on learning experiences because doing so would help all students learn and remember better. On the other hand, others say that it's possible to learn without doing and that schools should use their money for other educational purposes rather than trying to make everything hands-on learning. I believe that the best learning comes from hands-on work.

I know from experience that I learn better when I can actually do something myself. When students do projects such as growing plants, they really learn about the science because they are part of making that science work. This is analogous to learning how to ride a bike. A child can read about it, watch videos on it, and even watch someone actually ride a bike, but he doesn't learn how to do it until he gets on a bike and pedals away. Thus, it is important that the teacher provide opportunities for students to do as much hands-on learning as possible. However, those who think that students don't learn anything unless they actually do it are wrong. There are ideas that can't be experimented with. How can students re-create the Big Bang or evolution? But just because they can't actually do this doesn't mean students don't learn. There is a lot that can be learned from reading and learning from experts. However, if there is a choice between learning by doing and not having that opportunity, learning by doing is the better way to teach and learn.

On the other hand, other people think that experiential education is important only for students who will work in a career that requires that they do things themselves, such as engineering and technology. It is important that students who will enter careers that are skill based have the opportunity to practice this in school. School is supposed to teach what is needed for students later in life, and knowing how to do experiments or re-create what others have done should be part of this. But the people who argue for this say it is important only for students who will need it in their future careers. This means that some students, particularly those who don't know what career they want, will not get the benefit of hands-on experiences. That splits students into two groups: those who learn by doing and those who don't. All students learn well by doing, so it would not be fair to offer it only to some students. How can teachers know what is appropriate for students in their future careers if even the students don't yet know? This solution is not a good one because it assumes things that can't be supported.

Finally, it is shortsighted to argue that rather than create opportunities for hands-on learning, schools should spend their money on other things because learning by doing is expensive and may not be good for all students. There's always the problem that not all students learn in the same way so there's no one kind of learning that is best for everyone. But that doesn't mean teachers shouldn't provide hands-on opportunities. Actually, this is a good way to reach all students because it involves working with your hands, maybe some reading and talking too, and critical thinking, so it uses lots of ways of learning. It is foolish to have the opportunity to do something important and not do it just because some people may not benefit from it or it will cost money. Teachers should give students the opportunity to learn in a hands-on way as much as possible.

In the real world, when we need to learn something new, like how to cook or use a computer program, if it's possible to learn by doing while having someone help and direct us, that is the best way to learn and the way that schools should teach. Studies, and my own experience, show that everyone can benefit from hands-on education; that is the way we learn and remember best.

CHAPTER 22

Writing Prompt II

Directions: This is a test of your writing skills. You will have **forty** (40) minutes to write an essay in English. Before you begin planning and writing your essay, read the writing prompt carefully to understand exactly what you are being asked to do. Your essay will be evaluated on the evidence it provides of your ability to:

- clearly state your own perspective on the issue and analyze the relationship between your perspective and at least one other perspective
- develop and support your ideas with reasoning and examples
- organize your ideas clearly and logically
- communicate your ideas effectively in standard written English

Essay Task

Write a unified, coherent essay in which you evaluate multiple perspectives on attendance policies. In your essay, be sure to:

- clearly state your own perspective on the issue and analyze the relationship between your perspective and at least one other perspective
- develop and support your ideas with reasoning and examples
- organize your ideas clearly and logically
- communicate your ideas effectively in standard written English

Your perspective may be in full agreement with any of the others, in partial agreement, or wholly different. Whatever the case, support your ideas with logical reasoning and detailed, persuasive examples.

Planning Your Essay

Use a blank sheet of paper to generate ideas and plan your essay. You may wish to consider the following as you think critically about the task:

Strengths and weaknesses of the three given perspectives

- What insights do they offer, and what do they fail to consider?
- Why might they be persuasive to others, or why might they fail to persuade?

Your own knowledge, experience, and values

- What is your perspective on this issue, and what are its strengths and weaknesses?
- How will you support your perspective in your essay?

Attendance Policies

Students are required to be in attendance during the school day unless they are ill, have a doctor's appointment, or need to attend a funeral. Parents are allowed to take students out of school for other reasons, but prior approval is often required. Truancy, or unexcused absenteeism, is a problem that many schools have yet to solve. Since reducing truancy increases student success, should schools be doing more to prevent unexcused absences? Considering that students rely on educators to offer guidance and support, it is wise for schools to assist students in attending school as regularly as possible.

Read and carefully consider these perspectives. Each suggests a particular approach regarding truancy.

Perspective One	Perspective Two	Perspective Three
Schools should contact law enforcement officers to report students who skip school regularly. In addition to receiving detention for unexcused absences, students who engage in truancy should be given criminal records. This additional consequence will help discourage students from missing school.	Truancy is a symptom rather than a core issue. Students who skip school regularly often do so because of transportation difficulties, social problems, violence concerns, or lack of interest. Addressing the core issues is the key to increasing student attendance, and schools should develop programs to help students overcome obstacles that prevent them from coming to school.	Schools should offer helpful alternative instruction for students who regularly miss school. Whether students are allowed to attend school on the weekends or are required to take classes online, schools should provide students every opportunity to complete their courses and graduate.

ANSWERS AND EXPLANATIONS

EXAMPLE ESSAY

"Be cool; stay in school," is the type of saying that may sound silly to high school students. Even though that phrase isn't really sophisticated, it does provide very wise advice. Attending school is incredibly important, and some people argue that unexcused absences should be reported to the police. Other people want to focus on treating the underlying causes of truancy rather than doling out harsh punishments. Still others think that schools should provide alternative instruction options for students who have trouble getting to school on a regular basis. All three options have the same goal, which is to help students most at risk for missing school, and I think that schools should incorporate the best parts of all three approaches into their truancy-reduction policies.

The idea of having a police record because I skipped school is extremely scary and would certainly prevent me from missing school. If students know that their school will report them to the police after a specific number of unexcused absences, they will be more likely to find a way to get to school. Teenagers don't always do the right thing because it's a good idea but rather because not doing the right thing will get them in a lot of trouble. For example, many high school students turn in their assignments on time because they don't want teachers to deduct points for late submissions. The fear of consequence can promote good behavior in both homework habits and school attendance.

While avoiding a harsh consequence is a good reason to get to school, it's sometimes not compelling enough for students who are struggling with issues that make attending school very difficult. The best way to increase attendance for these students is to address the underlying problems. If students have transportation trouble, schools should help coordinate carpools and bus schedules. School counselors should be available to help students who have social issues or violence concerns. As for lack of interest, schools can offer before- and after-school activities such as intramural sports and social clubs to give students a reason to stay throughout the day.

Even with the best efforts, some students will invariably struggle with attendance. For those students, schools should offer as many opportunities for them to complete their coursework as possible. It is in society's best interest to facilitate education, especially for at-risk youth. Now that technology allows students to learn from nearly anywhere, schools should offer students the option to study remotely. Students will benefit from a high school diploma, of course, and they will be able to say that their teachers did everything they could to give them the best chance at a good life.

Attending school isn't just about learning facts. The school environment provides students with the opportunity to learn how to employ necessary social skills, collaborate with peers, and communicate effectively. The only way for students to develop these skills is to actually attend school. Every measure should be taken to reduce truancy, including the threat of a criminal record, the mitigation of underlying causes, and the option to pursue alternative instruction. That way, students don't have to just take our "be cool; stay in school" word for it — they'll show up because, really, with all those measures in place, how could they not?

SUMMARY

Checkup time!

Record what score you believe your essay would earn. Now, identify three items that you believe went very well. Next, identify three items you could improve to raise your score on Test Day. Did your essay have a strong introduction and conclusion, with five paragraphs total? Did you use real-world examples? Did you discuss at least one of the three perspectives?

Keep practicing using the other prompts in this book. With a regular cycle of review and practice, you'll soon be a master of the ACT Writing test!

Practice Tests

ACT Practice Test One
ANSWER SHEET

ENGLISH TEST

1. A B C D	11. A B C D	21. A B C D	31. A B C D	41. A B C D	51. A B C D	61. A B C D	71. A B C D
2. F G H J	12. F G H J	22. F G H J	32. F G H J	42. F G H J	52. F G H J	62. F G H J	72. F G H J
3. A B C D	13. A B C D	23. A B C D	33. A B C D	43. A B C D	53. A B C D	63. A B C D	73. A B C D
4. F G H J	14. F G H J	24. F G H J	34. F G H J	44. F G H J	54. F G H J	64. F G H J	74. F G H J
5. A B C D	15. A B C D	25. A B C D	35. A B C D	45. A B C D	55. A B C D	65. A B C D	75. A B C D
6. F G H J	16. F G H J	26. F G H J	36. F G H J	46. F G H J	56. F G H J	66. F G H J	
7. A B C D	17. A B C D	27. A B C D	37. A B C D	47. A B C D	57. A B C D	67. A B C D	
8. F G H J	18. F G H J	28. F G H J	38. F G H J	48. F G H J	58. F G H J	68. F G H J	
9. A B C D	19. A B C D	29. A B C D	39. A B C D	49. A B C D	59. A B C D	69. A B C D	
10. F G H J	20. F G H J	30. F G H J	40. F G H J	50. F G H J	60. F G H J	70. F G H J	

READING TEST

1. A B C D	6. F G H J	11. A B C D	16. F G H J	21. A B C D	26. F G H J	31. A B C D	36. F G H J
2. F G H J	7. A B C D	12. F G H J	17. A B C D	22. F G H J	27. A B C D	32. F G H J	37. A B C D
3. A B C D	8. F G H J	13. A B C D	18. F G H J	23. A B C D	28. F G H J	33. A B C D	38. F G H J
4. F G H J	9. A B C D	14. F G H J	19. A B C D	24. F G H J	29. A B C D	34. F G H J	39. A B C D
5. A B C D	10. F G H J	15. A B C D	20. F G H J	25. A B C D	30. F G H J	35. A B C D	40. F G H J

ENGLISH TEST

45 Minutes—75 Questions

Directions: In the following five passages, certain words and phrases are underlined and numbered. In the right-hand column are alternatives for each underlined portion. Select the one that best conveys the idea, creates the most grammatically correct sentence, or is the most consistent with the style and tone of the passage. If you decide that the original version is best, select NO CHANGE. You may also find questions that ask about the entire passage or a section of the passage. These questions will correspond to small numbered boxes in the text. For these questions, decide which choice best accomplishes the purpose set out in the question stem. After you've selected the best choice, fill in the corresponding oval in your Answer Grid. For some questions, you'll need to read the context in order to answer correctly. Be sure to read until you have enough information to determine the correct answer choice.

PASSAGE I

THE PARTHENON

[1]

If you are like most visitors to Athens, you will make your way to the <u>Acropolis, the hill</u> [1] that once served as a fortified, strategic position over-looking the Aegean Sea—to see the Parthenon. This celebrated temple was dedicated in the fifth century B.C. to the goddess Athena. There is no more famous building in all of Greece; to

1. A. NO CHANGE
   B. Acropolis. The hill
   C. Acropolis—the hill
   D. Acropolis

GO ON TO THE NEXT PAGE

climb up its marble steps is <u>to have beheld</u> [2] a human creation that has attained the stature of a natural

2. F. NO CHANGE
   G. to behold
   H. beholding
   J. to be holding

phenomenon like the Grand Canyon. <u>You should also make an attempt to sample Athenian cuisine while you're there.</u> [3]

3. A. NO CHANGE
   B. Also make an attempt to sample Athenian cuisine while you're there.
   C. While you're there, you should also make an attempt to sample Athenian cuisine.
   D. OMIT the underlined portion.

[2]

Generations of architects <u>have proclaimed</u> [4] the Parthenon to be the most brilliantly conceived structure in the Western world. The genius of its construction

4. F. NO CHANGE
   G. has proclaimed
   H. proclaims
   J. are proclaiming

is <u>subtle for example</u> [5] the temple's columns were made to bulge outward slightly in order to compensate for

5. A. NO CHANGE
   B. subtle; for example
   C. subtle. For example
   D. subtle. For example,

the <u>fact, viewed from distance, that straight columns appear concave.</u> [6] Using this and other techniques, the

6. F. NO CHANGE
   G. fact that straight columns, viewed from a distance, appear concave.
   H. view from a distance: straight columns appearing concave.
   J. fact, when viewed from far away, that straight columns appear concave.

architects strove to create an optical <u>illusion of; uprightness,</u> [7] solidity, and permanence.

7. A. NO CHANGE
   B. illusion of: uprightness
   C. illusion of, uprightness
   D. illusion of uprightness,

GO ON TO THE NEXT PAGE

[3]

<u>Because of this</u>,[8] the overall impression you'll get of the Parthenon will be far different from the one the ancient Athenians had. Only by standing on the marble steps of the Parthenon and allowing your imagination to transport you back to the Golden Age of <u>Athens. You will</u>[9] be able to see the temple's main attraction, the legendary statue of Athena Parthenos. It was 38 feet high and made of ivory and over a ton of pure gold. <u>Removed from the temple in the fifth century C.E.,</u>[10] all that remains is the slight rectangular depression on the floor where it stood.

8. F. NO CHANGE
   G. Thus
   H. Rather
   J. Of course

9. A. NO CHANGE
   B. Athens; you will
   C. Athens will you
   D. Athens. You may

10. F. NO CHANGE
    G. Having been removed from the temple in the fifth century c.e.,
    H. Given its removal from the temple in the fifth century c.e.,
    J. The statue was removed from the temple in the fifth century c.e.;

[4]

Many of the ornate carvings and sculptures that adorned the walls of the Acropolis <u>is</u>[11] no longer there, either. In the early nineteenth century, the British diplomat Lord <u>Elgins decision to</u>[12] "protect" the ones that survived by removing them from the Parthenon and carrying them back to Britain (he had the permission of the Ottoman Turks, who controlled Greece at the time, to do so).

11. A. NO CHANGE
    B. will be
    C. have been
    D. are

12. F. NO CHANGE
    G. Elgin's deciding that
    H. Elgin decided to
    J. Elgin's decision to

[5]

After they gained independence from the Turks, <u>they</u>[13] began to demand the sculptures and carvings back from the British, to no avail. Thus, if you want to gain a complete picture of what the Parthenon once looked like, you'll have to visit not only the Acropolis of Athens, but the British Museum in London as well.

13. A. NO CHANGE
    B. the Turks
    C. the Greeks
    D. who

GO ON TO THE NEXT PAGE

Questions 14–15 ask about the preceding passage as a whole.

14. The writer wishes to insert the following material into the essay:

> Some of them were destroyed in 1687 when attacking Venetians bombarded the Acropolis, setting off explosives that had been stored in the Parthenon.

The new material best supports and therefore would most logically be placed in paragraph:

F. 1.
G. 2.
H. 3.
J. 4.

15. Suppose the editor of an architecture journal had requested that the writer focus primarily on the techniques the ancient Greek architects used in constructing the Parthenon. Does the essay fulfill this request?

A. Yes, because the essay makes it clear that the Parthenon was an amazing architectural achievement.
B. Yes, because the essay explains in the second paragraph the reason the temple's columns bulge outward slightly.
C. No, because the Parthenon's construction is only one of several topics covered in the essay.
D. No, because the author never explains what the architects who designed the Parthenon were trying to accomplish.

GO ON TO THE NEXT PAGE

PASSAGE II

THE LEGENDARY ROBIN HOOD

Although there is no conclusive evidence that a man named Robin Hood ever actually existed, the story of Robin Hood and his band of merry men has become one of the most popular traditional tales in English literature. Robin is the hero in a series of ballads dating from at least the fourteenth century. These ballads are telling [16] of discontent among the lower classes in the north of England during a turbulent era culminating in the Peasants' Revolt of 1381. A good deal of the rebellion against authority stemmed from restriction of hunting rights. These early ballads reveal the cruelty that was a part of medieval life. Robin Hood was a rebel, and many of the most striking episodes depict him and his companions robbing and killing representatives of authority and they gave [17] the gains to the poor. Their most frequentest [18] enemy was the Sheriff of Nottingham, a local agent of the central government. Other enemies included wealthy ecclesiastical landowners.

While Robin could be ruthless with those who abused their power, he was kind to the oppressed. He

16. F. NO CHANGE
G. telling
H. tell
J. they are telling

17. A. NO CHANGE
B. they were giving
C. giving
D. gave

18. F. NO CHANGE
G. even more frequenter
H. frequent
J. frequently

GO ON TO THE NEXT PAGE

was a people's hero as King Arthur was a noble's. (The Broadway musical *Camelot* and Walt Disney's *The Sword in the Stone* are based on the legend of King Arthur.) [19] Some scholars have sought to prove that there was an actual Robin Hood. However, references to the Robin Hood legends by medieval writers make it clear that the ballads were the only evidence for Robin's existence available to them. [20] A popular modern belief that Robin was of the time of Richard I probably stems from the antiquary Richard Stukely's fabrication [21] of a "pedigree." [22]

In the eighteenth century, the nature of the legend was distorted by the suggestion that Robin was as a [23]

19. A. NO CHANGE
B. (The Broadway musical and the movie, respectively, *Camelot* and Walt Disney's *The Sword in the Stone*, are based on the legend of King Arthur.)
C. (Movies and musicals, including *The Sword in the Stone* and *Camelot*, are derived from the legend of King Arthur.)
D. OMIT the underlined portion.

20. F. NO CHANGE
G. him.
H. it.
J. those writing ballads about him.

21. A. NO CHANGE
B. Stukelys fabrication
C. Stukelys fabrication,
D. Stukely's, fabrication

22. Suppose that at this point in the passage, the writer wanted to add more information about Richard Stukely. Which of the following additions would be most relevant to the passage as a whole?
F. A discussion of relevant books on England during the realm of Richard I
G. A definition of the term *antiquary*
H. An example of Stukely's interest in King Arthur
J. A description of the influence Stukely's fabricated pedigree has had on later versions of the Robin Hood tale

23. A. NO CHANGE
B. was like as if he was
C. was a
D. is as a

GO ON TO THE NEXT PAGE

fallen nobleman. Writers adopted this new element as eagerly as puppies. Robin was also given a love
24

24. F. NO CHANGE
G. eagerly
H. eagerly, like a puppy
J. like a puppy's eagerness

interest; Maid Marian. Some critics say that these ballads lost much of their vitality and poetic value by losing the social impulse that prompted their creation.
25

25. A. NO CHANGE
B. interests—Maid
C. interest: Maid,
D. interest—Maid

Consequently, in the twentieth century, the legend of Robin Hood has inspired several movies and a
26

26. F. NO CHANGE
G. (Do NOT begin new paragraph) In the twentieth century, on the one hand,
H. (Begin new paragraph) In the twentieth century,
J. (Begin new paragraph) In the twentieth century, therefore,

television series. Even a Broadway musical basing on the tale. So, whether or not a Robin Hood actually lived in
27

27. A. NO CHANGE
B. has been based
C. to base
D. OMIT the underlined portion.

ancient Britain, and the legendary Robin has lived in the popular imagination for more than 600 years.
28

28. F. NO CHANGE
G. Britain,
H. Britain, therefore
J. Britain;

GO ON TO THE NEXT PAGE

Questions 29–30 ask about the preceding passage as a whole.

29. Suppose this passage were written for an audience that was unfamiliar with the legend of Robin Hood. The writer could most effectively strengthen the passage by:

A. citing examples of legendary rebels from Spanish and French literature.

B. including further evidence of Robin Hood's actual existence.

C. quoting a few lines from a Broadway musical about ancient Britain.

D. including a brief summary of the Robin Hood legend.

30. This passage was probably written for readers who:

F. are experts on how legends are handed down.

G. are authorities on ancient British civilization and culture.

H. are convinced that Robin Hood was an actual historical personage.

J. have some familiarity with the Robin Hood legends.

GO ON TO THE NEXT PAGE

PASSAGE III

HOW MOTHER NATURE JUMP-STARTED MY CAREER

The following paragraphs may or may not be in the most logical order. Each paragraph is numbered in brackets, and question 45 will ask you to choose the most logical order of the paragraphs.

[1]

When Mt. St. Helens erupted, my training as a private pilot paid off. My editor asked me to write a feature story on the volcano. Only scientists and reporters were allowed within a ten-mile radius (31) of the mountain. Eager to see Mt. St. Helens for himself, my brother Jeff volunteered to accompany me as an assistant on the flight. He had never flown with me before, and I looked forward at the opportunity to show off my skills. (32)

31. A. NO CHANGE
    B. radius, consisting of ten miles,
    C. measurement of a ten-mile radius
    D. radius, measuring ten miles,

32. F. NO CHANGE
    G. but looked forward to the opportunity of showing off my skills.
    H. and I looked forward to the opportunity to show off my skills.
    J. nevertheless I anticipated being able to show off my skills.

[2]

If I could read a newspaper, (33) I entertained thoughts of becoming a photojournalist. I always envisioned myself (34) in some faraway exotic place performing dangerous deeds as a foreign correspondent. I was thrilled when I was hired for my first job as a cub reporter for the local newspaper in my rural hometown. However, some of the glamour began to fade after I

33. A. NO CHANGE
    B. Since I found it easy to read a newspaper,
    C. Although I could read a newspaper,
    D. Ever since I could read a newspaper,

34. F. NO CHANGE
    G. I
    H. me
    J. it

GO ON TO THE NEXT PAGE

covered the umpteenth garden party. Then one day, Mother Nature intervened, [35] giving me the opportunity to cover an international event.

35. A. NO CHANGE
B. intervened:
C. intervened;
D. —intervened—

[3]

When we arrived at the airport, filing my flight plan; giving [36] my credentials as a reporter for the Gresham *Outlook*. As we departed Troutdale airport, my Cessna 152 ascended slowly on its way toward Mt. St. Helens. As we neared the crater, I kept a careful [37] watch for other airplanes in the vicinity. A few other pilots were also circling around the crater. I had to maintain a high enough altitude to avoid both the smoke being emitted from: the crater [38] and the ashen residue already in the atmosphere. Too much exposure to the volcanic particles could put my plane out of service. This element of danger served to increase not only my awareness, but also my excitement.

36. F. NO CHANGE
G. I filed my flight plan and gave
H. filing my flight plan, giving
J. my flight plan was filed by me, and I gave

37. The best placement for the underlined portion would be:
A. where it is now.
B. after the word *other.*
C. after the word *we.*
D. before the word *crater.*

38. F. NO CHANGE
G. (from: the crater)
H. from, the crater,
J. from the crater

[4]

Jeff and I were at first speechless and mute [39] at the awesome sight below us as we circled the crater. It was as if the spectacular beauty of a Fourth of July celebration were contained in one natural phenomenon. Jeff helped me, steadying the plane and took notes, [40] while

39. A. NO CHANGE
B. and also mute
C. —and mute—
D. OMIT the underlined portion.

40. F. NO CHANGE
G. steadying the plane and taking notes,
H. steadied the plane and taking notes,
J. steadies the plane and takes notes

GO ON TO THE NEXT PAGE

I shot pictures and dictated story ideas to him. [41]

[5]

My story appeared as the front-page feature the following day. <u>However,</u> [42] I have realized many of my early dreams, working as a foreign correspondent in many different countries. And yet none of my experiences has surpassed that special pride and excitement I felt covering my first "international" story.

41. The writer could most effectively strengthen the passage at this point by adding which of the following?

A. A description of Mt. St. Helens

B. The sentence, "Jeff, take this plane lower!" to add excitement

C. The statement, "A volcano is a vent in the earth's crust through which lava is expelled," to inform the reader

D. A discussion of other recent volcanic eruptions to provide a contrast

42. F. NO CHANGE

G. Since that time,

H. Furthermore,

J. Nevertheless,

Questions 43–45 ask about the preceding passage as a whole.

43. Readers are likely to regard the passage as best described by which of the following terms?

A. Optimistic

B. Bitter

C. Nostalgic

D. Exhausted

44. Is the author's use of the pronoun *I* appropriate in the passage?

F. No, because, as a rule, one avoids *I* in formal writing.

G. No, because it weakens the passage's focus on volcanoes.

H. Yes, because it gives immediacy to the story told in the passage.

J. Yes, because *I* is, as a rule, appropriate in writing.

45. Choose the sequence of paragraph numbers that will make the passage's structure most logical.

A. NO CHANGE

B. 2, 1, 3, 4, 5

C. 3, 4, 5, 1, 2

D. 4, 5, 1, 2, 3

GO ON TO THE NEXT PAGE

PASSAGE IV

SIR ARTHUR CONAN DOYLE

[1]

Sherlock Holmes, the ingenious and extremely clever (46) detective, with the deer-stalker hat, pipe, and magnifying glass, is a universally recognizable character. Everyone knows of Holmes's ability to solve even the most bizarre mysteries through the application of cold logic. Therefore, everyone (47) is familiar with the phrase "elementary, my dear Watson," Holmes's perennial response to the requests of his baffled sidekick, Dr. Watson, for an explanation of his amazing deductions. Strictly speaking, of course, Holmes's "deductions" were not deductions at all, but inductive inferences. (48)

[2]

But how many people know anything about the creator of Sherlock Holmes, Sir Arthur Conan Doyle? Fans of Holmes might be surprised to discover that he (49) did not want to be engraved forever in the memory of the people (50) as the author of the Sherlock Holmes stories. In fact, (51) Conan Doyle sent Holmes to his death at the end of the second book of short stories and

46. F. NO CHANGE
    G. ingenious
    H. ingenious, extremely clever
    J. cleverly ingenious

47. A. NO CHANGE
    B. Although everyone
    C. For this reason, everyone
    D. Everyone

48. F. NO CHANGE
    G. (Strictly speaking, of course, Holmes's "deductions" were not deductions at all, but inductive inferences.)
    H. Holmes's "deductions" were, strictly speaking, not deductions at all, but inductive inferences.
    J. OMIT the underlined portion.

49. A. NO CHANGE
    B. Conan Doyle
    C. they
    D. the detective

50. F. NO CHANGE
    G. to go down in the annals of history
    H. to be permanently thought of forever
    J. to be remembered

51. A. NO CHANGE
    B. Despite this,
    C. Regardless,
    D. Yet

GO ON TO THE NEXT PAGE

subsequently felt a great sense of relief. Having had enough of his famous character by that time, Sherlock Holmes would never divert him again from more serious writing, he promised himself. (52) It took eight years and the offer of a princely sum of money before Conan Doyle could be persuaded to revive the detective.

52. F. NO CHANGE
G. the diversion of Sherlock Holmes, he promised himself, would never again keep him from more serious writing.
H. more serious writing consumed all his time from then on.
J. he promised himself that Sherlock Holmes would never again divert him from more serious writing.

Soap opera characters are sometimes brought back to life after they've been pronounced dead, too. (53) [1] Admirers of Holmes's coldly scientific approach to his detective work may also be taken aback when they learn

53. A. NO CHANGE
B. (Soap opera characters are sometimes brought back to life after they've been pronounced dead, too.)
C. Sometimes you'll see soap opera characters who were dead being brought back to life, just like Holmes.
D. OMIT the underlined portion.

that Conan Doyle has been deeply immersed (54) in spiritualism. [2] Convinced by these experiences of the validity

54. F. NO CHANGE
G. is deeply immersed
H. was deeply immersed
J. has been immersed deeply

of paranormal phenomena, that he lectured (55) on spiritualism in towns and villages throughout Britain. [3] For example, he and his family attempted to communicate

55. A. NO CHANGE
B. phenomena, he lectured
C. phenomena was he that he lectured
D. phenomena. He lectured

with the dead by automatic writing, thought to be a method of talking with those no longer among the living, (56) and through a spiritual medium, an individual who supposedly could contact those in the world beyond. [4] Conan Doyle claimed to have grasped materialized hands and watched heavy articles swimming through

56. F. NO CHANGE
G. a means of getting in touch with those beyond the grave.
H. thought to be a method of talking with the dead.
J. OMIT the underlined portion.

GO ON TO THE NEXT PAGE

the air during sessions led by the medium. [57]

[3]

Doyle seems never to have asked <u>himself: why they</u> (58) would manifest themselves in such curious ways, or to have reflected on the fact that many of these effects are the standard trappings of cheating mediums. One has to wonder, <u>what would Sherlock Holmes have to say?</u> (59)

57. For the sake of unity and coherence, sentence 2 should be placed:

A. where it is now.
B. before sentence 1.
C. after sentence 3.
D. after sentence 4.

58. **F.** NO CHANGE
G. himself—why they
H. himself why those in the other world
J. himself why they

59. **A.** NO CHANGE
B. what would Sherlock Holmes have said?
C. what is Sherlock Holmes going to say?
D. what had Sherlock Holmes said?

Question 60 asks about the preceding passage as a whole.

60. Which of the following would be the most appropriate subtitle for the passage?

F. The Truth about Spiritualists
G. Rational or Superstitious?
H. The Secret Life of Sherlock Holmes
J. His Religious Beliefs

GO ON TO THE NEXT PAGE

PASSAGE V

VISUAL LEARNING

Traditional educational theories stressed lecture-based methods in which students learned by listening to an instructor, but contemporary studies have noted that students learn best when they see, hear, and experience. Based on these studies, current educational theories emphasize auditory, visual, and experiential learning. Such theories are not groundbreaking (61). For example, medical education has stressed this model for decades. Young doctors in their residency training often repeat the mantra, "see it, do it, teach it." Interestingly, much of the development in the area of (62) visual and experiential learning fields has come from the business world. Many businesses, from corporate management to consulting, utilize presentations. Traditionally, business presentations had included slides filled with dense text that merely repeated the presenter's words. Though these slides did provide a visual aspect, the slides (63) were difficult to read, which detracted from their effectiveness.

[1] Over the past decade, technological advances have created (64) additional presentation options, business leaders have teamed with public speaking experts to continue to refine the visual presentation style.

61. **A.** NO CHANGE
B. were not groundbreaking
C. had been groundbreaking
D. in groundbreaking

62. **F.** NO CHANGE
G. subject of
H. topic of
J. OMIT the underlined portion.

63. **A.** NO CHANGE
B. the slides'
C. the slide's
D. they

64. **F.** NO CHANGE
G. technological advances were creating
H. as technological advances have created
J. that technological advances have created

GO ON TO THE NEXT PAGE

[2] <u>A very important development revealed</u> that less cluttered visual aids work better than denser ones. [3] This development led to the understanding that text repeating a presenter's script did not <u>enhance or improve</u> student or audience learning. [4] Studies showed that visual aids should not simply present a speaker's words, but instead <u>demonstrate or add to them</u> in some way. [5] These studies emphasized the efficacy of visual representations of the presenter's dialogue in the form of graphs, charts, art, or pictures. [68]

65. **A.** NO CHANGE
B. On the other hand, a very important development revealed
C. A very important development similarly revealed
D. In contrast, a very important development revealed

66. **F.** NO CHANGE
G. lead to an improvement in
H. better enhance or improve
J. improve

67. **A.** NO CHANGE
B. they can be demonstrated or added to
C. demonstrating or adding to them
D. demonstrate adding for them

68. After reviewing the essay, the writer is considering inserting the following true statement in this paragraph:

> Audio aids, though infrequently used, can also help audiences focus on a presentation.

Should this sentence be added to this paragraph, and if so, what is the most logical placement for it?

F. Yes, after Sentence 2.
G. Yes, after Sentence 4.
H. Yes, after Sentence 5.
J. No, the sentence should NOT be added.

GO ON TO THE NEXT PAGE

Several studies <u>in listeners have been published in respected journals, that reveal that aesthetically appealing presentations improve comprehension.</u> 69

69. A. NO CHANGE
B. revealing that aesthetically appealing presentations improve comprehension in listeners have been published in respected journals.
C. in listeners that reveal that aesthetically appealing presentations improve comprehension in respected journals have been published.
D. have been published in respected journals by revealing in listeners that aesthetically appealing presentations improve comprehension.

<u>It has been determined by researchers that a learning aid can be created from any pleasing image, even one that is irrelevant.</u> 70 Using this model, many presenters have begun projecting nature scenes or famous paintings to

70. F. NO CHANGE
G. Researchers have determined that any pleasing image, even an irrelevant one, can serve as a learning aid.
H. As researchers have determined, that any pleasing image, even an irrelevant one, can serve as a learning aid.
J. A pleasing image, even an irrelevant one, researchers have determined it can serve as a learning aid.

accompany <u>presentations. Audience</u> 71 members report not being distracted by the irrelevant images. In fact, most audience members find the pleasing images helpful in creating a positive environment which, in turn, helps <u>him or her</u> 72 focus on the presentation.

71. A. NO CHANGE
B. presentations, audience
C. presentations, and that audience
D. presentations and that audience

72. F. NO CHANGE
G. one
H. you
J. them

[1] <u>Even more recently, of late,</u> 73 cognitive psychologists have noted that students and audience members

73. A. NO CHANGE
B. Not so long ago, in recent times,
C. Lately, in addition,
D. Recently,

GO ON TO THE NEXT PAGE

<u>use multiple senses to take in information.</u> [2] In fact,
74
many experts believe that a teacher's or presenter's body language is the most important factor in student or audience reaction. [3] Therefore, many education and public speaking experts <u>are interested in investigating other factors in student and audience reaction.</u> [4]
75
While these developments have not coalesced to form one paradigm for public speaking and presenting, they have underscored many of the new theories in the field of communication. [5] These developments continue to influence trends in the academic world.

74. Given that all of the following are true, which choice would provide the most effective and logical link between Sentences 1 and 2?

F. NO CHANGE
G. learn not only from images, but also from body language.
H. pay more attention to visual images that incorporate color or suggest movement.
J. recall more information when they are asked by the presenter or speaker to take notes or write questions.

75. At this point, the writer would like to show how education and public speaking experts have been influenced by the theory about the importance of body language. Given that all of the following are true, which choice best achieves the writer's purpose?

A. NO CHANGE
B. now teach presenters to make purposeful movements and focused gestures.
C. have adjusted the focus of their public speaking workshops for teachers and business professionals.
D. question how the size of an audience affects the power of a presenter's body language.

IF YOU FINISH BEFORE TIME IS CALLED, YOU MAY CHECK YOUR WORK ON THIS SECTION ONLY. DO NOT TURN TO ANY OTHER SECTION IN THE TEST. **STOP**

READING TEST

35 Minutes—40 Questions

Directions: There are four passages in this test. Each passage is followed by several questions. After reading a passage, choose the best answer to each question and fill in the corresponding oval on your answer document. You may refer to the passages as often as necessary.

PASSAGE I

PROSE FICTION

This passage is an excerpt from the short story "Graduation," by John Krupp.

Rosemary sat at her kitchen table, working at a crossword puzzle. Crosswords were nice; they filled the time, and kept the mind active. She needed just one word to complete this morning's puzzle; the clue was "a Swiss river," and the first of its three letters was "A." Unfortunately, Rosemary had no idea what the name of the river was, and could not look it up. Her atlas was on the desk, and the desk was in the guest room, currently being occupied by her grandson Victor. Looking up over the tops of her bifocals, Rosemary glanced at the kitchen clock: it was almost 10 A.M. *Land sakes!* Did the boy intend to sleep all day? She noticed that the arthritis in her wrist was throbbing, and put down her pen. At eighty-seven years of age, she was glad she could still write at all. She had decided long ago that growing old was like slowly turning to stone; you couldn't take anything for granted. She stood up slowly, painfully, and started walking to the guest room.

The trip, though only a distance of about twenty-five feet, seemed to take a long while. Late in her ninth decade now, Rosemary often experienced an expanded sense of time, with present and past tense intermingling in her mind. One minute she was padding in her slippers across the living room carpet, the next she was back on the farm where she'd grown up, a sturdy little girl treading the path behind the barn just before dawn. In her mind's eye, she could still pick her way among the stones in the darkness, more than seventy years later... Rosemary arrived at the door to the guest room. It stood slightly ajar, and she peered through the opening. Victor lay sleeping on his side, his arms bent, his expression slightly pained. *Get up, lazy bones,* she wanted to say. Even in childhood, Rosemary had never slept past 4 A.M.; there were too many chores to do. How different things were for Victor's generation! Her youngest grandson behaved as if he had never done a chore in his life. Twenty-one years old, he had driven down to Florida to visit Rosemary in his shiny new car, a gift from his doting parents. Victor would finish college soon, and his future appeared bright—if he ever got out of bed, that is.

Something Victor had said last night over dinner had disturbed her. Now what was it? Oh yes; he had been talking about one of his college courses—a "gut," he had called it. When she had asked him to explain the term, Victor had said it was a course that you took simply because it was easy to pass. Rosemary, who had not even had a high school education, found the term repellent. If she had been allowed to continue her studies, she would never have taken a "gut"...The memory flooded back then, still painful as an open wound all these years later. It was the first day of high school. She had graduated from grammar school the previous year, but her father had forbidden her to go on to high school

GO ON TO THE NEXT PAGE

that fall, saying that she was needed on the farm. After much tearful pleading, she had gotten him to promise that next year, she could start high school. She had endured a whole year of chores instead of books, with animals and rough farmhands for company instead of people her own age. Now, at last, the glorious day was at hand. She had put on her best dress (she owned two), her heart racing in anticipation. But her father was waiting for her as she came downstairs.

"Where do you think you're going?" he asked.

"To high school, Papa."

"No you're not. Take that thing off and get back to work."

"But Papa, you promised!"

"*Do as I say*!" he thundered.

There was no arguing with Papa when he spoke that way. Tearfully, she had trudged upstairs to change clothes. Rosemary still wondered what life would have been like if her father had not been waiting at the bottom of the stairs that day, or if somehow she had found the strength to defy him…

Suddenly, Victor stirred, without waking, and mumbled something unintelligible. Jarred from her reverie, Rosemary stared at Victor. She wondered if he were having a nightmare.

1. According to the passage, Victor is Rosemary's:

A. nephew.
B. son.
C. grandson.
D. great-grandson.

2. It can be inferred from the passage that Rosemary is disturbed by Victor's:

F. intention to drop out of college.
G. disregard of her harsh upbringing.
H. willingness to take courses that are easy to pass.
J. inability to get out of bed in the morning.

3. The passage suggests that in the year after she finished grammar school, Rosemary most wanted:

A. an escape from her father's company.
B. the opportunity to go to college.
C. the chance to study challenging subjects.
D. the company of people her own age.

4. The passage suggests that Rosemary's attitude toward the physical afflictions of old age is generally one of:

F. sadness.
G. acceptance.
H. resentment.
J. optimism.

5. According to the passage, Rosemary does crossword puzzles in order to:

A. keep her mind active.
B. practice her handwriting.
C. learn new geographical facts.
D. make her more aware of time.

6. The focus of the passage as a whole is on:

F. Rosemary's concern at Victor's lack of motivation.
G. the harsh treatment Victor received from his father.
H. the contrast between Victor's and Rosemary's attitudes toward education.
J. Rosemary's struggle to suppress painful memories.

GO ON TO THE NEXT PAGE

7. It can be inferred from the passage that Victor's "shiny new car" (line 49) is mentioned in order to illustrate:

   A. the excessive generosity of Rosemary's parents.
   B. the contrast between Rosemary's generation and his.
   C. the strength of Victor's prospects for the future.
   D. the lack of physical hardship in Victor's life.

8. The third paragraph (lines 53–80) primarily portrays Rosemary in her youth as:

   F. resentful of her father's conduct.
   G. eager to continue her education.
   H. undecided about her future career.
   J. proud of her appearance.

9. Rosemary's recollection of growing up on the farm (lines 29–36) is mentioned as an example of her:

   A. nostalgia for her childhood experiences.
   B. determination to overcome her physical disabilities.
   C. ability to recall past and present events at the same time.
   D. disappointment at being denied an education.

10. The statement that Victor's "future appeared bright" (lines 51–52) most likely reflects the opinion of:

    F. Rosemary.
    G. Victor.
    H. Victor's parents.
    J. Rosemary's father.

PASSAGE II

SOCIAL SCIENCE

These two passages reflect two different views concerning the origins of modern liberal economic regulation in the United States. Passage A is from a 1980 newspaper article about the beginning of progressive reforms to the American economy. Passage B was written in the 1990s by a noted economic historian.

PASSAGE A

The Sherman Antitrust Act was introduced into Congress by Senator John Sherman of Ohio, and, after being first rewritten by pro-business Eastern senators, was passed into law in 1890. The Act made illegal "every contract, combination in the form of trust or otherwise, or conspiracy in the restraint of trade." Many have charged, at that time and since, that the decidedly vague wording introduced by the pro-business revisers resulted in the emasculation of the law's anti-monopoly message. Nevertheless, the Act was the first law to fight, even symbolically, against economic monopolies in the "open" market economy of the United States.

From the birth of the nation, many politicians and influential business leaders had felt that the most natural and ideal democratic economy was one in which the government played a very limited role in regulating commerce. It was argued that, by permitting businesses to pursue their own interests, the government was promoting the interests of the nation as a whole, or as GM chairman Charles E. Wilson reportedly quipped, "What's good for General Motors is good for the nation." Many of the leaders of trusts and monopolies in the 1800s co-opted the then cutting-edge terminology of Charles Darwin's theory of natural selection, arguing that in an unrestrained economy, power and wealth would naturally flow to the most capable according to the principles of "Social Darwinism." Their monopolies were thus natural

GO ON TO THE NEXT PAGE

and efficient outcomes of economic development.

Towards the close of the 1800s, however, an increasingly large and vocal number of lower- and middle-class dissenters felt that the *laissez-faire*[1] policies of the federal government allowed monopolistic trusts like Standard Oil to manipulate consumers by fixing prices, exploit workers by cutting wages, and threaten democracy by corrupting politicians. Most directly, the trusts and monopolies completely destroyed the opportunities for competitors in their industries to do business effectively. The concerns of these working-class dissenters thus created a groundswell of support for the Sherman Antitrust Act, which attempted to outlaw these monopolies and trusts. Even more important than the direct effects of the Act, however, was the sign of a new era of reform against monopolistic economic corruption, and the rise of deliberate economic regulation in America. The federal government had finally realized that it had to take a more active role in the economy in order to protect the interests and rights of consumers, workers, and small businesses while tempering the dominating power of big business.

PASSAGE B

Some political historians contend that alterations to the powers or role of the federal government are a violation of the democratic principles and goals on which the United States was founded. I hold that the evolution of democracy in America has been absolutely necessary and has led to positive reform to correct injustices and suit the needs of changing times. In no arena is this more evident than in the field of economic policy, especially during the presidency of Franklin D. Roosevelt.

Roosevelt was a liberal Democrat who looked on his election in 1932 as a mandate from the nation's voters to forge a bold path out of the crippled economy, massive unemployment, and plummeting farm prices brought on by the Great Depression[2]. Traditionally, it was believed that in democratic nations the government should balance its own budget and not attempt to manipulate the economy as a whole by expending money. According to traditional or conservative capitalist economists, busts and booms in an open, unregulated economy were normal and healthy, part of a natural cycle that self-regulated excess or overproduction. There was thus no need for government intervention during recessions. It seemed evident to Roosevelt, however, that the Great Depression would not "naturally" recede, and that he must, in his own words, "reform democracy in order to save it." Roosevelt "pump-primed" the economy using government funds for the first time in American history by intentional deficit spending. In the Agricultural Adjustment Act, for example, Roosevelt controlled one of the causes and symptoms of the economic recession, agricultural overproduction, by using government funds to pay farmers to produce fewer crops. Perhaps more than any other, this act signaled the end of the *laissez-faire* economics era and ushered in the modern era of liberal economic regulation.

Our nation's founders had planned for a minimalist federal government that would balance its own books and mind its own business, and, for some 150 years, this attitude seemed intrinsic to the role of the federal government. The deficit spending and deliberate manipulation of the national economy by the Roosevelt administration marked a radical revision of the role of the federal government, and it's likely that only the severe crises of the Depression could have compelled Americans to fully embrace the notion that government intervention in the economy was both beneficial and necessary. The success of this approach in pulling the nation out of a crippling depression was undeniable. Also undeniable was the larger conclusion that the national government must adapt in both scope and purpose to fit the needs of changing times.

[1] from the French "to allow to do," an economic policy of non-intervention

[2] a prolonged and severe economic recession in America during the 1930s

GO ON TO THE NEXT PAGE

Questions 11–13 ask about Passage A.

11. The revisions mentioned in line 3 illustrate the:

A. support for Social Darwinism common in the nineteenth century.
B. resistance from business proponents to antitrust reform.
C. lengthy period of debate that preceded the passage of the Sherman Act.
D. ineffective nature of Congressional legislation in the 1890s.

12. The phrase "Social Darwinism" (lines 33–34) is included in Passage A as:

F. an illustration of the similarities between economic evolution and biological evolution.
G. an argument to assert that only the strongest corporations could survive in a free market economy.
H. a demonstration of the terms that monopolists utilized to justify their control of industries.
J. an example of the influence of scientific theories on social and economic policy.

13. Based on information in the third paragraph of Passage A (lines 36–59), it seems most likely that the author of Passage A would agree with which of the following?

A. All monopolistic trusts fixed prices and exploited workers.
B. The overall effects of stifled competition were negative for many Americans.
C. Outlawing monopolies was a necessary reform to save democracy.
D. Standard Oil was prevented from freely competing by the Sherman Antitrust Act.

Questions 14–16 ask about Passage B.

14. The author cites the Agricultural Adjustment Act (lines 93–94) as:

F. an important twentieth century antitrust act.
G. an act that led to a resurgence of *laissez-faire* economic policy.
H. a factor leading to the Great Depression.
J. an example of aggressive government intervention in the economy.

15. In the last paragraph of Passage B (lines 102–121), the author primarily:

A. argues that an alteration to the original plans for the American federal government was beneficial.
B. shows that Roosevelt's economic reforms were unnecessary.
C. cites an exception to his generalization that Roosevelt normally passed only beneficial legislation.
D. explores weaknesses in the original design of the American federal government.

16. In the second paragraph of Passage B, the author includes the opinion of "conservative capitalist economists" (lines 80–81) as:

F. a demonstration of the conservative nature of the economic reforms introduced during the Roosevelt era.
G. evidence in support of the Agricultural Adjustment Act.
H. a view about the necessity of government economic regulation that the author will later refute.
J. an argument that only severe poverty can force radical changes in America.

GO ON TO THE NEXT PAGE

Questions 17–20 ask about both passages.

17. Both passages cite which of the following as a necessary reform to the original design of the American democracy?

A. Lessening government control of the economy
B. Abandoning *laissez-faire* economic policy
C. Preventing unfair industry domination
D. Passing laws to limit agricultural overproduction

18. The author of Passage B would most likely respond to the description of monopolies as "natural and efficient outcomes of economic development" (lines 34–35) by:

F. arguing that theories of Social Darwinism were used as justification to promote the interests of the most wealthy.
G. noting that the most "natural" state of the economy is not necessarily the most preferable.
H. agreeing that government intervention in the economy is an abandonment of the ideals upon which the country was founded.
J. noting that the economic policies of Franklin Roosevelt were highly effective in battling such monopolies.

19. What aspect of government economic regulation is emphasized in Passage B, but not in Passage A?

A. Antitrust laws
B. Deficit spending
C. Congressional legislation
D. *Laissez-faire* policies

20. According to each passage, the term *laissez-faire* describes:

F. an economic policy that is beneficial to consumers and a period in history that has yet to conclude.
G. a natural, ideal democratic economy and a government's attempt to balance its own budget without creating interference.
H. a philosophy that Roosevelt championed and a presidential legacy that is in effect to this day.
J. an approach that allowed trusts to manipulate consumers and an era that the Agricultural Adjustment Act ended.

PASSAGE III

HUMANITIES

This passage is an excerpt from A Short History of Western Civilization, *Volume 1, by John B. Harrison, Richard E. Sullivan, and Dennis Sherman, © 1990 by McGraw-Hill, Inc. Reprinted by permission of McGraw-Hill, Inc.*

Enlightenment ideas were put forth by a variety of intellectuals who in France came to be known as the *philosophes. Philosophes* is French for philosophers, and in a sense these thinkers were rightly considered philosophers, for the questions they dealt with were philosophical: How do we discover truth? How should life be lived? What is the nature of God? But on the whole the term has a meaning different from the usual meaning of "philosopher." The philosophes were intellectuals, often not formally trained or associated with a university. They were usually more literary than scientific. They generally extended, applied, popularized, or propagandized ideas of others rather than originating those ideas themselves. The

GO ON TO THE NEXT PAGE

philosophes were more likely to write plays, satires, pamphlets or simply participate in verbal exchanges at select gatherings than to write formal philosophical books.

It was the philosophes who developed the philosophy of the Enlightenment and spread it to much of the educated elite in Western Europe (and the American colonies). Although the sources for their philosophy can be traced to the Scientific Revolution in general, the philosophes were most influenced by their understanding of Newton, Locke, and English institutions.

The philosophes saw Newton as the great synthesizer of the Scientific Revolution who rightly described the universe as ordered, mechanical, material, and only originally set in motion by God, who since then has remained relatively inactive. Newton's synthesis showed to the philosophes that reason and nature were compatible: Nature functioned logically and discernibly, and what was natural was also reasonable. Newton exemplified the value of reasoning based on concrete experience. The philosophes felt that his empirical methodology was the correct path to discovering truth.

John Locke (1632–1704) agreed with Newton but went further. This English thinker would not exempt even the mind from the mechanical laws of the material universe. In his *Essay Concerning Human Understanding* (1691), Locke pictured the human brain at birth as a blank sheet of paper on which nothing would ever be written except sense perception and reason. What human beings become depends on their experiences—on the information received through the senses. Schools and social institutions could therefore play a great role in molding the individual from childhood to adulthood. Human beings were thus by nature far more malleable than had been assumed. This empirical psychology of Locke rejected the notion that human beings were born with innate ideas or that revelation was a reliable source of truth. Locke also enunciated liberal and reformist political ideas in his *Second Treatise of Civil Government* (1690), which influenced the philosophes. On the whole Locke's empiricism, psychology and politics were appealing to the philosophes.

England, not coincidentally the country of Newton and Locke, became the admired model for many of the philosophes. They tended to idealize it, but England did seem to allow greater individual freedom, tolerate religious differences, and evidence greater political reform than other countries, especially France. England seemed to have gone furthest in freeing itself from traditional institutions and accepting the new science of the seventeenth century. Moreover, England's approach seemed to work, for England was experiencing relative political stability and prosperity. The philosophes wanted to see in their own countries much of what England already seemed to have.

Many philosophes reflected the influence of Newton, Locke, and English institutions, but perhaps the most representative in his views was Voltaire (1694–1778). Of all leading figures of the Enlightenment, he was the most influential. Voltaire, the son of a Paris lawyer, became the idol of the French intelligentsia while still in his early twenties. His versatile mind was sparkling; his wit was mordant. An outspoken critic, he soon ran afoul of both church and state authorities. First he was imprisoned in the Bastille; later he was exiled to England. There he encountered the ideas of Newton and Locke and came to admire English parliamentary government and tolerance. In *Letters on the English* (1732), *Elements of the Philosophy of Newton* (1738), and other writings, he popularized the ideas of Newton and Locke, extolled the virtues of English society, and indirectly criticized French society. Slipping back into France, he was hidden for a time and protected by a wealthy woman who

GO ON TO THE NEXT PAGE

became his mistress. Voltaire's facile mind and pen were never idle. He wrote poetry, drama, history, essays, letters, and scientific treatises—ninety volumes in all. The special targets of his cynical wit were the Catholic church and Christian institutions. Few people in history have dominated their age intellectually as did Voltaire.

21. The philosophes can best be described as:

A. writers swept up by their mutual admiration of John Locke.

B. professors who lectured in philosophy at French universities.

C. intellectuals responsible for popularizing Enlightenment ideas.

D. scientists who furthered the work of the Scientific Revolution.

22. Which of the following would most likely have been written by Voltaire?

F. A treatise criticizing basic concepts of the Scientific Revolution

G. A play satirizing religious institutions in France

H. A collection of letters mocking the English Parliament

J. A sentimental poem expounding the virtues of courtly love

23. According to the passage, Locke felt that schools and social institutions could "play a great role in molding the individual" (lines 57–58) primarily because:

A. human beings were born with certain innate ideas.

B. human nature becomes more malleable with age.

C. society owes each individual the right to an education.

D. the human mind is chiefly influenced by experience.

24. Based on the information in the passage, which of the following best describes Newton's view of the universe?

I. The universe was initially set in motion by God.

II. Human reason is insufficient to understand the laws of nature.

III. The universe operates in a mechanical and orderly fashion.

F. I only

G. I and II only

H. I and III only

J. II and III only

25. According to the passage, which of the following works questioned the idea that revelation was a reliable source of truth?

A. *Letters on the English*

B. *Second Treatise of Civil Government*

C. *Elements of the Philosophy of Newton*

D. *Essay Concerning Human Understanding*

26. The passage supports which of the following statements concerning the relationship between Newton and Locke?

F. Locke's psychology contradicted Newton's belief in an orderly universe.

G. Locke maintained that Newton's laws of the material universe also applied to the human mind.

H. Newton eventually came to accept Locke's revolutionary ideas about the human mind.

J. Newton's political ideas were the basis of Locke's liberal and reformist politics.

GO ON TO THE NEXT PAGE

27. According to the passage, the philosophes believed that society should:

I. allow individuals greater freedom.
II. free itself from traditional institutions.
III. tolerate religious differences.

A. I only
B. I and II only
C. II and III only
D. I, II, and III

28. It can be inferred from the passage that the author regards England's political stability and economic prosperity as:

F. the reason why the philosophes did not idealize England's achievement.
G. evidence that political reforms could bring about a better way of life.
H. the result of Voltaire's activities after he was exiled to England.
J. an indication that the Scientific Revolution had not yet started there.

29. The passage suggests that the French political and religious authorities during the time of Voltaire:

A. allowed little in the way of free speech.
B. overreacted to Voltaire's mild satires.
C. regarded the philosophes with indifference.
D. accepted the model of English parliamentary government.

30. How does the passage support the point that the philosophes were "more literary than scientific" (line 14)?

F. It demonstrates how the philosophes' writings contributed to the political change.
G. It compares the number of works that Voltaire authored to Newton's output.
H. It traces the influences of English literary works on French scientists.
J. It describes the kinds of literary activities the philosophes commonly engaged in.

PASSAGE IV

NATURAL SCIENCE

This passage explores the theory that a large asteroid collided with the Earth 65 million years ago.

Sixty-five million years ago, something triggered mass extinctions so profound that they define the geological boundary between the Cretaceous and Tertiary periods (the K-T Boundary). Approximately 75 percent of all animal species, including every species of dinosaur, were killed off; those that survived lost the vast majority of their numbers. The Earth exists in a region of space teeming with asteroids and comets, which on collision have frequently caused enormous environmental devastation, including extinctions of animal species. Yet few traditional geologists or biologists considered the effect such impacts may have had on the geologic and biologic history of the Earth. Since gradual geologic processes like erosion or repeated volcanic eruptions can explain the topographical development of the Earth, they felt that there was no need to resort to extraterrestrial explanations.

An important theory proposed in 1980 by physicists Luis and Walter Alvarez challenged

GO ON TO THE NEXT PAGE

this view. The Alvarezes argued that an asteroid roughly six miles in diameter collided with the Earth in the K-T Boundary. Although the damage caused by the meteorite's impact would have been great, the dust cloud that subsequently would have enveloped the planet, completely blotting out the sun for up to a year—the result of soil displacement—would have done most of the harm, according to this theory. The plunge into darkness—and the resulting drastically reduced temperatures —would have interrupted plant growth, cutting off the food supply to herbivorous species, the loss of which in turn would have starved carnivores. Additional species would have perished as a result of prolonged atmospheric poisoning, acid rain, forest fires, and tidal waves, all initiated by the asteroid's impact.

Some subsequent research not only tended to support the Alvarez theory, but suggested that similar impacts may have caused other sharp breaks in Earth's geologic and biologic history. Research in the composition of the Earth revealed a 160-fold enrichment of iridium all over the world in a thin layer of sediments formed at the K-T Boundary. The presence of this element, which is extremely uncommon in the Earth's crust but very common in asteroids and comets, suggested that a meteorite must have struck Earth at that time. Additional physical evidence of such a strike was found in rock samples, which contained shocked quartz crystals and microtektites (small glass spheres)—both byproducts of massive collisions.

Observation of the lunar surface provided further evidence of the likelihood of a massive strike. Since the moon and the Earth lie within the same swarm of asteroids and comets, their impact histories should be parallel. Although some lunar craters were of volcanic origin, over the last four billion years at least five impact craters ranging from 31 to 58 miles in diameter have marred the lunar surface. Therefore, over the same time span, Earth must have experienced some 400 collisions of similar magnitude. Although such an impact crater had not been found, Alvarez supporters didn't consider finding it necessary or likely. They reasoned that geologic processes over 65 million years, like erosion and volcanic eruptions, would have obscured the crater, which in any case probably formed on the ocean floor.

Traditional biologists and geologists resisted the Alvarez theory. They pointed to the absence of any impact crater; to the fact that iridium, while rare at the Earth's surface, was common at its core and could be transported to the surface by volcanic activity; and to the fact that the Alvarezes, though eminent physicists, were not biologists, geologists, or paleontologists.

31. According to the Alvarez theory, the mass extinctions of animal species at the end of the Cretaceous period were caused by:

A. animals being crushed by an enormous asteroid.

B. processes like erosion and repeated volcanic eruptions.

C. extreme global warming causing a global firestorm.

D. environmental conditions following a meteorite impact.

32. Based on the information in the passage, the author probably believes that those who held the traditional views about the topographical development of the Earth were:

F. proven incorrect by the Alvarezes.

G. unrivaled at the present time.

H. correct in challenging alternative views.

J. unreceptive to new evidence.

GO ON TO THE NEXT PAGE

33. As it is used in line 50, the word *enrichment* most nearly means:

A. wealth.

B. improvement.

C. increase in amount.

D. reward.

34. The views of scientists who opposed the Alvarez theory would have been strengthened if:

F. major deposits of iridium were found in the lava flows of active Earth volcanoes.

G. iridium were absent in sediments corresponding to several episodes of mass extinction.

H. iridium were absent in fragments of several recently recovered meteorites.

J. the Alvarezes were biologists as well as physicists.

35. The author's attitude toward the Alvarez theory is best characterized as:

A. dismissive.

B. neutral.

C. skeptical.

D. supportive.

36. According to the passage, which of the following is the correct order of events in the Alvarez theory explaining the mass extinction of species at the end of the Cretaceous period?

F. Soil displacement, disappearance of the sun, decline of plant life, fall in temperature

G. Soil displacement, disappearance of the sun, fall in temperature, decline of plant life

H. Fall in temperature, decline of plant life, soil displacement, disappearance of the sun

J. Disappearance of the sun, fall in temperature, decline of plant life, soil displacement

37. It can be inferred from paragraph 2 that the author discusses the Alvarezes' description of environmental conditions at the end of the Cretaceous period in order to:

A. demonstrate that an immense meteorite hit the Earth.

B. explain why no trace of an impact crater has yet been found.

C. show that the Earth is vulnerable to meteorite collisions.

D. clarify how a meteorite may account for mass extinctions.

38. The author's statement (lines 9–10) that "Earth exists in a region of space teeming with asteroids and comets" is important to:

F. the Alvarezes' claim that an asteroid's impact caused. atmospheric poisoning, acid rain, forest fires, and tidal waves.

G. the Alvarezes' view that the resulting dust cloud, rather than the impact of the meteorite, did most of the harm.

H. Alvarez supporters' argument based on the numbers of impact craters on the surface of the moon.

J. traditionalists' view that to pographical development of the Earth can be explained by gradual geologic processes.

GO ON TO THE NEXT PAGE

39. Supporters of the Alvarezes' theory believe finding the impact crater is not necessary because:

I. the crater probably is on the ocean floor.

II. iridium occurs at the Earth's core.

III. processes like erosion and volcanic eruptions obscured the crater.

A. I only

B. I and II only

C. I and III only

D. II and III only

40. According to the passage, species died in mass extinctions as a result of all of the following EXCEPT:

F. shocked quartz crystals and microtektites.

G. reduced sunlight for up to a year.

H. loss of food supplies.

J. prolonged atmospheric poisoning.

IF YOU FINISH BEFORE TIME IS CALLED, YOU MAY CHECK YOUR WORK ON THIS SECTION ONLY. DO NOT TURN TO ANY OTHER SECTION IN THE TEST. **STOP**

WRITING TEST

Directions: This is a test of your writing skills. You will have **forty** (40) minutes to read the prompt, plan your response, and write an essay in English. Before you begin working, read all material in this test booklet carefully to understand exactly what you are being asked to do.

You will write your essay on the lined pages in the **answer document** provided. Your writing on those pages will be scored. You may use the unlined pages in this test booklet to plan your essay. Your work on these pages will not be scored.

Your essay will be evaluated based on the evidence it provides of your ability to:

- clearly state your own perspective on a complex issue and analyze the relationship between your perspective and at least one other perspective
- develop and support your ideas with reasoning and examples
- organize your ideas clearly and logically
- communicate your ideas effectively in standard written English

Lay your pencil down immediately when time is called.

DO NOT OPEN THIS BOOKLET UNTIL TOLD TO DO SO.

GO ON TO THE NEXT PAGE

ESSAY TASK

Write a unified, coherent essay in which you evaluate multiple perspectives on the relevance of student feedback in lesson planning. In your essay, be sure to:

- clearly state your own perspective on the issue and analyze the relationship between your perspective and at least one other perspective
- develop and support your ideas with reasoning and examples
- organize your ideas clearly and logically
- communicate your ideas effectively in standard written English

Your perspective may be in full agreement with any of the others, in partial agreement, or wholly different. Whatever the case, support your ideas with logical reasoning and detailed, persuasive examples.

PLANNING YOUR ESSAY

You may wish to consider the following as you think critically about the task:

Strengths and weaknesses of the three given perspectives

- What insights do they offer, and what do they fail to consider?
- Why might they be persuasive to others, or why might they fail to persuade?

Your own knowledge, experience, and values

- What is your perspective on this issue, and what are its strengths and weaknesses?
- How will you support your perspective in your essay?

GO ON TO THE NEXT PAGE

Student Engagement

Studies show that students not only retain more information but also enjoy learning more when they actively participate in the classroom. Teachers therefore strive to optimize engagement to foster a positive, effective instructional environment. In an effort to increase student interaction in the high school classroom, some educators argue that curriculum should take into account the interests and suggestions of students. Since teachers cannot allow students to choose every aspect of a lesson, is it worth the time and effort to actively seek relevant student feedback? As high schools aim to improve the quality of the education they offer to students, student opinion may prove to be valuable.

Read and carefully consider these perspectives. Each discusses the relevance of student feedback in lesson planning.

Perspective One	Perspective Two	Perspective Three
Many colleges require students to complete a course survey before they are eligible to receive their semester grades. Colleges use students' responses to evaluate course materials to ensure quality education. High schools would benefit from implementing a similar system of regular feedback on classroom lesson plans by students.	Students are not qualified to provide insight regarding lesson planning or curriculum design. Improving the quality of education is the responsibility of educators, and they are rightfully in charge of making effective changes.	Many school districts evaluate teachers using students' test scores and by conducting in-classroom observations. Information gathered from student surveys could not only inform lesson design, but also provide another source of evaluation by which to measure teacher effectiveness.

GO ON TO THE NEXT PAGE

IF YOU FINISH BEFORE TIME IS CALLED, YOU MAY CHECK YOUR WORK ON THIS SECTION ONLY. DO NOT TURN TO ANY OTHER SECTION IN THE TEST. **STOP**

Practice Test One
ANSWER KEY

ENGLISH TEST

1. C	**11.** D	**21.** A	**31.** A	**41.** A	**51.** A	**61.** C	**71.** A
2. G	**12.** H	**22.** J	**32.** H	**42.** G	**52.** J	**62.** J	**72.** J
3. D	**13.** C	**23.** C	**33.** D	**43.** C	**53.** D	**63.** D	**73.** D
4. F	**14.** J	**24.** G	**34.** F	**44.** H	**54.** H	**64.** H	**74.** G
5. D	**15.** C	**25.** D	**35.** A	**45.** B	**55.** B	**65.** A	**75.** B
6. G	**16.** H	**26.** H	**36.** G	**46.** G	**56.** J	**66.** J	
7. D	**17.** C	**27.** B	**37.** A	**47.** D	**57.** D	**67.** A	
8. J	**18.** H	**28.** G	**38.** J	**48.** J	**58.** H	**68.** J	
9. C	**19.** D	**29.** D	**39.** D	**49.** B	**59.** B	**69.** B	
10. J	**20.** F	**30.** J	**40.** G	**50.** J	**60.** G	**70.** G	

READING TEST

1. C	**6.** H	**11.** B	**16.** H	**21.** C	**26.** G	**31.** D	**36.** G
2. H	**7.** B	**12.** H	**17.** B	**22.** G	**27.** D	**32.** H	**37.** D
3. D	**8.** G	**13.** B	**18.** G	**23.** D	**28.** G	**33.** C	**38.** H
4. G	**9.** C	**14.** J	**19.** B	**24.** H	**29.** A	**34.** F	**39.** C
5. A	**10.** F	**15.** A	**20.** J	**25.** D	**30.** J	**35.** D	**40.** F

ANSWERS AND EXPLANATIONS

ENGLISH TEST

PASSAGE I

1. C

Category: Punctuation
Difficulty: High
Getting to the Answer: At first glance, there may not seem to be anything wrong here. However, the dash after *Aegean Sea* alerts you that the writer has chosen to set off the parenthetical phrase describing *Acropolis* with dashes instead of commas. This means that you have to replace the comma after *Acropolis* with a dash, in order to have a matching pair. If there was a comma after *Aegean Sea,* this underlined part of the sentence would not need to be changed. Knowing that you need to "make it all match" will help you score points on ACT English.

2. G

Category: Sentence Sense
Difficulty: Medium
Getting to the Answer: This question tests your sense of parallelism. Your ear can often help you identify unparallel constructions. "To climb…is to have beheld" is unparallel. They should be in the same form: "to climb…is to behold."

3. D

Category: Writing Strategy
Difficulty: Low
Getting to the Answer: You have the option to OMIT in this question, which you should definitely take. Athenian cuisine has nothing to do with the subject of the paragraph or the passage, which is the Parthenon.

4. F

Category: Verb Tenses
Difficulty: Medium
Getting to the Answer: This verb is appropriately plural—the subject, *generations,* is plural—and in the present perfect tense. Choices G and H are singular verbs, while J is wrong because generations of architects can't all be proclaiming at the present time.

5. D

Category: Sentence Sense
Difficulty: High
Getting to the Answer: Run-on sentences are common on the English test. There are a couple of ways to deal with this run-on sentence. You could put a semicolon after *subtle* to separate the clauses, or you could put a period after *subtle* and make the clauses into separate sentences. Because the choices offer you both options, there must be something more. And there is: you need a comma after *For example* to set it off from the rest of the sentence. Choice (D) fixes both errors.

6. G

Category: Sentence Sense
Difficulty: Medium
Getting to the Answer: This part of the sentence sounds strange; it seems that *the fact* is what is being "viewed from a distance," not the *straight columns*. "Viewed from a distance" is a misplaced modifier that has to be moved to a position where it clearly modifies *columns*. Choice (G) accomplishes this.

7. D

Category: Punctuation
Difficulty: Medium
Getting to the Answer: Read the sentence out loud and you'll hear that it has punctuation problems. There is no need for a semicolon or any other kind of punctuation mark between *of* and *uprightness*. Don't place a comma before the first element of a

series, C, and don't place a colon between a preposition and its objects, B.

8. J

Category: Connections
Difficulty: Medium
Getting to the Answer: The phrase "because of this" doesn't make sense here. The optical illusion the architects created is not the reason you'll get a different impression of the Parthenon from the one the ancient Athenians had; the reason is that the statue of Athena Parthenos isn't there anymore. The introductory phrase that makes sense won't suggest conclusion or contrast, it will emphasize the information in the sentence, making (J) correct.

9. C

Category: Sentence Sense
Difficulty: Medium
Getting to the Answer: "Only by standing…Golden Age of Athens" is a sentence fragment that has to be hooked up somehow to the sentence after it. You can't just use a semicolon to join the two, B, because then the first clause of the new sentence will still be only a fragment. You have to reverse the subject and verb of the second sentence to attach the fragment to it, as (C) does.

10. J

Category: Sentence Sense
Difficulty: High
Getting to the Answer: What was removed from the temple? The underlined part of the sentence is an introductory modifying phrase that you know describes the statue, but the word *statue* isn't anywhere in the sentence. As a result, the sentence doesn't make sense at all; it's impossible that "all that remains" in the temple was removed in the fifth century c.e. Choice (J) makes the sentence make sense.

11. D

Category: Verb Tenses
Difficulty: Low
Getting to the Answer: Quite a few words come between the subject and the verb of this sentence. You shouldn't be fooled, though; *many* is the subject of the sentence, not *carvings, walls*, or *Acropolis*. Because *many* is plural, the verb of the sentence has to be plural as well. *Is* has to be changed to *are*, (D).

12. H

Category: Sentence Sense
Difficulty: High
Getting to the Answer: This sentence is really only a sentence fragment; it has a subject, *decision*, but no verb. Choice (H) rewords the underlined portion to make *Lord Elgin* the subject and *decided* the verb.

13. C

Category: Word Choice
Difficulty: Low
Getting to the Answer: *They* is an ambiguous pronoun because it's not immediately clear what group *they* refers to. You can figure out from the context that *they* is the Greeks; no other group could have won independence from the Turks and demanded the carvings back from the British. To make the first sentence clear, you have to replace *they* with the Greeks.

14. J

Category: Writing Strategy
Difficulty: Medium
Getting to the Answer: What could have been destroyed by explosions in the Parthenon? Carvings. The fact that some of the carvings were destroyed during a war is another good reason that many of them can no longer be found in the Parthenon, as paragraph 4 states. Therefore, the new material belongs in paragraph 4.

15. C

Category: Writing Strategy

Difficulty: Medium

Getting to the Answer: The answer to the question is clearly "no." The writer did not fulfill the request because only the second paragraph discusses techniques of construction at all; even then, only one technique, the bulging of the columns, is described in any detail. The author covers several topics in the essay in addition to construction techniques, including the statue of Athena Parthenos and the fate of the carvings.

PASSAGE II

16. H

Category: Verb Tenses

Difficulty: Low

Getting to the Answer: The previous sentence tells you that "Robin is the hero"; look for a verb form that matches the present tense *is*, because the sentence continues the discussion of the ballads. In (H), *tell* is in the right tense. Choice F switches to another tense, the present progressive, which makes it sound as if the ballads were literally speaking. Choice G lacks a main verb, creating a sentence fragment. Choice J has the same tense problem as F and compounds it by adding an extra, unnecessary subject, *they*.

17. C

Category: Sentence Sense

Difficulty: Medium

Getting to the Answer: You need a verb that is parallel to *robbing* and *killing*, so *giving*, (C), is the correct choice.

18. H

Category: Word Choice

Difficulty: Medium

Getting to the Answer: The adjective *frequent* is the correct choice to modify *enemy*. The underlined choice uses both the word *most* and the suffix *-est* to indicate the highest degree, or superlative form. Use one or the other, but not both. Likewise, G incorrectly uses *more* and the suffix *-er* together. Both of these express the comparative form—but again, you'd use one or the other, not both at once. In J, *frequently* is an adverb and so can't describe a noun.

19. D

Category: Writing Strategy

Difficulty: Medium

Getting to the Answer: When you see the OMIT option, ask yourself if the underlined portion is really necessary. The parentheses are a clue that the underlined part isn't really relevant. It goes off on a tangent about modern adaptations of the King Arthur legend, whereas Robin Hood is the focus of the passage. Choices B and C reword the irrelevant sentence.

20. F

Category: Word Choice

Difficulty: Medium

Getting to the Answer: This is correct as is. *Them* matches the plural noun it's standing in for: *writers*. Choice G, *him*, and H, *it*, are singular, so they don't. Choice J is wordy.

21. A

Category: Punctuation

Difficulty: Low

Getting to the Answer: This is correct because we need the possessive apostrophe. Choices B and C are wrong because they are the plural, not the possessive, form of Stukely, and there obviously aren't a lot of Stukelys running around. Choice D is wrong because if you read it out loud, you can tell that no pause—and so no comma—is called for.

22. J

Category: Writing Strategy

Difficulty: Medium

Getting to the Answer: Because this passage is aimed at discussing the historical development of the Robin Hood legend, (J) is most in keeping with the subject matter. Choice F goes way off track; you're asked to add more information on Stukely, not on English history. Choices G and H do relate their points to Stukely, but they pursue details. The main topic of the passage is Robin Hood, not antiquaries, G. (Remember, you want a choice that is most relevant to the passage as a whole.) As for H, King Arthur was mentioned earlier in the passage, but then only to make a point about Robin Hood. A discussion of Stukely's interest in King Arthur would stray from the topic of the passage.

23. C

Category: Sentence Sense
Difficulty: Low
Getting to the Answer: The shortest answer is the best choice. Choices A and D wrongly imply a comparison between Robin and a nobleman, when the claim was that Robin was a nobleman. B is incoherent.

24. G

Category: Writing Strategy
Difficulty: Medium
Getting to the Answer: The comparison with a puppy is silly in this context because it doesn't match the matter-of-fact tone of this passage; all choices except (G) can be eliminated. (The ACT will sometimes use a phrase that simply doesn't go with the passage's tone.)

25. D

Category: Punctuation
Difficulty: Medium
Getting to the Answer: The only choice that will tie in both parts of the sentence is (D). A dash in this context correctly makes an emphatic pause between *love interest* and its appositive, *Maid Marian*. All the rest of the choices have punctuation errors. Semicolons are used between independent clauses, and the part that would follow the semicolon in A isn't a clause. The plural form of the noun, *interests*, B, doesn't agree with the singular article. Choice C can be ruled out because there is no reason to pause in the middle of a name, and so the comma is incorrectly placed.

26. H

Category: Connections
Difficulty: High
Getting to the Answer: All the choices, with the exception of (H), have inappropriate connecting words. The passage moves to a discussion of a new time period, so you should begin a new paragraph, ruling out G. In addition, "on the one hand" should be followed by "on the other hand." *Consequently*, F, and *therefore*, J, wrongly imply that what follows is a result of something in the previous sentence.

27. B

Category: Verb Tenses
Difficulty: Medium
Getting to the Answer: The correct verb tense, and the only choice that doesn't create a sentence fragment, is (B). *Basing*, A, and *to base*, C, create sentence fragments. Of course, the omission of the verb would also result in a sentence fragment, so D is incorrect.

28. G

Category: Connections
Difficulty: Medium
Getting to the Answer: Choice (G) is the only choice that fits the rest of the sentence both logically and grammatically. *And* doesn't make sense as a connecting word in the original. Choice H also uses a connecting word that doesn't logically fit; *therefore* inaccurately suggests a cause-and-effect relationship. Choice J is wrong because a semicolon should be used between independent clauses, and the first clause can't stand alone.

29. D

Category: Writing Strategy

Difficulty: Medium

Getting to the Answer: You're told that the audience is unfamiliar with the story, so it would make sense to include a summary of the Robin Hood legend, (D), something the passage lacks. Choices A and C would do nothing for a reader curious about Robin Hood, because they go off on tangents about other issues. As the passage states that Robin Hood's existence is questionable (*legendary*), B doesn't fit in with the stance of the writer.

30. J

Category: Writing Strategy

Difficulty: Low

Getting to the Answer: Rarely are ACT English passages written for authorities or experts; they're usually written for the general public, as (J) correctly states in this question. If the passage were directed toward *experts*, F, or *authorities*, G, much of the basic information it presents would be unnecessary and not included. The passage states that the existence of Robin Hood is legendary, so the passage can't be aimed at readers craving confirmation that he "was an actual historical personage," so H is wrong.

PASSAGE III

31. A

Category: Wordiness

Difficulty: Low

Getting to the Answer: The shortest answer is correct. *Ten-mile* is correctly punctuated: the hyphen makes it an adjective modifying *radius*. The other answers are wordy and awkward.

32. H

Category: Word Choice

Difficulty: Medium

Getting to the Answer: You don't look forward *at* something. You look forward *to* something. Choice G wrongly implies that it is the brother who looks forward to the opportunity to show off the narrator's skills. Choice J wrongly implies a contrast between the two parts of the sentence. Actually, it is precisely because she hasn't flown with her brother that the writer anticipates showing off her skills to him.

33. D

Category: Connections

Difficulty: Medium

Getting to the Answer: *Ever since* means from the time the narrator first could read to the present time of the narrative. This span of time makes sense, since the writer is telling us how long she had planned on a journalism career. *If* in A signals a hypothetical situation, rather than a period of time. *Since* in B implies a cause-and-effect relationship that doesn't hold up. Why would her ability to easily read a newspaper be a reason for her career decision? *Although* in C signals a contrast, but there isn't one.

34. F

Category: Word Choice

Difficulty: Low

Getting to the Answer: It's true that you use *I* and *me*, in G and H, when you're writing about yourself. However, you can't say "I always envisioned I" or "I always envisioned me." Per the rules of grammar, you have to say "I always envisioned myself."

35. A

Category: Punctuation

Difficulty: Medium

Getting to the Answer: Choice (A) is correct because all you need to do is pause before the word *giving*, and this pause is signaled by the comma. You don't need a colon, as in B. Colons signal lists or definitions. You don't need a semicolon in C either—a semicolon should be placed between clauses that could stand alone as sentences, but the second part of this sentence can't. Choice D creates a sentence with no verb.

36. G

Category: Sentence Sense
Difficulty: Medium
Getting to the Answer: This is an example of a misplaced modifier. Choices F and H make it sound as if it is the airport, and not the pilot, that is filing the flight plan. Choice J is awkward (it uses a passive construction) and wordy. Choice (G) is concise, and the verbs *filed* and *gave* are parallel.

37. A

Category: Sentence Sense
Difficulty: Low
Getting to the Answer: The adjective *careful* should be placed before *watch*, the noun it modifies. Choice B is wrong because the reference is not to "careful airplanes." *Neared* requires an adverb such as *carefully* before it, not an adjective. Choice D is wrong because it is the people, not the crater, that are *careful.*

38. J

Category: Punctuation
Difficulty: Medium
Getting to the Answer: The colon in the original interrupts the flow of the sentence. Colons often function like equal signs. ("Here's what we need for the picnic: salami, ham, cheese, and bread.") Colons signal lists or definitions, but nothing needs to be equated in this sentence.

39. D

Category: Wordiness
Difficulty: Low
Getting to the Answer: Because *speechless* and *mute* mean the same thing, it's redundant to use both of them.

40. G

Category: Verb Tenses
Difficulty: Medium
Getting to the Answer: *Steadying* and *took* should be in parallel form. This makes (G) correct. The verbs in J are parallel, but they're in the present tense, which doesn't fit with the past tense verbs *shot* and *dictated* in the nonunderlined part of the sentence.

41. A

Category: Writing Strategy
Difficulty: Medium
Getting to the Answer: Jeff and the narrator are circling the mountain, so "a description of Mt. St. Helens" would be appropriate. Choice B contradicts the information in the passage; we're told that the plane must stay high enough to avoid smoke and ash. In any case, the tone of B doesn't suit the calm tone of the rest of the passage. Choice C sounds as if it belongs in a science textbook rather than in a story. Choice D wanders too far from the direct observation of the Mt. St. Helens volcano, which is the paragraph's focus.

42. G

Category: Connections
Difficulty: Medium
Getting to the Answer: "Since that time" is an appropriate transition. It makes clear the time shift between the day at Mt. St. Helens and the present. The other choices contain inappropriate connecting words. *However* in F and *nevertheless* in J signal contrasts, but there isn't one in the passage. *Furthermore* suggests an elaboration of what came before, but there is no elaboration in the passage.

43. C

Category: Writing Strategy
Difficulty: Medium
Getting to the Answer: Because the author is favorably recalling a memorable past experience, *nostalgic* in (C) is the best choice. The passage is positive in tone. It's definitely not *bitter*, B, or *exhausted*, D. *Optimistic* is close but wrong. *Optimistic* means "hopeful." The passage focuses on the excitement of the past, not on the good things that might happen.

44. H

Category: Writing Strategy

Difficulty: Medium

Getting to the Answer: The use of *I* is appropriate because this is a firsthand account. First-person narratives do tend to draw the reader in. Choice J is not true, because *I* is not appropriate in all types of writing. The passage is personal and chatty; it's not an example of "formal writing." The passage isn't focused on volcanoes in general, as G says, but on the Mt. St. Helens eruption, the narrator's first international story.

45. B

Category: Organization

Difficulty: High

Getting to the Answer: The passage reads best if the first and second paragraphs are switched. Choices A, C, and D confuse the time sequence of the narrative, which follows the narrator from her early dreams of becoming a photojournalist, to the memorable Mt. St. Helens story, to her present experience as a foreign correspondent.

PASSAGE IV

46. G

Category: Wordiness

Difficulty: Low

Getting to the Answer: The description of Sherlock Holmes as "ingenious and extremely clever" is redundant because ingenious and extremely clever mean the same thing. You need to use only one of the two to get the point across.

47. D

Category: Connections

Difficulty: High

Getting to the Answer: *Therefore* is supposed to be a signal that the sentence that follows is a logical conclusion based on information from the preceding sentence or sentences. The use of *therefore* doesn't make any sense here because you can't conclude that everyone knows the phrase "elementary, my dear Watson" just because everyone knows of Holmes's detective abilities. Choice C is wrong for the same reason—"for this reason" and *therefore* mean the same thing in this context. *Although*, B, indicates some sort of contrast; this would be wrong because there is no contrast within this sentence or between this sentence and the previous one. Really, there is no need for a structural signal here at all. Choice (D) is correct.

48. J

Category: Writing Strategy

Difficulty: Medium

Getting to the Answer: Note that this question has an OMIT option—a strong clue that the underlined portion is irrelevant to the paragraph. The theme of the first paragraph is "everyone knows who Sherlock Holmes is (or was)." The last sentence has absolutely nothing to do with this main idea, so it should be omitted. Putting parentheses around the sentence, as in G, will not make it more relevant, so that is not the way to solve the problem.

49. B

Category: Word Choice

Difficulty: Medium

Getting to the Answer: *He* is an ambiguous pronoun because it's unclear whether *he* refers to Conan Doyle or to Sherlock Holmes. You know after reading the entire sentence that *he* is Conan Doyle, so you have to replace *he* with *Conan Doyle* for the sake of clarity.

50. J

Category: Wordiness

Difficulty: Medium

Getting to the Answer: From a grammatical point of view, there is nothing wrong here; it's just unnecessarily wordy. The ACT prizes clarity and simplicity in style, which often means that the shortest answer is the best one. "To be remembered" is the most concise, and therefore the correct, answer.

51. A

Category: Connections
Difficulty: Medium
Getting to the Answer: *In fact* is the appropriate signal phrase here. *Despite this*, *regardless*, and *yet* would all indicate a contrast between this sentence and the previous one. There is no contrast, however; Conan Doyle did not want to be remembered as the author of Sherlock Holmes stories, so he killed the detective off (at least for a while).

52. J

Category: Sentence Sense
Difficulty: Medium
Getting to the Answer: A modifying phrase that begins a sentence refers to the noun or pronoun immediately following the phrase. According to that rule, the phrase "having had enough of his famous character by that time" modifies *Sherlock Holmes*, which doesn't make sense at all. The sentence has to be rearranged so that the introductory phrase describes Conan Doyle. Choice (J) is the choice that accomplishes this.

53. D

Category: Writing Strategy
Difficulty: Low
Getting to the Answer: Once again, take note of the OMIT choice. What do soap opera characters have to do with Arthur Conan Doyle and Sherlock Holmes? Nothing. This sentence disrupts the flow of the paragraph by being almost completely irrelevant, so it has to be omitted.

54. H

Category: Verb Tenses
Difficulty: Medium
Getting to the Answer: The verb is in the wrong tense. "Has been deeply immersed" is in the present perfect tense, which is used to describe an action that started in the past and continues to the present or that happened a number of times in the past and may happen again in the future. Conan Doyle's immersion in spiritualism is over and done with, so use the simple past: "was deeply immersed."

55. B

Category: Sentence Sense
Difficulty: Medium
Getting to the Answer: This is a sentence fragment because there is no subject and verb; all you have is an introductory phrase and a subordinate clause starting with *that*. By omitting *that*, you can turn the subordinate clause into a main clause, making "he lectured" the subject and verb, (B). Choice C would work if the sentence began with "so convinced." Choice D is wrong because the introductory phrase can't stand alone as a sentence.

56. J

Category: Wordiness
Difficulty: Low
Getting to the Answer: Because this sentence says that Conan Doyle and his family attempted to communicate with the dead by automatic writing, it's redundant to explain that automatic writing was thought to be a means of communicating with "those no longer among the living." Omit the underlined portion of the sentence.

57. D

Category: Organization
Difficulty: High
Getting to the Answer: The second sentence refers to "these experiences," so it should come directly after the sentence that describes the paranormal experiences Conan Doyle seemed to have had. The fourth sentence is the one that talks about materialized hands and heavy articles swimming through the air, so the second sentence should come after the fourth.

58. H

Category: Word Choice

Difficulty: Medium

Getting to the Answer: There are two problems with the underlined portion of the sentence: the colon does not belong there, and the pronoun *they* is ambiguous because it doesn't refer to anything in particular in the previous sentence. Choice (H) takes care of both of these problems by dropping the colon and by spelling out what the pronoun was supposed to refer to.

59. B

Category: Sentence Sense

Difficulty: Medium

Getting to the Answer: Here, you just have to pick the choice that makes sense. Sherlock Holmes is only a fictional character, so A, C, and D are wrong; Holmes could not possibly have said anything about Conan Doyle's spiritualism, nor will he ever. You can still wonder, however, what the esteemed detective would have said, if he were real. This is the idea behind the last sentence.

60. G

Category: Writing Strategy

Difficulty: High

Getting to the Answer: The passage contrasts the logical, deductive thinking used by Conan Doyle's fictional character, Sherlock Holmes, with Conan Doyle's own exploration of the paranormal. An appropriate subtitle must reflect this contrast. Choice (G) is the only choice that does.

PASSAGE V

61. A

Category: Verb Tenses

Difficulty: Medium

Getting to the Answer: Use context to determine correct verb tense usage. The first clause in the sentence uses the present tense "emphasize," so "are not groundbreaking" is correct in the second clause. NO CHANGE is needed. Choices B and C introduce inconsistent verb tenses. Choice D makes a sentence fragment.

62. J

Category: Wordiness

Difficulty: High

Getting to the Answer: "OMIT the underlined portion" is an answer choice, so you know that Wordiness is a potential issue. Check to see if the underlined selection repeats something that is stated elsewhere in the sentence. Reading the entire sentence tells you that "area of" is redundant; "fields," as it is used here, means essentially the same thing. OMIT is the correct choice. Choices G and H use similarly redundant language: "subject" and "topic," respectively.

63. D

Category: Wordiness

Difficulty: Medium

Getting to the Answer: If a clear, unambiguous antecedent is present, a pronoun will be correct. Because "the slides" is the only plural noun in this sentence, the pronoun "they" is the best choice here; (D) is correct. Choice A repeats "the slides" unnecessarily. Choices B and C incorrectly change the plural to the possessive.

64. H

Category: Sentence Sense

Difficulty: High

Getting to the Answer: There are several ways to join independent clauses, but only one choice will do so without introducing additional errors. As written, the sentence is a run-on. Choice (H) correctly inserts "as" to make the first clause dependent. Choice G does not address the error. Choice J creates a grammatically incorrect sentence.

65. A

Category: Connections
Difficulty: Medium
Getting to the Answer: When two answer choices have transitions that convey the same meaning and create grammatically correct sentences, you can eliminate both choices, because they can't both be right. This sentence is correct as written. Choices B and D use transitions indicating a contrast, but the idea that people are working on improving visual presentation style does not contrast with the idea that "less cluttered" aids work better than "denser ones." Choice C uses the transition "similarly," but the second sentence is an example supporting the first.

66. J

Category: Wordiness
Difficulty: Low
Getting to the Answer: When the underlined selection consists of two words joined by "and" or "or," consider whether they mean essentially the same thing. If they do, the correct answer choice will eliminate one of them. "Enhance" and "improve," in this context, mean the same thing. Choice (J) omits the redundancy. Choice G is unnecessarily wordy. Choice H does not address the error.

67. A

Category: Sentence Sense
Difficulty: Medium
Getting to the Answer: Verbs in comparative structures, such as "not simply...but instead," require parallel structure, as do compounds joined by "and" or "or." This sentence uses correct parallel structure in both cases; NO CHANGE is needed here. Choices B and C violate the rules of parallel structure. Choice D changes the meaning of the sentence by indicating that "adding" is the thing that is demonstrated.

68. J

Category: Writing Strategy
Difficulty: Medium
Getting to the Answer: In questions like this one, first answer the "yes" or "no" part of the question; you'll be able to eliminate at least one answer choice, and usually more. This paragraph focuses solely on how "visual presentation style" is being refined. The topic sentence of the paragraph doesn't discuss audio aids, nor does any other sentence in the paragraph. Therefore, the sentence should NOT be added; (J) is correct.

69. B

Category: Sentence Sense
Difficulty: High
Getting to the Answer: When you need to determine the correct order of words in a long sentence like this one, start by focusing on the correct placement of descriptive phrases and eliminate your way to the correct answer. "In respected journals" needs to follow the verb phrase "have been published." This eliminates C. "In listeners" belongs with "improve comprehension," which eliminates A and D. Choice (B) is correct here.

70. G

Category: Sentence Sense
Difficulty: Medium
Getting to the Answer: The passive voice will not always be wrong on the ACT, but passive constructions are generally wordier than active ones, so check for an active version of any underlined passives. "It has been determined by researchers" is a wordy and indirect way of saying "Researchers have determined"; (G) is the best choice here. Choice H is a sentence fragment with no independent clause. Choice J uses incorrect grammatical structure.

71. A

Category: Punctuation
Difficulty: Medium
Getting to the Answer: Don't expect to find an error in every underlined selection. About one-fourth of the English Test questions will require NO CHANGE. The end of one sentence and the beginning of the next are underlined, so determine if the sentences should be combined. None of the answer choices offers an option for correctly joining two independent clauses; NO CHANGE is needed. Choice B creates a run-on sentence. Choices C and D leave the meaning of the second clause incomplete.

72. J

Category: Word Choice
Difficulty: Medium
Getting to the Answer: When a pronoun is underlined, check that it agrees with its antecedent—the noun it replaces. The underlined pronoun refers back to the "audience members," so the third-person plural pronoun "them" is correct. Choices F and G use singular pronouns, which don't agree with the plural noun "audience members." Choice H uses the second person "you," but the writer is not directly addressing the reader.

73. D

Category: Wordiness
Difficulty: Medium
Getting to the Answer: Check underlined selections for words that mean essentially the same thing. "Recently" and "of late" mean essentially the same thing, so using them together is redundant. Only (D) eliminates all redundant language. B is also redundant; something that happened "in recent times" by definition happened "not so long ago." Choice C adds the transition "in addition," but the observations of psychologists are not a logical addition to the reactions of audience members discussed in the previous paragraph.

74. G

Category: Connections
Difficulty: High
Getting to the Answer: You need to pick the best Connection between sentences 1 and 2, so read sentence 2 before going to the answer choices. Sentence 2 discusses the importance of body language in presentations; the most effective link to this sentence will introduce this topic. Only (G) mentions body language. Choice F is much more general than (G), repeating ideas that have already been stated in the passage. Choice H focuses on visual images, which were discussed in the previous paragraph, not sentence 2 of this paragraph. Choice J is unnecessarily wordy, using the passive voice and redundant language.

75. B

Category: Writing Strategy
Difficulty: Medium
Getting to the Answer: Read the question stems carefully. Frequently, more than one answer choice will be both relevant and consistent, but only one will meet the specific criteria of the question. The writer wants to show how the theory about body language has "influenced" the education and public speaking experts who are the subject of the sentence. Choice (B) explains a specific way these experts have been influenced; they now focus on teaching presenters how to effectively use body language. Choices A and C are both too general; neither shows the specific influence of the body language theory. Choice D is out of scope; audience size isn't discussed in the passage.

READING TEST

PASSAGE I

1. C

Category: Detail
Difficulty: Low
Getting to the Answer: Line 11 explicitly states that Victor is Rosemary's grandson. Choice (C) is correct.

2. H

Category: Inference
Difficulty: Medium
Getting to the Answer: Rosemary's unease with Victor's behavior is broadly in response to what she perceives as his laziness, but "laziness" isn't an answer choice. Choice J may be tempting, but Victor isn't unable to get out of bed, he's unwilling to. Paragraph 3 does specifically talk about something he had said that had "disturbed" her—his willingness to take an easy class, which matches (H). There is no evidence that Victor plans to drop out, so F is not correct, and her upbringing is never discussed with him, so G is incorrect.

3. D

Category: Inference
Difficulty: Medium
Getting to the Answer: The answer is strongly implied in the passage. Paragraph 3 notes that Rosemary wanted to go to high school after finishing grammar school. Her father would not permit her to go, so she had to spend time "with animals and rough farmhands for company instead of people her own age," (D). Choice B is flatly contradicted by paragraph 3, which indicates that Rosemary wanted to go to high school, not college. Choices A and C make inferences that are not supported by the passage.

4. G

Category: Inference
Difficulty: Medium
Getting to the Answer: Lines 19–20 say that Rosemary "had decided long ago that growing old was like slowly turning to stone." This sentiment suggests that she is resigned to the physical problems that accompany old age. *Acceptance*, (G), therefore, is correct. *Sadness*, F, and *resentment*, H, are too negative in tone, while *optimism*, J, is too positive. Rosemary, in short, isn't at all emotional about the aging process.

5. A

Category: Detail
Difficulty: Low
Getting to the Answer: Rosemary's interest in crossword puzzles is discussed in the opening sentences of paragraph 1. She does them for two reasons: to pass the time and to keep her mind active, (A). The other choices distort details in paragraphs 1 and 2. Choice B plays on Rosemary's happiness at still being able to write at 87, C plays on her need to consult an atlas to look up the Swiss river, and D plays on her experience of "an expanded sense of time" as she grows older.

6. H

Category: Generalization
Difficulty: Medium
Getting to the Answer: Most of the passage is about the different attitudes of Rosemary and Victor toward education, (H). The first two paragraphs serve as a lead-in to this topic, while the remainder of the passage concentrates on Rosemary's thoughts and memories about education. Rosemary mentions Victor's laziness, F, but this isn't the main focus of the passage. Education is the primary focus. There's no information at all to suggest that Victor's father has mistreated him, G. Indeed, just the opposite is implied: Victor's "doting parents," after all, have given him a new car. Finally, J doesn't mention education. Moreover, Rosemary doesn't try to suppress her memories.

7. B

Category: Inference
Difficulty: High
Getting to the Answer: A question that contains a line reference requires you to understand the context in which the reference appears. In the lines that precede the mention of Victor's "shiny new car," Rosemary considers his easy upbringing, how he looks as if he's never done a chore. In other words, Victor's car is a symbol of his generation, which has had a much easier time of it than Rosemary's. So (B) is correct. Rosemary's parents, A—her father anyway—can't be described as generous. Besides, her parents have nothing to do with Victor's car. Similarly, while Rosemary seems to feel that Victor's future prospects are bright, C, and that his life lacks hardship, D, neither has anything to do with his car.

8. G

Category: Detail
Difficulty: Medium
Getting to the Answer: Paragraph 3 says that Rosemary is disturbed by Victor's dismissive attitude toward his education. She doesn't like the idea that his only reason for taking a course is that he can pass it. In contrast to Victor's attitude, Rosemary, in her youth, was eager to continue her education, (G). Choices F and J refer to details from the wrong paragraphs, while H introduces an issue that the passage never tackles.

9. C

Category: Detail
Difficulty: Medium
Getting to the Answer: A few lines before Rosemary recalls what it was like growing up on the farm, the passage says that "Rosemary often experienced an expanded sense of time, with present and past tense intermingling in her mind," (C). Choice D, on the other hand, alludes to recollections from the wrong paragraphs. Choices A and B distort details in paragraph 2.

10. F

Category: Inference
Difficulty: Low
Getting to the Answer: The reference to Victor's bright future comes at the end of paragraph 2, which precedes Rosemary's opinion: "if he (Victor) ever got out of bed." It's clear from the text that it's Rosemary, (F), who thinks that he has a good future. The passage never says what Victor thought about his own future, G. Nor does it say what his parents thought about his future, H. And it's extremely unlikely that Victor and Rosemary's father, J, were even alive at the same time.

PASSAGE II

11. B

Category: Detail
Difficulty: High
Getting to the Answer: Use evidence in the passage and your own common sense to form a prediction before looking at the answer choices. The passage states that these revisions were written by "pro-business Eastern senators," and that these revisions worked to weaken the effectiveness of the Act. (B) is correct; the pro-business senators resisted the purpose of the bill. A is a misused detail; Social Darwinism is not discussed until the next paragraph, and the author makes no direct connection between it and the revisions. C is a distortion; there is evidence of "debate," because the bill got rewritten, but there is no evidence that the debate took a long time. D is extreme; the author is only discussing this bill, not the nature of all Congressional legislation at that time.

12. H

Category: Detail
Difficulty: High
Getting to the Answer: Remember to keep straight the opinion of the author and other opinions cited in the passage. The trust leaders used the theory of "Social Darwinism" to explain why it was natural for

them to have monopolies. The author must have included this in order to explain how some people justified the existence of monopolies. Choice (H) is correct; this matches your prediction. F is a distortion; this is what the monopolists thought, not what the author thinks. G is out of scope; the author is not exploring what kind of corporations survived, except to the extent that monopolists artificially stifled competition. J is out of scope; the author is discussing a specific instance, not exploring the general "influence" of science on policy.

13. B

Category: Inference
Difficulty: Medium
Getting to the Answer: When a question stem refers you to a section of the passage but does not provide enough information to make a prediction, it is often helpful to take a quick scan through the passage before looking at the answer choices. The third paragraph states that *laissez-faire* policies created monopolies that had many negative effects. Many people objected to this, which eventually led to the Sherman Antitrust Act and other similar measures. (B) fits with the description of the many negative effects of the trusts. A is extreme; there is not enough evidence in the passage to use the word *all*. C is a misused detail; this idea comes from the second passage. The author of Passage A never states that it was necessary; maybe there were other ways to handle the situation. D is a distortion; the author would argue that all businesses, even big trusts like Standard Oil, could compete freely after the act.

14. J

Category: Detail
Difficulty: Medium
Getting to the Answer: Because the answer is in the passage, you should be able to move quickly through Detail questions, saving time for those you find more difficult. Read in the immediate vicinity of the given reference. The prior sentence states that Roosevelt used "government funds for the first time" in "intentional deficit spending." The sentence after the reference points out that this "ushered in the modern era of liberal economic regulation . . ." The Act is an example of active manipulation of the economy by the government, which matches (J). F is a misused detail; Passage A, not Passage B, refers to antitrust acts. G is opposite; the passage states that "this act signaled the end of the *laissez-faire* economics era . . ." H is opposite; the author says that the Agricultural Adjustment Act helped boost the nation out of the Great Depression.

15. A

Category: Generalization
Difficulty: High
Getting to the Answer: The first and last sentence of a paragraph will often help clue you into the author's purpose. Interestingly, the passage is not primarily about economics; the author simply uses economics as an example to make his larger point, that the role of the national government must change over time. In the last paragraph, the author reinforces this by saying that Roosevelt went against traditional attitudes about the role of government in the economy, and that he was very successful in doing so. In the last sentence, the author sums up by saying that "the national government must adapt in both scope and purpose to fit the needs of changing times." This matches (A). B is opposite; the author argues that reforms were quite necessary. C is out of scope; the author does not "cite" any exceptions. D is a distortion; the author is saying that the government must change because circumstances change. This does not mean that there were "weaknesses in the original design" of the government.

16. H

Category: Detail
Difficulty: Medium
Getting to the Answer: opposite choices can be tricky if you do not take the time to read carefully. Many people, including the "conservative capitalist

economists," felt that the economy would naturally rise and fall, and that the government should not interfere in that process. The author then goes on to state that Roosevelt felt the economy would not naturally recover and so he instituted policies and spent money to fix it. The author feels that Roosevelt was right to do so. (The author says that Roosevelt's success was "undeniable.") So, the author explains the viewpoint of the "conservative capitalist economists" in order to then argue that they were wrong, and that Roosevelt was right in working to change the economy. (H) fits nicely with the sentiments of the author. F is opposite; Roosevelt took the opposite view from the "conservative capitalist economists." G is opposite; the viewpoint of the "conservative capitalist economists" was in direct contradiction to policies like the Agricultural Adjustment Act. J is a misused detail; this does not come up until the final paragraph.

17. B

Category: Detail
Difficulty: Medium
Getting to the Answer: Watch out for choices that only apply to one of the Paired Passages. Both passages refer to economic reform. Passage A talks about preventing monopolies and trusts, and Passage B speaks in more general terms about spending money to pull the nation out of the Great Depression. Look for something that deals with government intervention in the economy. (B) is mentioned in both passages. A is opposite; both authors seem to agree that some degree of governmental control is necessary. C is a misused detail; this only appears in Passage A. D is a misused detail; this only appears in Passage B.

18. G

Category: Inference
Difficulty: Medium
Getting to the Answer: When you are trying to infer how one author would react to an idea in another passage, look for a concept that the author specifically addresses. The author of Passage B argues that it is often a good idea for the government to intervene in the economy. Therefore he would probably not accept the argument that something should continue to exist simply because it is the most natural state of affairs. (G) is correct; this fits with Author B's view of *laissez-faire* economic policy. F is out of scope; we do not know how the author of Passage B feels about the theory of Social Darwinism. C is opposite; this viewpoint is what Author B is arguing against. D is a distortion; Author B never mentions monopolies.

19. B

Category: Detail
Difficulty: Low
Getting to the Answer: Use the passages to research your answer. It is tough to make a specific prediction here, so jump into the answer choices, and compare each one against the passages. (B) is correct; Passage B mentions Roosevelt's plan to "pump-prime" the depressed American economy through government deficit spending. A is opposite; this appears in Passage A but not Passage B. C is opposite; this is from Passage A, not Passage B. D is opposite; this appears in both passages.

20. J

Category: Detail
Difficulty: High
Getting to the Answer: In the third paragraph of Passage A, the author cites many negative consequences of *laissez-faire* policies, and the trusts and monopolies that arose from these policies. In the third paragraph of Passage B, the author states that the Agricultural Adjustment Act "signaled the end of the *laissez-faire* economics era." These details match (J). F is opposite; Passage A describes how *laissez-faire* policies negatively affected consumers and Passage B states that the *laissez-faire* era ended by the end of the 19th century. G includes misused details that are mentioned in each passage but do

not address the question. H is out of scope; Roosevelt's presidential legacy is not discussed.

PASSAGE III

21. C

Category: Detail
Difficulty: Medium
Getting to the Answer: This question asks for a description of the *philosophes*, so it's back to the first two paragraphs. Lines 15–17 say that they took the ideas of others and popularized them. The first sentence of paragraph 2 goes on to state that they "developed the philosophy of the Enlightenment and spread it to much of the educated elite in Western Europe (and the American colonies)." Thus, (C) is correct. Choices B and D are contradicted by information in the first paragraph, which states that the philosophes were generally neither professors nor scientists. Choice A, on the other hand, is too narrow in scope: true, the philosophes were influenced by Locke, but they were also influenced by Newton and English institutions.

22. G

Category: Inference
Difficulty: Low
Getting to the Answer: Your passage map of the passage should have sent you directly to the last paragraph, where Voltaire is discussed. This paragraph says that Voltaire criticized both French society and religious institutions, so you can infer that he might have attacked French religious institutions, (G). Choice H is contradicted by information in the paragraph, which states that Voltaire "came to admire" English government. It's unlikely that he would have criticized the Scientific Revolution, F, because the philosophes were disciples of this revolution. Finally, the passage says nothing about Voltaire's views of "courtly love," J, so you can't infer what his position on this issue would have been.

23. D

Category: Detail
Difficulty: Medium
Getting to the Answer: The answer to a question that contains a line reference is found in the lines around that reference. Locke's idea that "schools and social institutions could...play a great role in molding the individual" comes up right after his belief that humans are shaped by their experiences, (D). Choice A is contradicted by lines 50–53, while B and C distort details in paragraph 4.

24. H

Category: Inference
Difficulty: High
Getting to the Answer: Your passage map should have pointed you to paragraph 3, where Newton is discussed. This paragraph says that Newton believed that "the universe [was]...originally set in motion by God," option I, and that "the universe operates in a mechanical and orderly fashion," option III. However, this paragraph doesn't say that Newton believed that "human reason is insufficient to understand the laws of nature," option II; if anything, it implies just the opposite. Choice (H), options I and III only, is correct.

25. D

Category: Detail
Difficulty: Medium
Getting to the Answer: Lines 61–64 reveal that it was Locke who questioned the notion that "revelation was a reliable source of truth." Thus, you're looking for a work written by him, so you can immediately eliminate A, *Letters on the English*, and C, *Elements of the Philosophy of Newton*, both of which were authored by Voltaire. The remaining two works, *Second Treatise of Civil Government*, B, and *Essay Concerning Human Understanding*, (D), were both written by Locke; but *Second Treatise of Civil Government*, B, is a political, not a philosophical, work, so it can be eliminated as well. That leaves (D) as the correct answer.

26. G

Category: Inference

Difficulty: Medium

Getting to the Answer: The first sentence of paragraph 4 states that Locke "agreed with Newton but went further." Specifically, Locke also thought that the human mind was subject to "the mechanical laws of the material universe" (lines 48–49), (G). The other choices distort details in paragraphs 3 and 4.

27. D

Category: Generalization

Difficulty: Medium

Getting to the Answer: The philosophes—as paragraph 5 shows—were greatly influenced by an England that allowed more individual freedom, was more tolerant of religious differences, and was freer of traditional political institutions than other countries, particularly France. Indeed, the philosophes wanted other countries to adopt the English model. Thus (D), statements I, II, and III, is correct.

28. G

Category: Writer's View

Difficulty: High

Getting to the Answer: This question also asks about England, so refer back to paragraph 5. In the second-to-last sentence of the paragraph, the philosophes cite England's political stability and prosperity as evidence that England's system worked. The last sentence of the paragraph goes on to say that the philosophes "wanted to see in their own countries much of what England already seemed to have." Choice (G), therefore, is correct. Choice F, on the other hand, flatly contradicts the gist of paragraph 5. Finally, H and J distort details from the wrong part of the passage.

29. A

Category: Inference

Difficulty: Low

Getting to the Answer: The French political and religious authorities during the time of Voltaire are discussed in paragraph 6. Voltaire got in hot water with the authorities over his outspoken views, so it's safe to assume that they weren't advocates of free speech, (A). They first imprisoned and then exiled him, so they clearly didn't regard the philosophes with indifference, C. The passage doesn't say precisely what Voltaire was imprisoned and exiled for, so you can't infer that the authorities "overreacted to Voltaire's mild satires," B, which, in any case, weren't that mild. Finally, because Voltaire was an advocate of the English system of government, it's also safe to assume that the French hadn't accepted this model, making D wrong.

30. J

Category: Generalization

Difficulty: Medium

Getting to the Answer: The notion that the philosophes were "more literary than scientific" appears in the middle of paragraph 1. A few lines further down, the paragraph furnishes a list of the types of literary works produced by the philosophes, so (J) is correct. The passage never mentions any "political change," F. Nor does it compare the literary outputs of Newton and Voltaire, G. Finally, H is out because the philosophes were not scientists.

PASSAGE IV

31. D

Category: Detail

Difficulty: Low

Getting to the Answer: This question emphasizes the importance of reading all the choices before selecting one. The second paragraph tells us that the Alvarezes believe conditions created by the impact of a meteorite led to mass extinctions. The impact of the asteroid, A, caused great damage, but it didn't do "most of the harm"—see the third sentence. Processes like B and C are the explanations of the traditional scientists.

32. H

Category: Writer's View
Difficulty: High
Getting to the Answer: This isn't easy, but (H) is the only possible choice. The author is an objective scientist or science journalist who wouldn't want opponents to give up their view until the new theory has been fully tested against all their criticisms. The traditionalists' arguments are given only briefly, and the author clearly believes the Alvarezes have added something valuable to the study of mass extinctions, but the traditional view has not proven wrong conclusively, F. And as the last paragraph indicates, traditionalists have produced their own theories to account for new evidence, such as iridium reaching the Earth's surface via volcanic activity, J. Choice G is clearly not true; the author believes the new theory challenged the old one.

33. C

Category: Vocab-in-Context
Difficulty: Medium
Getting to the Answer: As it is used in the sentence, *enrichment* means "increase in amount." It wouldn't make sense for the Earth to have wealth, A, improvement, B, or reward of iridium, D.

34. F

Category: Generalization
Difficulty: Low
Getting to the Answer: The arguments of Alvarez-theory opponents are given in the last paragraph: no crater, iridium comes from the Earth's core, and the Alvarezes are only physicists. If sufficient iridium deposits come from the Earth's core in lava flows, (F), Alvarez supporters can't rely on them as evidence of impact. The Alvarezes didn't say extinctions never occurred without asteroid impact, G, or that all meteorites contain iridium, H. Choice J contradicts one of the opponents' arguments.

35. D

Category: Writer's View
Difficulty: Medium
Getting to the Answer: In the first sentence of paragraph 2, the author calls the Alvarez theory important. The bulk of the passage explains and supports this theory. The implication is that the author believes the Alvarezes were on the right track, so we want a positive answer. Choices A and C are negative, and B is neutral.

36. G

Category: Detail
Difficulty: High
Getting to the Answer: According to the information in the second paragraph, soil displacement was the immediate result of a meteorite's impact; it "blotted out" the sun, which reduced temperatures and caused plants to die.

37. D

Category: Inference
Difficulty: Medium
Getting to the Answer: Look back at the second paragraph; details there clarify how the impact led to extinctions—the crater didn't simply smash all species into extinction. Choice A uses the wrong verb. The lack of a known crater site, B, is mentioned at the end of paragraph 4, but that's not relevant to the discussion in paragraph 2. The conditions that result from meteorite collisions aren't evidence that the Earth is vulnerable to such collisions, C.

38. H

Category: Generalization
Difficulty: Medium
Getting to the Answer: The large number of asteroids implied by *teeming* in paragraph 1 explains why Alvarez supporters believe frequent collisions must have occurred in Earth's history (paragraph 4). The fact that an impact would result in certain effects, F, or the idea that the dust cloud would do more harm than the impact itself, G, or the traditional

view about gradual processes, J, are not related to the number of impacts that are likely.

39. C

Category: Detail
Difficulty: Medium
Getting to the Answer: The two sentences at the end of paragraph 4 offer the answer; only I and III explain this position. Iridium relates to a different argument entirely.

40. F

Category: Detail
Difficulty: Low
Getting to the Answer: As we've seen, the disastrous consequences of an asteroid's impact are covered in paragraph 2, where G, H, and J are mentioned. Choice (F) is evidence of impact from paragraph 3.

WRITING TEST

MODEL ESSAY

Below is an example of what a high-scoring essay might look like. Notice the author states her position clearly in the introductory paragraph and supports that position with evidence in the following paragraphs. This essay also uses transitions, some advanced vocabulary, and an effective "hook" to draw in the reader.

Teenagers have lots of opinions, many of which we share rather loudly. Taking into consideration the students' feelings about the courses they study in high school has both pros and cons. Some argue that schools should provide students a way to make their preferences known, others feel students are too young to make good decisions about what to study, and others argue that surveying students can help make the curriculum more relevant to them and provide another way to evaluate a teacher's effectiveness. I agree that students' interests should be surveyed as long as they are not, in and of themselves, the basis for creating a curriculum.

From the first perspective, it is argued that high schools should do what colleges do and survey students to see how they feel about their classroom lessons. Studies show that when high school students are engaged because they enjoy their studies and understand the relevance of what they are learning, they are more participatory in class and remember more of what they learn. However, one problem is that schools cannot let students create the lessons, since this would lead to chaos with so many students expressing different opinions. However, if it were made clear that not all suggestions would be used but that there would be some way to pare down the suggestions, implementing only those with most student support, it would be possible for the students' preferences to be included in a lesson. Schools could survey students, compile a list of five top suggestions, then have students vote on them. In this way at least some student suggestions, and hopefully the most popular ones, would be part of the curriculum and promote more interaction and learning in a classroom. Surely this is the goal of education, and therefore it should be encouraged.

On the other hand, there are those who think that only the teachers should be in charge of the curriculum because students are not qualified to make those changes. It's true that students don't have the education, knowledge, and maturity to design lessons, but the argument doesn't say that the curriculum would be totally in the hands of the students, but only that student preferences should be considered. Those who argue that students aren't capable of designing the curriculum have misunderstood the statement. Every-body can benefit from suggestions, including educators, so there is nothing wrong with finding out what students want and trying to incorporate at least some of it into the curriculum. Any good teacher does this already. For example, she tries to make her examples relevant to what the students are interested in, such as teaching math by using basketball or baseball examples. So the argument is already partially in force, and those who misread it by thinking that the entire curriculum would be made up by students are misinterpreting the argument and coming to a wrong conclusion.

Finally, some argue that allowing student surveys could make lessons more interesting and also be a way of evaluating a teacher's effectiveness. I personally think that this would be a better way to evaluate teachers than using test scores, which don't always reflect real learning. But surveys are completely subjective, and it would be very difficult to tell which responses really reflect student satisfaction and which are just written because the student needs to write something. So this option is better than cold test scores, but I also see problems in it and so can't support it fully.

If a school administration makes it really clear that, just because students are being asked to make lesson plan suggestions doesn't mean that all suggestions will be used and that students are not in charge of making the curriculum, then the first perspective—allowing students to give their opinion about what they would like to study—is a good one. This one will make at least some lesson plans more interesting and relevant, and that will lead to better learning.

ACT Practice Test Two
ANSWER SHEET

ENGLISH TEST

1. Ⓐ Ⓑ Ⓒ Ⓓ	11. Ⓐ Ⓑ Ⓒ Ⓓ	21. Ⓐ Ⓑ Ⓒ Ⓓ	31. Ⓐ Ⓑ Ⓒ Ⓓ	41. Ⓐ Ⓑ Ⓒ Ⓓ	51. Ⓐ Ⓑ Ⓒ Ⓓ	61. Ⓐ Ⓑ Ⓒ Ⓓ	71. Ⓐ Ⓑ Ⓒ Ⓓ
2. Ⓕ Ⓖ Ⓗ Ⓙ	12. Ⓕ Ⓖ Ⓗ Ⓙ	22. Ⓕ Ⓖ Ⓗ Ⓙ	32. Ⓕ Ⓖ Ⓗ Ⓙ	42. Ⓕ Ⓖ Ⓗ Ⓙ	52. Ⓕ Ⓖ Ⓗ Ⓙ	62. Ⓕ Ⓖ Ⓗ Ⓙ	72. Ⓕ Ⓖ Ⓗ Ⓙ
3. Ⓐ Ⓑ Ⓒ Ⓓ	13. Ⓐ Ⓑ Ⓒ Ⓓ	23. Ⓐ Ⓑ Ⓒ Ⓓ	33. Ⓐ Ⓑ Ⓒ Ⓓ	43. Ⓐ Ⓑ Ⓒ Ⓓ	53. Ⓐ Ⓑ Ⓒ Ⓓ	63. Ⓐ Ⓑ Ⓒ Ⓓ	73. Ⓐ Ⓑ Ⓒ Ⓓ
4. Ⓕ Ⓖ Ⓗ Ⓙ	14. Ⓕ Ⓖ Ⓗ Ⓙ	24. Ⓕ Ⓖ Ⓗ Ⓙ	34. Ⓕ Ⓖ Ⓗ Ⓙ	44. Ⓕ Ⓖ Ⓗ Ⓙ	54. Ⓕ Ⓖ Ⓗ Ⓙ	64. Ⓕ Ⓖ Ⓗ Ⓙ	74. Ⓕ Ⓖ Ⓗ Ⓙ
5. Ⓐ Ⓑ Ⓒ Ⓓ	15. Ⓐ Ⓑ Ⓒ Ⓓ	25. Ⓐ Ⓑ Ⓒ Ⓓ	35. Ⓐ Ⓑ Ⓒ Ⓓ	45. Ⓐ Ⓑ Ⓒ Ⓓ	55. Ⓐ Ⓑ Ⓒ Ⓓ	65. Ⓐ Ⓑ Ⓒ Ⓓ	75. Ⓐ Ⓑ Ⓒ Ⓓ
6. Ⓕ Ⓖ Ⓗ Ⓙ	16. Ⓕ Ⓖ Ⓗ Ⓙ	26. Ⓕ Ⓖ Ⓗ Ⓙ	36. Ⓕ Ⓖ Ⓗ Ⓙ	46. Ⓕ Ⓖ Ⓗ Ⓙ	56. Ⓕ Ⓖ Ⓗ Ⓙ	66. Ⓕ Ⓖ Ⓗ Ⓙ	
7. Ⓐ Ⓑ Ⓒ Ⓓ	17. Ⓐ Ⓑ Ⓒ Ⓓ	27. Ⓐ Ⓑ Ⓒ Ⓓ	37. Ⓐ Ⓑ Ⓒ Ⓓ	47. Ⓐ Ⓑ Ⓒ Ⓓ	57. Ⓐ Ⓑ Ⓒ Ⓓ	67. Ⓐ Ⓑ Ⓒ Ⓓ	
8. Ⓕ Ⓖ Ⓗ Ⓙ	18. Ⓕ Ⓖ Ⓗ Ⓙ	28. Ⓕ Ⓖ Ⓗ Ⓙ	38. Ⓕ Ⓖ Ⓗ Ⓙ	48. Ⓕ Ⓖ Ⓗ Ⓙ	58. Ⓕ Ⓖ Ⓗ Ⓙ	68. Ⓕ Ⓖ Ⓗ Ⓙ	
9. Ⓐ Ⓑ Ⓒ Ⓓ	19. Ⓐ Ⓑ Ⓒ Ⓓ	29. Ⓐ Ⓑ Ⓒ Ⓓ	39. Ⓐ Ⓑ Ⓒ Ⓓ	49. Ⓐ Ⓑ Ⓒ Ⓓ	59. Ⓐ Ⓑ Ⓒ Ⓓ	69. Ⓐ Ⓑ Ⓒ Ⓓ	
10. Ⓕ Ⓖ Ⓗ Ⓙ	20. Ⓕ Ⓖ Ⓗ Ⓙ	30. Ⓕ Ⓖ Ⓗ Ⓙ	40. Ⓕ Ⓖ Ⓗ Ⓙ	50. Ⓕ Ⓖ Ⓗ Ⓙ	60. Ⓕ Ⓖ Ⓗ Ⓙ	70. Ⓕ Ⓖ Ⓗ Ⓙ	

READING TEST

1. Ⓐ Ⓑ Ⓒ Ⓓ	6. Ⓕ Ⓖ Ⓗ Ⓙ	11. Ⓐ Ⓑ Ⓒ Ⓓ	16. Ⓕ Ⓖ Ⓗ Ⓙ	21. Ⓐ Ⓑ Ⓒ Ⓓ	26. Ⓕ Ⓖ Ⓗ Ⓙ	31. Ⓐ Ⓑ Ⓒ Ⓓ	36. Ⓕ Ⓖ Ⓗ Ⓙ
2. Ⓕ Ⓖ Ⓗ Ⓙ	7. Ⓐ Ⓑ Ⓒ Ⓓ	12. Ⓕ Ⓖ Ⓗ Ⓙ	17. Ⓐ Ⓑ Ⓒ Ⓓ	22. Ⓕ Ⓖ Ⓗ Ⓙ	27. Ⓐ Ⓑ Ⓒ Ⓓ	32. Ⓕ Ⓖ Ⓗ Ⓙ	37. Ⓐ Ⓑ Ⓒ Ⓓ
3. Ⓐ Ⓑ Ⓒ Ⓓ	8. Ⓕ Ⓖ Ⓗ Ⓙ	13. Ⓐ Ⓑ Ⓒ Ⓓ	18. Ⓕ Ⓖ Ⓗ Ⓙ	23. Ⓐ Ⓑ Ⓒ Ⓓ	28. Ⓕ Ⓖ Ⓗ Ⓙ	33. Ⓐ Ⓑ Ⓒ Ⓓ	38. Ⓕ Ⓖ Ⓗ Ⓙ
4. Ⓕ Ⓖ Ⓗ Ⓙ	9. Ⓐ Ⓑ Ⓒ Ⓓ	14. Ⓕ Ⓖ Ⓗ Ⓙ	19. Ⓐ Ⓑ Ⓒ Ⓓ	24. Ⓕ Ⓖ Ⓗ Ⓙ	29. Ⓐ Ⓑ Ⓒ Ⓓ	34. Ⓕ Ⓖ Ⓗ Ⓙ	39. Ⓐ Ⓑ Ⓒ Ⓓ
5. Ⓐ Ⓑ Ⓒ Ⓓ	10. Ⓕ Ⓖ Ⓗ Ⓙ	15. Ⓐ Ⓑ Ⓒ Ⓓ	20. Ⓕ Ⓖ Ⓗ Ⓙ	25. Ⓐ Ⓑ Ⓒ Ⓓ	30. Ⓕ Ⓖ Ⓗ Ⓙ	35. Ⓐ Ⓑ Ⓒ Ⓓ	40. Ⓕ Ⓖ Ⓗ Ⓙ

ENGLISH TEST

45 Minutes—75 Questions

Directions: In the following five passages, certain words and phrases are underlined and numbered. In the right-hand column are alternatives for each underlined portion. Select the one that best conveys the idea, creates the most grammatically correct sentence, or is most consistent with the style and tone of the passage. If you decide that the original version is best, select NO CHANGE. You may also find questions that ask about the entire passage or a section of the passage. These questions will correspond to small, numbered boxes in the test. For these questions, decide which choice best accomplishes the purpose set out in the question stem. After you've selected the best choice, fill in the corresponding oval on your Answer Grid. For some questions, you'll need to read the context in order to answer correctly. Be sure to read until you have enough information to determine the correct answer choice.

PASSAGE I

AMERICAN JAZZ

<u>One of the earliest</u> [1] music forms to originate in the United States was Jazz. Known as truly Mid-American because of <u>it's</u> [2] having origins in several locations in middle America, this music developed almost simultaneously in New Orleans, Saint Louis, Kansas City, and Chicago.

At the start of the twentieth century, musicians all along the Mississippi River familiar with West African

1. A. NO CHANGE
   B. One of the most earliest
   C. The most early
   D. The earliest

2. F. NO CHANGE
   G. its
   H. its's
   J. its,

GO ON TO THE NEXT PAGE

folk music [3] blended it with European classical music from the early nineteenth century. This combination was adopted by artists in the region who began to use minor chords and syncopation, in their own music, ragtime and blues. At the same time, brass bands and gospel choirs adopted Jazz music, and it became a true blend of cultures. Eventually, a unique music style developed; based on a blend of the many different cultures in America at the time. It was American Jazz and became the first indigenous American style to affect music in the rest of the world.

[1] One of the true greats of American Jazz was Cabell "Cab" Calloway III. [2] He was born in New York in 1907, but his family moved to Chicago during

3. At this point, the writer is considering adding the following phrase:

   —rich with syncopation—

   Given that it is true, would this be a relevant addition to make here?

   A. Yes, because it can help the reader have a better understanding of the music being discussed.
   B. Yes, because it helps explain to the reader why this music became popular.
   C. No, because it fails to explain the connection between this music and the button accordion.
   D. No, because it is inconsistent with the style of this essay to mention specific musical forms.

4. **F.** NO CHANGE
   G. syncopation in their own music,
   H. syncopation, in their own music
   J. syncopation in their own music

5. **A.** NO CHANGE
   B. style developed based on
   C. style developed based on,
   D. style, developed based on

6. **F.** NO CHANGE
   G. This style, known as American Jazz,
   H. Being known as American Jazz, it
   J. It being American Jazz first

GO ON TO THE NEXT PAGE

his teen years. [3] Growing up, Cab made his living (7) working as a shoe shiner and he was (8) a waiter. [4] During these years, he also spent time at the racetrack, where he walked horses to keep them in good shape. [9] [5] After graduating from high school in Chicago, where (10) Cab got his first performance job in a revue called "Plantation Days." [6] His strong

7. Which of the following alternatives to the underlined portion would NOT be acceptable?
   A. earned his living by
   B. made his living from
   C. made his living on
   D. earned his living

8. F. NO CHANGE
   G. as well
   H. being
   J. OMIT the underlined portion

9. The writer is considering deleting the following clause from the preceding sentence (placing a period after the word *racetrack*):

   where he walked horses to keep them in good shape.

   Should the writer make this deletion?
   A. Yes, because the information is unrelated to the topic addressed in this paragraph.
   B. Yes, because the information diminishes the musical accomplishments and successes of Cab Calloway.
   C. No, because the information explains the reference to the racetrack, which might otherwise puzzle readers.
   D. No, because the information shows how far Cab Calloway came in his life.

10. F. NO CHANGE
    G. it was there that
    H. was where
    J. OMIT the underlined portion

GO ON TO THE NEXT PAGE

and impressive voice soon gained him popularity in the top Jazz circles of the United States. [12]

11. A. NO CHANGE
B. popularity: in the top Jazz circles
C. popularity, in the top Jazz circles,
D. popularity in the top Jazz circles,

12. Upon reviewing this paragraph and finding that some information has been left out, the writer composes the following sentence incorporating that information:

He became widely known as "The man in the zoot suit with the reet pleats."

This sentence would most logically be placed after sentence:

F. 3.
G. 4.
H. 5.
J. 6.

Many others have followed Cab's lead and have moved from the east coast to middle America. Like other folk music forms, American Jazz has a rich history and unique sound that means it'll stick around for a while.

13. Given that all the choices are true, which one would most effectively tie together the two main subjects of this essay?
A. NO CHANGE
B. and have added to the rich tradition of American Jazz.
C. such as George Duke and Earl Klugh.
D. and have signed large recording contracts.

14. F. NO CHANGE
G. causes it to be an enduring institution with a timeless appeal.
H. makes many people enjoy it.
J. ensures its continued vitality.

GO ON TO THE NEXT PAGE

Question 15 asks about the essay as a whole.

15. Suppose the writer's goal was to write a brief essay focusing on the history and development of American Jazz music. Would this essay successfully fulfill this goal?
   A. Yes, because the essay describes the origins of American Jazz music and one of its important figures.
   B. Yes, because the essay mentions the contributions American Jazz music has made to other folk music traditions.
   C. No, because the essay refers to other musical forms besides American Jazz music.
   D. No, because the essay focuses on only one American Jazz musician, Cab Calloway.

PASSAGE II

MY GRANDFATHER'S INTERNET

My grandfather is possibly the least technologically capable writer in the <u>world. He refused</u> [16] to use anything but his pen and paper to write until last year. (He <u>said,</u> [17] he didn't need any keys or mouse pads between his words and himself.) Consequently, when he <u>has went</u> [18] to buy a computer—

16. F. NO CHANGE
   G. world he refused
   H. world refusing,
   J. world, and has been refusing

17. A. NO CHANGE
   B. said
   C. said, that
   D. said, that,

18. F. NO CHANGE
   G. had went
   H. went
   J. goes

GO ON TO THE NEXT PAGE

because of the knowledge that his editor refused to read another hand-written novel—he resisted connecting it to the Internet for several months. He said he had no need to find information on a World Wide Web. [20]

19

Grandpa's editor, however, was clever and, knowing exactly how my grandfather could use it, described how the Internet would improve his life. However, Grandpa could get instant feedback, and praise from the publishing company, read online reviews, and do research for his characters much faster. Finally, Grandpa connected to the Internet, and he hasn't logged off yet.

21

22

Grandpa is fascinated by all the things he can do on the World Wide Web. He has found that chat rooms are wonderful places to have long conversations with people interesting enough to be characters in his books. For example, he says, by clicking the "close" button he

23

19. **A.** NO CHANGE
B. due to the fact that
C. because
D. so

20. Given that all are true, which of the following additions to the preceding sentence (after *World Wide Web*) would be most relevant?
F. that was on his computer.
G. when he had a set of encyclopedias right there in his office.
H. with other people on it.
J. where he might get a computer virus.

21. **A.** NO CHANGE
B. Additionally, Grandpa
C. Conversely, Grandpa
D. Grandpa

22. **F.** NO CHANGE
G. feedback and, praise
H. feedback and praise
J. feedback and praise,

23. **A.** NO CHANGE
B. To illustrate,
C. On the one hand,
D. On the other hand,

GO ON TO THE NEXT PAGE

can just ignore <u>them</u> [24] who aren't interesting. Grandpa's favorite website is Google.com. Google.com is a search engine that searches millions of sites for whatever word he types in, which is very <u>convenient when</u> [25] he needs to know how the native people of Africa developed the game Mancala. <u>For him, Grandpa says that, in merely a few seconds, to be able to find anything he wants is a source of pure joy.</u> [26]

24. F. NO CHANGE
G. the people
H. it
J. their talking

25. A. NO CHANGE
B. convenient, when
C. convenient. When
D. convenient; when

26. F. NO CHANGE
G. For him, Grandpa says that to be able to find anything he wants, is a source of pure joy for him, in merely a few seconds.
H. Grandpa says a source of pure joy for him is that he is able to find anything he wants, in merely a few seconds.
J. Grandpa says that being able to find anything he wants in merely a few seconds is source of pure joy for him.

[1] As for his writings, Grandpa uses the Internet not only for research but also for making them more creative and checking his word choice. [2] Explaining his new vocabulary to his editor, <u>Grandpa points</u> [27] to his new computer and admits that an Internet connection was a good idea after all. [3] I am sure Grandpa hasn't

27. A. NO CHANGE
B. pointing
C. having pointed
D. Grandpa has pointed

GO ON TO THE NEXT PAGE

explored the entire Internet yet, <u>but I am sure he will continue to find new and better ways of using it.</u> [28] [29]

28. F. NO CHANGE

G. and he probably won't explore the rest of it either.

H. and so his editor will have to teach him to find things faster.

J. and his editor knows just that.

29. Upon reviewing Paragraph 5 and realizing that some information has been left out, the writer composes the following sentence:

> He uses the dictionary and thesaurus websites religiously.

The most logical placement for this sentence would be:

A. before sentence 1.

B. after sentence 1.

C. after sentence 2.

D. after sentence 3.

Question 30 asks about the essay as a whole.

30. The writer is considering deleting the first sentence of Paragraph 1. If the writer removed this sentence, the essay would primarily lose:

F. information about aspects of technology that his grandfather does not use.

G. humor that sets the mood for the piece.

H. important details about the Internet that his grandfather might enjoy.

J. a justification for his grandfather's reluctance to use the Internet.

GO ON TO THE NEXT PAGE

PASSAGE III

CHICKASAW WANDERING

In[31] the twilight of a cool autumn evening, I walked with a gathering of people to the center of a field in

31. A. NO CHANGE
    B. On
    C. With
    D. From

Oklahoma. Although I didn't know more of the people who[32] walked with me,

32. F. NO CHANGE
    G. more of the people whom
    H. most of the people who
    J. most of the people whom

a few of them I did know quite well.[33] We were Chickasaw Indians, and some of us had waited for years

33. The writer wants to balance the statement made in the earlier part of this sentence with a related detail that suggests the unity of the people. Given that all of the following choices are true, which one best accomplishes this goal?
    A. NO CHANGE
    B. we each had our own reasons for being there.
    C. I hoped I would get to know some of them.
    D. I felt a kinship with them.

to make this journey across[34] the Chickasaw territory to the ornately

34. Which of the following alternatives to the underlined portion would NOT be acceptable?
    F. among
    G. over
    H. on
    J. through

GO ON TO THE NEXT PAGE

decorated capital of Tishomingo. [35]

35. The writer is considering revising the preceding sentence by deleting the phrase "to the ornately decorated capital of Tishomingo" (placing a period after the word *territory*). If the writer did this, the paragraph would primarily lose:

A. information comparing the narrator's own journey to similar ones made by members of other tribes.
B. details describing the destination of the people the narrator is traveling with.
C. details that establish the time and place of the events of the essay.
D. interesting but irrelevant information about the Chickasaw.

For my whole life I had been shown <u>other Chickasaw's pictures</u>[36]— many of them the ancestors of the <u>people, who walked along with me</u>[37], to the Festival that evening. <u>My father and grandmother helped preserve tribal history by collecting books and newspaper clippings.</u>[38] Books about the history and traditions of our tribe were stacked on the bookshelves, and framed portraits of members of our tribe decorated the walls of these rooms. When I was growing up, I would often find my father or grandmother in one of the rooms, my father reading a book and my grandmother listening to ancient tribal music

36. **F.** NO CHANGE
G. pictures in which other Chickasaw were present
H. pictures of other Chickasaw
J. other Chickasaw whose pictures had been taken

37. **A.** NO CHANGE
B. people who, walked along with me
C. people, who walked along, with me
D. people who walked along with me

38. **F.** NO CHANGE
G. Some of those pictures had been reprinted in books my father and grandmother collected.
H. My grandmother and father proudly displayed these pictures in their homes.
J. Like other Chickasaw, my father and grandmother had each set aside a room in their own home to the tribe.

GO ON TO THE NEXT PAGE

<u>That room</u> held everything I knew about being a <u>Chickasaw, and unlike</u> many Chickasaw, my family had moved away from Oklahoma all the way to Seattle. Once a year, the tribe held a Festival and Annual Meeting <u>that was always well attended.</u> Before they moved to Seattle, my grandmother and father had always attended this event. However, the tribe owned no land in Seattle on which a ceremonial house could be built and <u>Chickasaw ceremonies conducted.</u> Since I had never been to Oklahoma, I had never been to a Chickasaw event or walked in our territory. <u>Still,</u> I had never even known any other Chickasaw children. Finally, my father, grandmother, and I all took a trip to participate in the Festival. As we walked together through the open plain, hundreds of <u>crickets chirping</u> softly from the grass. The insects accompanied our march <u>like</u> the spirits of our ancestors singing to us on our way home.

(39: That room; 40: Chickasaw, and unlike; 41: that was always well attended.; 42: Chickasaw ceremonies conducted.; 43: Still,; 44: crickets chirping; 45: like)

39. A. NO CHANGE
B. Her rooms
C. Those rooms
D. This room

40. F. NO CHANGE
G. Chickasaw unlike
H. Chickasaw, unlike
J. Chickasaw. Unlike

41. Given that all of the choices are true, which one provides information most relevant to the main focus of this paragraph?
A. NO CHANGE
B. notable for its exquisite dancing.
C. in south central Oklahoma.
D. that lasted several days.

42. F. NO CHANGE
G. Chickasaw ceremonies were conducted there.
H. there were Chickasaw ceremonies conducted there.
J. the conducting of Chickasaw ceremonies.

43. A. NO CHANGE
B. Meanwhile
C. In fact,
D. On the other hand,

44. F. NO CHANGE
G. crickets, which chirped
H. crickets that chirped
J. crickets chirped

45. A. NO CHANGE
B. just as
C. as like
D. such as

GO ON TO THE NEXT PAGE

PASSAGE IV

TOPPING THE WASHINGTON MONUMENT

During the midday hours of December 6, <u>1884, engineers</u> [46] and workers braced themselves for the <u>days</u> [47] dangerous mission. Winds that rushed past the workers at speeds of nearly sixty miles per hour <u>threatened</u> [48] to postpone <u>and delay</u> [49] the capstone ceremony marking the placement of the capstone atop the Washington Monument. [50]

46. F. NO CHANGE
    G. 1884, and engineers
    H. 1884. Engineers
    J. 1884; engineers

47. A. NO CHANGE
    B. days'
    C. day's
    D. days's

48. F. NO CHANGE
    G. had been threatened
    H. will have threatened
    J. threatens

49. A. NO CHANGE
    B. to a later time
    C. by delaying
    D. OMIT the underlined portion

50. The writer is considering deleting the following from the preceding sentence:

    marking the placement of the capstone atop the Washington Monument.

    If the writer were to delete this phrase, the essay would primarily lose:

    F. a minor detail in the essay's opening paragraph.
    G. an explanation of the term *capstone ceremony.*
    H. the writer's opinion about the significance of the capstone ceremony
    J. an indication of the capstone ceremony's significance to the American people.

GO ON TO THE NEXT PAGE

Eighty-five years of fundraising and planning had brought about this moment. In 1799, attorney and Congressman [51] John Marshall proposed a monument to honor the young nation's Revolutionary War hero and first president. [52] Architect Robert Mills, who planned [53] the monument that would memorialize Washington. Meanwhile, the [54] monument would be in the form of a 500-foot obelisk made of marble and topped with a 100-pound capstone of aluminum.

In 1861, construction on the monument was halted because supplies and men were needed to fight the Civil War. During the war, the monument stood only 176 feet tall, and the ground around it served as grazing land for livestock used to feed the Union army. Fifteen years

51. **A.** NO CHANGE
B. attorney, and Congressman
C. attorney and Congressman,
D. attorney, and Congressman,

52. If the writer were to delete the preceding sentence, the paragraph would primarily lose:
F. an explanation of Washington's heroic acts of war.
G. details about what John Marshall thought the monument he envisioned should look like.
H. background information about why Washington was being honored with a monument.
J. biographical information about John Marshall.

53. **A.** NO CHANGE
B. Mills, planner of
C. Mills planned
D. Mills creating

54. **F.** NO CHANGE
G. Therefore, the
H. However, the
J. The

GO ON TO THE NEXT PAGE

passed before work resumed on the monument. The
55
workers had the entire monument's history in their

55. A. NO CHANGE
    B. started
    C. began
    D. restarted again

minds during they're attempt to place its capstone.
56

56. F. NO CHANGE
    G. they're attempt to place it's
    H. their attempt to place its
    J. their attempt to place it's

The crowd cheered as, attached to the top of the
57
monument, the capstone was hoisted up. More than
57

57. A. NO CHANGE
    B. As the crowd cheered, the capstone was hoisted up and attached to the top of the monument.
    C. As the crowd cheered, attached to the top of the monument, the capstone was hoisted up.
    D. The capstone was hoisted up as the crowd cheered and attached to the top of the monument.

eight decades and more than eighty years of planning
58

58. F. NO CHANGE
    G. decades amounting to more than eighty years
    H. decades–over eighty years–
    J. decades

and building had come to a conclusion, and the
59
Washington Monument was finally complete.

59. Which of the following alternatives would be LEAST acceptable in terms of the context of this sentence?
    A. reached completion,
    B. come to a halt,
    C. come to an end,
    D. ended,

GO ON TO THE NEXT PAGE

Question 60 asks about the essay as a whole.

60. Suppose the writer had intended to write a brief essay that describes the entire process of designing and building the Washington Monument. Would this essay successfully fulfill the writer's goal?

F. Yes, because it offers such details as the materials used to make the capstone and shaft of the monument.

G. Yes, because it explains in detail each step in the design and construction of the monument.

H. No, because it focuses primarily on one point in the development of the monument rather than on the entire process.

J. No, because it is primarily a historical essay about the early stages in the development of the monument.

PASSAGE V

WHY LIONS ROAR

Research by biologists and environmental scientists has found several reasons that lions roar. Lions, which live in groups called prides, are very social creatures that communicate with one another in many ways. Roaring, [61] the sound most often associated with lions, perform [62] several key functions within the pride.

61. **A.** NO CHANGE
B. Roaring
C. Roaring:
D. Roaring is

62. **F.** NO CHANGE
G. perform,
H. performs,
J. performs

GO ON TO THE NEXT PAGE

One of these defense involves protecting the pride's land. When prides take large pieces of land and claim them as their own, they will roar to keep away intruders, those are usually other lions. This "No Trespassing" warning serves to keep the peace because it helps prevent competing prides from fighting over food or for mates.

Lions also roar to stay in contact with one another when members of a pride are separated by long distances. Like all large cats, lions have intense hearing, which makes it possible for them to hear other members of their pride from great distances. Frequently, everyday

63. A. NO CHANGE
B. One of these, defense,
C. One of these being defense,
D. One of these is defense and it

64. F. NO CHANGE
G. most often these are
H. and are typically
J. usually

65. Which of the following alternatives to the underlined portion would be the LEAST acceptable?
A. although
B. in that
C. since
D. as

66. F. NO CHANGE
G. It's also the case that roaring is employed
H. In addition, roaring is a way
J. Roaring is also used

67. A. NO CHANGE
B. cunning
C. acute
D. vivid

68. F. NO CHANGE
G. Quite regularly, everyday
H. Many times, everyday
J. Everyday

GO ON TO THE NEXT PAGE

activities like hunting <u>call upon animals' sharp instincts;</u> (69) in order to reunite, the pride members roar to find one another.

69. Given that all of the choices are true, which is the best replacement for the underlined selection to provide a logical reason for the action described in the second clause of the sentence?
   - **A.** NO CHANGE
   - **B.** disperse a pride over large areas of land
   - **C.** require the pride to travel some distance
   - **D.** involve the entire pride

<u>Finally,</u> (70) lions use roars to attract potential mates. During mating season, males will try to attract females from the pride by roaring, displaying their manes, <u>they rub</u> (71) against females and fighting one another. Often a male that does not belong to a pride will try to enter the pride and mate with females inside the pride. When this occurs, the <u>alpha or, dominant, male</u> (72) instructs all the other males in the pride to roar toward the outsider. <u>The outsider is scared during his preparation for the fight partly by the roaring.</u> (73) The combined roaring of the

70.
   - **F.** NO CHANGE
   - **G.** Nevertheless,
   - **H.** Second,
   - **J.** Thus,

71.
   - **A.** NO CHANGE
   - **B.** rubbing
   - **C.** rubbed
   - **D.** rub

72.
   - **F.** NO CHANGE
   - **G.** alpha, or dominant, male
   - **H.** alpha or dominant male,
   - **J.** alpha or, dominant male

73.
   - **A.** NO CHANGE
   - **B.** The purpose of the roaring is to help scare the outsider during his preparation for the fight.
   - **C.** Fear in the outsider is raised, during preparation for the fight, by the roaring.
   - **D.** The roaring helps scare the outsider during his preparation for the fight.

GO ON TO THE NEXT PAGE

males make the pride sound much larger than it actually is. 74

Future research on lions will help us understand more about the reasons they roar. What is already clear, is that often the lion's roar is meant to be heard. Whether communicating with one another or threatening intruders, lions roar to get attention. 75

74. F. NO CHANGE
G. have the effect of making
H. are intended to make
J. makes

75. A. NO CHANGE
B. clear is that,
C. clear is, that
D. clear is that

IF YOU FINISH BEFORE TIME IS CALLED, YOU MAY CHECK YOUR WORK ON THIS SECTION ONLY. DO NOT TURN TO ANY OTHER SECTION IN THE TEST. **STOP**

READING TEST

35 Minutes—40 Questions

Directions: There are four passages in this test. Each passage is followed by several questions. After reading a passage, choose the best answer to each question and fill in the corresponding oval on your Answer Grid. You may refer to the passages as often as necessary.

PASSAGE I

PROSE FICTION

This passage is adapted from Nathaniel Hawthorne's short story "Rappaccini's Daughter."

Giovanni still found no better occupation than to look down into the garden beneath his window. From its appearance, he judged it one of those botanic gardens that were of earlier date in Padua than elsewhere in Italy or in the world. Or, not improbably, it might once have been the pleasure-place of an opulent family; for there was the ruin of a marble fountain in the center, sculptured with rare art, but so woefully shattered that it was impossible to trace the original design from the chaos of remaining fragments. The water, however, continued to gush and sparkle into the sunbeams as cheerfully as ever. A little gurgling sound ascended to the young man's window, and made him feel as if the fountain were an immortal spirit that sung its song unceasingly and without heeding the vicissitudes around it, while one century embodied it in marble and another scattered the perishable embellishments on the soil. All about the pool into which the water subsided grew various plants that seemed to require a plentiful supply of moisture for the nourishment of gigantic leaves, and, in some instances, flowers gorgeously magnificent. There was one shrub in particular, set in a marble vase in the midst of the pool, that bore a profusion of purple blossoms, each of which had the luster and richness of a gem; and the whole together made a show so resplendent that it seemed enough to illuminate the garden, even had there been no sunshine. Every portion of the soil was peopled with plants and herbs, which, if less beautiful, still bore tokens of assiduous care, as if all had their individual virtues, known to the scientific mind that fostered them. Some were placed in urns, rich with old carving, and others in common garden pots; some crept serpent-like along the ground or climbed on high, using whatever means of ascent was offered them. One plant had wreathed itself round a statue of Vertumnus, which was thus quite veiled and shrouded in a drapery of hanging foliage, so happily arranged that it might have served a sculptor for a study.

While Giovanni stood at the window he heard a rustling behind a screen of leaves, and became aware that a person was at work in the garden. His figure soon emerged into view, and showed itself to be that of no common laborer, but a tall, emaciated, sallow, and sickly-looking man, dressed in a scholar's garb of black. He was beyond the middle term of life, with gray hair, a thin, gray beard, and a face singularly marked with intellect and cultivation, but which could never, even in his more youthful days, have expressed much warmth of heart.

Nothing could exceed the intentness with which this scientific gardener examined every shrub that grew in his path: it seemed as if he were looking into their inmost nature, making observations in regard to their creative essence, and discovering why one leaf grew in this shape and another in that, and why such and such flowers differed among themselves in hue and perfume. Nevertheless, in spite of this deep intelligence on his part, there was no approach to intimacy between himself and these vegetable existences. On the contrary, he avoided their actual touch or

GO ON TO THE NEXT PAGE

the direct inhaling of their odors with a caution that impressed Giovanni most disagreeably; for the man's demeanor was that of one walking among malignant influences, such as savage beasts, or deadly snakes, or evil spirits, which, should he allow them one moment of license, would wreak upon him some terrible fatality. It was strangely frightful to the young man's imagination to see this air of insecurity in a person cultivating a garden, that most simple and innocent of human toils, and which had been alike the joy and labor of the unfallen parents of the race. Was this garden, then, the Eden of the present world? And this man, with such a perception of harm in what his own hands caused to grow—was he the Adam?

The distrustful gardener, while plucking away the dead leaves or pruning the too luxuriant growth of the shrubs, defended his hands with a pair of thick gloves. Nor were these his only armor. When, in his walk through the garden, he came to the magnificent plant that hung its purple gems beside the marble fountain, he placed a kind of mask over his mouth and nostrils, as if all this beauty did but conceal a deadlier malice; but, finding his task still too dangerous, he drew back, removed the mask, and called loudly, but in the infirm voice of a person affected with inward disease.

1. Of the plants mentioned in the passage, which of the following did Giovanni find to be the most exceptional?

A. The plant wreathed around the statue
B. The plant that crept along the ground
C. The plant with the gigantic leaves
D. The plant with the purple blossoms

2. In order to ensure that he is safe from the plants, the gardener:

I. handles them only indirectly.
II. avoids looking directly at them.
III. avoids breathing their odors.

F. I and II only
G. I and III only
H. II and III only
J. I, II, and III

3. It can reasonably be inferred from the passage that the gardener, as compared with Giovanni, is a:

A. more religious man.
B. less cautious man.
C. more cautious man.
D. less religious man.

4. Which of the following actions performed by the gardener disturbs Giovanni?

I. Indicating disregard or disapproval of the plants
II. Avoiding directly inhaling the odors of the plants
III. Looking at the inmost nature of the plants

F. I only
G. II only
H. III only
J. I and II only

GO ON TO THE NEXT PAGE

5. As described in the third paragraph (lines 56–82), the gardener's actions suggest that he is a man who:

A. is very alert.

B. knows all there is to know about plants.

C. loves nature.

D. resembles Adam.

6. The narrator suggests that the plant with "a profusion of purple blossoms" (lines 26–27) could:

F. sprout gems.

G. produce light.

H. overrun the garden.

J. grow very quickly.

7. The narrator takes the point of view of:

A. a gardener.

B. Giovanni.

C. a scientist.

D. an unknown third party.

8. When Giovanni questions whether the garden is "the Eden of the present world" and whether the gardener is Adam (lines 79–82), he is expressing his belief that the gardener:

F. goes about his work with great care.

G. has every reason to be distressed by the plants.

H. should treat the plants with reverence.

J. should not appear so afraid of the plants.

9. According to the passage, Giovanni characterizes the area beneath his window as a:

A. botanic garden.

B. center for rare art.

C. place for people with plants.

D. pleasure-place for the community.

10. In the third paragraph (lines 56–82), the author suggests that the gardener's relationship with the plants was partly characterized by:

F. the gardener's impatience with the plants.

G. the gardener's interest in understanding the plants.

H. the gardener's desire to harm the plants.

J. the gardener's anger toward the plants.

PASSAGE II

SOCIAL SCIENCE

This passage is adapted from "Look First to Failure" by Henry Petroski, which appeared in the October 2004 issue of Harvard Business Review. *It discusses a paradox in the field of engineering.*

Engineering is all about improvement, and so it is a science of comparatives. "New, improved" products are ubiquitous, advertised as making teeth whiter, wash fluffier, and meals faster. Larger engineered systems are also promoted for their comparative edge: the taller building with more affordable office space, the longer bridge with a lighter-weight roadway, the slimmer laptop with greater battery life. If everything is a new, improved version of older technology, why do so many products fail, proposals languish, and systems crash?

To reengineer anything—be it a straight pin, a procurement system, or a Las Vegas resort—we first must understand failure. Successes give us confidence that we are doing something right, but they do not necessarily tell us what or why. Failures, on the other hand, provide incontrovertible proof that we have done something wrong. That is invaluable information.

Reengineering anything is fraught with risk. Take paper clips. Hundreds of styles were introduced in the past century, each claiming to be an improvement over the classic Gem. Yet none displaced it. The Gem maintains its privileged position because, though far from perfect, it strikes

GO ON TO THE NEXT PAGE

an agreeable balance between form and function. Each challenger may improve on one aspect of the Gem but at the expense of another. Thus, a clip that is easier to attach to a pile of papers is also more likely to fall off. Designers often focus so thoroughly on the advantages that they fail to appreciate (or else ignore) the disadvantages of their new design.

Imagine how much more complex is the challenge of reengineering a jumbo jet. The overall external form is more or less dictated by aerodynamics. That form, in turn, constrains the configuration of the interior space, which must accommodate articulated human passengers as well as boxy luggage and freight. As much as shipping clerks might like fuselages with square corners, they must live with whale bellies. It is no wonder that Boeing invited stakeholders, including willing frequent flyers, to participate in designing its Dreamliner—so the users would buy into the inevitable compromises. The resulting jetliner will succeed or fail depending on how convincingly those compromises are rationalized.

Logically speaking, basing a reengineering project—whether of a product or a business process—on successful models should give designers an advantage: They can pick and choose the best features of effective existing designs. Unfortunately, what makes things work is often hard to express and harder to extract from the design as a whole. Things work because they work in a particular configuration, at a particular scale, and in a particular culture. Trying to reverse-engineer and cannibalize a successful system sacrifices the synergy of success. Thus John Roebling, master of the suspension bridge form, looked for inspiration not to successful examples of the state of the art but to historical failures. From those he distilled the features and forces that are the enemies of bridges and designed his own to avoid those features and resist those forces. Such failure-based thinking gave us the Brooklyn Bridge, with its signature diagonal cables, which Roebling included to steady the structure in winds he knew from past example could be its undoing.

But when some bridge builders in the 1930s followed effective models, including Roebling's, they ended up with the Tacoma Narrows Bridge, the third-longest suspension bridge in the world and the largest ever to collapse in the wind. In the process of "improving" on Roebling's design, the very cables that he included to obviate failure were left out in the interests of economy and aesthetics.

When a complex system succeeds, that success masks its proximity to failure. Imagine that the Titanic had not struck the iceberg on her maiden voyage. The example of that "unsinkable" ship would have emboldened success-based shipbuilders to model larger and larger ocean liners after her. Eventually the Titanic or one of those derivative vessels would probably have encountered an iceberg with obvious consequences. Thus, the failure of the Titanic contributed much more to the design of safe ocean liners than would have her success. That is the paradox of engineering—and of reengineering.

11. All of the following are mentioned as constraints on the design of a jumbo jet EXCEPT:

A. the shape of the human body.

B. fuel consumption.

C. aerodynamics.

D. freight handling.

12. When the author says Boeing wants stakeholders to "buy into" the Dreamliner's inevitable compromises (line 45), he means the company hopes that:

F. passengers will be willing to invest in the company to support Dreamliner development.

G. engineers will be able to satisfy all the needs of passengers, freight handlers, and pilots.

H. users will be willing to pay extra to have their specific needs met.

J. users will understand and accept that the jet will not meet all their needs perfectly.

GO ON TO THE NEXT PAGE

13. The author believes the sinking of the Titanic contributed more to the safety of ocean travel than its success would have because:

A. engineers realized they could not be so careless.

B. later ships carried more lifeboats.

C. shipbuilders were able to learn from mistakes in the Titanic's design before they built more ships with the same weakness.

D. passengers were more likely to take out insurance before a voyage.

14. The purpose of the passage is to convey the idea that:

F. failed systems often have more to teach us than do successful ones.

G. sophisticated engineering projects are more difficult than they seem.

H. the best way to design a system is to reverse-engineer successful models.

J. today's engineering is so technically advanced that there is little to learn from the past.

15. Based on the passage, which of the following contributed to the failure of the Tacoma Narrows Bridge?

A. The engineers copied the design for the Brooklyn Bridge too closely.

B. The wind at Tacoma Narrows was stronger than in Brooklyn.

C. The engineers ignored the aesthetic aspect of the design.

D. The final design omitted diagonal cables.

16. The author inserts the final paragraph (lines 79–90) in order to:

F. emphasize that the designers of the Titanic should have studied earlier ships more thoroughly.

G. make the point that all ocean liners will eventually encounter icebergs and sink.

H. illustrate how the failure of a complex design may contribute more to long-term technical development than its success would have.

J. point out that the designs of ocean liners and bridges both involve significant risks.

17. The main purpose of the Gem paper clip example is to show that:

A. paper clips are indispensable to modern business.

B. attempting to redesign a paper clip is a waste of time.

C. engineers should study the effectiveness of the paper clip before beginning a design project.

D. redesigning a successful product risks damaging its effectiveness.

18. According to the passage, the Gem paper clip continues to be the most popular because:

F. it features an excellent compromise between ease of attachment and security.

G. it was invented long before alternative designs.

H. people are familiar with the name and don't want to risk trying new products.

J. it is unlikely to fall off in use.

GO ON TO THE NEXT PAGE

19. In the context of this passage, "failure-based thinking" (line 67) refers to:

A. a counterproductive habit that engineers adopt that inhibits their creativity.

B. the process of taking inspiration from analyzing the causes of past failures.

C. an example of how cannibalizing a successful system can create synergy.

D. an approach to design that was discredited with the collapse of the Tacoma Narrows Bridge.

20. When the author says engineering is a "science of comparatives" (line 2), he means that:

F. engineers are always compared to other scientists.

G. engineered products are only better if they are bigger or faster than other products.

H. engineers' designs are generally evaluated based on whether they offer improvements over previous designs of the same product.

J. engineering tools are used to compare the discoveries of scientists.

PASSAGE III

HUMANITIES

The following passages are excerpted from two books that discuss fairy tales. Passage A was written by a specialist in psychology and children's literature and was published in 1965. Passage B was written by a folklore methodologist and was published in 1986.

PASSAGE A

Most of the stories that our society tells have only enjoyed a comparatively short period of popularity in comparison with the sweep of human history, flaming into popular consciousness in books, television, or film for a period reaching anywhere from a few months to a few centuries. Fads come and go as fickle as the weather, and today's hit may be tomorrow's forgotten relic. But one particular kind of story that our society tells, the fairy tale, has a kind of popularity that is uniquely persistent. Literally since time immemorial, fairy tales have been told and retold, refined and adapted across generations of human history. Folk tales that spoke to people in some deeper way, and thus proved popular, endured and were passed down through the ages. Tales that had only temporal and fleeting appeal are long since lost. Since, as we know, it is a truism that time sifts out the literary wheat and discards the chaff, fairy tales can be said to have undergone the longest process of selection and editing of any stories in human history.

Consider, for example, the story of Snow White. Here is reflected the tale of the eternal struggle for supremacy between the generations. The evil mother queen grows jealous of the competition of the young Snow White for supremacy in the realm of youth and beauty, so she contrives to do away with her rival. The innocent Snow White survives by a twist of whim and circumstance, and then retreats into the forest—the traditional symbol of the site of psychological change—where she hides among the Seven Dwarves. Small supernatural spirits or homunculi, often depicted in folk tales as tiny elves, spirit men, trolls, or fairies, represent unconscious forces, and thus Snow White must care for and nurture the Seven Dwarves while she undergoes her psychological transformation. The dwarves' mining activities can be said to symbolize this process of mental delving into the depths in hopes of uncovering the precious materials of the developing psyche.

Yet Snow White's road to her new identity is not without incident. The breaching of the secure space by the disguised queen mother and Snow White's giving in to the temptation of the apple—representative of the same youth and beauty that the queen seeks to deprive her of—causes her to fall into the slumberous mock death. Only the prince can deliver Snow White and metaphorically resurrect

GO ON TO THE NEXT PAGE

her with a kiss, itself a motif that suggests her entry into the identity of a mature person ready to leave the dwarves and forest of the unconscious behind and take on adult responsibilities.

The popularity of this tale, and others like it, across time and in widely scattered societies confirms its power in tapping into unconscious forces and common motifs that all humans share. All humans in all ages experience generational rivalry and the impact that it has on patterns of growth and maturity. The specific symbols used to represent these dynamics are less important than their universality; indeed the very adaptability of the symbolism is what allows tales to remain popular over time. By dramatizing these psychological progressions, the fairy tale helps its audience to process the ill-understood unconscious psychological forces that are a part of human life. Can it be any wonder that such powerful avenues to the cosmic unconscious can be shown to have remained popular across the eons?

PASSAGE B

The contention that folklore represents a cosmic tale that encapsulates cross-cultural human universalities in narrative form is naïve in the extreme. The notion that folk tales somehow embody a symbolically encoded map of human consciousness suffers from a fundamental flaw: It assumes that each tale has a more-or-less consistent form. In fact, the forms of most folk tales that we have today recorded in collections and in the popular media represent nothing more than isolated snapshots of narratives that have countless forms, many of which are so different as to drastically change the interpretations that some critics want to say are universal.

Consider, for example, the story of Little Red Riding Hood. Some psychological interpretations might conjecture, for example, that this is a tale about obedience and parental authority. Straying from the path in the forest, in this context, might represent rebelling against that authority, and the wolf then symbolizes the dangerous unconscious forces from which parents seek to protect Little Red. The red color of the riding hood might be seen as representing the subdued emotions of anger and hostility. Being consumed by the wolf signifies a period of isolation and transformation. Finally, the rescuing huntsman at the end of the story then symbolizes the return of parental authority to deliver the innocent child from being metaphorically consumed by ill-understood emotional states.

It is an apparently consistent analogy, and one that is difficult to dispute, until one investigates the circumstances of the composition and recording of the version of Little Red Riding Hood that we have today. Earlier editions of the story simply don't have many of the components that critics would like to present as so-called "universal symbols." For example, in the vast majority of the older and simpler versions of this tale, the story ends after the wolf eats the girl. So there can be no theme of parental rescue because, in all but a few of the examples of this tale, there is no rescue and no kind huntsman. In some versions the girl even saves herself, completely contradicting the assumption that it is a story about rescue. Story elements such as the path, the hunter, and the happy ending, which are seen as essential symbolic components of our interpretation above, were introduced to this ancient tale by the Brothers Grimm in the 19th century. Even the introduction of the "symbolic" red garment dates only from the seventeenth century, when it was put into the story by Charles Perrault.

In fact, every fairy tale known to the study of folklore has so many different versions that there are encyclopedic reference books to catalog the variations and the differences between them. A creature that is an elf in one country and era might be a troll in another. A magic object represented as a hat in one version of a tale might be a cloak in ten other tellings. If folk tales actually represent universal human truths in symbolic form, the symbols in them would have to reflect universal consistency across time. Any attempt to pinpoint a consistent symbolic meaning or underlying scheme in such a field of moving, blending, and ever-changing targets is doomed to fail before it even begins. Instead, we should embrace all such variations on a theme, searching for insights into the cultural conditions that prompt such divergence.

GO ON TO THE NEXT PAGE

Questions 21–23 ask about Passage A.

21. The "motifs" mentioned in line 57 support the author's primary argument that motifs:

A. represent experiences that all humans have undergone.

B. reflect the views of critics.

C. signify the transition from childhood to adult identity.

D. embody unconscious forces that must be cared for and nurtured.

22. The word "avenues" in line 68 conveys the author's belief that fairy tales offer:

F. boulevards into the human subconscious.

G. beginnings of life-changing adventures.

H. approaches for understanding common experiences.

J. homecomings for people's true feelings toward others.

23. In discussing "fairy tales" in lines 7–21, the author of Passage A suggests that:

A. which stories endure and which are forgotten has nothing to do with the quality of the story.

B. stories written by a single author and not endlessly retold and edited may well not have the lasting appeal of fairy tales.

C. many folk tales that spoke deeply to their audiences have been lost and forgotten over the ages.

D. folk tales undergo the same degree of selection and editing as other kinds of literature.

Questions 24–26 ask about Passage B.

24. The final sentence of Passage B provides information about:

F. the author's opinion that only fairy tales written in modern times can be accurately interpreted.

G. folklore methodologists that seek out oral versions of folk tales themselves instead of getting them from books.

H. the earliest recorded versions of folk tales, which are more accurate and authoritative than later versions.

J. the variations among versions of fairy tales, which can tell us something about the cultures in which these versions developed.

25. The author of Passage B specifically disagrees with critics who extract simple symbolic interpretations from fairy tales because of their:

A. disregard for the rigorous principles of modern psychology.

B. willingness to assume that minor details of a specific version of a folk tale are universal.

C. failure to make proper use of reference materials pertaining to folklore methodology.

D. naïve view of the complexity of human nature.

GO ON TO THE NEXT PAGE

26. The statement that "there can be no theme of parental rescue . . . huntsman" in Passage B (lines 115–118) suggests that fairy tales:

F. cannot be said to have a single authoritative form.
G. are generally not interested in historical accuracy.
H. should make a greater effort to capture universal human themes.
J. are usually not concerned with themes of rescue.

Questions 27–30 ask about both passages.

27. The authors of both passages state that fairy tales are:

A. intuitively meaningful.
B. critically misunderstood.
C. historically changeable.
D. symbolically rich.

28. Which of the following best describes the primary disagreement that the author of Passage B would most likely raise against the statement in Passage A (lines 32–37) that "Small supernatural spirits . . . transformation"?

F. The specific details in different versions of this folk tale show too much variation to make any consistent interpretations based on this particular version.
G. The popularity of this tale is no indication of its value in expressing a psychological truth.
H. This version of the tale is not necessarily the most accurate, because it is recent and may have deviated too much from the true version over time.
J. Small supernatural spirits could represent many things other than unconscious forces.

29. The author of Passage A would probably respond to the statement in lines 78–84 of Passage B with the argument that:

A. many modern folk tales originated relatively recently and haven't been subjected to centuries of editing.
B. the changes in the symbolism of more-recent revisions of folk tales are less important psychologically than the broad themes.
C. there is no evidence that the symbolism of folk tales is related to psychological forces.
D. Snow White is a poor example to use as evidence because it has changed so much over time.

30. With which of the following statements about fairy tales would the authors of both passages most likely agree?

F. The popularity of fairy tales is due to their deeper meanings.
G. Fairy tales speak to all humans in the language of universal psychological symbols.
H. Fairy tales have resulted from a compositional process very different from that of modern literature written by a single author.
J. The study of folklore is undergoing extensive changes because of new information about different versions of particular tales.

GO ON TO THE NEXT PAGE

PASSAGE IV

NATURAL SCIENCE

This passage is adapted from a Wikipedia.com entry on particle accelerators. It describes two different devices used to accelerate subatomic particles.

In linear accelerators, particles are accelerated in a straight line, with the target at the end of the line. Low energy accelerators such as cathode ray tubes and X-ray generators use a single pair of electrodes with a DC voltage of a few thousand volts between them. In an X-ray generator, the target is one of the electrodes.

Higher energy accelerators use a linear array of plates to which an alternating high energy field is applied. As the particles approach a plate, they are accelerated toward it by an opposite polarity charge applied to the plate. As they pass through a hole in the plate, the polarity is switched so that the plate now repels the particles, which are now accelerated by it toward the next plate. Normally, a stream bunches particles that are accelerated, so a carefully controlled AC voltage is applied to each plate to repeat this for each bunch continuously.

As the particles approach the speed of light, the switching rate of the electric fields becomes so high as to operate at microwave frequencies, and so microwave cavities are used in higher energy machines instead of simple plates. High energy linear accelerators are often called linacs.

Linear accelerators are very widely used. Every cathode ray tube contains one, and they are also used to provide an initial low-energy kick to particles before they are injected into circular accelerators. They can also produce proton beams, which can produce "proton-heavy" medical or research isotopes, as opposed to the "neutron-heavy" ones made in reactors.

In circular accelerators, the accelerated particles move in a circle until they reach sufficient levels of energy. The particle track is bent into a circle using dipole magnets. The advantage of circular accelerators over linacs is that components can be reused to accelerate the particles further, as the particle passes a given point many times. However, they suffer a disadvantage in that the particles emit synchrotron radiation.

When any charged particle is accelerated, it emits electromagnetic radiation. As a particle travelling in a circle is always accelerating towards the center of the circle, it continuously radiates. This has to be compensated for by some of the energy used to power the accelerating electric fields, which makes circular accelerators less efficient than linear ones. Some circular accelerators have been deliberately built to generate this radiation (called synchrotron light) as X-rays—for example, the Diamond Light Source being built at the Rutherford Appleton Laboratory in England. High energy X-rays are useful for X-ray spectroscopy of proteins, for example.

Synchrotron radiation is more powerfully emitted by lighter particles, so these accelerators are invariably electron accelerators. Consequently, particle physicists are increasingly using heavier particles, such as protons, in their accelerators to achieve higher levels of energy. The downside is that these particles are composites of quarks and gluons, which makes analyzing the results of their interactions much more complicated.

The earliest circular accelerators were cyclotrons, invented in 1929 by Ernest O. Lawrence. Cyclotrons have a single pair of hollow "D"-shaped plates to accelerate the particles and a single dipole magnet to curve the track of the particles. The particles are injected in the center of the circular machine and spiral outwards toward the circumference.

Cyclotrons reach an energy limit because of relativistic effects at high energies, whereby particles gain mass rather than speed. As the Special Theory of Relativity means that nothing can travel faster than the speed of light in a vacuum, the particles in an accelerator normally travel very close to the speed of light. In high energy accelerators, there is a diminishing return in speed as the particle approaches the speed of light. The effect of the energy injected using the electric

GO ON TO THE NEXT PAGE

fields is therefore to increase their mass markedly, rather than their speed. Doubling the energy might increase the speed a fraction of a percent closer to that of light, but the main effect is to increase the relativistic mass of the particle.

Cyclotrons no longer accelerate electrons when they have reached an energy for about 10 million electron volts. There are ways of compensating for this to some extent—namely, the synchrocyclotron and the isochronous cyclotron. They are nevertheless useful for lower energy applications.

To push the energies even higher—into billions of electron volts—it is necessary to use a synchrotron. This is an accelerator in which the particles are contained in a doughnut-shaped tube, called a storage ring. The tube has many magnets distributed around it to focus the particles and curve their track around the tube, and microwave cavities similarly distributed to accelerate them. The size of Lawrence's first cyclotron was a mere four inches in diameter. Fermilab now has a ring with a beam path of four miles.

31. The main idea of the passage is that:

A. linear accelerators are more efficient than circular accelerators.

B. particles in accelerators cannot travel at the speed of light.

C. linear and circular accelerators have important, but different, uses.

D. the cyclotron is a useful type of circular accelerator.

32. The passage states that magnets affect particles by:

F. influencing the direction particles travel.

G. creating curved particles.

H. increasing the acceleration of particles.

J. causing an increase in the particles' energy levels.

33. The passage states that which of the following causes an increase in particle mass?

A. A particle reaching the speed of light

B. Acceleration of a particle in a vacuum

C. Using heavier particles

D. Injecting energy using electric fields

34. As it is used in line 62, the word *quarks* most nearly refers to:

F. objects made up of electrons.

G. objects made up of radiation.

H. components of protons.

J. components of gluons.

35. According to the passage, which of the following CANNOT be a result of using a circular accelerator?

A. Particles that emit electromagnetic radiation

B. Reuse of components to accelerate particles

C. Particles that emit synchrotron radiation

D. An initial low kick of energy in particles

36. Which of the following statements would the author most likely agree with?

F. Linear accelerators are of limited use.

G. Using particles such as protons in such experiments is not possible, since they are composites of quarks and gluons.

H. Circular accelerators have improved little since Lawrence's first cyclotron.

J. Depending on the desired result, both linear and circular accelerators are valuable tools.

GO ON TO THE NEXT PAGE

37. According to the passage, what is one effect of particles passing through the hole in the plate of higher energy accelerators?

   A. The mass of the particles increases.

   B. The charge of the particles changes.

   C. The particles lose energy.

   D. The particles are repelled and accelerated toward the next plate.

38. The passage suggests that the greatest difference between a cyclotron and a synchrotron is that:

   F. cyclotrons are not useful.

   G. synchrotrons accelerate particles in a circle.

   H. synchrotrons can overcome limitations that cyclotrons cannot.

   J. synchrotrons are capable of causing particles to curve more closely to the edge of the tube.

39. How does the information about the size of Lawrence's first cyclotron and the size of Fermilab's ring function in the passage?

   A. It suggests that, over time, there has been progress in improving the size and capabilities of particle accelerators.

   B. It proves that cyclotrons are important for particle acceleration because they were invented by Lawrence.

   C. It indicates that the inventors at Fermilab were more capable than Lawrence was.

   D. It emphasizes the difference between cyclotrons and synchrotrons.

40. What is the main idea of the ninth paragraph (lines 73–87)?

   F. Cyclotrons can accelerate particles to nearly the speed of light.

   G. As the speed of particles in an accelerator approaches the speed of light, they gain more mass than speed.

   H. The speed of particles diminishes when particles get close to the speed of light.

   J. Energy limits are reached in cyclotrons because the mass of the particles becomes too high.

IF YOU FINISH BEFORE TIME IS CALLED, YOU MAY CHECK YOUR WORK ON THIS SECTION ONLY. DO NOT TURN TO ANY OTHER SECTION IN THE TEST. **STOP**

WRITING TEST

Directions: This is a test of your writing skills. You will have **forty** (40) minutes to read the prompt, plan your response, and write an essay in English. Before you begin working, read all material in this test booklet carefully to understand exactly what you are being asked to do.

You will write your essay on the lined pages in the **answer document** provided. Your writing on those pages will be scored. You may use the unlined pages in this test booklet to plan your essay. Your work on these pages will not be scored.

Your essay will be evaluated based on the evidence it provides of your ability to:

- clearly state your own perspective on a complex issue and analyze the relationship between your perspective and at least one other perspective
- develop and support your ideas with reasoning and examples
- organize your ideas clearly and logically
- communicate your ideas effectively in standard written English

Lay your pencil down immediately when time is called.

DO NOT OPEN THIS BOOKLET UNTIL TOLD TO DO SO.

GO ON TO THE NEXT PAGE

ESSAY TASK

Write a unified, coherent essay in which you evaluate multiple perspectives regarding academic programs that assist students in choosing appropriate fields of study. In your essay, be sure to:

- clearly state your own perspective on the issue and analyze the relationship between your perspective and at least one other perspective
- develop and support your ideas with reasoning and examples
- organize your ideas clearly and logically
- communicate your ideas effectively in standard written English

Your perspective may be in full agreement with any of the others, in partial agreement, or wholly different. Whatever the case, support your ideas with logical reasoning and detailed, persuasive examples.

PLANNING YOUR ESSAY

You may wish to consider the following as you think critically about the task:

Strengths and weaknesses of the three given perspectives

- What insights do they offer, and what do they fail to consider?
- Why might they be persuasive to others, or why might they fail to persuade?

Your own knowledge, experience, and values

- What is your perspective on this issue, and what are its strengths and weaknesses?
- How will you support your perspective in your essay?

GO ON TO THE NEXT PAGE

Collegiate Fields of Study

Students pursuing higher education with the intent to commit to a particular field of study often determine that a different concentration is a better fit and subsequently make a change. Many students base their initial field of study on their interests, strengths, and experiences in high school. Some students complete the program they originally selected, but many others find that college unearths new passions and prospects. Additionally, collegiate study often exposes students to job markets, which help students evaluate the availability of jobs in their desired field; this is often a driving factor in changing their concentration since students seek financial security upon graduation. Should high schools incorporate career-oriented programs to help students make better decisions regarding their majors? Making better-informed choices before entering college will help students wisely allocate their time and money during their college careers, and will prevent graduates from entering a career field without background knowledge regarding job availability.

Read and carefully consider these perspectives. Each discusses the importance of providing high school students with the necessary knowledge to choose appropriate fields of study in college.

Perspective One	Perspective Two	Perspective Three
High schools should hold career-oriented seminars at least once a semester during the regular school day to help students make more directed decisions when choosing collegiate fields of study. These seminars will help students explore career options, post-graduate position availability, and job requirements. Armed with this knowledge, students can make better-informed choices that will help them to avoid spending unnecessary time and money in both college and job markets.	High schools should retain their current primary focus, but should offer optional after-school career-focused seminars conducted by professionals so students can learn about options before attending college. Students who take advantage of this resource will be able to make better decisions, and these seminars will allow teachers to continue to focus on the core curriculum and assist students academically.	High schools should partner with colleges and professionals to embed career-oriented options into current courses. The job market information will be relevant to the class in which it is presented. Although students will only receive career-based information centered on the courses in which they are enrolled, this approach guarantees that each student is offered course-specific advice.

GO ON TO THE NEXT PAGE

GO ON TO THE NEXT PAGE

IF YOU FINISH BEFORE TIME IS CALLED, YOU MAY CHECK YOUR WORK ON THIS SECTION ONLY. DO NOT TURN TO ANY OTHER SECTION IN THE TEST. **STOP**

Practice Test Two

ANSWER KEY

ENGLISH TEST

1. A	**11.** A	**21.** D	**31.** A	**41.** C	**51.** A	**61.** A	**71.** B
2. G	**12.** J	**22.** H	**32.** H	**42.** F	**52.** H	**62.** J	**72.** G
3. A	**13.** B	**23.** D	**33.** D	**43.** C	**53.** C	**63.** B	**73.** D
4. G	**14.** J	**24.** G	**34.** F	**44.** J	**54.** J	**64.** J	**74.** J
5. B	**15.** A	**25.** A	**35.** B	**45.** A	**55.** A	**65.** A	**75.** D
6. G	**16.** F	**26.** J	**36.** H	**46.** F	**56.** H	**66.** F	
7. C	**17.** B	**27.** A	**37.** D	**47.** C	**57.** B	**67.** C	
8. J	**18.** H	**28.** F	**38.** J	**48.** F	**58.** J	**68.** J	
9. C	**19.** C	**29.** B	**39.** C	**49.** D	**59.** B	**69.** B	
10. J	**20.** G	**30.** J	**40.** J	**50.** G	**60.** H	**70.** F	

READING TEST

1. D	**6.** G	**11.** B	**16.** H	**21.** A	**26.** F	**31.** C	**36.** J
2. G	**7.** D	**12.** J	**17.** D	**22.** H	**27.** C	**32.** F	**37.** D
3. C	**8.** J	**13.** C	**18.** F	**23.** D	**28.** F	**33.** D	**38.** H
4. J	**9.** A	**14.** F	**19.** B	**24.** J	**29.** B	**34.** H	**39.** A
5. A	**10.** G	**15.** D	**20.** H	**25.** B	**30.** H	**35.** D	**40.** G

ANSWERS AND EXPLANATIONS

ENGLISH TEST

PASSAGE I

1. A
Category: Word Choice
Difficulty: Low
Getting to the Answer: The superlative adjective form will use *-est* or *most*—not both. This sentence needs (A), NO CHANGE. "Earliest" is the correct superlative adjective to refer to all "music forms." Choice B uses "most" with "earliest," which is grammatically incorrect. Choice C uses "most early," which is also incorrect; "most" is only used with words that do not have an *-est* superlative form. Choice D uses the right adjective, but creates a subject–verb agreement error; "The earliest…forms" does not agree with the singular verb form "was."

2. G
Category: Punctuation
Difficulty: High
Getting to the Answer: "It's" is a contraction of *it is* or *it has*. If neither of these makes sense when substituted for the contraction, the contraction is incorrect. It doesn't make sense to say "because of it is (or has) having," so we know F is incorrect. Choice (G) substitutes the correct singular possessive adjective, *"its,"* meaning that the "origins" belong to American Jazz. Choices H and J use spellings that are never correct.

3. A
Category: Writing Strategy
Difficulty: High
Getting to the Answer: Just determining whether or not the suggested information is relevant gives you a 50–50 chance of getting the question right. First, determine if the new information is relevant or not. Here, it is, since the paragraph discusses the way that different musical forms came together to form American Jazz; eliminate C and D. Choice B is out of scope for the paragraph, which concerns the development, not the popularity, of American Jazz. Choice (A) is correct.

4. G
Category: Punctuation
Difficulty: Medium
Getting to the Answer: If a phrase is set off by a comma or commas, the sentence must make sense without it. The phrase "ragtime and blues" should be set of from the rest of the sentence with a comma because it is not essential to the meaning of the sentence; (G) is correct. Removing the phrase set off by commas in F does not result in a logical sentence. Choice H incorrectly separates a prepositional phrase from the rest of the sentence. Choice J eliminates the commas, making the sentence difficult to understand.

5. B
Category: Punctuation
Difficulty: Medium
Getting to the Answer: If a semicolon is used to combine clauses, the clauses must be independent. This sentence incorrectly places a semicolon between an independent and a dependent clause. Choice (B) eliminates the incorrect semicolon. Choice C incorrectly inserts a comma between a preposition and its object. Choice D separates a subject from its verb with a comma, which is also incorrect.

6. G
Category: Word Choice
Difficulty: Medium
Getting to the Answer: When an underlined selection includes a pronoun, make sure its antecedent is clear and unambiguous. There are several singular nouns in the sentence previous to this one ("style," "blend," "America," "the time") that could be antecedents for the pronoun "It." Choice (G) replaces the pronoun with the appropriate noun. Choices H and J do not address the ambiguity issue.

7. C

Category: Word Choice

Difficulty: Medium

Getting to the Answer: When an English Test question has a stem, read it carefully. This one asks you to determine the unacceptable choice, which means three of the choices will be correct in context. Although "made his living on" is a properly constructed idiom, it is inappropriate in this context, since it refers to the location where the living was made, rather than the occupation itself. Choice (C) is the correct choice here. Choices A, B, and D are all acceptable in the sentence.

8. J

Category: Connections

Difficulty: Medium

Getting to the Answer: When OMIT is an option, check to see if the underlined selection is necessary to the meaning of the sentence. "He was" isn't necessary here; "working as a shoe shiner and a waiter" properly provides a compound object for the preposition, so (J) is correct. Choice G uses incorrect grammatical structure and H leaves the meaning of the second clause incomplete.

9. C

Category: Writing Strategy

Difficulty: High

Getting to the Answer: When facing a question about deleting information, read the sentence without the suggested deletion. The information that Cab Calloway "spent time at the racetrack" doesn't make sense coming directly after a sentence that discusses the jobs he held, unless we also know that Calloway worked at the track. Choice (C) is correct; without this explanation, readers might be confused. Choice A is incorrect; the information does relate to the topic at hand. Choice B is also wrong; the information has nothing to do with Calloway's accomplishments or successes. Other information in the sentence tells us how far Cab Calloway came in his life; it's not necessary to keep this clause for the reason that D suggests.

10. J

Category: Sentence Sense

Difficulty: Medium

Getting to the Answer: Although OMIT will not always be the correct answer when it's offered, always consider the possibility that the selection is either redundant or used incorrectly. As written, this sentence is a fragment, with no independent clause. Eliminating "where," as (J) suggests, corrects this error. Choice G is unnecessarily wordy. Choice H does not address the fragment error.

11. A

Category: Punctuation

Difficulty: Medium

Getting to the Answer: The ACT tests only a few very specific punctuation rules; make sure your answer choice follows these rules. Choice (A) is correct; no punctuation is needed here. Choice B inserts a colon which, on the ACT, will only be correct when used to introduce a brief explanation, definition, or list. Choice C treats the phrase "in the top Jazz circles" as nonessential information, but the sentence does not make sense when read without it. Choice D inserts an unneeded comma before a prepositional phrase.

12. J

Category: Organization

Difficulty: Medium

Getting to the Answer: Because NO CHANGE is not an answer choice, the sentence must be relevant; you'll need to determine its most logical placement. "Widely known" is a good context clue. It doesn't make sense that he was well-known when he was a shoe-shiner and waiter, when he was walking racehorses, and when he first began performing, so you can eliminate F, G, and H. Choice (J) places the sentence logically.

13. B

Category: Writing Strategy

Difficulty: Low

Getting to the Answer: Your Reading skills will be helpful in answering questions like this one. The two topics of this essay are Cab Calloway and American Jazz. Choice (B) is the only choice that mentions both of these topics and relates them to one another. Choices A, C, and D all fail to mention American Jazz, the second main subject of the passage.

14. J
Category: Writing Strategy
Difficulty: Medium
Getting to the Answer: In addition to following the rules of grammar, style, and usage, the correct answer choice must also be consistent with the tone of the passage. The phrase "it'll stick around for a while" is too informal and slangy for the rest of this passage. Choice (J) matches the tone of the essay and provides a logical conclusion. Choice G is unnecessarily wordy. Choice H doesn't provide a logical conclusion to the passage; it concerns Jazz's popularity rather than its endurance.

15. A
Category: Writing Strategy
Difficulty: Medium
Getting to the Answer: Once you determine whether or not the passage satisfies the conditions in the question stem, you can immediately eliminate two of the four choices. First, you'll need to determine whether or not this essay focuses on "the history and development of American Jazz music." Since it does, you can eliminate both "no" choices, C and D. Now focus on the reasoning. Choice B misstates the information in the passage, which tells us that Jazz developed from folk music, not the other way around. Choice (A) is the correct choice here.

PASSAGE II

16. F
Category: Sentence Sense
Difficulty: Medium
Getting to the Answer: Approximately 25% of ACT English Test questions will require NO CHANGE. This sentence contains no error; (F) is correct. Choice G creates a run-on sentence. Choice H would be acceptable if the comma were placed after "world," but is incorrect punctuated this way. Choice J introduces a verb tense that is inappropriate in context.

17. B
Category: Punctuation
Difficulty: Medium
Getting to the Answer: When commas are the issue, remember your tested rules. This sentence does not meet any of the tested conditions for proper comma usage; (B) is correct. Choice A separates the verb from its object. Choices C and D do not address the error; "said that" would be acceptable without the commas but, as written, these choices are incorrect.

18. H
Category: Verb Tenses
Difficulty: Medium
Getting to the Answer: Unless context tells you that more than one time frame is referred to, verb tenses should remain consistent. This sentence discusses something that happened in the past; (H) is correct. Choices F and G incorrectly use "went" with "has" and "had," respectively; the correct past participle for the verb *to go* is "gone." Choice J uses the present tense, which is incorrect in context.

19. C
Category: Wordiness
Difficulty: Low
Getting to the Answer: Many ACT Style questions will have four answer choices that are grammatically correct; your goal is to find the best one. "Because" is all that is needed here; (C) is the best choice. Choices A and B are unnecessarily wordy. Choice D creates an illogical relationship between the clauses; the editor's refusal to read hand-written manuscripts was the cause, not the result, of the grandfather's decision to buy a computer.

20. G
Category: Writing Strategy
Difficulty: High
Getting to the Answer: An added sentence or clause must be relevant to the topic of the passage and consistent with its tone. The theme of this passage up to this point is the grandfather's preference for

the old-fashioned way of doing things. Choice (G) provides a low-tech alternative to the Internet: "a set of encyclopedias." Choices F and H are redundant; we already know the World Wide Web is on the computer and that other people use it. Choice J is out of scope; nothing in the passage indicates that the writer's grandfather is concerned about computer viruses.

21. D

Category: Connections
Difficulty: Medium
Getting to the Answer: Make sure Connections words are both logical and necessary. This sentence needs nothing to link it to the sentence that precedes it. Choice (D) eliminates the unnecessary words. Choice A incorrectly uses "however" to link the two sentences. This would indicate that the second sentence contradicts the first, which it does not. Choice B uses "additionally," which means the second sentence is building upon the first sentence. This is not the case here either. "Conversely," in C, indicates a contradiction to what came before, which is inappropriate here.

22. H

Category: Punctuation
Difficulty: Medium
Getting to the Answer: Use commas only between items in a series of three or more items; a compound does not require a comma. This sentence treats the compound "feedback and praise" as two separate items in this series of clauses. The conjunction "and," however, is not correct between the first two items in a longer series. Choice (H) eliminates the incorrect comma. Choice G places a comma after the conjunction "and," which is not correct in a series. Choice J treats "from the publishing company" as an item in the series, which does not make sense in a list of uses for a computer.

23. D

Category: Connections
Difficulty: Medium
Getting to the Answer: Make sure Connections words properly relate the words or clauses they connect. The second sentence here provides a different point than the first; Grandpa is saying that he can talk to interesting people for a long time or he can ignore uninteresting people. Choice (D) uses the appropriate connection. Choices A and B indicate that the second sentence will provide a specific example of the first, but this is not the case. Choice C suggests that the writer will introduce a contrasting perspective after discussing Grandpa's use of the "close" button, but she does not do so.

24. G

Category: Word Choice
Difficulty: Low
Getting to the Answer: When the underlined word is a pronoun, make sure its antecedent is clear and that it is in the proper case. Since you wouldn't say "them people," F is incorrect; *those* would be the proper pronoun here. However, since *those* is not among the answer choices, you'll need to find a logical replacement for the pronoun. Choice (G) correctly indicates who isn't interesting. Choice H incorrectly uses "it" to refer to people. Choice J creates a sentence that is grammatically incorrect.

25. A

Category: Punctuation
Difficulty: Medium
Getting to the Answer: If you read the sentence and don't find a problem with it, don't be afraid to choose NO CHANGE. It will be the correct choice about 25% of the time. This sentence contains no error; (A) is correct here. Choice B treats the phrase "which is very convenient" as nonessential information, but the sentence does not make sense without it. The second sentence created by C is a fragment. Choice D misuses the semicolon splice, which is only correct when combining two independent clauses.

26. J

Category: Sentence Sense
Difficulty: High
Getting to the Answer: When an entire sentence is underlined, choose the clearest revision. As written, this sentence is wordy and convoluted. While not much briefer, (J) is easier to understand; "in

merely a few seconds" is placed directly after the phrase it modifies, "being able to find anything he wants," and "for him" follows the phrase it modifies, "a source of pure joy." Choices F, G, and H are all less concise and more awkward than (J); additionally, Choice G incorrectly places a comma between the sentence's subject and predicate verb.

27. A
Category: Verb Tenses
Difficulty: Medium
Getting to the Answer: Unless context makes it clear that more than one time frame is being referenced, verb tenses should remain consistent. This sentence needs (A), NO CHANGE; the present tense is correct in context. Choices B and C create sentence fragments. Choice D introduces a verb tense that is inappropriate in context.

28. F
Category: Sentence Sense
Difficulty: Low
Getting to the Answer: Don't just read for errors in grammar and usage; read for logic as well. Here, (F) is the only choice that is both consistent with the passage and uses the proper contrast transition "but." Nothing in the passage indicates that Grandpa won't continue to explore the Internet, as G suggests, or that his editor believes this to be the case, as in J. Choice H doesn't follow logically from the first clause of the sentence.

29. B
Category: Organization
Difficulty: Medium
Getting to the Answer: When asked to add information, read the new sentence into the passage at the suggested points to determine its best placement. This sentence adds information about how Grandpa uses the websites he accesses, so placing it before sentence 1, as A suggests, is illogical. Choices C and D both place the new information too far from the discussion of Grandpa's use of the Internet. Choice (B) is the most logical place for this new sentence.

30. J
Category: Writing Strategy
Difficulty: Medium
Getting to the Answer: Whenever you are asked to consider deleting something, think about why the author included that information—what purpose does it serve? The first sentence of this passage tells us that Grandpa does not know how to use technology. This explains why Grandpa did not want to use the Internet; (J) is correct. Choice F misstates a detail from the passage; the sentence in question tells us only that Grandpa does not like to use technology, not the specific technologies he avoids. The first sentence is not particularly humorous, which eliminates G. Choice H can be eliminated as well, since no justification for Grandpa's technophobia is provided.

PASSAGE III

31. A
Category: Word Choice
Difficulty: Low
Getting to the Answer: Most Idioms question will hinge on preposition usage. This sentence needs (A), NO CHANGE; "In the twilight" is the appropriate idiom in this context. Choice B is idiomatically incorrect usage. Choices C and D would require more information to be correct; neither "With the twilight" nor "From the twilight" is an acceptable idiom by itself.

32. H
Category: Word Choice
Difficulty: High
Getting to the Answer: Some constructions might be grammatically correct but inappropriate in context. Although "more of the people who" is a grammatically correct construction, it is used incorrectly here, so F is incorrect. It was "most of the people" the writer did not know; (H) makes the correction without introducing a new error. Choice G does not address the error; additionally, it uses the objective pronoun form "whom" where "who" is correct. Choice J corrects the incorrect use of "more", but adds a new error by changing "who" to "whom."

33. D

Category: Writing Strategy

Difficulty: Medium

Getting to the Answer: Read question stems carefully and use Keywords to determine the correct answer choice. The Keyword in this question stem is "unity." Choice (D) mentions "kinship," which suggests a family-like relationship between the writer and the other walkers. Choice A indicates that the writer knew some of the people, but you can know people without feeling unity with them. Choice B's mention of each walker having his or her own reasons for being there suggests the opposite of unity. Being interested in knowing people, as C suggests, does not convey unity.

34. F

Category: Word Choice

Difficulty: Low

Getting to the Answer: Read question stems carefully to determine what the question is asking. Here, you are looking for the one unacceptable answer, which means that three of the choices will be appropriate in context. You can "journey over," "journey on," and "journey through" a territory; you cannot "journey among" it. Choices G, H, and J would be acceptable and (F) would not be acceptable, so (F) is the correct choice here.

35. B

Category: Writing Strategy

Difficulty: Medium

Getting to the Answer: Questions like this one require you to use the "purpose of a detail" skills from your Reading lessons. When a question stem asks you to determine what a paragraph would lose with information deleted, it's asking the purpose of that information. Here, what's being deleted is the information about the writer's destination; (B) is the correct choice. The phrase in question does not compare "the narrator's. . .journey" to any others or "establish the time and place of the events of the essay" as A and C suggest, nor is it "about the Chickasaw," as D suggests.

36. H

Category: Sentence Sense

Difficulty: High

Getting to the Answer: When all of the answer choices are wordier than the original selection, ask yourself if there is a grammatical or logical need for a longer phrase. As written, the sentence does not make clear whether the writer is talking about pictures *of* other Chickasaw or pictures *belonging to* other Chickasaw, so F is incorrect. Choice (H) makes this clear. Choice G is unnecessarily wordy. Choice J changes the meaning of the phrase, indicating that it was "Chickasaw," and not "pictures," that the writer had been shown.

37. D

Category: Punctuation

Difficulty: Medium

Getting to the Answer: Only very specific comma uses are tested on the ACT. If commas are used in any other way, they will be incorrect. The underlined selection does not meet any of the tested requirements for comma usage; (D) is correct. Choice A treats the phrase "who walked along with me" as nonessential information, but the sentence does not make sense without it. Choice B inserts a comma within a phrase modifying "people." Choice C treats another necessary phrase, "who walked along," as nonessential.

38. J

Category: Connections

Difficulty: High

Getting to the Answer: Each sentence in the passage must lead logically into the next. Look at the sentence preceding the selection and the one that follows. You need to find a choice that transitions from the idea of the pictures the writer had been shown and somewhere that "Books...were stacked on the bookshelves." (J) does this best. Choices F, G, and H all explain where the pictures came from but do not lead logically into the sentence that follows.

39. C

Category: Word Choice

Difficulty: Low

Getting to the Answer: Remember to read for logic as well as grammar and usage. We know there are two rooms: the father's and the grandmother's; (C) correctly conveys this. Choices A and D refer to a single room, but the writer has been talking about two rooms. Choice B seems to indicate that both rooms belong to the writer's grandmother, but this contradicts the passage.

40. J

Category: Connections

Difficulty: Medium

Getting to the Answer: Connection words, such as conjunctions, must logically join the ideas they are used to combine. The two clauses here do not relate to one another in a way that makes it logical for them to be joined into a single sentence; one clause concerns the rooms displaying pictures of Chickasaw and the other the writer's family's move to Seattle, so a change is needed and F is wrong. Choice (J) makes each clause a separate sentence. Choices G and H create run-on sentences.

41. C

Category: Writing Strategy

Difficulty: High

Getting to the Answer: When NO CHANGE is offered as an option, you'll need to determine the logic and relevance of any potential new material. The information in the underlined sentence, while related to the topic being discussed, does not logically lead from the idea that the writer and his family had moved to Seattle to the reason they were then unable to attend the Annual Meetings. This means you can eliminate A. By pointing out the location of these meetings, (C) connects the two ideas: the meetings were too far away from the family's new home. Choice B is out of scope—dancing at the Festivals is never mentioned in the passage—and still fails to logically connect the ideas. Choice D also fails to provide a logical reason for the writer's family not attending the meetings.

42. F

Category: Wordiness

Difficulty: Medium

Getting to the Answer: Be wary of answer choices that are significantly longer than the original selection. Barring errors of grammar or logic, these will be incorrect. There is no need to make this sentence any longer; (F) is correct. Choices G, H, and J are all wordier than the original and violate the parallel structure required for the compound "built and... conducted."

43. C

Category: Connections

Difficulty: Low

Getting to the Answer: Connections words and phrases must logically combine the ideas they connect. This sentence builds on the preceding one by giving more evidence to make the point of the first sentence. Choice (C) correctly reflects this relationship. Choices A and D use inappropriate contrast connections. Choice B indicates two events occurring simultaneously, which is illogical in context.

44. J

Category: Sentence Sense

Difficulty: Medium

Getting to the Answer: A sentence can have multiple verbs and still be a fragment. Remember, the *-ing* verb form by itself can never be the predicate (main) verb in a sentence. As written, this sentence is a fragment; neither clause is independent. Choice (J) gives the sentence a correct predicate verb, "chirped." Choices G and H do not address the error.

45. A

Category: Word Choice

Difficulty: Medium

Getting to the Answer: Some idiomatic phrases are only correct as part of a longer construction. Choice (A) is correct here; "like" can stand alone as a comparison in this context. Choice B does not properly complete the idiomatic construction "just as...so." Choice C uses the grammatically incorrect "as like." Choice D uses an idiom that means "for example," which is inappropriate in context.

PASSAGE IV

46. F
Category: Punctuation
Difficulty: Medium
Getting to the Answer: An introductory clause should be set off with a comma. This sentence is punctuated appropriately; (F) is correct. Choice G incorrectly places a comma and a coordinating conjunction between an independent clause and a prepositional phrase. The first sentence created by H is a fragment. Choice J improperly places a semicolon between an independent clause and a prepositional phrase.

47. C
Category: Punctuation
Difficulty: Medium
Getting to the Answer: When apostrophe use is the issue, use context to determine whether a plural or a possessive is required; eliminate answer choices that use the apostrophe in ways that are never correct. As written, this sentence uses the plural "days," which doesn't make sense in context, so you can eliminate A. Although there are circumstances in which a noun ending in *s* will be made possessive by adding 's, the rules for this usage are quite complicated and are not tested on the ACT; eliminate D. Since the sentence is discussing one specific day (December 6, 1884), the plural possessive in B can also be eliminated. "Day's," the singular possessive, is what is called for here; (C) is correct.

48. F
Category: Verb Tenses
Difficulty: Low
Getting to the Answer: Use context to determine the appropriate tense of underlined verbs. There is no contextual reason to change verb tenses in this sentence; since "rushed" is in the past tense, (F) "threatened" is correct. Choice G changes the meaning of the sentence, making the wind the object of the threat, rather than its cause. Choice H uses a tense that indicates actions that will happen in the future, but these actions have already occurred. Choice J uses the singular verb form "threatens" with the plural noun "winds."

49. D
Category: Wordiness
Difficulty: Low
Getting to the Answer: Whenever OMIT is presented as an option, check the underlined selection for relevance and redundancy. Here, "postpone" and "delay" mean essentially the same thing, so eliminate A; (D), OMIT, is the correct choice here. Choice B still contains redundant wording; "to a later time" is understood in "postpone." Choice C is also redundant; there is no other way to "postpone" something than "by delaying" it.

50. G
Category: Writing Strategy
Difficulty: Medium
Getting to the Answer: Remember your "purpose of a detail" skills from ACT Reading; that's what question stems like this one are asking for. Here, the phrase marked for deletion is the definition of "capstone ceremony"; (G) correctly explains what the essay would lose if the clause were deleted. Since the term "capstone ceremony" is not something most people are familiar with, this "detail" is not "minor," as F suggests. Nothing in the phrase reflects the writer's opinion or the ceremony's significance to the American people, which eliminates H and J.

51. A
Category: Punctuation
Difficulty: Medium
Getting to the Answer: Remember your tested comma rules; if a comma is used in any other way in the underlined selection, it will be incorrect. None of the conditions for comma usage are met by this sentence, so (A) is correct. Choices B and D insert commas between the two parts of a compound; this is never correct comma usage. Choice C treats "attorney and Congressman" as nonessential information, but leaving it out makes it unclear who John Marshall was.

52. H
Category: Writing Strategy
Difficulty: High
Getting to the Answer: When a question stem suggests deleting a sentence, first determine the

sentence's purpose in the passage. The sentence in question says that the monument was proposed to honor a war hero and president; (H)'s "background information about why Washington was being honored" is the purpose of this detail in the passage. Choice F is out of scope; the sentence merely tells us that Washington was a Revolutionary War hero, not what he did to become one. Choice G is also out of scope; nowhere in the passage is this discussed. Choice J is out of scope as well; the passage contains no biographical information about John Marshall.

53. C
Category: Sentence Sense
Difficulty: Medium
Getting to the Answer: A sentence may be a fragment even if it contains multiple nouns and verb forms. As written, this sentence consists of a single dependent clause, so eliminate A. Only (C) creates a complete sentence by adding an appropriate predicate verb, "planned." Choices B and D do not address the fragment error.

54. J
Category: Connections
Difficulty: Low
Getting to the Answer: When evaluating Connections words, consider the possibility that no Connection is needed. This sentence needs nothing to link it to the sentence that precedes it; (J) is the best choice here. Choice F indicates that the actions in the two sentences occurred concurrently, which is illogical. Choice G indicates that the second sentence is the result of the first, which also doesn't make sense in context. Choice H links the two sentences with a contrast Connection, which is inappropriate here as well.

55. A
Category: Word Choice
Difficulty: Medium
Getting to the Answer: If two answer choices mean the same thing and work in grammatically similar ways, you can eliminate them both, since only one answer choice can be correct. Since work was done on the monument, stopped, and then started again, "resumed," (A), is the most appropriate. Choices B and C do not convey the idea that this work was a continuation of work that was done in the past. Choice D is redundant; "again" is indicated by the prefix *re–* in "restarted."

56. H
Category: Word Choice
Difficulty: Medium
Getting to the Answer: Replacing contractions with the full phrase can help you determine correct usage. "They're" is a contraction of they are, so first determine if the contraction is appropriate here. Since "during they are attempt" doesn't make sense, you can quickly eliminate F and G. Now turn to the difference between the remaining choices: the possessive "its" versus the contraction "it's." Try replacing the contraction with it is or it has; neither makes sense, so you can eliminate J as well. Choice (H) is correct here.

57. B
Category: Sentence Sense
Difficulty: Medium
Getting to the Answer: In most cases, a descriptive phrase will modify the first noun that follows it. As written, this sentence refers to the capstone as "attached to the top of the monument." However, this doesn't make sense, since the sentence concerns placing the capstone there, so eliminate A. Choice (B) creates the most logical sentence: The crowd cheers while the capstone is hoisted up, then the capstone is attached. Choices C and D make it sound as if the crowd, not the capstone, was "attached to the top of the monument."

58. J
Category: Wordiness
Difficulty: Low
Getting to the Answer: Look for words and phrases that mean the same thing; using them together will not be correct on the ACT. "Eight decades" and "eighty years" are the same amount of time. Choice (J) eliminates the redundancy. Choices F, G, and H all include redundant information.

59. B
Category: Writing Strategy
Difficulty: High
Getting to the Answer: Read question stems carefully. This one asks for the LEAST acceptable alternative, which means that three choices will work in context. "Conclusion," "completion," "end," and "halt" all have similar meanings but, in this context, "come to a halt" implies that the project was not completed. Since context tells us the project was completed, Choice (B) is the least acceptable choice. Choices A, C, and D would all be acceptable in context.

60. H
Category: Writing Strategy
Difficulty: Medium
Getting to the Answer: Question stems like this one appear frequently on the ACT. Answer the "yes" or "no" part of the question first, then tackle the reasoning behind your choice. The question stem asks if this essay would satisfy an assignment to write about "the entire process of designing and building the Washington Monument." Since the passage focuses primarily on the capstone ceremony, you can immediately eliminate the "yes" choices, F and G. Choice J's reasoning is that the essay focuses on "the early stages" of the monument's construction, but the opposite is true. Choice (H) is correct here.

PASSAGE V

61. A
Category: Punctuation
Difficulty: Medium
Getting to the Answer: Keep tested punctuation rules in mind; uses other than these will be incorrect on the ACT. This sentence is punctuated correctly; the phrase separated out by the commas is not essential to the meaning of the sentence. Choice (A) is correct. By eliminating the first comma, B incorrectly leaves the subject and verb of the sentence separated by a comma. Choice C misuses the colon which, on the ACT, will only be correct when used to introduce or emphasize a brief explanation, description, or list. Choice D creates a sentence that is grammatically incorrect.

62. J
Category: Word Choice
Difficulty: Medium
Getting to the Answer: The test maker frequently places a plural object near a verb with a singular subject. Always determine the proper subject of an underlined noun; it will generally not be the noun closest to it in the sentence. The singular "Roaring," not the plural "lions," is the subject of the verb "perform," so eliminate F. Choice (J) puts the verb in the proper singular form without introducing any additional errors. Choice G does not address the error and also incorrectly places a comma between the verb and its object. Choice H corrects the agreement error, but also inserts the incorrect comma.

63. B
Category: Punctuation
Difficulty: High
Getting to the Answer: Always read for logic as well as usage and style. As written, this sentence uses the plural "these" to modify the singular "defense." This is incorrect, so eliminate A. By putting commas around "defense," (B) makes "One of these" refer to "functions," and identifies "defense" as a function of roaring. Choice C creates a sentence that is grammatically incorrect. Choice D is unnecessarily wordy.

64. J
Category: Sentence Sense
Difficulty: Medium
Getting to the Answer: There are several ways to correct a run-on sentence, but only one answer choice will do so without introducing any new errors. This sentence is a run-on; the underlined selection begins a new independent clause, which means F is incorrect. Choice (J) corrects the error by making the final clause dependent. Choice G does not address the error. Choice H eliminates the run-on error, but it is unnecessarily wordy.

65. A
Category: Connections
Difficulty: Low
Getting to the Answer: Read question stems carefully. You can determine the least acceptable Connections word simply by finding the one that is inconsistent with the other three. Because NO CHANGE is not given as an option, you're looking for the connection that cannot be substituted for "because." "In that," "since," and "as" can all mean "because"; therefore, B, C, and D are all considered acceptable. "Although" indicates contrast, not cause-and-effect, and is therefore considered unacceptable, so (A) is correct.

66. F
Category: Wordiness
Difficulty: Low
Getting to the Answer: Be suspicious of answer choices that are significantly longer than the original selection. They won't always be incorrect, but make sure the longer phrase is necessary for logic or grammatical correctness. There is no reason for a longer sentence; (F) is correct. Choices G, H, and J are all unnecessarily wordy.

67. C
Category: Word Choice
Difficulty: High
Getting to the Answer: Some Word Choice questions will require you to use skills you've learned in your Reading sessions. "Intense" means *extreme* or *forceful*, "cunning" means *clever*, "acute" means *extremely sharp or intense*, and "vivid" means *having the clarity and freshness of immediate experience*. Of these, the one most logical to modify "hearing" in this context is (C), "acute."

68. J
Category: Wordiness
Difficulty: Medium
Getting to the Answer: Use context clues to determine when words are used redundantly. Something that is described as "everyday" can be assumed to be done "frequently"; (J) eliminates the redundancy. Choices F, G, and H all use words or phrases that are redundant with "everyday."

69. B
Category: Writing Strategy
Difficulty: High
Getting to the Answer: Remember the first rule in the Kaplan Method: Read until you have enough information to answer the question. The second clause here tells us the pride members have to "reunite," so the logical answer choice will concern their being separated. Choice (B) is the choice most consistent with the question stem. Neither A nor D involve the pride becoming separated. Although C mentions the pride traveling, it does not indicate that they become separated when they do so.

70. F
Category: Connections
Difficulty: Medium
Getting to the Answer: Connections words and phrases must logically transition between the ideas they combine. Each paragraph in this essay describes a way in which roaring helps lions survive. This paragraph discusses the final use lions have for their roars; "Finally" is the best Connection here, so (F) is correct. Choice G uses "nevertheless," which indicates a contrast that is not present here. Choice H uses "second," but this is the essay's third point. Choice J signifies a conclusion, which is inappropriate in this context.

71. B
Category: Sentence Sense
Difficulty: Low
Getting to the Answer: Run-on sentences can be corrected in a number of ways, but only one answer choice will do so without introducing additional errors. As written, this sentence is a run-on, so you can eliminate A right away. Choices (B), C, and D all make the second clause dependent, but only (B) follows the rules of parallel structure required in the series "roaring...displaying...and fighting."

72. G

Category: Punctuation

Difficulty: High

Getting to the Answer: Commas are never correct when used to separate a subject and verb. As written, the sentence treats the word "dominant" as nonessential information, so F is incorrect; however, the sentence does not make sense without it. Choice (G) correctly sets off the phrase "or dominant" from the rest of the sentence; the sentence is still both logical and grammatically correct with this information removed. Choice H incorrectly places a comma between a subject and its predicate verb. Choice J places a comma after a non-coordinating conjunction, which is also incorrect.

73. D

Category: Sentence Sense

Difficulty: Medium

Getting to the Answer: In most cases, the passive voice will make a sentence unnecessarily wordy and may cause modifier errors as well. This sentence is written in the passive voice, making it unclear what the phrase "by the roaring" is intended to modify, so A is incorrect. Choice (D) creates the clearest sentence. The passive voice in B and C makes them unnecessarily wordy.

74. J

Category: Word Choice

Difficulty: Medium

Getting to the Answer: Don't mistake the object of a preposition for the subject of a verb. Here, the plural "males" is the object of the preposition "of"; the subject of the verb here in the singular "roaring." Choice F is incorrect; G, H, and (J) all correct the agreement error, but G and H are unnecessarily wordy.

75. D

Category: Punctuation

Difficulty: Medium

Getting to the Answer: Remember your tested comma rules. If a sentence doesn't satisfy one or more of those requirements, commas will be incorrect. This sentence does not meet any of the tested requirements for comma usage; (D) is correct. Choice A puts a comma between the sentence's subject and its predicate verb. Choice B incorrectly places a comma between "that" and the clause it introduces. The comma in C separates the verb "is" from its object.

READING TEST

PASSAGE I

1. D

Category: Detail

Difficulty: Medium

Getting to the Answer: Good notes will help lead you quickly to the section of the passage you need to research. In lines 25–30, Giovanni notices "one shrub in particular" that seems to "illuminate the garden." The plant he is speaking about is the one with "a profusion of purple blossoms." In the next sentence, he considers other plants that are "less beautiful" than the one with purple blossoms. This should lead you to (D). Choice A is a misused detail; the plant that is wreathed around the statue (lines 39–43) is shown in a positive light, but these lines do not indicate that Giovanni finds the plant to be exceptional. Choice B is a misused detail; in lines 37–39, there is information about plants that "crept serpent-like along the ground," yet no specific plant is mentioned, nor are any viewed as being special. Choice C is a misused detail; in line 23, "gigantic leaves" are mentioned, but not a specific plant's leaves.

2. G

Category: Detail

Difficulty: Medium

Getting to the Answer: If you are able to determine that a certain statement is correct (or incorrect), you can include (or eliminate) all answer choices that include that statement. Normally, you would start with the statement that appears most frequently, but all statements here appear an equal number of times. Your notes should indicate that the narrator discusses the gardener's interaction with the plants principally in paragraphs 3 and 4. Skim those paragraphs for the information in the three statements. In lines 67–68, you see that the gardener avoids the "actual touch or the direct inhaling of [the plants'] odors." Based on this, you know that Statements I and III are valid; eliminate all choices that don't include both of them (F and H). Paragraph 4 offers alternate confirmation of these two statements. A quick skim of the paragraphs offers no support for Statement II; eliminate J. Choice (G) is correct; the passage supports both statements. Choice F is a distortion; this lacks Statement III. Choice H is a distortion; this lacks Statement I. Choice J is out of scope; the passage doesn't support the second statement.

3. C

Category: Generalization
Difficulty: Medium
Getting to the Answer: Generalization questions can be challenging because the answers will not be directly stated in the passage. Remember, though, that the answers will be supported by information within the passage, usually in more than one spot. Your notes should help you to see that the gardener is shown as being very cautious when he gardens. For instance, in lines 85–86, it is stated that the gardener wears gloves to protect himself. He also wears other "armor," the mask that he puts over his mouth and nostrils, in lines 89–90. In lines 67–74, Giovanni is disturbed by the fact that the gardener takes so much caution with the plants, indicating that Giovanni himself would not take these types of precautions. A good prediction is *cautious man*. Choice (C) matches this. Choice A is a distortion; Giovanni alludes to Adam and the Garden of Eden, but this does not indicate that the gardener is more religious. Choice B is opposite; the narrator depicts the gardener as being very cautious, behavior that disturbs Giovanni. Choice D is a distortion; Giovanni alludes to Adam and the Garden of Eden, but this does not indicate that the gardener is less religious.

4. J

Category: Detail
Difficulty: Medium
Getting to the Answer: In Roman numeral questions, start with the statements that appear more frequently. Statements I and II appear more frequently than the third one does, so start there. In line 69, the gardener "impressed Giovanni most disagreeably" by avoiding the inhalation of the plants' odors; Statement II is valid then. Eliminate F and H. (Note that this means you don't have to investigate Statement III.) In the following lines, Giovanni becomes upset that "the man's demeanor was that of one walking among malignant influences," which supports Statement I. Choice (J) is the correct choice. Choice F is a distortion; this does not include Statement II. Choice G is a distortion; this does not include Statement I. Choice H is a misused detail; the narrator describes the gardener as doing this, but not that it disturbs Giovanni.

5. A

Category: Generalization
Difficulty: Medium
Getting to the Answer: Some questions will ask you to read between the lines. Although this can sometimes be difficult, remember that the answer will always be supported by information in the passage. The gardener, in lines 67–68, avoids directly touching the plants or "inhaling… their odors." He is also described as a "scientific gardener," who seems to be "looking into" the nature of the plants. You can infer that he is observant and seems to understand the essence of the plants. Predict that he is *focused* or *attentive*. Choice (A) matches this prediction. Choice B is extreme; lines 56–63 indicate that the gardener knows a lot about plants. The narrator suggests, however, that he discovers this information as he works, not that he already knows all there is to know about plants. Choice C is opposite; the fact that he refuses to touch or smell the plants goes against the idea that he loves nature. Choice D is a misused detail; Giovanni mentions Adam in lines 80–82, but there is no indication that the gardener actually resembles him.

6. G

Category: Inference
Difficulty: Medium
Getting to the Answer: Don't "over-infer." The correct choice will be closely related to something stated in the passage. In lines 30–31, the plant is described as seemingly able to "illuminate the garden, even had there been no sunshine." From this, you can infer that the plant seemed capable of producing light, which matches (G). Choice F is a distortion; in lines 27–28 the narrator states that each blossom "had the luster and richness of a gem." To say that the plant could sprout gems stretches the metaphor too far. Choice H is a distortion; the narrator suggests that the plant could shed light on the garden, not overrun it like a weed. Choice J is out of scope; nowhere in the passage is there any indication that the plant grows very quickly.

7. D

Category: Writer's View
Difficulty: Low
Getting to the Answer: Take the time to predict an answer before looking at the answer choices; this will help you avoid being tempted by incorrect answer choices. The passage is not told directly from Giovanni's point of view; the reader understands what Giovanni is thinking, yet this information comes from an unidentified narrator. Look for this among the choices; (D) matches. Choice A is a misused detail; the narrator refers to the gardener in the third person. Choice B is a misused detail; the narrator refers to Giovanni in the third person. Choice C is a misused detail; the gardener is described as being scientific, yet that does not indicate that the narrator is a scientist.

8. J

Category: Function
Difficulty: Medium
Getting to the Answer: Read the referenced lines carefully to determine the author's intent. These statements are made after the narrator describes Giovanni as being disturbed by the insecurities the gardener shows while cultivating the garden. The narrator mentions Eden and Adam to show how far the gardener's behavior is from these ideals—he should display more positive feelings for the plants he tends. Choice (J) matches this prediction. Choice F is a misused detail; Giovanni seems to recognize this in the gardener earlier in the paragraph, but this has no relation to the references to Adam and Eden. Choice G is opposite; Giovanni finds the gardener's behavior inexplicable. Choice H is a distortion; while these are Biblical references, Giovanni never implies that the gardener should show the plants respect, religious or otherwise.

9. A

Category: Detail
Difficulty: Low
Getting to the Answer: When you don't receive line references, good notes will help you know where to research. Your notes should indicate that every paragraph but the first focuses on Giovanni's observation of the gardener, so look to the first paragraph. Scan the choices first, then look for the match. Choice (A) is correct; in lines 3–4, Giovanni refers to the garden as "one of those botanic gardens," different from most in the world. Choice B is a distortion; rare art is mentioned in line 9, but this refers specifically to the marble fountain, not to the garden as a whole. Choice C is a distortion; this answer is a misreading of lines 31–32, where the narrator states that "the soil was peopled with plants and herbs." He is not referring to actual people. Choice D is a distortion; in lines 6–7, the narrator states that the garden "might once have been the pleasure-place of an opulent family." He never states that it was such a locale for "the community."

10. G

Category: Generalization
Difficulty: High
Getting to the Answer: When given line references in the question stem, go back to those lines in the text and, if necessary, read the sentences before and after those lines. The paragraph begins by describing the gardener as examining the plants intently and "looking into [the plants'] inmost nature,"

"discovering why one leaf grew in this shape and another in that" (lines 61–62). He seems interested in understanding what the plants are made up of. The remainder of the paragraph discusses his apparent fear of the plants. Look for one of these ideas in the correct choice. Choice (G) matches the first part of the paragraph. Choice F is opposite; the paragraph indicates that he is quite patient, intently seeking to understand the plants' inmost qualities. Choice H is a distortion; the gardener seems to fear the plants may harm him, but he does not seem to want to harm the plants. Choice J is out of scope; there is no indication that the gardener is angry with the plants.

PASSAGE II

11. B

Category: Detail
Difficulty: Low
Getting to the Answer: You are looking for three things that ARE mentioned and one that IS NOT. Don't get the two confused. First check your notes to see that the author mentions jumbo jet design in paragraph 4. Research the passage and cross off each choice that is referenced in the paragraph. Choice (B) is not referenced in this paragraph. Choice A is opposite; the author mentions this in line 39. Choice C is opposite; the author mentions this in line 37. Choice D is opposite; the author mentions this in line 40.

12. J

Category: Vocab-in-Context
Difficulty: Medium
Getting to the Answer: The test maker frequently gives you uncommon usages of common words. You need to read carefully to understand the intended meaning of the phrase. The Boeing example starts by pointing out that the plane's design will be limited in ways that will make it impossible to satisfy everyone. You can assume that the company wants to come close enough to satisfying all the plane's users that those users will be happy with the final design. Choice (J) matches the thrust of the text. Choice F is out of scope; the author doesn't discuss such investments. Choice G is extreme; the passage tells you that there will be compromises. Choice H is out of scope; the cost to users is not mentioned.

13. C

Category: Detail
Difficulty: Medium
Getting to the Answer: You need to find the details used as evidence for this belief. Therefore, your answer will come straight from the passage. Your passage notes should send you to the last paragraph. The author asks you to "imagine" that the Titanic hadn't sunk on her first trip. In the author's opinion, there would have been many ships designed just like the Titanic and potentially many more disasters. Look for an answer choice that reflects this idea. Choice (C) is correct. Choice A is out of scope; there is no evidence that ship designers were careless before the Titanic sank. Choice B is out of scope; the number of lifeboats is not mentioned. Choice D is out of scope; the passage never discusses insurance.

14. F

Category: Generalization
Difficulty: Medium
Getting to the Answer: The answer should come from your overall understanding of the passage, not from specific details. Your active reading told you that this passage is about the importance of learning from failure. The passage title—"Look First to Failure"—is an excellent clue. Therefore, look for an answer choice that mentions the positive aspects of studying failures. Choice (F) matches this prediction. Choice G is out of scope; the author does not address whether or not projects "seem" difficult. Choice H is opposite; in lines 58–60, the author tells you that reverse engineering "sacrifices the synergy of success." Choice J is opposite; the author says that studying past failures is an excellent way to learn.

15. D

Category: Detail
Difficulty: Medium
Getting to the Answer: Use your notes to find the correct paragraph and predict the answer before

looking at the choices; you will reach your answer more quickly and be less likely to fall into traps set by the test maker. Based on your notes, you should go directly to paragraph 6. It tells you that the engineers for the Tacoma Narrows Bridge tried to improve on Roebling's design for the Brooklyn Bridge and left out "the very cables that he included to obviate failure." The prior paragraph identifies those cables. Choice (D) is correct. Choice A is opposite; deviations from the design of the Brooklyn Bridge were the cause of the failure of the Tacoma Narrows Bridge. Choice B is out of scope; the author doesn't discuss any difference in the wind strength between the two bridges. Choice C is opposite; the engineers' concern for "economy and aesthetics" were what caused them to leave out the critical cables.

16. H

Category: Function
Difficulty: High
Getting to the Answer: Use your notes to help you understand the writer's purpose in selecting this specific example. Because this is the final paragraph, it is likely that its meaning will be closely related to the overall purpose of the passage. Lines 80–84 state that Titanic's failure contributed more to ocean liner safety than its success would have. Note that the correct choice may not be stated so specifically; (H) is correct. Choice F is a distortion; the author's point is about design in general, not just the Titanic. Choice G is a distortion; the article is not about the fate of ocean liners. Choice J is out of scope; this is true, but it's not the function of the paragraph.

17. D

Category: Function
Difficulty: Medium
Getting to the Answer: Focus on how an example fits into the overall point the author is making. Use your notes to locate the paper clip example—paragraph 3. The author points out that challengers to the Gem may be able to improve on one aspect of its design but not another. This reiterates the topic sentence, "Reengineering anything is fraught with risk." The example is probably meant to emphasize this point. Choice (D) is correct. Choice A is out of scope; the paragraph is not about the importance of paper clips. Choice B is extreme; the example points out the risks of reengineering in general. Choice C is a distortion; the author does not suggest any redesign of the paper clip.

18. F

Category: Detail
Difficulty: Low
Getting to the Answer: Use your notes to research paragraph 3. To avoid traps, predict your answer before reading the choices. The paragraph tells you that the Gem clip is easy to use and doesn't fall off. Challengers have improved on one aspect of the Gem clip but have sacrificed the other. Choice (F) addresses the compromise predicted. Choice G is out of scope; function, not timing, determines success. Choice H is out of scope; brand awareness and familiarity are not mentioned. Choice J is a distortion; this mentions only one of the benefits the author lists.

19. B

Category: Detail
Difficulty: Medium
Getting to the Answer: When dealing with unfamiliar or passage-specific terms, read around the reference carefully. "Failure-based thinking" in this reference is related to Roebling's *successful* design of the Brooklyn Bridge. A careful reading shows you that Roebling was able to succeed because he understood where others had failed. You need to look for a positive use of "failure" in your answer choice. Choice (B) matches this prediction. Choice A is out of scope; the author doesn't discuss such a habit. Choice C is a distortion; this choice can be tempting because it uses several key words from the paragraph, but the passage says cannibalizing can *sacrifice* synergy, not *create* it. Choice D is opposite; the Tacoma Bridge collapse supports the author's theory because the designers of that bridge failed to use "failure-based thinking."

20. H

Category: Vocab-in-Context

Difficulty: Medium

Getting to the Answer: To answer this question, you need to understand the author's use of the term *in context*. First, read the entire sentence and, if necessary, the sentences before and after. "So" in the middle of the sentence tells you that the first and second halves of the sentence are closely linked. From this, you conclude that "comparatives" relates to improvements. Choice (H) is correct. You need to look for an answer choice that tells you that engineering is measured by its ability to make improvements. Choice F is out of scope; the comparison is between products, not individuals. Choice G is a distortion; "bigger" and "faster" are only two possible measures of improvement. Choice J is out of scope; the author doesn't deal with such comparisons.

PASSAGE III

21. A

Category: Generalization

Difficulty: Medium

Getting to the Answer: When a line reference occurs in the first line of a paragraph, you'll often need to read the following sentence to answer the question fully. Research the passage to find that the "motifs" mentioned are a shared reality with the common human experience, so predict something such as, *all humans go through such experiences*. This prediction matches (A). Choice B is out of scope; the author doesn't mention "critics." Choice C is a distortion; this comes up in the prior paragraph, but it doesn't fit with the author's intention here. Choice D is out of scope; the paragraph doesn't address this.

22. H

Category: Writer's View

Difficulty: Low

Getting to the Answer: Read the sentence referenced in the question stem to make a prediction. The passage says that these avenues are used to get at "the cosmic unconscious," so predict that the author believes fairy tales are one method to help people process human experiences. Choice (H) matches this prediction. Choice F reflects the standard meaning of the word, which doesn't fit here. Choices G and J don't make sense in context.

23. D

Category: Inference

Difficulty: Low

Getting to the Answer: Correct answers to Inference questions will only be a step removed from what is stated in the passage. The lines indicated in the passage, along with those preceding them, discuss how popular fairy tales survive, while unpopular ones die out ("time . . . discards the chaff"). Look for an answer close to that. Choice (D) matches the passage's emphasis on "editing" and "appeal." A Choice A is out of scope; "quality" is not discussed at this point. Choice B is a distortion; fairy tales "can be said to have" undergone an editing process, but not to "the same degree" as other forms of writing. Choice C is opposite; such tales would have "endured."

24. J

Category: Detail

Difficulty: Medium

Getting to the Answer: Don't range too far from the text given and the ideas in that text when drawing your conclusion. The final sentence of Passage B says that we should acknowledge the many variations among versions of fairy tales and search "for insights into the cultural conditions which prompt such divergence." In other words, we should question what these variations tell us about the specific cultures in which they appear. This matches (J) nicely. Choice F is a distortion; the author of Passage B indicates that there is no "accurate" interpretation of such tales. Choice G is out of scope; the passage doesn't explore the difference between written and "oral versions" of the stories. Choice H is a distortion; the author of Passage B does not suggest that any version of a tale is more valid or authoritative than any other.

25. B

Category: Detail

Difficulty: Medium

Getting to the Answer: Remember not to confuse something said by one author with something said by the other author. You know that the author of Passage B disagrees with the kinds of symbolic interpretations made in Passage A, and this question asks specifically why. Predict something about the way that they fail to take multiple versions of tales into account. Choice (B) matches this prediction. Choice A is opposite; if anything, Author B thinks that Author A pays too much attention to "psychology." Choice C is out of scope; the problem that Author B sees goes beyond simple failure to use reference materials. Choice D is a misused detail; it's not the "naïve view of . . . human nature," but rather the naïve view of folklore methodology.

26. F

Category: Inference

Difficulty: High

Getting to the Answer: Beware of answer choices that pull from details in the passage but have nothing to do with the inference at hand. The indicated section of the passage makes the argument that an interpretation based on details about the huntsman can't be valid when most versions of the folk tale don't have a huntsman in them. Predict something along the lines of fairy tales having too many variations to interpret. Choice (F) is the best match for this prediction. Choice H is a distortion; this original idea comes from Passage A. Choice G is out of scope; the passage doesn't raise the question of historical accuracy. Choice J is a distortion; "themes of rescue" are not what the author is striving for here.

27. C

Category: Detail

Difficulty: Low

Getting to the Answer: Some questions don't lend themselves easily to prediction; work your way through the answer choices if you need to. This question calls for a detail that the passages have in common, but it doesn't give you any real hints as to where to look. Eliminate wrong answers, paying special attention to those that come from one passage only. Choice (C) is the correct choice. Both authors admit that fairy tales have changed over time. Choice A is a distortion; only Passage A states this. Choice B is a distortion; this idea appears only in Passage B. Choice D is a distortion; this appears only in Passage A. The author of Passage B would not agree that symbolic interpretation of folk tales is valid.

28. F

Category: Generalization

Difficulty: Medium

Getting to the Answer: Return to the main point made by Author B. The correct answer should be consistent with this overall idea. The main argument made by Author B is that it isn't possible to interpret the symbolism of specific tales as reflecting general psychological truth, so eliminate any answer choice that contradicts that idea. Only (F) captures the central argument of Author B against this type of interpretation. Choice G is out of scope; Author B does not address the "popularity" of such tales. Choice H is a distortion; Author B does not believe that there is such a thing as a definitive version of a tale. Choice J is a distortion; this choice doesn't reflect the overall opinion of Author B that interpretations can't be made at all.

29. B

Category: Inference

Difficulty: High

Getting to the Answer: In questions asking what one author might say to the other, be careful not to confuse the respective viewpoints of the authors. Author A mentions that these motifs are common to all humans in "widely-scattered" societies across time, so he'd probably argue that the specifics of a given version are less important than these universal psychological trends. This prediction matches (B). Choice A is out of scope; Author A makes no mention of recent versions of folk tales or advances in methodology. Choice C is opposite; Author A believes in the relevance of "psychological forces." Choice D is opposite; Author A chooses Snow White as the principal example of his argument.

30. H

Category: Inference

Difficulty: Low

Getting to the Answer: For broadly stated questions, work through the choices, eliminating clearly incorrect answers, and then return to the passages to support your choice. Because a prediction for this question might be difficult, check and eliminate answer choices that don't match both passages. Because both authors would concur that folk tales are developed and passed down through generations (certainly a unique "compositional process"), they would agree with (H). Choice F is a distortion; only Author A emphasizes this. Choice G is a distortion; the contention that folk tales have "universal" truth comes from Passage A only. Choice J is out of scope; neither passage says anything about "new information about . . . particular tales."

PASSAGE IV

31. C

Category: Generalization

Difficulty: Low

Getting to the Answer: Be sure to predict an answer before looking at the answer choices; predicting will help you avoid trap answers. Your notes should help you to predict an answer for this on every passage. Throughout this passage, the author discusses how linear and circular accelerators work and how they differ in their uses. Choice (C) matches this prediction well. Choice A is a misused detail; although this does appear, it is not the main idea of the entire passage. Choice B is a misused detail; this appears in the passage, but it is not the main idea. Choice D is a misused detail; based on the passage, cyclotrons do seem to be a useful type of circular accelerator, but this is not the main idea of the entire passage.

32. F

Category: Detail

Difficulty: Medium

Getting to the Answer: Think of Detail questions as matching questions. The answer choice will always match a detail stated directly in the passage. In lines 98–100, the author writes, "The tube has many magnets distributed around it to focus the particles and curve their track around the tube." The magnets, by focusing the particles and their curve, influence the direction in which the particles travel; use this as your prediction. Choice (F) matches this prediction well. Choice G is a distortion; this misconstrues the statement that the magnets curve the particles' track "around the tube" (line 100). The particles' track is curving, not the particles themselves. Choice H is a distortion; the microwave cavities accelerate the particles (lines 100–101), not the magnets. Choice J is out of scope; there is no indication that the magnets impact the energy levels of the particles.

33. D

Category: Detail

Difficulty: Medium

Getting to the Answer: On Detail questions, avoid incorrect choices that contain details from the passage not relevant to the question being asked. According to lines 81–83, "The effect of the energy injected using the electric fields is therefore to increase their mass." Choice (D) is correct. Choice A is a distortion; the passage states that particles do not reach the speed of light. Choice B is a distortion; this misconstrues the reference to a vacuum in line 77. Choice C is out of scope; there is no indication in the passage that using heavier particles will cause particle mass to increase.

34. H

Category: Vocab-in-Context

Difficulty: Medium

Getting to the Answer: The entire sentence that contains the vocabulary word to decipher its meaning; then look at the choices. In lines 58–61, the author states that heavier particles, such as protons, are being used in accelerators. In the following sentence, you see that "these particles are composites of quarks and gluons." It follows that quarks help make up protons. Choice (H) matches this prediction. Choice F is a misused detail; electron accelerators are mentioned in lines 56–58, but there is no indication that electrons are what make up a quark. Choice G is out of scope; there is no mention of radiation in this paragraph, nor is there any indication that a quark is made up of radiation. Choice J is a distortion; gluons and quarks seem to be roughly equivalent. Neither is a component of the other.

35. D

Category: Detail

Difficulty: Medium

Getting to the Answer: Some questions will ask you what CANNOT be possible. Make sure you take the time to read the question carefully, so that you don't select what is possible. In lines 27–29, the passage states that linear accelerators "are also used to provide an initial low-energy kick to particles before they are injected into circular accelerators." These lines show that linear accelerators provide this kick, not the circular accelerator, as (D) suggests. Choice A is opposite; in lines 42–43, the author states that "When any charged particle is accelerated, it emits electromagnetic radiation," which means that the circular accelerator can cause this. Choice B is opposite; in lines 37–38, the author states that parts of circular accelerators "can be reused to accelerate the particles further." Choice C is opposite; in lines 39–41, the author states that circular accelerators suffer a disadvantage in that the particles emit synchrotron radiation.

36. J

Category: Generalization

Difficulty: Medium

Getting to the Answer: Some questions will ask you to read between the lines. Although this can sometimes be difficult, remember that the answer will always be supported by information in the passage. The passage discusses how linear and circular accelerators work. Some information is also given on how they differ, how they can be used, and some different types of accelerators. Based on this information, it would seem that they have different uses, yet both linear and circular accelerators are valuable in their own ways; (J) is correct. Choice F is extreme; the author states, for example, that linear accelerators can be used to "provide an initial low energy kick." Choice G is extreme; the author states in lines 58–61 that physicists are using particles like protons in accelerators. Choice H is a distortion; besides the first circular accelerator invented by Lawrence in 1929, the passage mentions other types of circular accelerators, such as the synchrotron, which is able to push energies into the billions of electron volts versus the 10 million electron volts that a cyclotron can push energies to.

37. D

Category: Detail

Difficulty: Medium

Getting to the Answer: To get more points on Test Day, predict answers; this will keep you from being tempted to pick incorrect choices that distort or misuse information from the passage. Your notes can help direct you to the second paragraph. Lines 12–15 include the information needed to answer this question. Once the particles have passed through the hole in the plate, the plate repels the particles, which are accelerated towards the next plate. Choice (D) matches this. Choice A is out of scope; the author does not state this. Choice B is out of scope; the author does not state this. Choice C is out of scope; the author does not state this.

38. H

Category: Inference

Difficulty: High

Getting to the Answer: Remember that even though the answers for Inference questions will not be directly stated in the passage, they will be supported by information in the passage. Use your notes to find where the author discusses these items. The author writes that synchrotrons can push energy levels higher than cyclotrons can. Look for this distinction among the choices. Choice (H) is correct. Choice F is extreme; as stated in lines 92–93, cyclotrons are still useful for lower energy applications. Choice G is a distortion; circular accelerators accelerate particles in a circle, and cyclotrons and synchrotrons are both types of circular accelerators. Choice J is out of scope; the author never indicates that synchrotrons cause particles to move closer to the edge of the tube.

39. A

Category: Function
Difficulty: Medium
Getting to the Answer: When you come across Function questions, remember that context is crucial to understanding the purpose of a particular passage element. After discussing the "storage ring," the author recalls the earliest cyclotron, from 1929, and shows the size difference between it and a modern counterpart. You can predict that the author means to *show the progress made in the technology*. Choice (A) matches this prediction. Choice B is a misused detail; the passage indicates that cyclotrons are important, but not because Lawrence invented them. Choice C is a distortion; simply due to the passage in time and the natural pace of progress, this is likely true. This is not, however, the author's purpose in making this statement. Choice D is a distortion; this is not the purpose of this reference.

40. G

Category: Generalization
Difficulty: Medium
Getting to the Answer: Go back and read the lines mentioned in the question. Taking the time to research the passage will help ensure that the answer you choose is supported by the passage, which means more points on Test Day. Throughout this paragraph, the main focus is on how particles in high energy accelerators approach the speed of light, and that when they do so, the main effect is an increase in the relativistic mass of the particle. Choice (G) matches this. Choice F is a misused detail; the author references this in line 79, but it is not the main idea of the paragraph. Choice H is a distortion; this choice is a misinterpretation of the information in lines 79–81. Choice J is a distortion; energy limits are not reached because the mass increases. The mass increases in particles as they come closer to traveling at the speed of light.

WRITING TEST

LEVEL 6 ESSAY

High school is a time to master a solid educational base and explore future opportunities, therefore high schools need to expose students to career opportunities. The best way to accomplish this goal is to require students to attend in-school seminars that are held on a regular basis. Having information about a variety of careers provides an excellent basis to keep exploring, and that basis should be introduced in high school to give students a jump start on their thinking about careers.

Because exploring options is so important to deciding on a career, students should be required to attend career seminars in assemblies held during the regular school day. While attending such events once a semester is a good start, it would make sense for the number of seminars to increase as graduation approaches. Freshmen should be expected to attend just two seminars a year, as they are likely least sure of their future careers, while juniors and seniors should attend a few each semester. The seminars for freshmen and sophomores should focus on the myriad of options available to entice students to study hard and earn the grades required to be admitted to competitive college programs. For juniors and seniors, the information should be more focused and provide real-life examples of what someone can actually do with a Gen Ed degree versus a bachelors in STEM. Students need to learn whether it's worth it to spend tens of thousands of dollars on a degree that will require additional training after graduation, such as a Bachelor of Philosophy. If students know that the job market is looking for people with Bachelors degrees in the sciences, technology, engineering, and math fields, hopefully they'll pursue degrees that will provide options for paying back mountains of student debt.

At my high school in Miami, only about half of the graduating class each year goes directly on to college, leaving hundreds of students who are entering into the job market without much guidance. The students who need these seminars the most are the least likely to spend their free time after school attending a lecture about jobs, so it is imperative that schools make students attend job information sessions during the day. Many of those students do not have a family background that encourages college or professional careers, and those students would likely not attend seminars that they feel is of no interest to them. By bringing professions right into the school day , students will learn their options after graduation. Someone who is considering continuing to work part-time at a restaurant could learn from a career lecture how much career advancement is possible in companies many students don't think of often, such as rental car companies like Hertz and retail clothing stores like Banana Republic.

The idea to embed career-oriented options into current courses misses the fact that not all students take the same courses, so those who do not take courses with career options embedded in them will not be exposed to these opportunities. Also, if the options are taught in a class relevant to it, who would choose which classes and options to incorporate? Furthermore, this option would take up class time and teachers may not be able to teach everything they need to. The argument states that all students would be given course-specific advice, but to guarantee that every student gets that advice means that there will have to be a lot of options offered in every class, from art to history, and a lot of classes interrupted. This approach takes up school time. The same professionals and college representatives can give seminars and not have to develop whole programs that would go into high school classes. This may be overkill. We don't need to have entire embedded programs to be exposed to career possibilities.

When all students have the opportunity to learn about careers and future financial security, they can make better decisions about what to study in college, and presumably graduate into a society which values and recompenses their expertise.

SCORE EXPLANATION (6666)

This essay stays squarely focused on the prompt, explores the implications of all three perspectives, and presents the author's opinion in both the opening and closing paragraphs. Specific examples are provided, including types of Bachelors degrees, companies that offer career advancement, reference to art and history classes, students who will and will not take advantage of seminars, and those who cannot attend after-school seminars.

Ideas and Analysis (6)

The essay is centered around a precise thesis: schools should incorporate career seminars into school-day assemblies once or more per semester. The context is what is best for students, a critical consideration from the writer's point of view. The writer has considered other options and provides good reasoning for why they are not the best solutions, thus presenting an argument with multiple perspectives but clearly signaling her agreement with one only.

Development and Support (6)

The author's position is well reasoned and supported, and critical thinking is clearly displayed. It is evident that this writer has understood the prompt and different points of view, considered the pros and cons of two, and taken a solid stand of her own. She reviews the general issue, summarizing it concisely, then clearly states her point of view.("Because exploring options is so important to deciding on a career, I agree that students should be required to attend career seminars at least once a semester, and that they should be given by college representatives and career professionals.") She goes beyond the basic argument to add her own thoughts about how many seminars to give and how to focus each according to the needs and status of the audience. Support is well stated and relevant to her argument, strengthening her conclusion.

Organization (6)

The essay is well organized into paragraphs, each with a thesis statement followed by support for the statement. Transition words and phrases are well placed (*Some, Others, Furthermore*), and though not every paragraph opens with a transition, each paragraph is clearly separate and discusses one of the three options. There is a logical progression of ideas, creating a coherent argument centered on the theme. The opening paragraph introduces the question and opposing points of view. The body paragraphs explain the author's point of view while logically discussing pros and cons of the alternatives, and the conclusion is a concise restatement of her points. Each paragraph has a thesis statement, if not a transition, and all in all, the essay shows a smooth and logical progression.

Language Use (6)

The writer displays good use of the conventions of writing, including high-level vocabulary with phrases such as "core curriculum," "embedded," and "solid educational base." Though the writer also uses lower-level words (*overkill, ok*), they do not reduce the impact of the writing. Grammar and punctuation are generally correct.

LEVEL 4 ESSAY

Though there are several opinions on how to do it, the general idea that high school students should be given information about future careers is an important one. School is the logical place to do this, given a captive audience and academic focus. Since we already spend enough time in school without having to go to lectures after school, seminars should be scheduled during the school day when we are already there, but should not take up class time because we have a great deal of work to do in all of our classes. Even though career education can be helpful, it shouldn't be added to class time.

Most schools hold weekly assemblys, and it's an unfortunate fact that many students consider them a waste of time and pay scant attention. How much more interesting and vital would it be to use that time to present information on careers and future earnings? Doing so recognizes that even though we are only teenagers, we are thinking about our future and need guidance to understand the range of career possibilities and earnings. Though enlisting professionals is mentioned only in option two, there is no reason that professionals could not talk to students during school day assemblys. Not only would the information be much more important to students, but the mere fact that the speaker is not the usual teacher or principal will hold student interest that much better. From a personal experience, I once met a phlebotomist, a job I didn't know even existed. When he explained the work, and though I don't want to spend my working life drawing blood from people's veins, I did learn about a new career, and one which is in demand in the medical world. If all students were exposed to things like that, as they would be in once a semester career assemblys, it would open their eyes to work they've never thought about but which might be of great interest.

After-school seminars can benefit those who can attend, but they might be just a small percentage of the entire student body. Many students have after-school activities, from football practice to paid jobs, and cannot afford to miss these for an optional seminar. As for having professionals address specific classes, the problem is obvious. Only those students in the class would recieve the information, but many others not taking the class could also benefit from it. It's also true that some students are in a particular class, for example, physics, because they are required. This doesn't reflect their personal interests which may drive their career choices, so it can't be assumed that physics students—and only physics students—are the best audience for physic's career advice.

In-school assemblys are the best way to get information about careers to students since we'll actually pay attention, we won't have to stay after school, and we won't take up important class time. Career advice is important to all high school students, and should be provided for all students in a convenient way.

SCORE EXPLANATION (4444)

The writer provides a clear perspective and stays on topic throughout the essay, while somewhat discussing the alternative perspectives.

Ideas and Analysis (4)

The writer's point of view is clear—career-oriented seminars should be presented in assemblies once per semester—and analyzed in terms of their outreach to all students, best use of assembly time, audience interest, and exposure to new career choices. Though the writer does not specifically reference alternatives, she does analyze them clearly enough to bring out the implications and problems with each. The argument is logical and engaging, emphasizing the writer's point of view while giving attention to the alternatives.

Development and Support (4)

The writer's argument is clearly presented in the opening paragraph and thoroughly supported in the next, though it lacks a further supporting paragraph. The personal example of meeting a phlebotomist is relevant, and the writer expands it from the personal to the general, stating that if all students had the opportunity to be exposed to new careers, "it would open their eyes to work they've never thought about but which might be of great interest." Further support is provided by reference to teens' consideration of their future and the importance of having a wide understanding of careers. The writer's discussion of alternatives, though less-well developed than her own thesis, is well stated and supported.

She gives specific reasons why she does not agree with these alternatives, including interference with after-school activities and the fact that taking a physics class does not always reflect the students' interest in physics as a career.

Organization (4)

The essay is clearly arranged in paragraphs, with the first introducing the author's thesis, the second expanding on it, and the third discussing alternatives, and the fourth reiterates the thesis. Though they are not introduced by transition words, the specific content of each paragraph is clear, and transition words are used throughout the passage ("even though," "not only"). Though the alternatives are not named, they are discussed in such a way as to make the perspectives unambiguous. The progression of ideas is clear, logical, and cohesive, and the essay holds together well.

Language Use (4)

The writing style and word choices are adequate, and the few spelling errors (*assemblys, recieve*) are not sufficiently egregious to detract from understanding. Style could be improved by use of fewer contractions, giving a more formal tone, but the use of a rhetorical question ("How much more interesting and vital would it be to use that time to present information on careers and future earnings?") and proper use of dashes ("physics students—and only physics students—") indicate high-level and inventive writing. Sentence structure, grammar, and punctuation follow normal English usage.

LEVEL 2 ESSAY

I think that learning about careers should be optional, so that means it should be done in after-school seminars. Many students already know what they want to do after college and don't need anyone to tell them differently. I already no I will work in my uncles garage and hes going to teach me everything I need to know about it.

Since I already have my future planned out, it would be silly for me to spend time listening to someone try to interest me in something diffrent, and other students probably feel the same way. They can learn about other jobs if they want to, so they would go to after-school seminars. But that would be they're decision, not something school requires for everyone. Experts may know a lot about they're own jobs, but they dont have the same background as my friends and me do and dont no anything about our lives. Even if we learned about some interesting job, we probly couldn't go to colege because of the money and time it costs.

After-school seminars are best because there not required for all students and only those who have the time and interest need to go.

SCORE EXPLANATION (2222)

The essay scores poorly because it lacks good reasoning, a well written argument, and proper conventions of English.

Ideas and Analysis (2)

Though the author presents her perspective, the essay is very poorly written and shows little, if any, logical reasoning. The author has a definite point of view, but it is not analyzed critically or with any support other than her own experience and her assumptions about herself and her friends. She has not fully considered any point of view other than her own aside from a fleeting, derogatory reference to one alternative and those who may present job information. The essay fails to make an intelligible argument, and the writer's purpose is confusing. The author seems to have taken this task as an opportunity to vent her own somewhat angry feelings without logical reasons, support, or clarity.

Development and Support (2)

The author's argument is one-note and circular, completely centered on her own opinion and plans, and shows little coherent thought or development in its progression. Though she clearly has a point of view, it is stated without any logical or critical thinking and is not developed any further than her original statement. Her only support is that she already knows what she will do and needs no other information about careers.

Organization (2)

The essay does not include transition words or phrases to connect the writer's assertions. Ideas are poorly grouped together; in the body paragraph, the writer does not offer a transition between students' feelings and experts' insights. The concluding paragraph features just one sentence, which does not provide an adequate summary of the ideas presented in the essay.

Language Use (2)

Conventions of English are flouted in every category. There are numerous misspellings, including *no* for *know*, *diffrent* for *different*, and *colege* for *college*. Contractions lack apostrophes, and *they're* is confused with *their.* Though there are three paragraphs and a minimal conclusion, the second paragraph rambles, conflating two alternatives into the same paragraph with no transition. Word choice is very basic, and the writer shows little style. Overall, the argument is weak and poorly presented.

ACT Practice Test Three

ANSWER SHEET

ENGLISH TEST

1. A B C D	11. A B C D	21. A B C D	31. A B C D	41. A B C D	51. A B C D	61. A B C D	71. A B C D
2. F G H J	12. F G H J	22. F G H J	32. F G H J	42. F G H J	52. F G H J	62. F G H J	72. F G H J
3. A B C D	13. A B C D	23. A B C D	33. A B C D	43. A B C D	53. A B C D	63. A B C D	73. A B C D
4. F G H J	14. F G H J	24. F G H J	34. F G H J	44. F G H J	54. F G H J	64. F G H J	74. F G H J
5. A B C D	15. A B C D	25. A B C D	35. A B C D	45. A B C D	55. A B C D	65. A B C D	75. A B C D
6. F G H J	16. F G H J	26. F G H J	36. F G H J	46. F G H J	56. F G H J	66. F G H J	
7. A B C D	17. A B C D	27. A B C D	37. A B C D	47. A B C D	57. A B C D	67. A B C D	
8. F G H J	18. F G H J	28. F G H J	38. F G H J	48. F G H J	58. F G H J	68. F G H J	
9. A B C D	19. A B C D	29. A B C D	39. A B C D	49. A B C D	59. A B C D	69. A B C D	
10. F G H J	20. F G H J	30. F G H J	40. F G H J	50. F G H J	60. F G H J	70. F G H J	

READING TEST

1. A B C D	6. F G H J	11. A B C D	16. F G H J	21. A B C D	26. F G H J	31. A B C D	36. F G H J
2. F G H J	7. A B C D	12. F G H J	17. A B C D	22. F G H J	27. A B C D	32. F G H J	37. A B C D
3. A B C D	8. F G H J	13. A B C D	18. F G H J	23. A B C D	28. F G H J	33. A B C D	38. F G H J
4. F G H J	9. A B C D	14. F G H J	19. A B C D	24. F G H J	29. A B C D	34. F G H J	39. A B C D
5. A B C D	10. F G H J	15. A B C D	20. F G H J	25. A B C D	30. F G H J	35. A B C D	40. F G H J

ENGLISH TEST

45 Minutes—75 Questions

Directions: In the following five passages, certain words and phrases are underlined and numbered. In the right-hand column are alternatives for each underlined portion. Select the one that best conveys the idea, creates the most grammatically correct sentence, or is most consistent with the style and tone of the passage. If you decide that the original version is best, select NO CHANGE. You may also find questions that ask about the entire passage or a section of the passage. These questions will correspond to small, numbered boxes in the test. For these questions, decide which choice best accomplishes the purpose set out in the question stem. After you've selected the best choice, fill in the corresponding oval on your Answer Grid. For some questions, you'll need to read the context in order to answer correctly. Be sure to read until you have enough information to determine the correct answer choice.

PASSAGE I

MY OLD FASHIONED FATHER

My father, though he is only in his early 50s, is stuck in his old-fashioned <u>ways. He has a</u> (1) general mistrust of any innovation or technology that he can't immediately grasp and he always <u>tells us, that</u> (2) if something isn't broken, then you shouldn't fix it.

He <u>has run</u> (3) a small grocery store in town, and if you were to look at a snapshot of his back office taken when he opened the store in 1975, you would <u>see that not much has changed since</u> (4). He is the most disorganized person I know and still

1. A. NO CHANGE
   B. ways he has a
   C. ways having a
   D. ways, and still has a

2. F. NO CHANGE
   G. tells us, that,
   H. tells us that,
   J. tells us that

3. A. NO CHANGE
   B. was running
   C. runs
   D. ran

4. F. NO CHANGE
   G. not be likely to see very much that has changed since.
   H. be able to see right away that not very much has changed since.
   J. not change very much.

GO ON TO THE NEXT PAGE

uses a pencil and paper to keep track of his inventory.[5] His small office is about to burst with all the various documents, notes, and receipts he has accumulated over the years, his filing cabinets[6] have long since been filled up. The centerpiece of all the clutter is his ancient typewriter, which isn't even electric. In the past few years, Father's search for replacement typewriter ribbons has become an increasingly difficult task, because they are no longer being produced. He is perpetually tracking down the few remaining places that still have these antiquated ribbons in their dusty inventories. When people ask him why he doesn't get upgrade his equipment, he tells them, "Electric typewriters won't work in a blackout. All I need is a candle and some paper, and I'm fine." Little does Father know, however, is that[7] the "upgrade" people are speaking of is not to an electric typewriter but to a computer.

[1] Hoping to bring Father out of the dark ages, my sister, and I[8] bought him a brand new computer for his fiftieth birthday. [2] We offered to help him to transfer all of his records onto it and to teach him how to use it.

5. Assuming that all are true, which of the following replacements for "inventory" would be most appropriate in context?

A. inventory of canned and dry goods.
B. inventory, refusing to consider a more current method.
C. inventory, which he writes down by hand.
D. inventory of goods on the shelves and in the storeroom.

6. **F.** NO CHANGE
G. years; his filing cabinets
H. years, and besides that, his filing cabinets
J. years and since his filing cabinets

7. **A.** NO CHANGE
B. know, besides, that
C. know, however, that
D. know, beyond that,

8. **F.** NO CHANGE
G. me and my sister
H. my sister and I
J. my sister and I,

GO ON TO THE NEXT PAGE

[3] Eagerly, we told him about all the new spreadsheet programs that would help simplify his recordkeeping and organize his accounts; and emphasized the advantage of not having to completely retype any document when he found a typo. [4] Rather than offering us a look of joy for the life-changing gift we had presented him, however, he again brought up the blackout scenario. [5] To Father, this is a concrete argument, never mind the fact that our town hasn't had a blackout in five years, and that one only lasted an hour or two. [12]

My father's state-of-the-art computer now serves as a very expensive bulletin board for the hundreds of adhesive notes he uses to keep himself organized. Sooner than later, we fully expect it will completely disappear under the mounting

9. A. NO CHANGE
B. On the other hand,
C. In addition
D. Rather,

10. F. NO CHANGE
G. accounts and
H. accounts and,
J. accounts, we

11. A. NO CHANGE
B. although,
C. although
D. despite the fact that

12. The author wants to include the following statement in this paragraph:

We expected it to save him a lot of time and effort.

The most logical placement for this sentence would be:

F. before Sentence 1
G. after Sentence 1
H. after Sentence 4
J. after Sentence 5

13. A. NO CHANGE
B. Sooner rather than later,
C. Sooner or later,
D. As soon as later,

GO ON TO THE NEXT PAGE

files and papers in the back office. In the depths of that disorganized office, the computer will join the cell phone my mom gave him a few years ago. (14) Interestingly enough, every once in a while, that completely forgotten cell phone will ring

14. F. NO CHANGE
G. Deep in the disorganization of that office's, the computer will join the cell phone my mom gave him a few years back.
H. In the disorganized depths of the office, the computer will soon be joined by the cell phone my mom gave him a few years ago.
J. The computer will join the cell phone my mom gave him a few years back in the disorganized depths of that office.

from under the heavy clutter of the past. [15]

15. Which of the following would provide the most appropriate conclusion for the passage?
A. It's hard to say what else might be lost in there.
B. We tell my father it's a reminder that he can't hide from the future forever.
C. We have no idea who might be calling.
D. Maybe one day I will try to find it and answer it.

PASSAGE II

BREAKING BASEBALL'S COLOR BARRIER

A quick perusal of any modern major league baseball team will reveal a roster of players of multiple ethnicities from the farthest (16) reaches of the globe. Second only to soccer, baseball has evolved into a global sport and a symbol for equality among races.

16. F. NO CHANGE
G. from the most far
H. from the most farthest
J. from farther

It's (17) diversity today presents a stark contrast to the state of the sport just sixty years ago. As late as the 1940s, there existed an unwritten rule in baseball that

17. A. NO CHANGE
B. Its'
C. Its
D. Its own

GO ON TO THE NEXT PAGE

prevented all but white players <u>to participate</u> 18 in the major leagues. This rule was known as the "color barrier" or "color line." The color line in baseball actually predated the birth of the major leagues. Prior to the official formation of any league of professional baseball teams, there existed an organization of amateur baseball clubs known as the National Association of Baseball Players, <u>which was the precursor to today's National League.</u> 19 On December 11, 1868, the governing body of this association had unanimously adopted a rule that effectively barred any team that <u>had, any "colored persons"</u> 20 on its roster. However, when baseball started to organize into leagues of professional teams in the early <u>1880s; the</u> 21 National Association of Baseball Players' decree no longer had any weight, especially in the newly formed American

18. **F.** NO CHANGE
G. to be able to participate
H. from participating
J. to participation

19. Is the underlined portion relevant here?
A. Yes, because it helps familiarize the reader with the range of baseball associations that once existed.
B. Yes, because it helps clarify the development the author traces.
C. No, because the names of the organizations are not important.
D. No, because it is inconsistent with the style of the essay to provide specific historical data.

20. **F.** NO CHANGE
G. had any, "colored persons"
H. had any "colored persons"
J. had any "colored persons,"

21. **A.** NO CHANGE
B. 1880s, the
C. 1880s. The
D. 1880s, and the

GO ON TO THE NEXT PAGE

Association. <u>For a brief period in those early years, a few African Americans played side by side with white players on major league diamonds.</u> 22

22. The writer is considering deleting the underlined portion. Should the writer make this deletion?

F. Yes, because the information is not relevant to the topic of the paragraph.
G. Yes, because the information contradicts the first sentence of the paragraph.
H. No, because the information shows that white players did not object to integration.
J. No, because the statement provides a smooth transition to the specific information about early African-American players in the next paragraph.

[1] Most baseball historians believe that the first African American to play in the major leagues was Moses "Fleet" Walker. [2] <u>Walker was a catcher</u> 23 for the Toledo Blue Stockings of the American Association between 1884 and 1889. [3] During that time, a few other African Americans, <u>including</u> 24 Walker's brother Weldy, <u>would be joining him</u> 25 on the Blue Stockings. [4] Unfortunately, this respite from segregation did not last for very long; as Jim Crow laws took their hold on the nation, many of the most popular white ballplayers started to refuse to take the field with their African-American teammates. [5] By the 1890s, the

23. A. NO CHANGE
B. Walker, being a catcher
C. Walker, a catcher
D. Walker who was a catcher

24. F. NO CHANGE
G. which included
H. who would include
J. including among them

25. A. NO CHANGE
B. joined him
C. were to join him
D. will join him

GO ON TO THE NEXT PAGE

color barrier had fully returned to baseball, where it would endure for more than half a century. [26]

Jackie Robinson would become the first African American to cross the color line at the time when (27) he debuted for the Brooklyn Dodgers in 1947. For Robinson's landmark achievements on and off the diamond, he will forever be recognized as (28) a hero of the civil rights movement and a sports icon. The path that he blazed through the prejudices of American society during the 1940s and 1950s opened the door for the multi-racial and multi-national face of modern baseball, and fans of the sport worldwide will be in his debt for all time to come. (29)

26. Upon reviewing this paragraph, the author discovers that he has neglected to include the following information:

    A handful of African Americans played for other teams as well.

    This sentence would be most logically placed after:

    F. Sentence 1.
    G. Sentence 2.
    H. Sentence 3.
    J. Sentence 4.

27. **A.** NO CHANGE
    B. when
    C. while
    D. when the time came that

28. **F.** NO CHANGE
    G. one day be recognized
    H. forever recognize
    J. be admired by a lot of people for being

29. **A.** NO CHANGE
    B. will be forever in his debt.
    C. will owe him a lot.
    D. being in his debt forever.

GO ON TO THE NEXT PAGE

Question 30 asks about the essay as a whole.

30. Suppose the writer had been assigned to develop a brief essay on the history of baseball. Would this essay successfully fulfill that goal?

F. Yes, because it covers events in baseball over a period of more than a century.
G. Yes, because it mentions key figures in baseball history.
H. No, because people played baseball before 1868.
J. No, because the focus of this essay is on one particular aspect of baseball history.

PASSAGE III

THE BEAR MOUNTAIN BRIDGE

When the gleaming Bear Mountain Bridge officially opened to traffic on Thanksgiving Day in 1924, it [31] was known as the Harriman Bridge, after Edward H. Harriman, wealthy philanthropist and patriarch of the family most influential in the bridges [32] construction. Before the Harriman Bridge was constructed, there were no bridges spanning the Hudson River south of Albany. By the early 1920s, the ferry services used to transport people back and forth across the river had become woefully inadequate. In February of 1922, in an effort to alleviate some of the burden on the ferries and create a permanent link across the Hudson, the New York State Legislature

31. A. NO CHANGE
B. 1924; it
C. 1924. It
D. 1924 and it

32. F. NO CHANGE
G. bridges'
H. bridge's
J. bridges's

GO ON TO THE NEXT PAGE

had authorized a group of private investors, led by
33
Mary Harriman, to build a bridge. The group, known as the Bear Mountain Hudson Bridge Company (BMHBC), was allotted thirty years to build, construct,
34
and maintain the structure, at which time the span
34
would be handed over to New York State.

The BMHBC invested almost $4,500,000 into the suspension bridge and hired the world-renowned design team of Howard Baird and George Hodge as
35
architects. [36] Baird and Hodge enlisted the help of John A. Roebling and Sons,

33. A. NO CHANGE
B. authorized
C. was authorized
D. would authorize

34. F. NO CHANGE
G. build and construct and maintain
H. construct and maintain
J. construct, and maintain

35. A. NO CHANGE
B. of Howard Baird, and George Hodge
C. of Howard Baird and, George Hodge
D. of, Howard Baird and George Hodge

36. The author wants to remove the following from the preceding sentence:

invested almost $4,500,00 into the suspension bridge

If this language were deleted, the essay would primarily lose:

F. a piece of information critical to the point of the essay.
G. a necessary transition between the second and third paragraphs.
H. a detail contributing to the reader's understanding of the magnitude of the project.
J. an explanation of how the group raised money to invest in the bridge.

GO ON TO THE NEXT PAGE

who were instrumental in the steel work of the Brooklyn
37
Bridge and would later work on the Golden Gate and George Washington Bridges.

Amazingly, the bridge took only twenty months and eleven days to complete, and not one life was lost. [38] It was a technological marvel and would stand as a model for the suspension bridges of the future. At the time of the Harriman Bridge's completion, it was, at 2,257 feet, the longest single-span steel suspension bridge in the world.

Therefore, the two main cables used in the suspension
39
were 18 inches in diameter, and each contained 7,752 individual steel wires wrapped in 37 thick strands. If completely unraveled, the single wires in both cables would be 7,377 miles longer. The bridge links Bear
40
Mountain on the western bank of the Hudson to Anthony's Nose on the eastern side, and it lies so precisely on an east-west plane that one can check a compass by it. It carries Routes 6 and 202 across the Hudson, as well as being the point of river crossing for
41
the Appalachian Trail.

37. **A.** NO CHANGE
B. who was
C. a company
D. a company that had been

38. If the writer were to delete the preceding sentence, the essay would lose primarily:
F. information about how long the project had been expected to take.
G. a warning about the dangers of large-scale construction projects.
H. crucial information about the duration of the project.
J. a necessary transition between paragraphs 3 and 4.

39. **A.** NO CHANGE
B. Nonetheless, the
C. At the same time, the
D. The

40. **F.** NO CHANGE
G. long.
H. in total length.
J. lengthy.

41. **A.** NO CHANGE
B. and is as well
C. and is
D. besides being

In an attempt to recoup some of its investment after the bridge <u>opened, the BMHBC charged</u> [42] an exorbitant toll of eighty cents per crossing. Even with the high toll, however, it operated at a loss for thirteen of its first sixteen years. Finally it was acquired, more than ten <u>years—a full decade—</u>[43]earlier than planned, by the New York State Bridge Authority. The bridge was renamed the Bear Mountain Bridge. Today, the Bear Mountain Bridge sees <u>more than</u> [44] six million vehicles cross its concrete decks each year.

42. **F.** NO CHANGE
G. opened the BMHBC charged
H. opened: the BMHBC charged
J. opened; the BMHBC charged

43. **A.** NO CHANGE
B. years and a full decade
C. years, a full decade,
D. years

44. **F.** NO CHANGE
G. over
H. even more than
J. a higher amount than

Question 45 asks about the essay as a whole.

45. Suppose the author had been assigned to write a brief history of bridge building in the United States. Would this essay successfully fulfill that requirement?

A. Yes, because it provides information on the entire process from the initial funding through the opening of the bridge.
B. Yes, because Bear Mountain Bridge is historically significant.
C. No, because it focuses on only one bridge.
D. No, because the essay is primarily concerned with the financial aspects of building and maintaining the bridge.

GO ON TO THE NEXT PAGE

PASSAGE IV

THE DREAM OF THE AMERICAN WEST

As the sun was slowly rising (46) over the Atlantic Ocean and painted New York harbor a spectacular fiery orange, I started my old Toyota's engine. At this early hour, there was still some semblance of the night's tranquility left on the city sidewalks, but I knew that, as the minutes ticked by, the streets would flood with humanity. (47)

46. F. NO CHANGE
    G. rising slowly
    H. rose slowly
    J. continued to rise

47. The author wants to contrast the statement about the quiet of the night streets with a related detail about the daytime activity. Assuming that all of the choices are true, which of the following best accomplishes that goal?
    A. NO CHANGE
    B. some people might appear.
    C. everything would be different.
    D. the tranquility would be unbroken.

I smiled with (48) the thought that soon all the wonderful chaos of New York City would be disappearing behind me as I embarked on my trip to the other side of (49) the country.

48. F. NO CHANGE
    G. along with
    H. at
    J. all because of

49. A. NO CHANGE
    B. embarked on this journey across
    C. traveled to the other side of
    D. traveled across

As the morning sun climbed into the sky, (50)

50. Which of the following alternatives to the underlined portion would NOT be acceptable?
    F. At sunrise,
    G. Watching the morning sun climb into the sky,
    H. The morning sun climbed into the sky,
    J. As the sun rose,

GO ON TO THE NEXT PAGE

I shuddered with excitement to think that my final stop would be in California, where the sun itself ends its journey across America. 51 Like the sun, however, I still had quite a journey before me.

I had been planning this road trip across the United States for as long as I could remember. In my life, I had been fortunate enough to see some of the most beautiful countries in the world. However, it had always bothered me that although I'd stood in the shadow of the Eiffel Tower, marveled in the desert heat at the Pyramids of Giza, 52 I'd never seen any of the wonders of my own country, except those found in my hometown of New York City. All of that was about to change.

As I left the city, the tall buildings began to give way to smaller ones, then to transform into the quaint rows of houses that clustered the crowded suburbs. 53 Trees and grass, then the yellow-green of cornfields and the golden wash of wheat

51. The writer is considering revising this sentence by deleting the underlined portion. If she did so, the paragraph would primarily lose:

A. information about the reasons for the writer's trip.

B. information about the writer's destination.

C. a description of the writer's planned route.

D. a comparison between the sunrise in New York and the sunset in California.

52. F. NO CHANGE

G. Eiffel Tower and had marveled in the desert heat at the Pyramids of Giza,

H. Eiffel Tower and marveled in the desert heat at the Pyramids of Giza

J. Eiffel Tower, and had marveled, in the desert heat, at the Pyramids of Giza

53. Given that all are true, which of the following provides the most effective transition between the third paragraph and the description of the Midwest in the fourth paragraph?

A. NO CHANGE

B. In fact, there were changes on the horizon almost immediately.

C. My excitement hadn't diminished.

D. I realized that people who lived in other areas might feel the same way about visiting New York.

GO ON TO THE NEXT PAGE

were rapidly replacing the familiar mazes of cement and steel. My world no longer stretched vertically toward the sky, it now spread horizontally towards eternity.
54 55

54. Assuming that all are true, which of the following provides information most relevant to the main focus of the paragraph?

F. NO CHANGE
G. appearing before me.
H. racing past my window.
J. becoming monotonous.

55. A. NO CHANGE
B. the sky but it now spread
C. the sky; it now spread
D. the sky spreading

For two days I pushed through the wind-whipped farmlands of Mid-America, hypnotized by the beauty of the undulating yet unbroken lines. At night, the breeze from my car would stir the wheat fields to dance beneath the moon, and the silos hid in the shadows, quietly imposing their simple serenity upon everything.
56

56. F. NO CHANGE
G. For two days,
H. During two days,
J. During two days

Then, as the night's shadows gave way to light, there seemed to be a great force rising to meet the sun as it made its reappearance.
57 58

57. A. NO CHANGE
B. nights shadows
C. shadows from the night
D. night shadow

58. F. NO CHANGE
G. sun as it reappeared
H. reappearing sun
J. sun as it was also rising

Still, I had no idea what I was looking at. Then, there was no
59

59. A. NO CHANGE
B. Even so,
C. At first,
D. Eventually,

GO ON TO THE NEXT PAGE

mistaking it. The unbroken lines of Mid-America had
60
given way to the jagged and majestic heights of the Rockies and the gateway to the American west.

60. F. NO CHANGE
G. mistake to be made.
H. chance to mistake it.
J. having made a mistake.

PASSAGE V

TRAVELING AT THE SPEED OF SOUND

The term "supersonic" refers to anything that travels faster than the speed of sound. When the last of the supersonic Concorde passenger planes made its final trip across the Atlantic in November of 2003, an
61
interesting chapter in history was finally closed. The
61
fleet of supersonic Concorde SSTs, or "Supersonic Transports," which were jointly operated by Air France and British Airways, had been making the intercontinental trip across the Atlantic for almost thirty years. These amazing machines cruised at Mach 2 which is
62
more than twice the speed of sound. They flew to a height almost twice that of standard passenger
63
airplanes. The Concorde routinely made the trip from New York to London in less than three hours and was much more expensive than normal transatlantic flights. Though the majority of the passengers who traveled on the Concorde were celebrities or the extremely wealthy, it also attracted ordinary people who simply wanted to know how it felt to travel faster than the speed of sound.

61. A. NO CHANGE
B. November, of 2003 an interesting
C. November of 2003 an interesting
D. November of 2003; an interesting

62. F. NO CHANGE
G. Mach 2, which
H. Mach 2,
J. a speed of Mach 2, which is

63. A. NO CHANGE
B. at an altitude
C. toward an altitude
D. very high

GO ON TO THE NEXT PAGE

Some of these, [64] would save money for years just to gain that knowledge.

64. F. NO CHANGE
G. Among these were those who
H. Some
J. Some,

What is the speed of sound? Many people are surprised to learn that there is no fixed answer to this question. The speed that [65] sound travels through a given medium depends on a

65. A. NO CHANGE
B. to which
C. at which
D. where

number of factors. So that we may better begin to understand [66] the speed of sound, we must first understand what a "sound" really is.

66. F. NO CHANGE
G. In order that we may understand
H. To understand
J. For understanding

The standard dictionary definition of sound is "a vibration or disturbance transmitted, like waves through water, through a material medium such as a gas." Our ears are able to pick up those sound waves and convert [67] them into what we hear. This means that the speed at which sound travels through gas

67. Which of the following alternatives to the underlined portion would be the LEAST acceptable?
A. change
B. translate
C. alter
D. transform

directly depends on what gas it is traveling through, and the temperature and pressure of the gas. [68] When discussing aircraft breaking the speed of sound, that gas medium, of course, is

68. F. NO CHANGE
G. depends directly on the type, temperature, and pressure of the gas it is traveling through.
H. directly depends on what gas it is, and also on the temperature and pressure of that gas.
J. depends directly on the type, temperature, and pressure of the gas.

air. As air temperature and pressure decrease with altitude, [69] so does the speed of sound. An airplane flying at the speed of sound at sea level is traveling roughly at

69. A. NO CHANGE
B. with height
C. with a drop in altitude
D. at higher altitudes

GO ON TO THE NEXT PAGE

761 mph; <u>however</u>[70] when that same plane climbs to 20,000 feet, the speed of sound is only about 707 mph. This is why the Concorde's cruising attitude was so much higher than that of a regular passenger aircraft; <u>planes can reach supersonic speeds more easily at higher altitudes.</u>[71]

In the years since the Concorde <u>has been</u>[72] decommissioned, only fighter pilots and astronauts have been able to experience the sensation of breaking "the sound barrier." <u>But that is all about to change very soon.</u>[73] Newer and faster supersonic passenger planes are being developed that will be technologically superior to the Concorde and much cheaper to operate. <u>That means we can expect that in the very near future,</u>[74] supersonic passenger travel will be available not only to the rich and famous, <u>but also be for</u>[75] the masses, so they, too, can experience life at faster than the speed of sound.

70. **F.** NO CHANGE
G. however,
H. and so,
J. even so

71. Given that all are true, which of the following provides the most logical conclusion for this sentence?
A. NO CHANGE
B. they're much faster.
C. they use much more fuel than regular aircraft.
D. they're rarely visible because they fly above the cloud cover.

72. **F.** NO CHANGE
G. came to be
H. was
J. had been

73. **A.** NO CHANGE
B. Soon, however, that is about to change.
C. Soon, however, that will change.
D. That is about to change soon.

74. **F.** NO CHANGE
G. So then, in the near future
H. Soon,
J. We can expect, then, that in the near future

75. **A.** NO CHANGE
B. but also be available to
C. but also to
D. but for

IF YOU FINISH BEFORE TIME IS CALLED, YOU MAY CHECK YOUR WORK ON THIS SECTION ONLY. DO NOT TURN TO ANY OTHER SECTION IN THE TEST. **STOP**

READING TEST

35 Minutes—40 Questions

Directions: There are four passages in this test. Each passage is followed by several questions. After reading a passage, choose the best answer to each question and fill in the corresponding oval on your Answer Grid. You may refer to the passages as often as necessary.

PASSAGE I

PROSE FICTION

This passage is adapted from The Age of Innocence, *by Edith Wharton (1920).*

It was generally agreed in New York that the Countess Olenska had "lost her looks."

She had appeared there first, in Newland Archer's boyhood, as a brilliantly pretty little girl of nine or ten, of whom people said that she "ought to be painted." Her parents had been continental wanderers, and after a roaming babyhood she had lost them both, and been taken in charge by her aunt, Medora Manson, also a wanderer, who was herself returning to New York to "settle down."

Poor Medora, repeatedly widowed, was always coming home to settle down (each time in a less expensive house), and bringing with her a new husband or an adopted child, but after a few months she invariably parted from her husband or quarrelled with her ward, and, having got rid of her house at a loss, set out again on her wanderings. As her mother had been a Rushworth, and her last unhappy marriage had linked her to one of the crazy Chiverses, New York looked indulgently on her eccentricities, but when she returned with her little orphaned niece, whose parents had been popular in spite of their regrettable taste for travel, people thought it a pity that the pretty child should be in such hands.

Everyone was disposed to be kind to little Ellen Mingott, though her dusky red cheeks and tight curls gave her an air of gaiety that seemed unsuitable in a child who should still have been in black for her parents. It was one of the misguided Medora's many peculiarities to flout the unalterable rules that regulated American mourning, and when she stepped from the steamer her family was scandalized to see that the crepe veil she wore for her own brother was seven inches shorter than those of her sisters-in-law, while little Ellen wore a crimson dress and amber beads.

But New York had so long resigned itself to Medora that only a few old ladies shook their heads over Ellen's gaudy clothes, while her other relations fell under the charm of her high spirits. She was a fearless and familiar little thing, who asked disconcerting questions, made precocious comments, and possessed outlandish arts, such as dancing a Spanish shawl dance and singing Neapolitan love-songs to a guitar. Under the direction of her aunt, the little girl received an expensive but incoherent education, which included "drawing from the model," a thing never dreamed of before, and playing the piano in quintets with professional musicians.

Of course no good could come of this, and when, a few years later, poor Chivers finally died, his widow again pulled up stakes and departed with Ellen, who had grown into a tall bony girl with conspicuous eyes. For some time no more was heard of them; then news came of Ellen's marriage to an immensely rich Polish nobleman of legendary fame. She disappeared, and when a few years later Medora again came back to New York, subdued, impoverished, mourning a third husband, and in quest of a still smaller house, people wondered that her rich niece had not been able to do something for her. Then came the news that Ellen's own marriage had ended in disaster, and that she was herself returning home to seek rest and oblivion among her kinsfolk.

GO ON TO THE NEXT PAGE

These things passed through Newland Archer's mind a week later as he watched the Countess Olenska enter the van der Luyden drawing room on the evening of the momentous dinner. In the middle of the room she paused, looking about her with a grave mouth and smiling eyes, and in that instant, Newland Archer rejected the general verdict on her looks. It was true that her early radiance was gone. The red cheeks had paled; she was thin, worn, a little older-looking than her age, which must have been nearly thirty. But there was about her the mysterious authority of beauty, a sureness in the carriage of the head, the movement of the eyes, which, without being in the least theatrical, struck him as highly trained and full of a conscious power. At the same time she was simpler in manner than most of the ladies present, and many people (as he heard afterward) were disappointed that her appearance was not more "stylish"—for stylishness was what New York most valued. It was, perhaps, Archer reflected, because her early vivacity had disappeared; because she was so quiet—quiet in her movements, her voice, and the tones of her voice. New York had expected something a good deal more resonant in a young woman with such a history.

1. The author describes which of the following practices as undesirable to New York society?
   A. Playing the piano
   B. Performing Spanish shawl dances
   C. Traveling
   D. Adopting children

2. As a result of her "peculiarities" (line 31), Medora offends her family by:
   F. allowing Ellen to marry a Polish nobleman.
   G. wearing a veil that is too short for mourning.
   H. returning to New York with no money.
   J. refusing to dress stylishly when meeting Newland Archer.

3. It is most reasonable to infer that, after the death of Medora's third husband, Ellen did not help her aunt primarily because:
   A. Ellen was no longer wealthy, since her own marriage had failed.
   B. Medora had become embittered because she hadn't heard from Ellen for so long.
   C. Ellen resented the incoherent education she received from her aunt.
   D. receiving help from her niece would interfere with Medora's desire to be eccentric.

4. Based on the characterization of Newland Archer in the last paragraph, he can best be described as:
   F. reflective and nonjudgmental.
   G. likable but withdrawn.
   H. disinterested but fair.
   J. stylish and gregarious.

5. The third paragraph (lines 11–25) suggests that Medora's lifestyle was primarily viewed by others as:
   A. acceptably different from societal norms.
   B. a terrible example to set for her niece.
   C. unfortunate and pitiful.
   D. disturbingly inconsistent.

6. Which of the following conclusions about the relationship between Medora and Ellen is best supported by the passage?
   F. Ellen is grateful that her aunt unselfishly adopted her.
   G. Medora is jealous of her niece's marriage to a wealthy husband.
   H. Both women share a distaste for New York society.
   J. Ellen has adopted some of her aunt's unconventional traits.

GO ON TO THE NEXT PAGE

7. What does the narrator suggest is a central characteristic of Medora Manson?

A. Arrogance
B. Immodesty
C. Non-conformity
D. Orthodoxy

8. Which of the following characters learns to do something otherwise unheard of by New York society?

F. Ellen Mingott
G. Newland Archer
H. Medora Manson
J. Count Olenska

9. Newland Archer would most likely agree with which of the following characterizations of Ellen?

A. She is confident and poised.
B. She is lonely and unhappy.
C. She is intelligent and outspoken.
D. She is highly-educated and intimidating.

10. One can reasonably infer from the passage that on the occasion of the dinner, Newland and Ellen:

F. had not seen each other for some time.
G. were interested in becoming romantically involved.
H. were both disappointed with New York society.
J. had just met, but were immediately attracted to each other.

PASSAGE II

SOCIAL SCIENCE

The following passage is excerpted from a magazine article discussing scientific research on traditional methods of predicting the timing and character of the Indian monsoon.

Can traditional rules of thumb provide accurate weather forecasts? Researchers in Junagadh, India, are trying to find out. Most farmers in the region grow one crop of peanuts or castor per year. In a wet year, peanuts give the best returns, but if the rains are poor, the more drought-tolerant castor is a better bet. In April and May, before the monsoon comes, farmers decide what to plant, buy the seed, prepare the soil and hope for the best. An accurate forecast would be extremely helpful.

Little wonder, then, that observant farmers have devised traditional ways to predict the monsoon's timing and character. One such rule of thumb involves the blooming of the *Cassia fistula* tree, which is common on roadsides in southern Gujarat. According to an old saying which has been documented as far back as the 8th century, the monsoon begins 45 days after *C. fistula's* flowering peak. Since 1996, Purshottambhai Kanani, an agronomist at Gujarat Agricultural University, has been collecting data to test this rule. He records the flowering dates of trees all over the university's campus and plots a distribution to work out when the flowering peak occurs. While not perfect, *C. fistula* has so far done an admirable job of predicting whether the monsoon will come early or late.

Similarly, with help from local farmers, Dr Kanani has been investigating a local belief regarding the direction of the wind on the day of Holi, a Hindu festival in spring. The wind direction at certain times on Holi is supposed to indicate the strength of the monsoon that year. Wind from the north or west suggests a good monsoon, whereas wind from the east indicates drought. Each year before Holi, Dr Kanani sends out postcards to more than 400 farmers in Junagadh and neighbouring districts. The farmers note the wind direction at the

GO ON TO THE NEXT PAGE

specified times, and then send the postcards back.

In years of average and above-average monsoons (1994, 1997, 1998, and 2001), the wind on Holi tended to come from the north and west. In the drier years of 1995 and 1996 the majority of farmers reported wind from the east (Dr Kanani did not conduct the study in 1999 and 2000). As with the *C. fistula* results, the predictions are not especially precise, but the trend is right.

Dr Kanani first became interested in traditional methods in 1990, when an old saying attributed to a tenth-century sage named Bhadli—that a storm on a particular day meant the monsoon would come 72 days later—proved strikingly correct. This prompted Dr Kanani to collect other rules from old texts in Gujarati and Sanskrit.

Not all of his colleagues approve. Damaru Sahu, a meteorologist at Gujarat Agricultural University and a researcher for India's director-general of meteorology, says that traditional methods are "OK as a hobby." But, he goes on, they cannot be relied upon, and "may not be applicable to this modern age." Yet Dr Sahu concedes that meteorological science has failed to provide a useful alternative to traditional methods. For the past 13 years, he notes, the director-general for meteorology has predicted "normal monsoon" for the country. Every year, the average rainfall over the whole country is calculated, and this prediction is proved correct. But it is no use at all to farmers who want to know what will happen in their region.

Dr Kanani hopes that his research will put traditional methods on a proper scientific footing. He and his colleagues have even set up a sort of peer-review forum for traditional meteorology. Each spring, he hosts a conference for 100 local traditional forecasters, each of whom presents a monsoon prediction with supporting evidence—the behaviour of a species of bird, strong flowering in a certain plant, or the prevailing wind direction that season. Dr Kanani records these predictions and publishes them in the local press.

He has also started a non-governmental organisation, the Varsha Vigyan Mandal, or Rain Science Association, which has more than 400 members. Its vice-president, Dhansukh Shah, is a scientist at the National Directorate of Meteorology in Pune. By involving such mainstream meteorologists as Dr Shah in his work, Dr Kanani hopes to bring his unusual research to the attention of national institutions. They could provide the funding for larger studies that could generate results sufficiently robust to be published in peer-reviewed science journals.

11. According to the passage, all of the following traditional methods of weather prediction have been scientifically tested EXCEPT:

A. wind direction during the Hindi festival of Holi.

B. the behavior of certain bird species.

C. the flowering *Cassia fistula* trees.

D. a tenth century prediction connecting storm activity to later monsoons.

12. When the author uses the phrase "useful alternative" (line 62), she means that:

F. modern meteorology rarely provides an accurate forecast.

G. equipment needed for accurate forecasting is too expensive for many in India.

H. modern meteorology doesn't give as specific predictions as traditional methods do.

J. today's science cannot explain why traditional methods work so well.

GO ON TO THE NEXT PAGE

13. The main purpose of the last three paragraphs (lines 55–92) is to:

A. project the role of traditional weather prediction methods in the scientific community into the future.

B. suggest that both traditional and scientific methods can co-exist because they serve very different functions.

C. remind us that traditional methods have been around too long to be easily eclipsed by modern science.

D. introduce us to a general respect for ancient knowledge in the sciences.

14. The author's attitude toward traditional methods of weather forecasting may reasonably be described as:

F. curious as to their development.

G. cautious hopefulness that they are useful.

H. skeptical regarding their real scientific value.

J. regretful of the "fad" of interest in these methods.

15. Based on information in the passage, which of the discussed methods gives the most advanced prediction of monsoon arrival?

A. The behavior of the birds

B. The flowering of the fistula tree

C. The wind direction on Holi

D. Bhadli's prediction based on storms

16. The function of the second paragraph in relation to the passage as a whole is most likely to provide:

F. a reason that farmers need techniques to predict monsoons earlier.

G. examples of the inexact nature of predictions made from traditional methods.

H. an explanation of the ancient saying that the rest of the passage will examine.

J. an introduction to the modern research of traditional methods.

17. According to the passage, the purpose of Dr. Kanani's springtime conferences is to:

A. record the traditional methods of weather prediction before they disappear.

B. help gain acceptance for traditional methods in the academic community.

C. publish the methods in the local press.

D. facilitate the exchange of ideas between farmers from far-flung regions of India.

18. According to the passage, the reason farmers use traditional methods to predict the weather is that:

F. traditional methods are more accessible to rural populations.

G. "normal" monsoons can still be very different from each other.

H. they need to anticipate the local conditions for the coming growing season.

J. traditional methods get the basic trends right.

GO ON TO THE NEXT PAGE

19. The author uses the term "admirable job" (line 25) to indicate that:

A. the flowering of the fistula tree provides remarkably predictive data on the coming monsoon.

B. precision isn't everything.

C. predictions based on the peak of *C. fistula's* flowering do provide some reliable answers.

D. sometimes rules of thumb are better than complex formulas.

20. According to Damaru Sahu, traditional weather prediction:

F. can be curiously accurate.

G. has a defined place in meteorology.

H. is useful in some ways despite its lack of scientific foundation.

J. appeals to an instinct different than the rational brain.

PASSAGE III

HUMANITIES

One of the most enjoyable ways to analyze culture is through music. By analyzing musical styles and lyrics, one can explore quintessential characteristics of particular cultures.

PASSAGE A

Country music has its roots in the southern portions of the United States, specifically in the remote and undeveloped backcountry of the central and southern areas of the Appalachian mountain range. Recognized as a distinct cultural region since the late nineteenth century, the area became home to European settlements in the eighteenth century, primarily led by Ulster Scots from Ireland. Early inhabitants have been characterized as fiercely independent, to the point of rudeness and inhospitality. It was in this area that the region's truly indigenous music, now known as country music, was born.

Rooted in spirituals as well as folk music, cowboy songs, and traditional Celtic melodies, country music originated in the 1920s. The motifs are generally ballads and dance tunes, simple in form and accompanied mostly by guitar, banjo, and violin. Though today there are many genres of country music, all have their roots in this mélange of sources.

The term "country" has replaced the original pejorative term, "hillbilly." Hillbillies referred to Appalachian inhabitants who were considered poor, uneducated, isolated, and wary; the name change reflects a more accepting characterization of these mountain dwellers.

Hank Williams put country music on the map nationally, and is credited with the movement of country music from the South to more national prominence. Other early innovators include the Carter family, Ernest Tubb, Woody Guthrie, Loretta Lynn, and Bill Monroe, father of bluegrass music. More recently, Faith Hill, Reba McEntire, and Shania Twain have carried on the tradition.

What might be considered the "home base" of country music is in Nashville, Tennessee, and the legendary music hall, the Grand Ole Opry. Founded in 1925 by George D. Hay, it had its genesis in the pioneer radio station WSM's program *Barn Dance*. Country singers are considered to have reached the pinnacle of the profession if they are asked to become members of the Opry. While noted country music performers and acts take the stage at the Opry numerous times, Elvis Presley performed there only once, in 1954. His act was so poorly received that it was suggested he return to his job as a truck driver.

The offshoots and relatives of country music highlight the complexity of this genre. In a move away from its mountain origins, and turning a focus to the West, honky-tonk music became popular in the early twentieth century. Its name is a reference to its roots in honky-tonk bars, where the music was played. Additionally, Western Swing emerged as one of the first genres to blend country

GO ON TO THE NEXT PAGE

and jazz musical styles, which required a great deal of skill and creativity. Some of the most talented and sophisticated musicians performing in any genre were musicians who played in bluegrass string bands, another relative of country music.

Country music has always been an expression of American identity. Its sound, lyrics, and performers are purely American, and though the music now has an international audience, it remains American in its heart and soul.

PASSAGE B

A style of music closely related to country is the similarly indigenous music known as bluegrass, which originated in the Appalachian highland regions extending westwards to the Ozark Mountains in southern Missouri and northern Arkansas. Derived from the music brought over by European settlers of the region, bluegrass is a mixture of Scots, Welsh, Irish, and English melodic forms, infused, over time, with African-American influences. Indeed, many bluegrass songs, such as "Barbara Allen" and "House Carpenter" preserve their European roots, maintaining the traditional musical style and narratives almost intact. Storytelling ballads, often laments, are common themes. Given the predominance of coal mining in the Appalachian region, it is not surprising that ballads relating to mining tragedies are also common.

Unlike country music, in which musicians commonly play the same melodies together, bluegrass highlights one player at a time, with the others providing accompaniment. This tradition of each musician taking turns with solos, and often improvising, can also be seen in jazz ensembles. Traditional bluegrass music is typically played on instruments such as banjo, guitar, mandolin, bass, harmonica, and Dobro (resonator guitar.) Even household objects, including washboards and spoons, have, from time to time, been drafted for use as instruments. Vocals also differ from country music in that, rather than featuring a single voice, bluegrass incorporates baritone and tenor harmonies.

Initially included under the catch-all phrase "folk music," and later referred to as "hillbilly," bluegrass did not come into his own category until the late 1950s, and appeared first in the comprehensive guide, *Music Index*, in 1965. Presumably it was named after Bill Monroe's Blue Grass band, the seminal bluegrass band. A rapid, almost frenetic pace, characterizes bluegrass tempos. Even today, decades after their most active performing era, *The Foggy Mountain Boys* members Lester Flatt, a bluegrass guitarist and mandolinist, and Earl Scruggs known for his three-finger banjo picking style, are widely considered the foremost artists on their instruments.

Partially because of its pace and complexity, bluegrass has often been recorded for movie soundtracks. "Dueling Banjos," played in the movie *Deliverance*, exemplifies the skill required by the feverish tempo of the genre. The soundtrack for *O Brother Where Art Thou?* incorporates bluegrass, and its musical cousins folk, country, gospel, and blues. Bluegrass festivals are held throughout the country and as far away as the Czech Republic. Interactive, often inviting audience participation, they feature performers such as Dolly Parton and Alison Krauss.

Central to bluegrass music are the themes of the working class—miners, railroad workers, farmers. The phrase "high, lonesome sound" was coined to represent the bluegrass undertones of intensity and cheerlessness, symbolizing the hard-scrabble life of the American worker. As with so much of a nation's traditional music, and for better or worse, bluegrass music reflects America.

Questions 21–23 ask about Passage A.

21. According to the passage, country music originated from all of the following EXCEPT:

A. Celtic melodies.
B. spirituals.
C. jazz.
D. cowboy songs.

GO ON TO THE NEXT PAGE

that Pluto be made the first entry in a new catalog of TNOs for which precise orbits have been determined. It would then enter the textbooks as something like TN-1 (or TN-0, as some astronomers have suggested).

Marsden agrees that Pluto is a TNO, but he doesn't like the idea of establishing a new catalog of solar system objects, arguing that astronomers already have a perfectly serviceable list of numbered minor bodies (mostly asteroids). "The question is: Do we want to recognize [trans-Neptunian objects] with a different designation?" he asks. He points out that the Centaurs—TNOs that have been nudged well inside Neptune's orbit—have been classified as asteroids and says he sees "no reason for introducing a new designation system for objects of which we have representations in the current [catalog of minor bodies]."

Instead of making Pluto the founding member of a new catalog, Marsden wants to add it to the existing list. "The current number is 9826," he says. "With the current detection rate, we should arrive at number 10,000 somewhere in January or February." He notes that asteroids 1000, 2000, 3000, and so on have all been honored by the IAU with special names, including Leonardo and Isaac Newton. "What better way to honor Pluto than to give it this very special number?"

But the prospect of lumping Pluto with the solar system's riffraff outrages supporters of a new TNO category. "It's the most idiotic thing" she's ever heard, says Luu. "Pluto is certainly not an asteroid," she says.

To try to settle the issue, Mike A'Hearn of the University of Maryland, College Park, is collecting e-mail votes from 500 or so members of IAU divisions on the solar system, comets and asteroids, and other relevant topics. "I wanted to arrive at a consensus before Christmas [1998]," he says, "but it may take a while, since the community as a whole doesn't seem to have a consensus." Neither proposal has attracted a majority. Although many people opposed Marsden's proposal, a comparable number were unhappy with Binzel's idea, A'Hearn says, because Pluto would still be an anomaly, being much larger than the other trans-Neptunian objects. A'Hearn says that if no consensus can be reached, Pluto will probably not end up in any catalog at all, making it the ultimate outcast of the solar system.

However the debate settles out, Pluto's career as a planet seems to be ending, and even astronomers are wistful at the prospect. "No one likes to lose a planet," says Luu. A'Hearn agrees. "It will probably always be called the ninth planet" by the general public, he says.

31. According to the passage, regarding the view that Pluto should be categorized as an asteroid, Jane Luu expressed which of the following?

A. Shock

B. Excitement

C. Confusion

D. Forceful opposition

32. It can be inferred that Pluto's original designation as a planet would have never happened if scientists had:

F. understood its size from the beginning.

G. seen the icy core of Pluto sooner.

H. been able to detect the many smaller TNOs when Pluto was discovered.

J. understood the popular misconceptions about Pluto's planet-hood that would follow.

33. According to the passage, Pluto has historically been regarded as:

A. closer in relation to rocky planets such as Earth.

B. unlikely to keep its title as a planet.

C. an outlier among planetary bodies.

D. destined for an honorable place in astronomy history.

GO ON TO THE NEXT PAGE

34. According to the passage, large objects similar to the makeup and orbit of Pluto found nearer to the sun than Neptune are called:

F. Centaurs.
G. IAUs.
H. TNOs.
J. ice-dwarves.

35. According to lines 64–71, the central issue in the debate over Pluto is:

A. whether Pluto is more similar to rocky planets or the gas giants.
B. the distance of Pluto from the sun.
C. whether or not the issues raised by Pluto's differences from the other TNOs are substantial enough to create a new classification for it.
D. scientists' conception of Pluto versus the view of the general public.

36. As used in line 63, the term *serviceable* most nearly means:

F. able to be fixed.
G. adequate.
H. beneficial.
J. durable.

37. One slightly less scientific concern expressed by most of the scientists in the passage is:

A. the role of the IAU in making classification decisions.
B. respect for the views of the public.
C. who gets the credit for Pluto's reclassification.
D. the preservation of Pluto's fame and importance.

38. According to the passage, what is the major reason for lack of consensus regarding the status of Pluto?

F. The general population resists the scientific community's belief that Pluto is not a planet.
G. Pluto seems very different than the other members of any classification.
H. Pluto's strange orbit makes it asteroid-like, but its surface more closely resembles a planet.
J. There have been numerous discoveries of other Pluto-like objects nearer to the sun than to Neptune.

39. Details in the passage suggest that Pluto is much different from other planets in:

A. its distance from the sun and the shape of its orbit.
B. its size and the shape of its orbit.
C. the year of its discovery and its size.
D. its shape and surface composition.

40. Pluto's size accounts for:

F. its classification as a TNO.
G. its dissimilarity to asteroids.
H. its early discovery relative to other TNOs.
J. its bizarre orbit.

IF YOU FINISH BEFORE TIME IS CALLED, YOU MAY CHECK YOUR WORK ON THIS SECTION ONLY. DO NOT TURN TO ANY OTHER SECTION IN THE TEST. **STOP**

WRITING TEST

Directions: This is a test of your writing skills. You will have **forty** (40) minutes to read the prompt, plan your response, and write an essay in English. Before you begin working, read all material in this test booklet carefully to understand exactly what you are being asked to do.

You will write your essay on the lined pages in the **answer document** provided. Your writing on those pages will be scored. You may use the unlined pages in this test booklet to plan your essay. Your work on these pages will not be scored.

Your essay will be evaluated based on the evidence it provides of your ability to:

- clearly state your own perspective on a complex issue and analyze the relationship between your perspective and at least one other perspective
- develop and support your ideas with reasoning and examples
- organize your ideas clearly and logically
- communicate your ideas effectively in standard written English

Lay your pencil down immediately when time is called.

DO NOT OPEN THIS BOOKLET UNTIL TOLD TO DO SO.

GO ON TO THE NEXT PAGE

ESSAY TASK

Write a unified, coherent essay in which you evaluate multiple perspectives regarding government funding of scientific research. In your essay, be sure to:

- clearly state your own perspective on the issue and analyze the relationship between your perspective and least one other perspective
- develop and support your ideas with reasoning and examples
- organize your ideas clearly and logically
- communicate your ideas effectively in standard written English

Your perspective may be in full agreement with any of the others, in partial agreement, or wholly different. Whatever the case, support your ideas with logical reasoning and detailed, persuasive examples.

PLANNING YOUR ESSAY

You may wish to consider the following as you think critically about the task:

Strengths and weaknesses of the three given perspectives

- What insights do they offer, and what do they fail to consider?
- Why might they be persuasive to others, or why might they fail to persuade?

Your own knowledge, experience, and values

- What is your perspective on this issue, and what are its strengths and weaknesses?
- How will you support your perspective in your essay?

GO ON TO THE NEXT PAGE

Scientific Research

A great deal of pure research, undertaken without specific goals but generally to further humankind's understanding of itself and its world, is subsidized at least partly, if not fully, by the nation's government to help drive progress and promote outcomes that improve overall quality of life for citizens. Though pure research often involves considerable time, energy, and money without any assurances of positive outcomes, it can result in economic, medical, and technological benefits. However, it can also result in negative, harmful, and perhaps irreversible outcomes, in which case taxpayer dollars can be wasted and society put at risk. Should governments fund research when the outcome is unclear? Given that taxpayers prefer that their dollars be spent efficiently and effectively, it may be unwise to allocate significant funding to endeavors that may not benefit society as a whole.

Read and carefully consider these perspectives. Each discusses government funding of scientific research.

Perspective One

Governments should fund as much pure research as they can afford when the intent is to benefit the mass population. Without the government's money, many research projects would have to cease unless alternative funding is secured. Even research without clear, positive consequences should be pursued because the outcome may prove beneficial, and the research can always be paused or stopped entirely if negative repercussions begin to emerge.

Perspective Two

Governments should be very cautious and limit efforts to fund research programs with unclear consequences. Rather, these programs should demonstrate their worth and intended results in order to seek government money. Governments should evaluate the merit and benefit of each program and on a case-by-case basis, fund only those projects that are designed to create, and will likely achieve, clear and acceptable outcomes.

Perspective Three

Governments should partner with private contributors to fund research. Private contributors include companies doing research and development as well as nonprofit foundations. These partnerships will distance the government from taking responsibility for any unintended or undesired consequences and relieve the burden on the taxpayer for efforts that do not prove beneficial. Additionally, this approach incentivizes research teams to provide results-based research that can generateprivate funding, thus increasing the chance that the research will prove useful to multiple entities, including the government.

GO ON TO THE NEXT PAGE

IF YOU FINISH BEFORE TIME IS CALLED, YOU MAY CHECK YOUR WORK ON THIS SECTION ONLY. DO NOT TURN TO ANY OTHER SECTION IN THE TEST.

STOP

Practice Test Three

ANSWER KEY

ENGLISH TEST

1. A	**11.** C	**21.** B	**31.** A	**41.** C	**51.** B	**61.** A	**71.** A
2. J	**12.** G	**22.** J	**32.** H	**42.** F	**52.** G	**62.** H	**72.** H
3. C	**13.** C	**23.** A	**33.** B	**43.** D	**53.** A	**63.** B	**73.** C
4. F	**14.** F	**24.** F	**34.** H	**44.** F	**54.** F	**64.** H	**74.** H
5. B	**15.** B	**25.** B	**35.** A	**45.** C	**55.** C	**65.** C	**75.** C
6. G	**16.** F	**26.** H	**36.** H	**46.** H	**56.** G	**66.** H	
7. C	**17.** C	**27.** B	**37.** D	**47.** A	**57.** A	**67.** C	
8. H	**18.** H	**28.** F	**38.** J	**48.** H	**58.** H	**68.** J	
9. A	**19.** B	**29.** B	**39.** D	**49.** D	**59.** C	**69.** D	
10. G	**20.** H	**30.** J	**40.** G	**50.** H	**60.** F	**70.** G	

READING TEST

1. C	**6.** J	**11.** B	**16.** J	**21.** C	**26.** F	**31.** D	**36.** G
2. G	**7.** C	**12.** H	**17.** B	**22.** J	**27.** B	**32.** H	**37.** D
3. A	**8.** F	**13.** A	**18.** H	**23.** D	**28.** H	**33.** C	**38.** G
4. F	**9.** A	**14.** G	**19.** C	**24.** J	**29.** C	**34.** F	**39.** B
5. A	**10.** F	**15.** D	**20.** H	**25.** A	**30.** G	**35.** C	**40.** H

ANSWERS AND EXPLANATIONS

ENGLISH TEST

PASSAGE I

1. A
Category: Sentence Sense
Difficulty: Low
Getting to the Answer: When a period appears in the underlined portion, check to see if each "sentence" is complete. Here, each sentence is complete and correct; therefore (A), NO CHANGE, is correct. Choice B creates a run-on sentence. Choices C and D create sentences that are awkward and overly wordy.

2. J
Category: Punctuation
Difficulty: Medium
Getting to the Answer: The ACT tests very specific punctuation rules. If punctuation is used in a way not covered by these rules, it will be incorrect. No commas are required in the underlined selection; (J) is correct. Choices F, G, and H all contain unnecessary commas.

3. C
Category: Verb Tenses
Difficulty: Medium
Getting to the Answer: When a verb is underlined, make sure it places the action properly in relation to the other events in the passage. This passage is written primarily in the present tense; "runs," (C), is the best answer here. Choices A and B use verb tenses that do not make sense in context. The past tense verb in D is inconsistent with the rest of the passage.

4. F
Category: Wordiness
Difficulty: Medium
Getting to the Answer: Very rarely will a correct answer choice be significantly longer than the original selection. The underlined selection is grammatically and logically correct, so check the answer choices for a more concise version. You can eliminate G and H, both of which are wordier than the original. Choice J may be tempting because it's shorter than the underlined selection, but it changes the meaning of the sentence; the back office, not the reader, is what hasn't changed. Choice (F) is correct.

5. B
Category: Writing Strategy
Difficulty: Medium
Getting to the Answer: When an English Test question contains a question stem, read it carefully. More than one choice is likely to be both relevant and correct, but only one will satisfy the conditions of the stem. This paragraph deals with the author's father's refusal to give up his old-fashioned ways. Choice (B) is the most consistent choice. Choices A and D describe the items being inventoried, which is irrelevant to the point of the paragraph. Choice C is redundant; since we already know he uses paper and pencil to keep his inventory, it's understood that he's writing it by hand.

6. G
Category: Sentence Sense
Difficulty: Medium
Getting to the Answer: Commas cannot be used to combine independent clauses. Here, the comma connects two independent clauses. Choice (G) correctly replaces the comma with a semicolon. Choice H corrects the run-on error but is unnecessarily wordy. Choice J leaves the meaning of the second clause incomplete.

7. C
Category: Sentence Sense
Difficulty: High
Getting to the Answer: Beware of answer choices that make changes to parts of the selection that

contain no error; these choices will rarely be correct. As written, this sentence uses incorrect grammatical structure; the verb "is" is incorrect here, so you should eliminate A. Choice (C) eliminates it without introducing additional errors. Choices B and D correct the sentence's grammatical error, but neither uses the necessary contrast Connection to relate this sentence to the one before it.

8. H

Category: Punctuation
Difficulty: Low
Getting to the Answer: Commas are used in a series of three or more; they are incorrect in compounds. "My sister and I" is a compound; no comma is needed, so F is correct. Choice (H) corrects the error without adding any new ones. Choice G uses the incorrect pronoun case; since you wouldn't say "me bought him a brand new computer," "me" is incorrect in the compound as well. Choice J incorrectly separates the sentence's subject and its predicate verb with a comma.

9. A

Category: Connections
Difficulty: High
Getting to the Answer: When a Connections word or phrase is underlined, make sure it properly relates the ideas it connects. The underlined word is the Connection between the offer to help transfer records and the information about other ways the computer could be helpful. The second sentence is a continuation of the first, so you can eliminate B and D, both of which suggest a contrast. Choosing between (A) and C is a little more difficult, but remember that new errors may be introduced in answer choices. "In addition" in C would be acceptable if it were followed by a comma, but as written, it's incorrect.

10. G

Category: Punctuation
Difficulty: Medium
Getting to the Answer: Semicolons can only combine independent clauses. Here, the second clause is not independent, so the semicolon is incorrect; eliminate F. Choice (G) eliminates the semicolon. Choice H incorrectly places a comma after the conjunction. Choice J creates a run-on sentence.

11. C

Category: Wordiness
Difficulty: Medium
Getting to the Answer: If you don't spot a grammar or usage error, check for errors of style. This sentence is grammatically correct, but "although" in (C) is a much more concise way of saying "never mind the fact that." Choice B corrects the wordiness error but places an incorrect comma after "although." Choice D is still unnecessarily wordy.

12. G

Category: Writing Strategy
Difficulty: Medium
Getting to the Answer: When asked to add new information, read it into the passage at the points suggested to choose its most logical placement. There are three pronouns in this new sentence; clarity requires that it be placed somewhere that these pronouns have logical antecedents. Placing it after Sentence 1, as (G) suggests, gives each pronoun a clear antecedent: "we" is the author and his sister, "him" is their father, and "it" is the computer. Choice F puts the siblings' hopes about how a computer could help their father before the information that they bought him one. Choice H's placement makes the antecedent for "it" Father's "blackout scenario," which doesn't make sense in context. Placing the new sentence where Choice J suggests gives the pronoun the antecedent "blackout," which is also illogical.

13. C

Category: Word Choice
Difficulty: Medium
Getting to the Answer: Idioms questions often offer more than one idiomatically correct answer choice; use context to determine which is appropriate. "Sooner than later" is idiomatically incorrect, so you

should eliminate A; these are comparison words, but nothing is compared here. Both B and (C) offer proper idioms, but (C) is the one that's appropriate here. Choice D is also incorrect idiomatic usage.

14. F

Category: Sentence Sense
Difficulty: Medium
Getting to the Answer: Remember to read for logic as well as for grammar and usage. The best version of this sentence is the way it is written; (F) is correct. Choice G redundantly uses the possessive "office's" where possession has already been indicated by "of." Choice H misstates the information in the passage; the writer's father received the cell phone before the computer. In J, "the disorganized depths of that office" is where the writer's father received his cell phone, not where the cell phone ended up.

15. B

Category: Writing Strategy
Difficulty: Low
Getting to the Answer: When asked to add information, consider both subject matter and tone. This essay is about the author's father's resistance to technology. Choice (B) concludes the essay by referencing something stated at the beginning: that the writer's father tries to "hide" from the future. Choices A, C, and D, while relevant to the paragraph, do not provide strong conclusions to a passage about the father's aversion to technology.

PASSAGE II

16. F

Category: Word Choice
Difficulty: Medium
Getting to the Answer: *More* or *–er* adjectives are used to compare two items; for more than two, use *most* or *–est*. This sentence is correct as written, (F); "farthest" is appropriate when comparing all areas of the globe. Choice G uses "most far," but "most" is only correct with adjectives that don't have *–est* forms. Choice H combines "most" with the *–est* suffix, which is never correct. Choice J uses "farther," which indicates a comparison that is not present here.

17. C

Category: Punctuation
Difficulty: Medium
Getting to the Answer: "It's" has an apostrophe only when it's used as a contraction; possessive pronouns do not have apostrophes. To check for the correctness of "It's," substitute *It is* or *It has* for the contraction. Since "It is diversity today presents a stark contrast" does not make sense, the contraction is incorrect; eliminate A. Choice (C) is the appropriate possessive here. Choice B uses a spelling that is never correct. Choice D adds the word "own" unnecessarily.

18. H

Category: Word Choice
Difficulty: Medium
Getting to the Answer: Most ACT Idioms questions will hinge on preposition usage. "Prevented... to participate" is idiomatically incorrect, so you can eliminate F; the proper idiom in this context is "prevented from participating," (H). Choices G and J are both idiomatically incorrect.

19. B

Category: Writing Strategy
Difficulty: Medium
Getting to the Answer: When you're asked whether a piece of text is relevant, first determine the topic of the paragraph. This paragraph is about the evolution of the "color line" in baseball. Therefore, information that talks about the development of the industry and the shift in authority is relevant to the paragraph; (B) is correct. Choice A is incorrect because, although the text does talk about previous associations, knowing that range doesn't further the purpose of the paragraph. Choices C and D can be eliminated, since they indicate that the information is irrelevant.

20. H

Category: Punctuation

Difficulty: Medium

Getting to the Answer: A verb should not be separated from its object by a comma. As written, this sentence places an incorrect comma between the verb "had" and its object; eliminate F. Choice (H) eliminates the comma without introducing any additional errors. Choices G and J both add incorrect commas.

21. B

Category: Punctuation

Difficulty: Medium

Getting to the Answer: A semicolon can only be used to combine clauses if both of them are independent. The first clause of this sentence is not independent, so the semicolon is incorrect; a comma correctly joins it to the independent clause that follows. Choices A, C, and D all treat the first clause as independent. Choice (B) is correct.

22. J

Category: Writing Strategy

Difficulty: Medium

Getting to the Answer: Determining whether or not the underlined text should be deleted will help you quickly eliminate two answer choices. If you eliminate the underlined selection, the passage skips abruptly from the decree losing its force to a discussion of specific African-American players. The underlined text introduces those players generally, as a result of the decree losing its impact, and therefore provides a necessary transition, as indicated in (J). Choice F and G can be eliminated, since they advocate deleting the selection. The reasoning in H is not supported by the passage.

23. A

Category: Sentence Sense

Difficulty: Medium

Getting to the Answer: Expect about 25% of your English Test questions to have no error. This sentence is correct as written, (A). Choices B, C, and D all create sentence fragments.

24. F

Category: Word Choice

Difficulty: Medium

Getting to the Answer: Beware of answer choices that are longer than the original; barring errors of grammar or logic, they will not be correct. The phrase "including his brother Weldy" is properly used here to modify "a few other African Americans"; (F), NO CHANGE is needed. Choices G, H, and J all make the sentence wordier unnecessarily.

25. B

Category: Verb Tenses

Difficulty: Medium

Getting to the Answer: Use context to determine appropriate verb tense usage. The previous sentence says that Walker "was" a catcher; the introductory phrase in this sentence refers us to the same time period. Only (B) uses a consistent tense. Choices A, C, and D all refer to future actions.

26. H

Category: Writing Strategy

Difficulty: Medium

Getting to the Answer: Since NO CHANGE is not presented as an option, you'll need to find the most logical placement for the new sentence. "Other teams" must contrast with teams already mentioned, and the only place that happens is in Sentences 2 and 3. Sentence 2 talks about one player for the Blue Stockings and Sentence 3 mentions some additional players for the same team. Sentence 4 turns to the time when segregation returned, so the information about African Americans playing for other teams must come before that, between Sentences 3 and 4, (H).

27. B

Category: Wordiness

Difficulty: Low

Getting to the Answer: When you don't spot an error in grammar or usage, check for errors of style. "At the time when" is a longer way of saying "when"; (B) is correct here. Choice C uses "while," which indi-

cates a continuing period of time, but this sentence refers to a specific moment when Jackie Robinson crossed the color line. Choice D is even wordier than the original.

28. F

Category: Word Choice
Difficulty: Medium
Getting to the Answer: Make sure answer choices that are more concise than the original selection do not alter the meaning of the sentence. The best version of this sentence is the way it is written, (F). Choice G changes the meaning of the sentence, implying that Robinson has yet to be recognized as a hero. Choice H also changes the sentence's meaning, indicating that Robinson is doing the recognizing rather than being recognized. Choice J is unnecessarily wordy.

29. B

Category: Wordiness
Difficulty: Medium
Getting to the Answer: When looking for a more concise version of the underlined selection, keep style, tone, and point of view in mind as well. As written, this sentence is unnecessarily wordy, so A is incorrect; (B) is more concise without introducing any errors. Choice C is too casual for the tone of this passage. Choice D leaves the meaning of the second clause incomplete.

30. J

Category: Writing Strategy
Difficulty: Medium
Getting to the Answer: This question format appears frequently on the ACT; what it's asking for is the passage's main idea. This essay is about the color barrier in baseball; it would not fulfill an assignment to write about the history of baseball, so you can eliminate F and G. The fact that baseball was played before 1868, H, is not the reason this essay does not fulfill an assignment on baseball's history. Choice (J) correctly states the reasoning: the essay focuses only on one aspect of the game.

PASSAGE III

31. A

Category: Punctuation
Difficulty: Medium
Getting to the Answer: An introductory phrase should be separated from the rest of the sentence by a comma. The introductory phrase is set off by a comma; the sentence is correct as written, (A). Choices B and C incorrectly treat the introductory phrase as an independent clause. Choice D incorrectly connects a dependent and an independent clause with the conjunction "and."

32. H

Category: Punctuation
Difficulty: Low
Getting to the Answer: Possessive nouns use apostrophes; plural nouns do not. Here, the noun is possessive; the writer is discussing the construction of a bridge, so F is incorrect. Choice (H) places the necessary apostrophe correctly. Choice G uses the plural possessive, but only one bridge is referred to. (Don't be fooled by the fact that it's been known by two different names.) Choice J uses *'s* to make a plural noun possessive. While there are cases where this is correct, it is not here. (Plural possessives are not generally tested on the ACT, although they may appear in wrong answer choices.)

33. B

Category: Verb Tenses
Difficulty: Medium
Getting to the Answer: Make sure verb tenses make sense within the chronology of the passage. The past perfect is used in this sentence, but this tense is only correct when used to describe one past action completed before another. That is not the case here, so A is incorrect; (B) correctly replaces the verb with its past tense form. Choice C changes the meaning of the sentence (the legislature did the authorizing; it wasn't authorized by someone else) and creates a sentence that is grammatically incorrect. Choice D uses a conditional verb phrase, which is inappropriate in context.

34. H
Category: Wordiness
Difficulty: Low
Getting to the Answer: When the underlined selection contains a compound, check to see if the words mean the same thing. If so, the correct answer choice will eliminate one of them. "Build" and "construct" mean the same thing, so you can eliminate F and G right away. The only difference between (H) and J is a comma, which is incorrect in a compound; eliminate J.

35. A
Category: Punctuation
Difficulty: Medium
Getting to the Answer: Where the only difference among the answer choices is comma placement, remember your tested rules. This sentence needs NO CHANGE, (A). Choice B incorrectly places a comma between items in a compound. Choice C places a comma after the conjunction in a compound, which is also incorrect. Choice D incorrectly inserts a comma between a preposition and its object.

36. H
Category: Writing Strategy
Difficulty: Medium
Getting to the Answer: Read the sentence without the material in question to determine how its meaning changes. Looking at the paragraph as a whole, you can see that the author mentions the amount of money invested, the prominence of the architects, and the accomplishments of the firm the architects brought in to help. Removing one of these details detracts from that description; (H) is the best choice here. Choice F can be eliminated because this is not the only detail that supports the larger point; in and of itself, it's not critical. Removing this one phrase wouldn't impact the transition, as G suggests. Choice J is a trap. The segment in question does concern finances, but the text only mentions the amount of money invested, not how it was raised.

37. D
Category: Word Choice
Difficulty: High
Getting to the Answer: On the ACT, "who" will only be correct when used to refer to people. Despite the fact that it's named after a person, "John A. Roebling and Sons" is the name of a company, so "who" isn't appropriate. That eliminates A and B. Choice C might be tempting because it's shorter than (D), but when C is read into the sentence, it creates a grammatical problem: "a company...and would later" requires another verb. Choice (D) is correct.

38. J
Category: Writing Strategy
Difficulty: Medium
Getting to the Answer: Consider context when you're asked about the role a piece of text plays. A question that asks what would be lost if text were deleted is really just asking for the Function of that text. If you read the paragraphs before and after the sentence in question, you'll see that what is missing is a clear transition; (J) is correct. Choice F distorts the meaning of the sentence, which discusses how long the project actually took, not how long it was expected to take. Choice G is out of scope; danger is only mentioned in this one sentence and then only in terms of how few lives were lost constructing the bridge. Choice H overstates the significance of the detail regarding construction time.

39. D
Category: Connections
Difficulty: Medium
Getting to the Answer: When Connections words are underlined, focus on the relationship between the sentences or clauses they combine. The preceding sentence talks about the length of the bridge, and the sentence in which the underlined segment appears goes on to describe the cables in more detail. Since the second isn't a result of the first, you can eliminate A. Choice B inaccurately suggests an inconsistent or contradictory relationship between

the sentences. Choice C is illogical; these are facts about the bridge, not events occurring simultaneously. The best choice here is no transition at all, as in (D).

40. G

Category: Word Choice
Difficulty: Low
Getting to the Answer: Word Choice wrong answers may have the wrong word in context. They may also be wordy or passive. "Longer" means a comparison: one thing is longer *than* something else. Since this sentence doesn't offer a comparison, "longer" can't be correct. Eliminate F. Choices (G) and H are both grammatically correct in context, but H is unnecessarily wordy. "Lengthy," in J, is not correct when used to describe a specific length.

41. C

Category: Wordiness
Difficulty: Medium
Getting to the Answer: If all of the answer choices create grammatically correct sentences, check for errors of style. "As well as being" is just a wordier way of saying "and is"; (C) is the best choice here. Choices B and D are still unnecessarily wordy.

42. F

Category: Punctuation
Difficulty: Medium
Getting to the Answer: Introductory phrases and clauses should be set off from the rest of the sentence by a comma. The comma here is used correctly; (F), NO CHANGE is needed Choice G eliminates the comma, making the sentence difficult to understand. Both the colon in H and the semicolon in J would only work if the first clause were independent, which it is not.

43. D

Category: Wordiness
Difficulty: Low
Getting to the Answer: Look for words that restate information, either explicitly or implicitly. "Ten years" and "a decade" are the same thing, so A is incorrect; (D) removes the redundancy. Choices B and C do not address the error.

44. F

Category: Word Choice
Difficulty: Medium
Getting to the Answer: Use "over" for physical location and "more than" for numbers or amounts. This sentence is correct as written, (F). Choice G replaces "more than" with "over," which, despite its common usage, is actually a preposition and indicates location, not amount. Choice H is unnecessarily wordy. Choice J is also wordy and uses "amount," which is incorrect for a countable noun like "vehicles."

45. C

Category: Writing Strategy
Difficulty: Medium
Getting to the Answer: As you read ACT English passages, develop a sense of topic or "big idea," just like you do in Reading; this question format is very common on the ACT. This passage is about one specific bridge, so it would not satisfy the requirement set out in the question stem. You can therefore eliminate A and B right away. Now turn to the reasoning. Choice D misstates the topic of the passage; (C) is correct.

PASSAGE IV

46. H

Category: Verb Tenses
Difficulty: Medium
Getting to the Answer: Verbs in a compound should be in the same tense. The compound verb in this clause is "was...rising...and painted." Since the second verb is in the past tense, the first should be as well, so F is incorrect; (H) is correct. Choice G uses the gerund verb form without the necessary helping verb. Choice J is unnecessarily wordy.

47. A

Category: Writing Strategy
Difficulty: Medium
Getting to the Answer: Read English Test question stems carefully. Often, all of the choices will be relevant and grammatically correct, but only one will fulfill the requirements of the stem. This question stem asks for a detail that shows a contrast between the quiet night streets and the daytime activity. The original text does this best. The verb in B does not convey the difference in the streets at these two times as well as "flood" in (A). Choice C is too general. Choice D does not provide the necessary contrast.

48. H

Category: Word Choice
Difficulty: Medium
Getting to the Answer: There are no "rules" to learn that will help you answer idioms questions; use your Kaplan resources to familiarize yourself with commonly tested ones. Although all four answer choices form idioms that would be correct in some contexts, one smiles *at* someone or something; (H) is correct.

49. D

Category: Wordiness
Difficulty: Medium
Getting to the Answer: When you don't spot an error in grammar or usage, look for errors in style. The underlined selection is a wordy way of saying "traveled across," (D). Choices B and C are unnecessarily wordy.

50. H

Category: Sentence Sense
Difficulty: Low
Getting to the Answer: Read question stems carefully. This one asks which answer choice would NOT be acceptable, which means that three of the choices will be correct in context. Choices F, G, and J are appropriate introductory clauses, but (H) is an independent clause, which makes the sentence a run-on.

51. B

Category: Writing Strategy
Difficulty: Medium
Getting to the Answer: Use your Reading skills for questions like this one that ask for the function of a detail. The underlined portion tells us that the writer's journey will end in California. Choice (B) is correct. The underlined selection does not mention the reasons for the writer's trip, describe her route, or make any comparisons, so A, C, and D are incorrect.

52. G

Category: Punctuation
Difficulty: Medium
Getting to the Answer: Use commas in a list or series only if there are three or more items. Since the writer only mentions two places she has been, the first comma here is incorrect; eliminate F. Choice (G) corrects this without introducing any additional errors. Choice H eliminates the incorrect comma but removes the one at the end of the selection, which is needed to separate the introductory clause from the rest of the sentence. Choice J does not address the error.

53. A

Category: Connections
Difficulty: Medium
Getting to the Answer: To identify the most effective Connection, you'll need to read both paragraphs. Paragraph 3 is about how the author has traveled to foreign countries but, within the United States, only knows New York City. Paragraph 4 describes her drive through the Midwest. The text as written takes the reader from New York City (tall buildings) to the less populated areas, leading to the description of the cornfields. Choice (A), NO CHANGE, is the best choice here. Choice B misstates the passage; the cornfields didn't appear "almost immediately," but gradually. Choice C and D do not provide appropriate transitions between the paragraphs.

54. F

Category: Writing Strategy
Difficulty: Medium
Getting to the Answer: When you're asked to identify the "most relevant" choice, use context clues. The paragraph is about the change the author experiences as she drives from New York across the country. That contrast is clear in the passage as written; (F) is the best choice here. Choices G and H do not relate to the paragraph's topic. Choice J is opposite; the writer describes many different settings, which is the opposite of "monotonous."

55. C

Category: Sentence Sense
Difficulty: Medium
Getting to the Answer: There are a number of ways to correct a run-on sentence, but only one answer choice will do so without introducing any additional errors. Each of the clauses in this sentence is independent; (C) corrects the run-on by replacing the comma with a semicolon. Choice B omits the comma necessary with the coordinating conjunction "but." Choice D loses the contrast between the clauses that is present in the original.

56. G

Category: Punctuation
Difficulty: Medium
Getting to the Answer: Introductory phrases and clauses should be set off from the rest of the sentence with a comma. The underlined portion here is an introductory phrase, which should be followed by a comma, so F is incorrect; (G) makes the correction. Choice H corrects the error but changes "For" to "During," which is incorrect for a fixed period of time such as the one referred to here. Choice J does not address the error and also changes "For" to "During."

57. A

Category: Punctuation
Difficulty: Medium
Getting to the Answer: Only two apostrophe uses are tested on the ACT: possessive nouns and contractions. The noun here is possessive; the apostrophe is used correctly, (A). Choice B uses the plural "nights" instead of the possessive. Choice C is unnecessarily wordy and uses the idiomatically incorrect "shadows from the night." Choice D changes the meaning of the sentence.

58. H

Category: Wordiness
Difficulty: Medium
Getting to the Answer: If you don't spot a grammar or usage error, check for errors in style. As written, this sentence is unnecessarily wordy, so F is wrong; (H) provides the best revision. Choices G and J are still unnecessarily wordy.

59. C

Category: Connections
Difficulty: Medium
Getting to the Answer: When a Connections word or clause is underlined, determine the relationship between the ideas being connected. Look at the relationship between the sentences in this paragraph. The ideas are presented chronologically—that is, in the order in which they happened. Choice (C), "At first," is the best transition into this series of events. Choice A and B imply contradiction or qualification, which is incorrect in context. Choice D implies that a lot went on prior to the writer's not having any idea what she was looking at, but this is presented as the first in a series of events.

60. F

Category: Word Choice
Difficulty: High
Getting to the Answer: The correct answer will rarely be longer than the original selection. This question requires NO CHANGE, (F). The pronoun's antecedent appears in the previous sentence ("what I was looking at") and the *—ing* verb form is used correctly. Choices G, H, and J are wordy; additionally, G introduces the passive voice unnecessarily.

PASSAGE V

61. A

Category: Punctuation
Difficulty: Low
Getting to the Answer: Commas are used to combine an independent and a dependent clause. This sentence is correct as written, (A), with the comma properly placed after the introductory clause. Choice B places the comma incorrectly; "of 2003" is part of the introductory clause. Choice C omits the necessary comma. Choice D incorrectly uses a semicolon between a dependent and an independent clause.

62. H

Category: Wordiness
Difficulty: Medium
Getting to the Answer: Always read the shortest answer into the sentence to determine how much information can be omitted without changing the meaning of the sentence. Choice (H) eliminates everything but "Mach 2." If you read it back into the sentence, you see that the rest of the phrase isn't necessary. Choice (H) also adds the necessary comma that was omitted in F. Choice G adds the comma, but omits the verb, making the sentence grammatically incorrect. Choice J is unnecessarily wordy; we know from context that Mach 2 is a speed.

63. B

Category: Word Choice
Difficulty: Medium
Getting to the Answer: Word Choice questions require you to look at context; frequently words will have similar meanings but be used differently. "Height" means "the distance from the top to the bottom of something"; "altitude" means "height above sea level." Since "altitude" is correct in this context, you can eliminate A. Choices (B) and C both use "altitude," but "at an altitude" is the correct idiom here; (B) is correct. Choice D creates a grammatically incorrect sentence.

64. H

Category: Wordiness/Punctuation
Difficulty: Medium
Getting to the Answer: When an underlined segment contains more than one error, make sure your answer choice addresses all of them. The underlined segment contains a punctuation error. The subject and predicate of a sentence should not be separated by a single comma, so you can eliminate F and J. Of the remaining two choices, G is unnecessarily wordy. Choice (H) is correct.

65. C

Category: Word Choice
Difficulty: High
Getting to the Answer: Words like "that," which are commonly misused in everyday speech, can make a question more challenging. Sound doesn't travel a speed, it travels *at* a speed; eliminate A. Only (C) makes the correction. Sound doesn't travel *to* a speed, as in B; D, "where" will only be correct on the ACT when used to indicate location or direction.

66. H

Category: Wordiness
Difficulty: Medium
Getting to the Answer: Phrases like "In order to" are often superfluous. Check to see if the answer choices include a more concise version. Choice (H) is concise, without changing the meaning of the sentence. Choice G is still unnecessarily wordy. "For understanding" in J is a proper idiom, but it is not correct in this context.

67. C

Category: Word Choice
Difficulty: Medium
Getting to the Answer: Read English Test question stems carefully. This one asks for the LEAST acceptable alternative, which means that three of the choices will be correct in the sentence. All of the answer choices mean "change," so read each of them into the sentence. "Change them into," "translate them into," and "transform them into" are all ap-

propriate usage, but "alter them into" is not. Choice (C) is the correct choice here.

68. J

Category: Wordiness
Difficulty: High
Getting to the Answer: Look for constructions that repeat words unnecessarily; these will be incorrect on the ACT. The sentence tells us that the speed at which sound travels through gas depends on three things: what kind of gas it is, the temperature, and the pressure; "it is traveling through" is redundant, so F is incorrect. Choice (J) is the most concise answer, and it does not lose any of the meaning of the underlined selection. Choices G and H do not address the error.

69. D

Category: Word Choice
Difficulty: High
Getting to the Answer: Don't choose the shortest answer if it fails to make the writer's meaning clear. "Air temperature and pressure decrease with altitude" isn't clear; "air temperature" and "pressure" themselves do not have altitude, and we're not told "the altitude of what?" so A is incorrect. Choice (D) makes the writer's meaning clear; when altitudes are higher, the decrease in temperature and pressure occur. Choice B does not address the error and even compounds it by replacing "altitude" with "height." Choice C contradicts the facts in the passage; higher, not lower, altitudes have this effect.

70. G

Category: Punctuation
Difficulty: Medium
Getting to the Answer: Beware of answer choices that make unnecessary changes to the sentence. The information provided in the two clauses contrasts, so "however" is correct, but it requires a comma to separate it from the rest of the clause. Eliminate F. Choice (G) is correct. Choice H creates an inappropriate cause-and-effect relationship between the clauses. Choice J does not address the punctuation error.

71. A

Category: Writing Strategy
Difficulty: Medium
Getting to the Answer: When you're asked to choose the most logical conclusion, first determine the sentence's function within the paragraph. The first half of this sentence previews a reason that the Concorde cruises at a higher altitude than regular planes, and it ties that reason back to the contrast between the speed of sound at two different altitudes. You need, then, a conclusion to the sentence that both explains why the planes would fly higher and does so in light of the information about altitude in the preceding sentence. The best choice here is (A); the original version of the sentence is the most logical. Choice B doesn't provide a reason; it simply repeats information that has already been stated. Choice C is out of scope; fuel consumption isn't mentioned in the passage. Choice D is a result of the plane's higher altitude, not its cause.

72. H

Category: Verb Tenses
Difficulty: High
Getting to the Answer: The use of "since" creates a specific marking point in the past and requires a verb that does the same. You need a simple past verb with "since; (H) is correct. Choice F uses a tense that indicates an action that is ongoing, but the decommissioning of the Concorde has been completed. Choice G is unnecessarily wordy. The past perfect in J is only correct when used to indicate one past action competed prior to another stated past action, which is not the case here.

73. C

Category: Sentence Sense/Wordiness
Difficulty: Medium
Getting to the Answer: Sentences beginning with coordinating (FANBOYS) conjunctions will not be correct on the ACT. This sentence incorrectly begins with "But", so you should eliminate A; additionally, "about to" and "very soon" are redundant. Only (C) makes the necessary changes. Choices B and D do not address the redundancy error.

74. H

Category: Wordiness
Difficulty: Medium
Getting to the Answer: Try the shortest answer first; it will frequently be correct. Choice (H) replaces the long introductory clause with a single word without losing any of the sentence's meaning. Choices G and J are still unnecessarily wordy.

75. C

Category: Sentence Sense
Difficulty: Medium
Getting to the Answer: Here, the items combined by "not only...but also" are "to the rich and famous" and "be for the masses." Choice (C) corrects the error. Choices B and D do not address the error; additionally, D fails to correctly complete the idiom.

READING TEST

PASSAGE I

1. C

Category: Detail
Difficulty: Low
Getting to the Answer: Remember that the correct answer to Detail questions will be directly stated in the passage. Your notes should guide you as you locate specific references to the details in question. Line 23 mentions Ellen's parents' "regrettable taste for travel," and lines 22–23 make it clear that New York society agrees with this characterization. Predict something like *travel.* Choice (C) matches this prediction. Choice A is a misused detail; Medora does teach her niece to play the piano, but nothing in the passage suggests that this was undesirable. Choice B is a misused detail; Spanish shawl dances are described as "outlandish," but this description is never directly attributed to New York Society. Choice D is a misused detail; while Medora often adopted children, this is never described as undesirable.

2. G

Category: Detail
Difficulty: Low
Getting to the Answer: Each of the answer choices may be a detail from the passage, but only one will be the correct response to the question. Predicting an answer will help keep you from being distracted by the irrelevant details. The only time in the passage in which Medora's family is clearly upset is when they are "scandalized" that she wears a veil that is shorter than those of her sisters-in-law (lines 33–37); this makes an excellent prediction. Choice (G) is an exact match. Choice F is a distortion; the author tells you neither that Medora allowed Ellen to marry, nor that her family raised any objections. Choice H is a misused detail; although Medora does return to New York impoverished (line 60), the passage does not indicate that her family is upset by this. Choice J is a distortion; this refers to Countess Olenska, not Medora.

3. A

Category: Inference
Difficulty: Medium
Getting to the Answer: To answer Inference questions, you will have to go beyond what is directly stated in the passage. However, the correct answer choice will be supported by evidence from the passage, so make sure that you make a prediction that has solid textual support. You can predict, based on lines 55–66, that Ellen was unable to help her aunt because her own marriage to the immensely rich Polish nobleman "had ended in disaster." Choice (A) matches this prediction. Choice B is a distortion; although the passage does state that no one had heard from Ellen in some time, there is nothing to suggest that Medora had strong feelings about this. Choice C is a distortion; while the author tells you that Ellen had an incoherent education, nothing in the passage suggests that she resented this. Choice D is a distortion; though the passage makes it clear that Medora was eccentric, this is in no way related to receiving help from her niece.

4. F

Category: Generalization

Difficulty: Medium

Getting to the Answer: Generalization questions require you to synthesize information, sometimes from the entire passage. Predicting an answer is particularly important for questions like this. Make sure you can support your prediction with information in the passage. Lines 67–68 suggest that Newland has spent time thinking about Ellen, and lines 74–92 all describe Newland's observations of Ellen. Newland is not disappointed that Ellen is not as "stylish" as others expected (lines 84–86). You can predict that Newland is *thoughtful* and, unlike many of the other characters in the passage, *non-judgmental.* Choice (F) matches this prediction. Choice G is out of scope; It might seem reasonable to conclude that Newland is likeable, but the passage does not provide any evidence to directly support this. Also, there is nothing to suggest that he is withdrawn. Choice H is 0pposite; Newland's observations about Ellen in the last paragraph clearly indicate that he is interested in her. Choice J is a distortion; Newland's observation that Ellen is not as stylish as New York society might expect says nothing about his own stylishness. Also, the author never implies that Newland behaves in the same way as New York society, so there is no reason to believe that he is gregarious.

5. A

Category: Inference

Difficulty: Medium

Getting to the Answer: The answer to questions like this can be found in the passage, but you may have to put a few pieces of information together to get to the correct answer. Lines 20–21 state that "New York looked indulgently on her eccentricities." Predict that *Medora's eccentric nature was largely accepted.* Choice (A) matches your prediction. Choice B is extreme; although lines 24–25 state that others thought it was a pity that Ellen should be in Medora's care, to call Medora's lifestyle a "terrible example" goes too far. Choice C is a distortion; although Medora's life is described as unfortunate, the passage does not suggest that this is the way in which others viewed her life. Choice D is a distortion; it may be reasonable to describe Medora's life as inconsistent, but nothing suggests that others viewed her life that way.

6. J

Category: Generalization

Difficulty: Medium

Getting to the Answer: Answering Generalization questions like this might require you to pull together information from throughout the entire passage. It is clear from lines 38–50 and lines 82–86 that Ellen, like Medora, is unconventional and eccentric. Predict that *Ellen has taken on some of her Aunt's uniqueness and eccentricity.* Choice (J) matches this prediction. Choice F is out of scope; nothing in the passage suggests that Medora is necessarily grateful or that her aunt was unselfish in adopting her. Choice G is out of scope; nothing suggests that Medora is jealous of Ellen's marriage. Choice H is a distortion; while the passage makes it clear that New York society is suspicious of both Ellen and Medora, you don't necessarily know that they, in turn, dislike New York society.

7. C

Category: Generalization

Difficulty: Medium

Getting to the Answer: Make sure you have good evidence for your prediction, and the right answer choice will be easy to find. Line 21 mentions Medora's "eccentricities," line 31 mentions her "peculiarities," and line 44 mentions the "outlandish arts" that Medora teaches Ellen. From these descriptions, you can predict that Medora is *unconventional* or *eccentric.* Choice (C) matches this prediction. Choice A is out of scope; although Medora does not adhere to conventions, as indicated by lines 31–32, there is nothing to suggest that this is attributable to arrogance. Choice B is a distortion; the description of the short veil that Medora wore to her brother's funeral in lines 34–36 might suggest immodesty, but the author makes clear that this is evidence of Medora's willingness to flout social conventions. Choice D is opposite; you're told in lines 31–32 that one of her peculiarities is to "flout the unalterable rules that regulated American mourning."

8. F

Category: Detail
Difficulty: Low
Getting to the Answer: Detail questions like this one are straightforward, but it can sometimes be difficult to find exactly where in the passage the relevant information comes from. Make sure that you are answering the specific question being asked, so that other details don't distract you. Medora teaches Ellen "drawing from the model" (lines 48–49), which is described as "a thing never dreamed of before," so predict *Ellen* or *Countess Olenska*. Choice (F) matches your prediction. Choice G is out of scope; Newland is not described as having learned anything at all, let alone something controversial. Choice H is a distortion; Medora teaches Ellen, but the passage does not mention Medora learning anything herself. Choice J is a distortion; Count Olenska is only mentioned indirectly as the rich nobleman who Medora marries. The passage makes it clear that Ellen is *Countess* Olenska; don't be fooled by this initially tempting, but incorrect, choice.

9. A

Category: Inference
Difficulty: Medium
Getting to the Answer: You won't be able to predict an answer to Inference questions like this. Instead, examine each of the answer choices and find the one that is best supported by the passage. Although some details might seem to support several answer choices, only one will have strong support in the text. Most of the passage describes Ellen in her childhood, so focus on the last paragraph, which describes Ellen as Newland encounters her. Lines 78–82 describe her sureness, and her "conscious power." Later, in lines 88–90, she is also described as quiet. Choice (A) matches these characterizations. Choice B is a distortion; while the passage does state that Ellen's marriage had ended (lines 63–64), it's never inferred that Ellen is necessarily unhappy about it. Choice C is opposite; you might infer that Ellen is intelligent, but she is quiet, which contradicts describing her as *outspoken*. Choice D is extreme; Ellen is described as confident; *intimidating* goes too far.

10. F

Category: Inference
Difficulty: High
Getting to the Answer: Remember that Inference questions will have details in the wrong answer choices that are meant to throw you off. Making a good prediction before reviewing the choices will guard against this. The beginning of the passage (line 4) makes it clear that Newland knew Ellen when he was young. Lines 55–59 state that no one had heard from Ellen for some time, and after a few years, she came back to New York, as Medora had done before her. Predict that at the dinner, Newland and Ellen *had not seen one another for an extended period of time*. Choice (F) matches your prediction. Choice G is extreme; although Newland is clearly paying attention to Ellen in the last paragraph, there is nothing to suggest that either of them is interested in a romantic relationship. Choice H is extreme; while Ellen's lack of "stylishness" (lines 85–86) might suggest that she is not interested in New York society's conventions, it goes too far to say that she is disappointed. Choice J is opposite; the passage clearly portrays Ellen and Newland's encounter as a reacquaintance.

PASSAGE II

11. B

Category: Detail
Difficulty: Medium
Getting to the Answer: More difficult Detail questions can be approached using elimination and careful reading. Remember the EXCEPT. For "except" questions, review the answer choices methodically, eliminating those which fail to meet the conditions of

the question stem. The passage deals in some depth with both the flowering of the fistula tree, C, and the wind during Holi, A, so you can eliminate those first. Paragraph 5 states that Dr. Kanani became interested in traditional methods when a tenth century rule of thumb "proved strikingly correct," which suggests that D has been tested. In contrast, the bird behavior is merely listed as an example of a rule of thumb uncovered in one of Kanani's conferences, making (B) the correct answer.

12. H

Category: Inference

Difficulty: Medium

Getting to the Answer: Read through the part of the passage that uses the word or phase in question, using context to inform your prediction. Look at the sentence directly following the phrase. It compares the usefulness of modern predictions to the information provided by traditional methods. The farmers need more specific evidence than the averages over time and geography provided by meteorology. Predict that *Meteorology is not always useful for the farmers' purposes.* Choice (H) matches this prediction. Choice F is a distortion; the author here does not make a statement regarding the accuracy of meteorology, and, in fact, suggests that meteorologists have been right in the past. What's important is that the information they predict is of little use to farmers. Choice G is out of scope; the passage never makes a statement regarding the expense of equipment. Choice J is a distortion; the phrase quoted intends to *compare* modern and traditional meteorology, not to apply the modern to the traditional.

13. A

Category: Generalization

Difficulty: High

Getting to the Answer: Generalization questions that ask about multiple paragraphs often require you to interpret how the main ideas of each paragraph are related. Paraphrase the main idea of each paragraph, then note the way in which these ideas progress. The sixth paragraph deals with scientific skepticism for traditional methods. The seventh details efforts by those studying traditional methods to gain recognition in the mainstream. The last introduces you to new groups and projects to achieve the goals of the seventh. In general, you can see that *achieving acceptance of traditional methods by a skeptical scientific community* is the general story told by these paragraphs and a good prediction for the correct answer choice. Choice (A) clearly fits this view. Choice B is a misused detail; while the sixth paragraph mentions the differences in the methods, the next two still deal with the controversy over accepting traditional approaches. Choice C is opposite; the paragraphs tell the story of an uphill battle for advocates of traditional methods. Choice D is a out of scope; these paragraphs never leave the main topic of weather.

14. G

Category: Inference

Difficulty: Medium

Getting to the Answer: Inference questions encompassing the whole text will draw on evidence from the entire passage. A good prediction depends on your ability to synthesize the major ideas from throughout the passage. The passage mentions several traditional methods and their amazing accuracy. Even the scientific skepticism described in the passage admits a place for traditional methodology. The passage validates traditional methods, so predict that the author finds these methods to be *valuable*. Choice (G) matches this prediction. Choice F is out of scope; while the author briefly discusses the origins of each method, she never asks any questions. Choice H is a distortion; the skepticism gets relatively little treatment and is followed by a detailed discussion of the progress toward making a real science of traditional methods. Choice J is opposite; the author never casts interest in traditional methods as a "fad," and, as noted before, mentions the success of traditional methods more than once.

15. D
Category: Detail
Difficulty: Low
Getting to the Answer: Look to your notes to find specific locations for tested details. According to paragraph 5, Bhadli's storm method offers a 72-day warning. None of the other cited methods provide the same sort of accuracy over such a specific and extended time period, so look for Bhadli's method among the choices. Choice (D) matches this prediction. Choice A is a distortion; while the author suggests that bird behavior can serve as a predictor, this is never viewed as a particularly precise method. Choice B is a distortion; the flowering of the *fistula* tree does provide a specific and accurate prediction, but it gives only 45 days advance warning. Choice C is a distortion; while the passage describes a loose correlation between the character of the monsoon and the wind direction on Holi, this method doesn't predict when the monsoon will arrive.

16. J
Category: Function
Difficulty: Low
Getting to the Answer: Beware of answer choices that present details that are narrower than the main point of the paragraph or sum up surrounding paragraphs instead of the target of the question. Focus on the overall topic of the paragraph and how it helps build the story or argument in the passage. The passage in general describes the accuracy of traditional methods of weather prediction. The paragraph introduces you to Dr. Kanani and his interest in applying scientific rigor to these methods. Predict that the correct answer will describe this paragraph as an introduction to a central character and a description of his particular interests. Choice (J) matches this prediction. Choice F is a misused detail; this sums up the first paragraph. Choice G is a misused detail; this accounts only for the last sentence of the cited paragraph. Choice H is a distortion; while the ancient saying is examined in passage, this choice casts this examination as the central issue.

17. B
Category: Detail
Difficulty: Low
Getting to the Answer: For Detail questions, rely on your notes to direct your research to the relevant part of the passage. Lines 70–73 read: "Dr Kanani hopes that his research will put traditional methods on a proper scientific footing. He and his colleagues have even set up a sort of peer-review forum." Predict that the conference's goal is this *establishment of traditional methods as worthy subjects of scientific inquiry*. Choice (B) matches this prediction. Choice A is out of scope; the passage never discusses the disappearance of traditional methods. Choice C is a misused detail; while Dr. Kanani does, in fact, publish the methods in the local press, this is not the objective of the conference. Choice D is out of scope; the passage never mentions the exchange of ideas between geographically distant farmers.

18. H
Category: Inference
Difficulty: Medium
Getting to the Answer: Beware of general answer choices. Attack the question stem, get a good understanding of what it's really asking, and make a solid prediction. The question asks you for the reason farmers predict the weather using traditional methods. What do they hope to accomplish? When the question is rephrased, the answer seems more obvious; predict that the correct choice will show that *they want to know what to plant*, so they need to know what's coming. Choice (H) matches this prediction. Choice F is out of scope; the passage never mentions the accessibility of the methods. Choice G is a distortion; while "'normal' monsoons" are discussed in paragraph 6, this in reference to modern meteorology, not traditional methods of forcasting. Choice J is a distortion; while traditional methods do get the basics right, the question asks why the farmers are trying to get the basics right in the first place.

19. C

Category: Function
Difficulty: Medium
Getting to the Answer: Context clues can be important in Function questions in which simple replacement is difficult. Eliminate answers that are inconsistent with the central concerns of the passage. Reread the specific reference and the surrounding text, which talks about the flowering of *C. fistula* as a monsoon predictor that isn't "perfect," but still of value and interest. Predict that the correct choice will account for both an *appreciation of this traditional method* and *an awareness of its limitations*. Choice (C) matches this prediction. Choice A is extreme; while the author feels that the predictive data are useful and noteworthy, calling them *remarkable* goes too far. Choice B is out of scope; the author never attempts to generalize on the relative value of precision. Choice D is out of scope; again, the author neither casts traditional methods as rules of thumb and scientific methods as complex formulas nor attempts to elevate one over the other.

20. H

Category: Detail
Difficulty: Low
Getting to the Answer: Consult your notes to direct your research to the relevant text. Sahu says in lines 58–61 that traditional prediction may be "OK as a hobby," but "may not be applicable to this modern age," but then concedes that modern era forecasts are not always helpful to farmers in the way traditional methods claim to be. That *some utility exists despite scientific skepticism* serves as a good prediction and an accurate paraphrase of his attitude. Choice (H) summarizes Sahu's attitude and matches this prediction. Choice F is out of scope; Sahu does not comment directly on the accuracy of the methods. Choice G is opposite; Sahu rejects traditional methods from the scientific view. Choice J is out of scope; Sahu never mentions the "appeal" of the methods, only their trustworthiness as predictors.

PASSAGE III

21. C

Category: Detail
Difficulty: Medium
Getting to the Answer: It is very difficult to predict the answer to this type of question because the answer choices themselves give the clues. Go directly to the choices and research each one in the passage. Paragraph 2 includes information about the origins of country music. Choice (C) is correct because country music is not rooted in jazz. Rather, jazz was combined with country music to create Western Swing. Paragraph 6 states, "Additionally, Western Swing emerged as one of the first genres to blend country and jazz musical styles, which required a great deal of skill and creativity." Choice A is opposite; paragraph 2 describes the many sources of country music with the phrase, "Rooted in spirituals as well as folk music, cowboy songs, and traditional Celtic melodies, country music originated in the 1920s." Choice B is opposite; spirituals influenced the development of country music. Choice D is opposite; country music is rooted in cowboy songs.

22. J

Category: Detail
Difficulty: Medium
Getting to the Answer: The answer to a Detail question is stated in the passage. However, because all answer choices are in the passage, be careful to assess each one in terms of the actual question asked. A look at your notes, or a quick scan of the passage, should provide enough information to make a prediction about where to find the best country music. Match that prediction to the correct answer. Choice (J) is correct; in paragraph 5, the author writes "Country singers are considered to have reached the pinnacle of the profession if they are asked to become members of the Opry." To hear the best music, it makes sense to go to the place where those at the pinnacle, or top of their field, perform. Choice F is a misused detail; one would hear honky-tonk music, a derivative of country, but not country music itself,

in these bars. Choice G is a misused detail; Ireland is the original home of the Ulster Scots, many of whom settled in Appalachia. Choice H is a misused detail; though country music had its origins in the mixture of music created in Appalachia, the author does not state that it is the place to hear the best music.

23. D

Category: Inference
Difficulty: Medium
Getting to the Answer: An inference is a conclusion not directly stated in the passage, but one that must be true given the information that is stated. In the last paragraph, the author concludes his discussion of country music by putting it in the context of American identity. Look for an answer that is very close to this statement. Choice (D) is correct; in the last paragraph, the author clearly states, "Country music has always been an expression of American identity." The word "character" is another word that can mean the same thing as "identity," both describing qualities representative of a person or, in this case, a country. Choice A is a distortion; the word "most" makes this answer an extreme one, taking it far beyond the author's intended meaning. Furthermore, the author writes nothing about which genre is most influential. Choice B is a misused detail; though country music rose from the mountain people of Appalachia, the author calls this music reflective of the American identity, not specific to one area of the nation. Choice C is out of scope; the Grand Ole Opry is the hub of country music, but not necessarily the place where it is best performed. Indeed, the example of Presley's failure shows that some performances are quite bad.

24. J

Category: Inference
Difficulty: Low
Getting to the Answer: Though the answer is not directly stated in the passage, look for an answer that can be assumed based on what is stated. Locate where mining disasters are referred to, consider what kind of event this is, then which of the possible answers it would exemplify. Choice (J) is correct; ballads are mentioned in paragraph 1, where they are given as an example of the stories told in laments. That connects well with the meaning of high, lonesome sound, which is described as "the bluegrass undertones of intensity and cheerlessness, symbolizing the hard-scrabble life of the American worker." Choice F is out of scope; mining disasters are not relevant to the Blue Grass Band, and furthermore, there are no examples of the songs performed by the band. Choice G is out of scope; country music is the topic of Passage A, not Passage B. Choice H is a misused detail; though Scottish music is referred to as one of the sources of bluegrass, it is the actual genre of bluegrass, which is characterized by the phrase, "high, lonesome sound."

25. A

Category: Detail
Difficulty: Medium
Getting to the Answer: Locate the paragraph in which bluegrass instruments are described, and match those descriptions with the correct answer choice. Your notes point to only one paragraph in which musical instruments are mentioned. Scan the answer choices, then re-read the information in that paragraph to determine which answer choice characterizes the information given. Choice (A) is correct; musical instruments are described in the second paragraph, and include typical ones such as "banjo, guitar, mandolin, bass, harmonica, and Dobro (resonator guitar.)" But the paragraph goes on to include far less typical ones, such as "household objects, including washboards and spoons," which are not usually considered musical instruments, but are sometimes included in a bluegrass band. Choice B is a misused detail; African-American influences are provided as one more source of the bluegrass genre but do not refer to instrumentation. Choice C is a misused detail; this is an example of a bluegrass piece, which was used in a movie soundtrack. Choice D is out of scope; the reference to the Ozark mountains concerns the origin of bluegrass and has nothing to do with a description of musical instruments.

26. F

Category: Detail

Difficulty: High

Getting to the Answer: The answer to a Detail question is stated in the passage. Locate the paragraph in which the differences between country and bluegrass music are discussed. Paragraph 2 includes the information you need to answer the question. Be sure to keep straight which details describe each genre of music. Choice (F) is correct; paragraph 2 details two characteristics of bluegrass music; first, that "bluegrass highlights one player at a time, with the others providing accompaniment," and second, that "bluegrass incorporates baritone and tenor harmonies." Choice G is opposite; country music features a single voice. Choice H is opposite; country musicians commonly play the same melodies together. Choice J is opposite; both country music and bluegrass music feature banjo and guitar.

27. B

Category: Vocab-in-context

Difficulty: Medium

Getting to the Answer: Vocab-in-Context questions require that you understand the context of a cited word or phrase. Locate the reference and focus your research on the text immediately preceding and immediately following the word or phrase in question. The introductory paragraph states, "One of the most enjoyable ways to analyze culture is through music." Look for an answer choice that indicates that music can provide specific insight about a culture as a whole. Choice (B) matches this prediction. Choice A is a distortion; quintessential does not mean old-fashioned. Choice C is a distortion; quintessential does not mean charming. Choice D is opposite; quintessential means conventional, or typical.

28. H

Category: Inference

Difficulty: Medium

Getting to the Answer: When looking for something on which both authors would agree, first determine what each one actually states in the passage, then consider what must be true based on those statements. The evolution, or gradual change, in music, as with anything else, must start from somewhere, so look to the parts of each passage that detail the genesis of the music genres, then consider the progression from there. Choice (H) is correct; both authors detail the various music sources that became either country or bluegrass. In the first passage, the author mentions "folk music, cowboy songs, and traditional Celtic melodies," and in the second passage, the author refers to "Scots, Welsh, Irish, and English melodic forms, infused, over time, with African-American influences." Both authors affirm that the two music genres are "indigenous." Thus, it must be true that both country and bluegrass music have evolved from their various roots to become American music, supporting agreement on the fact that music can evolve. Choice F is out of scope; there is no reference to how popular these genres are. Though this might be assumed in Passage B, where the author notes that bluegrass festivals are held even in the Czech Republic, this is not matched by any similar information in Passage A. Choice G is a misused detail; the Grand Ole Opry showcases country music only, not bluegrass. Choice J is out of scope; neither passage indicates that the music is gaining in acceptance.

29. C

Category: Inference

Difficulty: Medium

Getting to the Answer: When asked to use a quote to find support in one paragraph for information in another, be sure to read the quote in the context of the paragraph. First find the paragraph in which the quote from Passage A appears, then match the quote to one in Passage B. Choice (C) is correct; Flatt and Scruggs are mentioned in Passage B, paragraph 3, in which they are characterized as "the foremost artists on their instruments." The best artists are certainly "talented and sophisticated." Choice A is a misused detail; this quote refers to bluegrass themes, whereas the question asks for one that supports talented and sophisticated musicians. Choice B is out of scope; music soundtracks are not support for the artistry of the musicians. Choice D is out of scope; the relation between bluegrass and country music refers to the kinship of the genres, not the musicians.

30. G

Category: Inference
Difficulty: Medium
Getting to the Answer: There are several points at which bluegrass and country music intersect. Focus on the one specifically asked for in the question. Locate the paragraphs that mention laments and high, lonesome sound, and consider what the author means by including these two themes. Choice (G) is correct; the reference to "laments" is in the first paragraph of Passage A, where it serves as an example of country music themes. The reference to "high, lonesome sound" is in the last paragraph of the second passage, and is an example of "the hard-scrabble life of the American worker." Passage A ends with the phrase "it remains American in its heart and soul," while Passage B states "for better or worse, bluegrass music reflects America." Thus, both kinds of music reflect American subject matter. Choice F is out of scope; Irish music is one of the sources of both bluegrass and country genres, which are included in the sources of the music, not the themes. Choice H is a misused detail; Shania Twain is an example of a country singer, and is mentioned in Passage A only. Choice J is a misused detail; though both types of music were originally called "hillbilly," this is the name for the genres, not the themes.

PASSAGE IV

31. D

Category: Inference
Difficulty: Medium
Getting to the Answer: After reading the question stem, you'll be aware of what to look for. Predict before looking at the answer choices and trust your judgment. Luu strongly disagrees with the view that Pluto should be labeled an asteroid (lines 82–86). She goes so far as to use the term "idiotic" in reference to others in her profession, so predict something like *indignation*. Choice (D) matches this prediction. Choice A is a distortion; while "shock" may be an initially tempting choice, it's clear that Luu's surprise stems from her disagreement with the opinion, not her lack of preparation to hear it. Choice B is opposite; excitement suggests some degree of positive response, which Luu clearly does not display. Choice C is opposite; Luu quite clearly expresses her feelings on the classification controversy.

32. H

Category: Inference
Difficulty: Medium
Getting to the Answer: If you get stuck, eliminating answers that have no support in the passage will greatly reduce the number of choices. The passage states that, if astronomers had known about the other TNOs, Pluto would not have been named a planet (lines 48–51). The size of Pluto is indicated as the reason it was discovered before the others. You can infer that a better system of detection would have discovered other TNOs, eliminating Pluto's status as a planet. Account for this in your prediction. Choice (H) matches your prediction. Choice F is opposite; Pluto's size separates it from other TNOs. Choice G is out of scope; the article never mentions Pluto's icy core. Choice J is a distortion; the controversy that would later surround Pluto's initial classification as a planet was never drawn into the discussion of the original classification.

33. C

Category: Generalization
Difficulty: Low
Getting to the Answer: Since you've been summarizing the main idea of each paragraph as you've moved through the passage, you're well equipped to predict an answer to Generalization questions. Think about overarching, recurrent themes. The majority of statements in the passage, including the title, should point you to the conclusion that Pluto was difficult to classify from the beginning. Your prediction should focus on this difficulty. Choice

(C) matches this prediction. Choice A is opposite; the passage only mentions such a comparison once, and describes Pluto as out of place among rocky planets such as earth. Choice B is a misused detail; while Pluto does appear likely to lose its planetary status within the scientific community, this has not historically been the case. Choice D is a misused detail; it is the current controversy, rather than the traditional view, that will ultimately give Pluto special status in the history of astronomy.

34. F

Category: Detail
Difficulty: Low
Getting to the Answer: Your notes on the passage should show the location of key details and terminology, so you can quickly find them as you research the question stem. Neptune is mentioned only a few times and all but once merely appeared as part of the longer name of TNOs, trans-Neptunian objects. This single reference is in connection with a description of Centaurs, one of the answer choices. Sure enough, an examination of the description reveals that *Centaurs*, a great prediction, are asteroids similar to Pluto "nudged" inside Neptune's orbit. Choice (F) matches this prediction. Choice G is a misused detail; the passage states that IAU stands for International Astronomical Union. Choice H is a misused detail; TNO stands for TRANS-Neptunian objects, things beyond Neptune. Choice J is a misused detail; the term "ice dwarf" is used in connection with the discovery of a TNO.

35. C

Category: Inference
Difficulty: Low
Getting to the Answer: Inference questions such as this ask that you interpret the referenced lines, drawing on your reading of the passage as a whole. The quote making up the majority of the referenced lines comes from a scientist who, in the passage, takes a position against creating a new classification. Your prediction should reflect the issue of *whether the existing categories are suitable*. Choice (C) matches this prediction. Choice A is a misused detail; this is certainly discussed in the passage, but this doesn't pertain to the cited lines or the speaker in question. Choice B is a misused detail; distance from the sun and from Neptune is significant to certain classification schemes, but this is not the central issue in Pluto's specific case. Choice D is a misused detail; that the scientific community and general public have differing opinions is irrelevant to the cited lines.

36. G

Category: Vocab-in-Context
Difficulty: High
Getting to the Answer: Vocab-in-Context questions require that you understand the context of a cited word or phrase. Locate the reference and focus your research on the text immediately preceding and immediately following the word or phrase in question. Investigating the word in question contextualizes it within the argument of a scientist who "doesn't like the idea of establishing a new catalog of solar system objects" (lines 61–62) and argues that "astronomers already have a perfectly serviceable list of numbered minor bodies" (lines 62–64). Predict something like *sufficient* to replace the word in question. Choice (G) matches this prediction. Choice F invokes the most common meaning of the word, which doesn't make sense in context and is usually a trap answer. Choices H and J don't work in context, since describing a particular classification system as "beneficial" or "durable" is awkward.

37. D

Category: Generalization
Difficulty: Low
Getting to the Answer: Remember that Generalization questions will attempt to make tempting answer choices out of issues discussed in the passage only briefly. A recurring theme throughout the passage is giving Pluto a "very special designation" (line 19) or "honor" (line 80), which differs from the predominantly scientific concerns over Pluto's classification discussed elsewhere. Predict an answer that touches on this

idea of honoring or distinguishing Pluto in some way. Choice (D) matches this prediction. Choice A is out of scope; the role of the IAU is never discussed by the cited experts. Choice B is a misused detail; the author does relay some information about the ways in which public opinion is unlikely to change, but this is not a significant concern for scientists dealing with deeper issues. Choice C is out of scope; none of the cited scientists seem particularly concerned with being credited for solving the problem.

38. G

Category: Inference
Difficulty: Medium
Getting to the Answer: Use your reading of the passage as a whole to guide your predictions when tackling Inference questions; the answer is in your ability to synthesize ideas that recur throughout. The passage ends the debate about Pluto's classification with a discussion of one scientist's attempt to find consensus. In this part of the passage, the major ideas are listed. Binzel's idea is rejected because Pluto "would still be an anomaly." Luu forcefully asserts that "Pluto is certainly not an asteroid." Both criticisms are based on the idea that neither category adequately describes Pluto, so predict that the correct answer will focus the inadequacy of any categorization scheme. Choice (G) matches this prediction. Choice F is a misused detail; the public's recognition of Pluto's controversial status or a potential change in category is not a significant issue to scientists. Choice H is a distortion; Pluto's orbit plays little role in the discussion of its classification, and its surface is never mentioned. Choice J is a misused detail; the existence of Pluto-like objects nearer to the sun than Neptune functions as a criticism of only one theory.

39. B

Category: Detail
Difficulty: Medium
Getting to the Answer: Detail questions will sometimes require a broad approach to information from a variety of locations in the text. Your notes will help you to sort out the specifics. Lines 24–27 discuss Pluto's size in relation to other planets and line 27 describes its orbit as anomalous. A good prediction will account for both. Choice (B) matches this prediction. Choice A is a misused detail; distance from the sun versus distance from Neptune is significant only in certain classification systems for non-planets. Choice C is out of scope; the year of Pluto's discovery in relation to those of other planets is never discussed. Choice D is out of scope; neither Pluto's shape nor surface composition are ever substantially compared to those of other planets.

40. H

Category: Detail
Difficulty: High
Getting to the Answer: Tougher Detail questions will require an investigation of several sections of text. Count on your notes to direct you, even when the search is fairly extensive. Lines 24–27 tell you that Pluto is smaller than other planets, which is why scientists need to reclassify it, yet its large size compared to asteroids and TNOs (lines 99–100) is what keeps many scientists confused about its proper category. Lines 45–48 cite Pluto's size as the exact reason that it was found 60 years before the next body like it. Your prediction should account for this classification difficulty as well as Pluto's early discovery. Choice (H) matches this prediction. Choice F is a distortion; categorizing of Pluto as a TNO is only a proposed solution to the classification problem and takes into consideration issues other than size. Choice G is opposite; it is Pluto's relatively small size that potentially allows it the same classification as an asteroid. Choice J is a misused detail; the passage never relates Pluto's size to the nature of the planet's orbit.

WRITING TEST

LEVEL 6 ESSAY

I fully agree that pure scientific research is vital to increase our understanding of ourselves and our world, and that this research, even without specific goals, can result in important benefits to society. To fund this research, a consortium of government, pharmaceutical companies, and nonprofit agencies should be formed, pooling money but giving no one group entire oversight or responsibility.

Many life-changing discoveries have been found without purposely looking for them. Alexander Fleming did not set out to discover penicilin, but in doing so accidentally saved millions of people from death. Putting a man on the moon did not help people on Earth, but it certainly taught us a lot about our universe. This kind of pure research must continue, and the cost should be shared by the government, drug companies, and nonprofit groups. This type of research can be prohibitively expensive; thus, monies must be drawn from various sources, each contributing as much as possible. No single organization can completely fund ongoing research, especially if there is no stated goal other than to hopefully discover something beneficial. Tax payers, pharmaceutical company investors, and nonprofit group members expect results, which may be long in coming, or, indeed, continually elusive. However, efforts must continue. As Thomas Edison said, "Just because something doesn't do what you planned it to do doesn't mean it's useless."

Consider also that pharmaceutical companies are always searching for new therapeutic drugs. They send scientists out into the field to come back with anything interesting, which is then researched and, if promising, developed into a new drug. Such is the relation between blood sugar and diabetes, leading to the insulin that my diabetic cousin takes; without insulin, he would not survive. If a drug company develops an important drug, it can make millions of dollars from the sale of it, leading to funding more research. Nonprofit organizations also have a stake in pure research, since another accidental discovery could prove to be financially beneficial. Finally, if the government shares the burden of underwriting research, it is not at risk for being fully blamed if the research does not produce positive results. Taxpayers would be more liable to accept a minimal loss in a good cause rather than a major loss in an unsure endeavor. A partnership would ensure continued funding and the funders, as well as all citizens, would benefit from discoveries.

On the other hand, people who say the government should fund only research which has demonstrated its worth do not understand the function of pure research. It is not possible for researchers to say with certainty that they are going to find a cure for cancer. Researchers have to be able to say they are searching for something as yet unknown with the hope that it will be beneficial. And what is a clear and acceptable outcome? If cancer researchers find a cure for diabetes, but not cancer, is that acceptable if it is not the stated intention? A great deal of science is luck and perserverance. According to this perspective, if a researcher wanted government funding to work in the Amazonian rain forest with the general intent of exploring indigenous plants, the government would be unable to fund the project because there is no clearly beneficial objective. But that is exactly how quinine, a now widely used treatment for malaria, was found, and the general exploration was certainly worth funding. Finally, it is unlikely that pure research, no matter who funds it, will result in disaster. Researchers are very careful to prevent this, and even if a disaster did happen, it would not be the fault of whom is funding the research.

It is quite clear that pure research is invaluable, as the examples of penicilin, quinine, and insulin support. It cannot be dependent on the whims, finances, and oversight of any one group but must be a concerted effort among all and for all who may benefit.

SCORE EXPLANATION (6666)

This essay is clearly focused on the prompt, shows complete understanding of the issue, logically assesses the implications of all three perspectives, and puts forth the author's point of view in both the first and fifth paragraphs. This is a cohesive, critical analysis of the perspectives, with a solid, well-supported thesis.

Ideas and Analysis (6)

The argument is driven by strong and clear analysis of each perspective, with good examination of implications. The writer's consistent focus on the benefits of pure research makes the essay cohesive and precise: pure research is worth pursuing and, for economic and oversight reasons, must be funded by a consortium of groups. Keeping this focus, the writer is able to explore each perspective, identify pros and cons, and provide strong support for her point of view. Critical, logical thinking is clearly displayed.

Development and Support (6)

The writer introduces her argument with a strong statement supporting pure research in general, and she immediately follows up with her perspective. That perspective is developed through reference to "life-changing discoveries," the cost of research, specific discussion of drug company research and benefits and what may constitute acceptable risk. Support is strong, referencing Alexander Fleming, penicillin, space exploration, quinine, and insulin, and it includes a relevant quote from Thomas Edison. Reasoning and support are well integrated, and the author never loses sight of the thesis. Both alternatives are discussed. One alternative is discussed in detail, while the other is given only passing, but still with strong consideration ("And what is a clear and acceptable outcome?" "Finally, it is unlikely that pure research, no matter who funds it, will result in disaster"). Development moves from the general to the specific, with excellent support for each point, and a clear and consistent perspective.

Organization (6)

There is a clear and strong introduction and a summary conclusion, both of which expand the specifics of the prompt to the larger issues involved. Each paragraph begins with a topic sentence, and the contrasting view is signaled with the phrase "On the other hand," while the third paragraph is introduced with a creative transition phrase "Consider also." The essay is cohesive and flows well, ideas are well connected, and support is explicit, relevant, and well positioned to enhance the argument.

Language Use (6)

The writing is mostly high-level, with the use of a rhetorical question and words such as *perseverance, accountable, consortium,* and *pharmaceutical*. Several sentences are varied and complex. The grammar and punctuation are mostly correct, though there are some spelling errors (*penicilin, perserverance*). The writer's style is appropriately formal, even with a personal example, and her word choice is effective in characterizing the perspectives and writing a persuasive argument.

LEVEL 4 ESSAY

Pure research is done for the purpose of discovery without a specific goal in mind. Even so, it has produced important breakthroughs such as treatment for Alzheimer's disease, and even the development of the GPS. Though scientific research is vitally important, people disagree about who should pay for it. Some people think that the government should fund the research if the goal is a good one. Others think that the government should only give money to research that can be shown will be helpful. Still others believe that the government and private companies should work together to give scientists the money they need, which is the best way to do it, and the perspective I agree with.

I know the importance of research because my little brother has asthma and requires daily medication. Though I don't know who paid for the research that helped make his meds, I'm quite sure that the research behind it took a long time and cost a great deal of money. Though the government may have enough money to fully fund research like this, it has other responsibilities as well and can't afford to fund research alone, especially if the outcome is unsure. However, with other money from drug companies and nonprofit agencies, research can continue to be funded without any one entity eating into their finances earmarked for other purposes. Even if the research doesn't show results for many years, a group of funders can provide enough money so that scientists can keep working until they discover something helpful and then continue to develop it.

The government can't do everything on its own and companies shouldn't have to work by themselves either. If they team up, lots of research can get done. Asthma is now manageable, but there are plenty of other illnesses that are very deadly. Everybody is hoping for a cure for cancer one day, and scientists need time and money to find one. Groups working together can give those scientists the time and money they need, since no one group is responsible for an immediate, beneifical result from the research it funds. The government and companies should pick an amount of money they want to spend each year on scientific research and give it to a variety of research groups. Then, if any of the groups make a major discovery, they can earn more money and invest it back into ongoing research.

On the other hand, some people think that scientists should have to show the government that their projects will be helpful in order to get money. That would exclude a lot of past and future research that was done purely in the hopes of discovery but without assurances. Louis Pasture wouldn't have gotten money from his government to make penicillin since it was a total accident. Being able to pinpoint the exact purpose and result of pure research is precisely the opposite of what pure research aims to do. Like all important things, research requires time, effort and money. The best way to fund it is to gather a group of government, private, and nonprofit agencies who can pool their resources to let scientists keep working. Some research may fail miserably, but some may change the course of the world. That possibility is surely worth funding.

SCORE EXPLANATION(4444)

The writer provides a minimal discussion of all three perspectives, but fails to fully consider the implications of the other perspectives. She doesn't fully consider counterarguments, but she does provide relevant support for her opinion.

Ideas and Analysis (4)

Ideas are clearly stated, if redundant. The argument centers around "time, effort, and money," with discussion of each taking up most of the essay. Her perspective is analyzed primarily through a personal anecdote about her brother, which is more related to research in general than to pure research. However, the author is consistent in her argument and able to critique another perspective while returning to her own point of view.

Development and Support (4)

The writer begins with a good statement defining pure research, immediately bringing in the examples of Alzheimer's and the GPS, though a brief explanation of their relevance would enhance the support. The first paragraph also introduces all perspectives. However, when the writer states her own opinion at the end of the introduction, she does not do so forcefully. The argument is developed with a personal statement about her brother's asthma, which leads into further discussion of funding. The writer continues this argument in the next paragraph, again referencing asthma and mentioning cancer, though both statements are fleeting and do not offer strong support. One other alternative is discussed in the fourth paragraph, nicely harking back to the definition of pure research (the incorrect reference to Pasteur and penicillin does not affect the support).

Organization (4)

The writer provides a clear introductory paragraph and a good conclusion, and she is able to tie the essay together by returning to the initial definition of pure research at the end of the fourth paragraph with "Being able to pinpoint the exact purpose and result of pure research is precisely the opposite of what pure research aims to do." The first paragraph shows good connection words between perspectives (*Some, Others, Still others*). However, there are few transitions other than the one introducing paragraph 4; better use of transitions would make the essay flow more smoothly. The essay is nonetheless cohesive in its perspective.

Language Use (4)

The writing style is adequate, with some spelling and grammar errors. Word choice could be improved by avoiding very informal words and phrases ("eating into their finances," "total accident," "meds," "plenty of other diseases") and expressing ideas with more high-level vocabulary and complex sentence structure. Less use of contractions would also raise the language to a more appropriately formal essay level.

LEVEL 2 ESSAY

Working with a real goal in mind is the best way to do a project and the goverment has lots of money, so I think the government should pay for research projects but only those which will succeed. I did a school sience project with too other kids but we ended up fighting and not finishing it, which is what would happen if lots of groups got together to fund something.

When my teacher assigns a sience project even though I get to choose which one to do she expects results. The goverment should think the same way because if they don't they will be spending money for something which could be useless. Just like my teacher does when she decides what grade to give my project, the goverment should think about how successful the research might be and save their money for research that will really come up with something important.

Like it says, "to many cooks spoil the broth" which means that when theres a whole group of people, chances are the end result is bad. That goes for the govement partnering *with other groups also they should pay for research by themselves but only if it looks like the research will come up with something good.*

SCORE EXPLANATION (2222)

Though the author addresses the prompt and takes a side, this essay is very poorly written and supported, and ideas and analysis are weak with little clarity.

Ideas and Analysis (2)

This essay indicates a lack of understanding of the prompt and task, and poor reasoning and writing skills. The author has focused primarily on the issues of money and the negative effects of working with partners, likening the latter to working with others on a science project. She has not analyzed any perspective in depth; instead, ideas are repetitive, with shallow support. The author has not looked beyond her own school experience, thus her argument is weak and analysis of the prompt is superficial.

Development and Support (2)

The author fails to develop her thesis beyond general, poorly supported statements, which repeat her two ideas that working together is detrimental to a project and government money should be spent on projects with demonstrated success. Her support is weak and irrelevant, focusing on a school project, equating it with pure research, and suggesting that the government should determine its funding in the same way that a teacher determines a grade. The saying that opens the third paragraph is a trite platitude, lacking any real analysis. The author's reasoning is inadequate and confused, and she fails to examine the argument logically.

Organization (2)

Though there are three separate paragraphs and the conclusion echoes the first paragraph's perspective, each paragraph is weak and disjointed, with no transition phrases to tie the essay together. Ideas are poorly grouped together; the author repeatedly compares a school project to governmental pure research funding.

Language Use (2)

There are numerous spelling and punctuation errors, word choice is simplistic, and the writing fails to be persuasive. *Government* and *science* are consistently misspelled, and there are several instances of improper pronoun/antecedent agreement. The author misuses the word *too*, omits the apostrophe from *there's*, and follows the missed apostrophe with a run-on sentence. Word choice and sentence structure are rudimentary, and the essay lacks the strength and style of writing which would make it persuasive and engaging.